KT-194-966

HOTEL
FRONT OFFICE
OPERATIONS AND MANAGEMENT

LEARNING CENTRE
HAMMERSMITH AND WEST
LONDON COLLEGE
GLIDDON ROAD
LONDON W14 9BL

JATASHANKAR R. TEWARI

*Babu Banarasi Das National Institute of
Technology and Management
Lucknow*

WITHDRAWN

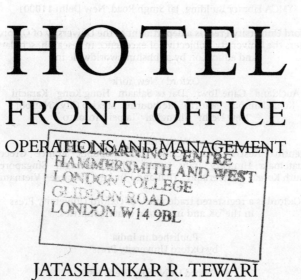

OXFORD

HAMMERSMITH WEST LONDON COLLEGE

338038

OXFORD

UNIVERSITY PRESS

YMCA Library Building, Jai Singh Road, New Delhi 110001

Oxford University Press is a department of the University of Oxford.
It furthers the University's objective of excellence in research, scholarship,
and education by publishing worldwide in

Oxford   New York
Auckland   Cape Town   Dar es Salaam   Hong Kong   Karachi
Kuala Lumpur   Madrid   Melbourne   Mexico City   Nairobi
New Delhi   Shanghai   Taipei   Toronto

With offices in
Argentina   Austria   Brazil   Chile   Czech Republic   France   Greece
Guatemala   Hungary   Italy   Japan   Poland   Portugal   Singapore
South Korea   Switzerland   Thailand   Turkey   Ukraine   Vietnam

Oxford is a registered trade mark of Oxford University Press
in the UK and in certain other countries.

Published in India
by Oxford University Press

© Oxford University Press 2009

The moral rights of the author/s have been asserted.

Database right Oxford University Press (maker)

First published 2009
Second impression 2009

All rights reserved. No part of this publication may be reproduced,
stored in a retrieval system, or transmitted, in any form or by any means,
without the prior permission in writing of Oxford University Press,
or as expressly permitted by law, or under terms agreed with the appropriate
reprographics rights organization. Enquiries concerning reproduction
outside the scope of the above should be sent to the Rights Department,
Oxford University Press, at the address above.

You must not circulate this book in any other binding or cover
and you must impose this same condition on any acquirer.

HAMMERSMITH AND WEST
LONDON COLLEGE
LEARNING CENTRE

2 6 APR 2010

338038   £14-99
647·94 TEW

Business

ISBN-13: 978-0-19-569919-7
ISBN-10: 0-19-569919-X

Typeset in Berthold Baskerville
by Recto Graphics, Delhi 110096
Printed in India by Radha Press, Delhi 110031
and published by Oxford University Press
YMCA Library Building, Jai Singh Road, New Delhi 110001

338038

This work is dedicated to my source of inspiration and strength–

My parents

Smt Kamla Devi & Shri Ram Prasad Tewari

For constantly inspiring and motivating me to pursue excellence in every field of life.

Preface

Today tourism is one of the largest and most dynamic sectors of the economy. It is growing at a fast pace, leading to infrastructure development, considerable volume of foreign currency inflows, and good job opportunities. So it affects various sectors of the economy, contributing to the social and economic development of the country as a whole. According to recent statistics, tourism provides about 10 per cent of the world's income and employs almost one tenth of the world's workforce. All considered, tourism's actual and potential economic impact is astounding.

The hospitality industry came into existence in order to accommodate tourists. When guests stay in a hotel and use the various services and facilities provided by the hotel, they seldom think about the complexity of hotel operations. The smallest of their demands, like for a cup of tea, requires coordination among a series of people. The hotel industry is a people-oriented industry. It is the effectiveness, efficiency, and courteous behaviour of the hotel employees that make a lasting impression on the guest's total experience.

The front office department of a hotel is the hub of guest activities. This department looks after the guests' needs—right from the booking of rooms to receiving and registering guests, to assigning rooms, to handling guests' mails and messages, to presenting bills and settling guests' accounts at the time of check-out. It is important for the front office staff to provide excellent and flawless services to guests, as it goes a long way in creating an indelible image of the hotel.

In India, the subject of front office operations is taught in degree and diploma courses in hotel management, postgraduate diploma in accommodation, and also in postgraduate degree programmes like MSc/MA/MBA with hotel management as a main subject. Apart from the regular course in hotel management, front office management is also taught in courses in tourism management.

ABOUT THE BOOK

Hotel Front Office: Operations and Management is a comprehensive, syllabi-oriented textbook that has been developed especially for the students of hotel management and hospitality management courses. Students will find this book useful for its coverage of the key concepts of front office operations and management, explained through industry-related examples, flowcharts, tables, formats, and photographs. With its practice-oriented approach, the book would also be useful to front office professionals.

The book has been divided into three parts. The first part–*The Hospitality Industry*–gives an introduction to the hospitality industry and acquaints the reader with the classification and organization of hotels. The second part–*Front Office Operations*–explains front office organization, internal and external communication, and room tariff. The guest cycle, which includes the stages of pre-arrival (reservation), arrival (registration), stay (guest services), and departure (check-out and settlement of bills), is explained in detail. This section also includes chapters on front office accounting, night auditing, safety and security of guests, and computer applications in front office. The final part–*Front Office Management*–imparts an understanding of the key managerial concepts, such as revenue management, forecasting, budgeting, and human resource management. Contemporary issues like environmental management and total quality management are also explored in this section.

PEDAGOGICAL FEATURES

The various pedagogical features of the book are as under:
- Each chapter begins with concise learning objectives.
- The text has been streamlined for the easy understanding of students and has been written in simple, easy-to-understand language.
- Concepts are illustrated by suitable figures, formats, examples, tables, and photographs for the better comprehension of the reader.
- Chapter-end summary helps recapitulate what has been learnt in the chapter.
- A glossary of key terms is given at the end of every chapter to aid better understanding of the subject.
- Review questions at the end of each chapter help the students revise the concepts learnt in the chapter.
- Caselets enhance critical thinking and relate the concepts to real-life situations.
- The project work enhances the research, experimental, and analytical skills of the reader.

STRUCTURE

The first three chapters of the book constitute Part I–*The Hospitality Industry*. Chapter 1 introduces the hotel industry, Chapter 2 deals with the classification of hotels, and Chapter 3 provides indepth knowledge about hotel organization.

Part II of the book comprises ten chapters, concerning various aspects of *Front Office Operations*. Chapter 4 discusses the organization of a front office department, Chapter 5 discusses communication and its importance in the front office department, and Chapter 6 deals with the room tariff. Chapters 7, 8, and 9 deal with various operational aspects of the front office department, like making advance booking of rooms, receiving and registering guests, and extending various guest services, like handling of messages, keys, mails, and guest complaints; guest paging; facilitating guest room change; providing safety deposit locker and left luggage facilities, etc. Chapters 10, 11, and 12 deal with check-out procedures, front office accounting, and night auditing.

Chapter 13 provides an overview of the safety and security procedures followed in the hotel industry.

Part III of the book comprises seven chapters about *Front Office Management.* Chapter 14 deals with the use and applications of computers in the hotel industry. Chapters 15, 16, and 17 discuss the various methods of evaluating the performance of a hotel, the application of yield management techniques to increase revenue generation, budgeting, forecasting, and marketing of hospitality products. Chapter 18 elaborates on the human resource aspects like recruitment, selection, training, and evaluating performance of employees. Chapters 19 and 20 discuss the environmental concerns of the hotel industry and the application of total quality management concepts to attain perfection in carrying out hotel operations.

ACKNOWLEDGEMENTS

I am indebted to all those who very kindly extended their help to me in the preparation of this book. No endeavour achieves success without the advice and cooperation of others. I would like to acknowledge the people and organizations who have either directly or indirectly contributed towards the conceptualization and compilation of this book. I am thankful to Mr Dheeraj Kukreja (General Manager & VP–Operations, Piccadily Holiday Resorts Limited, Hotel Piccadily, Lucknow) for providing free access to the hotel to understand the various procedures and practices used in the front office operations and for providing photographs for the book.

I am also thankful to the students and faculty members of the Babu Banarasi Das National Institute of Technology and Management, Lucknow for their valuable suggestions. In this regard, I would also like to acknowledge the assistance of Mr Ashish Srivastava who sometimes helped me in the typing of the manuscript.

The entire editorial team from Oxford University Press, India deserves my gratitude for their professionalism and for bearing with me when I overshot my deadlines. I would also like to thank all the people at Oxford University Press, India who have contributed in some way or the other in the completion of this book. I also owe my gratitude to the anonymous peer reviewers whose valuable feedback enabled me to improve the text.

I would like to acknowledge the patience and support of my father, mother, wife Suman, daughter Shambhavi, and son Shivansh. Finally, I would like to thank all my well wishers, friends, students, and academicians, for having in some way influenced the development of this book.

Jatashankar R. Tewari

Contents

Part-II Front Office Operations

Part-III   Front Office Management

Part-I
The Hospitality Industry

- Introduction to the Hospitality Industry
- Classification of Hotels
- Hotel Organization

CHAPTER 1

Introduction to the Hospitality Industry

Learning Objectives:

After reading this chapter, you will be able to understand the following:
- Hospitality industry—its origin and growth.
- Travel and tourism—their evolution, importance, and related industries.
- Evolution and growth of the hotel industry in the world and in India.
- Hotel—definition and core areas.

The hospitality industry is among the oldest commercial activities in the world. It is, in fact, an integral part of the larger business enterprise known as travel and tourism, which provides a wide range of travel related services, such as modes of travel, accommodation, food and drinks, recreational activities, and other facilities required by the modern-age traveller. Hospitality seems to be a glamorous industry, but not many know that a tremendous amount of hard work goes behind the sheen and glitter that meets the eye.

This chapter is aimed at providing an insight into the evolution and growth of the hospitality industry in India and other parts of the world. Tourism is one of the most important commercial activities of the modern economy. The relationship between the tourism and hotel industries is also explained with reference to the diverse profile of the present-day client, who could be travelling for business, vacation, pleasure, adventure, or even medical treatment. An overview of hotels and their core departments is also provided for an overall understanding of hotel operations.

THE HOSPITALITY INDUSTRY

Catering to all needs of travel related activity, the hospitality sector is estimated to be a US $3.5 trillion industry in the world economy today. Hospitality refers to the relationship between a guest and a host, and it also refers to the act or practice of being hospitable. It includes cordial reception and entertainment of guests, visitors, or strangers. Hospitality is also known as the act of generously providing care and kindness to whoever is in need.

The hospitality industry is an umbrella term for a broad variety of service industries, including, but not limited to, hotels, restaurants, casinos, catering enterprises, resorts, and clubs. The industry is very diverse and global, and is greatly impacted by fluctuations within the economy as also by various happenings across the world.

Origin and Growth

The origin and development of the hospitality industry is a direct outcome of travel and tourism. There are many reasons for which a person may travel: business, pleasure, further studies, medical treatment, pilgrimage, or any other reason. When a person travels for a few or more days, he may carry his clothes with him, but it's not possible for him to carry his food and home. Thus, two of his three basic needs—food and shelter—are not taken care of when he is travelling. This is where the hospitality industry steps in.

Fig. 1.1 A caravan of camels

Before the wheel was invented, people undertook journeys on animals such as horses, camels, and elephants. In those days, they used to travel in groups called caravans (Fig. 1.1) for safety. However, there was a limit to the distance they could cover in a day. At nightfall they avoided travel due to the fear of wild animals and bandits, and also because of animal fatigue. Thus, for the night halt, they looked for a

Fig. 1.2 A tavern

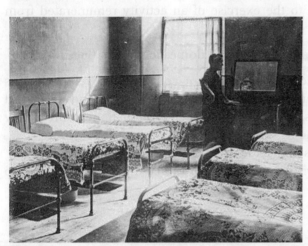

Fig. 1.3 An early inn

place that could provide them with water, fuel to cook food, and, above all, security from wild animals and bandits.

The primitive lodging houses or inns originated essentially to cater to these needs of the travellers. Throughout the world they were known by different names, such as *dharamshala* and *sarai* in India, *ryokans* in Japan, *paradors* in Spain, *pousadas* in Portugal, *coffee houses* in America, *taverns* (Fig. 1.2) and *inns* in Europe, c*abarets* and *hostelries* in France, *mansionis* and *hospitia* in Switzerland, *phatnal* in Greece, and *relay houses* in China.

The earliest inns were generally run by families or husband-wife teams who provided large halls to travellers to make their own beds and sleep on the floor. They also provided modest wholesome food and drinks like wine, port, ale, etc., and stable facilities for the animals. Entertainment and recreation were also provided on a modest scale. All this, of course, came for a price. These inns or lodging properties were housed in the private homes of the local people. They made a living by providing accommodation to travellers. These inns were not as clean and tidy as we see them today. They were also devoid of the frills and facilities as seen in the modern-day hospitality establishments. The travellers had to make their own beds and cook for themselves. Gradually, the inns started providing beds to travellers—typically, an inn would have a large hall with many beds (Fig. 1.3).

TOURISM INDUSTRY

Tourism is one of the world's fastest growing industries and a major source of foreign exchange and employment generation for many countries. It is regarded as one of the most remarkable economic and social phenomena of the past century. According to the data available with the United Nations World Tourism Organization

(UNWTO), a global forum for promoting tourism, the number of international arrivals in the world grew from 25 million in 1950 to a whopping 806 million in 2005—nearly 30 fold rise—registering an annual average growth rate of 6.5 per cent.

The word 'tour is' derived from the Latin word *tornus*, meaning 'a tool for making a circle'. Tourism may be defined as the movement of people from their normal place of residence to another place (with the intention to return) for a minimum period of twenty-four hours to a maximum of six months for the sole purpose of leisure and pleasure.

The Rome Conference on tourism in 1963 defined tourism as 'a visit to a country other than one's own or where one usually resides and works'. This definition, however, did not take into account domestic tourism, which has become an important money-spinner and job generator for the hospitality industry.

The UNWTO defines tourists as 'people who travel to and stay in places outside their usual environment for not more than one consecutive year for leisure, business and other purposes not related to the exercise of an activity remunerated from within the place visited'.

Tourism can be categorized as international and domestic tourism (Fig. 1.4):

International tourism When people visit a foreign country, it is referred to as international tourism. In order to travel to a foreign country, one needs a valid passport, visa, health documents, foreign exchange, etc. International tourists may be inbound or outbound (Fig. 1.4):

Inbound: This refers to tourists of outside origin entering a particular country.

Outbound: This refers to tourists travelling from the country of their origin to another country.

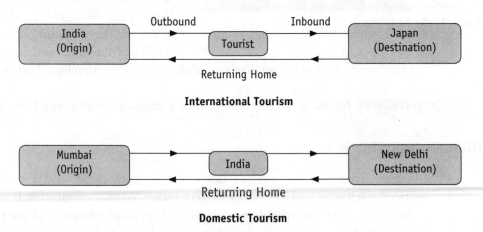

Fig. 1.4 International and domestic tourism

Domestic tourism   The tourism activity of people within their own country is known as domestic tourism. Travelling within the same country is easier because it does not require formal travel documents and tedious formalities like compulsory health checks and foreign exchange. In domestic tourism, a traveller generally does not face much language problem or currency exchange issues.

Importance of Tourism

Tourism and hospitality, which are inextricably linked to each other, are among the major revenue-earning enterprises in the world. They happen to be among the top employers too. There has been an upmarket trend in tourism over the last few decades as travel has become quite common. People travel for business, vacation, pleasure, adventure, or even medical treatment. The present-day tourist, who has higher levels of disposable income, international exposure, and refined tastes, wants specialized versions of products and services, such as quieter resorts, family-oriented holidays, or commercial hotels. This has led to a demand for better quality products and services, mainly regarding accommodation and travelling, thus feeding the growth of the hospitality industry as a whole.

The developments in technology and transport infrastructure, such as jumbo jets, low-cost airlines, and more accessible airports have made tourism affordable and convenient. There have also been changes in lifestyle—for example, now retiree-age people sustain tourism round the year. The sales of tourism products on the Internet, besides the aggressive marketing of tour operators and travel agencies, has also contributed to the growth of tourism.

With several business-related activities associated with tourism, the industry has a tremendous potential of generating employment as well as earning foreign exchange. There are many countries in the world, such as Mauritius, Malaysia, Singapore, Fiji, and Caribbean, whose economies are primarily driven by tourism. Tourism can contribute to the economic growth of a country in the following ways:

Employment generation   It creates a large number of jobs among direct service providers (such as, hotels, restaurants, travel agencies, tour operators, guide and tour escorts, etc.) and among indirect service providers (such as, suppliers to hotels and restaurants, supplementary accommodation, etc.).

Infrastructure development   Tourism spurs infrastructure development. In order to become an important commercial or pleasure destination, any location would require all the necessary infrastructure, like good connectivity via rail, road, and air transport, adequate accommodation, restaurants, a well-developed telecommunication network, and medical facilities, among others.

Foreign exchange   The people who travel to other countries spend a large amount of money on accommodation, transportation, sightseeing, shopping, etc. Thus, an inbound tourist is an important source of foreign exchange for any country.

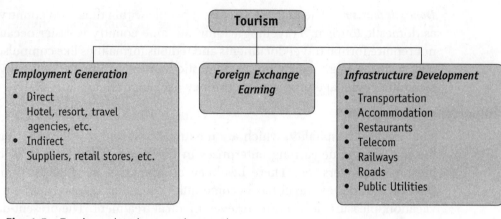

Fig. 1.5 Tourism related economic growth

Figure 1.5 provides an insight into the economic activities that are spurred by tourism. The World Travel and Tourism Council (WTTC) predicted in 1997 that the twenty-first-century economy would be dominated by three industries: telecommunications, information technology, and tourism. The travel and tourism industry has grown by 500 per cent in the last 25 years. In India, the travel and tourism industry is expected to contribute 2.3 per cent to gross domestic product (GDP) in 2008, while the total travel and tourism economy contribution to GDP is around 6.1 per cent. Tourism generates more than 230 million jobs (directly and indirectly) and contributes to more than 10 per cent of the world GDP. International tourist arrivals in 2006 were 842 million and the UNWTO forecasts 1.6 billion international tourist arrivals worldwide by 2020.

Notwithstanding these bright outlook and prospects, the tourism and hospitality industry is very vulnerable to the fluctuations of national economies and happenings in the world, especially terrorist attacks that have at times dealt severe blows to the business. In the recent years, there have been a few setbacks in tourism, such as the terrorist siege of the Taj and Oberoi hotels in Mumbai, India (26 November 2008); the attack on the World Trade Centre in the United States of America (11 September 2001); bombings in a hotel on the Indonesian island of Bali (12 October 2002); tsunami in Southeast Asia and South Asia on 26 December 2004, in which thousands of lives were lost and consequently tourism was hit. Nonetheless, the sectors are now getting back to business.

INDUSTRIES RELATED TO TOURISM

Over the years, tourism has become a popular global activity. Depending upon the nature and purpose of their travel, tourists need and demand certain facilities and services. This has given rise to a wide range of commercial activities that have acquired industry proportions. Thus, travel and tourism nowadays represents a broad range of related industries. Figure 1.6 presents an overview of the tourism industry and other sectors related to it.

Hotels   Hotels are commercial establishments that provide accommodation, meals, and other guest services. In general, to be called a hotel, an establishment must have a minimum of six guest rooms, at least three of which must have attached private bathroom facilities.

Although hotels are classified into 'star' categories, there is no standard method of assigning these ratings, and compliance with customary requirements is voluntary. An American hotel with a certain rating, for example, may look very different from a European or Asian hotel with the same rating, and would provide a different level of amenities, range of facilities, and quality of service. Although hotel chains assure uniform standards throughout, non-chain hotels (even within the same country) may not agree on the same standards.

In the travel and tourism industry, the hotel industry plays a very significant role, as all tourists need a place to stay at their destinations, and require many more services and facilities to suit their specific needs and tastes.

Restaurants   Restaurants are retail establishments that serve prepared food and beverages to customers. Though the term is generally applicable for eating on premises, it has also been used to include take-away establishments and food delivery services. Restaurants range from unpretentious dining places with simple

THE TOURISM INDUSTRY

Accommodation	Transportation	Food & Beverage	Retail Stores	Activities
Hotel	Trains	Restaurants	Shopping Malls	Seasonal Festivals
Motel	Passenger Ships	Bars	Gift Shops	Trade Fairs
Time-Share	Airlines	Pubs	Art & Craft Shops	Road Shows
Resort	Buses	Dhabas	Handicraft	Exhibitions
Holiday Village	Cars	Vendors	Handloom	Sports Events
Dak Bungalow	Bikes	Take Away	Emporium	Study Trips
Sarai	Limousines	Snakes Bar	Antique Shops	Excursions
Casino Hotel	Ferries	Retail Shops		Cultural Events
B & B Hotel	Steamers	Kiosks		Light Shows
Condominium	Cruise liners			
Circuit Houses				
Capsule Hotel				

Fig. 1.6   An overview of the tourism industry

food served in simple settings at low prices to expensive establishments serving refined food and wines in a formal setting. Typically, customers are seated at tables, their orders are taken by a waiter who serves food when it is ready, and the customers pay the bill before leaving. In finer restaurants, there is generally a host or hostess to welcome customers and to seat them. Other staff waiting on customers includes busboys and sommeliers. Restaurants often specialize in certain types of food, or present a certain unifying, and often entertaining, theme. For example, there are seafood restaurants, vegetarian restaurants, or ethnic restaurants.

In the travel and tourism industry, restaurants and other food and beverage outlets are very important as tourists like to experiment with local cuisines of the places they are visiting.

Retail and Shopping   The retail industry is very important as tourists shop for their day-to-day necessities as well as look for mementos and souvenirs. In the recent years, several cities in the world have been promoted as shopping destinations to attract people with a penchant for shopping by offering various products, such as garments, electronic goods, jewellery, and antiques, among others, at very low prices. Cities like Singapore, Dubai, and Bangkok attract shoppers with their state-of-the-art malls and plush shopping plazas, while cities like New York, Paris, London, and Milan in Italy are famous as fashion havens of the world. The recent years have seen the organization of events like shopping festivals to attract tourists with deep pockets.

Transportation   It is the movement of people and goods from one place to another. The term is derived from the Latin words *trans* meaning 'across' and *portare* meaning 'to carry'. Industries that are in the business of providing transport equipment and services are important in most national economies and are referred to as transport industries.

A well-developed transport industry, as well as infrastructure, is integral to the success of any travel and tourism enterprise. Good transport facilities and connectivity are basic for putting any place on a tourist map, whether domestic or international. At times, poor connectivity and transport has kept places, such as the northeastern states of India (Fig. 1.7), from

Fig. 1.7   A stream near Gangtok, Sikkim

exploiting their full tourism potential. In a bid to encourage travel to the northeast, several travel concessions are announced by the states as well as the Union government from time to time.

Travel Agencies A travel agency is a retailing business that sells travel-related products and services, particularly package tours, to customers on behalf of suppliers such as airlines, car rentals, cruise liners, hotels, railways, and sightseeing and tour operators. In addition to dealing with ordinary tourists, most travel agencies have a separate department devoted to making travel arrangements for business travellers. However, some travel agencies specialize in commercial and business travel only. There are also travel agencies that serve as general sales agents for foreign travel companies, allowing them to have offices in countries other than their countries of origin.

A travel agency's main function is to act as an agent selling travel products and services on behalf of a supplier. But, unlike other retail businesses, they do not keep a stock in hand. They do not buy a package holiday or a ticket from a supplier unless a customer requests it. Most travel agencies operate on a commission-basis, implying that the supplier—airlines, car rentals, cruise liners, hotels, railways, or sightseeing and tour operators—offers a fixed percentage of the sale to the agencies as commission for booking clients. The agencies may offer a discount on a holiday package or ticket to the customers by shrinking their commission. Some travel agencies, especially large chains, undertake other commercial operations, such as the sale of in-house insurance, travel guide books, timetables, car rentals, and the services of an on-site *bureau de change,* dealing in the most popular currencies.

Travel agencies play a very important role as they plan out the itinerary of their clients and make the necessary arrangements for their travel, stay, and sightseeing, besides facilitating their passport, visa, etc.

Tour Operators A tour operator assembles the various elements of a tour. It typically combines tour and travel components to create a holiday. The most common example of a tour operator's product would be a seat on a charter airline plus a transfer from the airport to a hotel, and the services of a local representative, all for one price. Niche tour operators may specialize in destinations and activities, or a combination thereof.

The original *raison d'être* (reason for existence) of tour operators was the difficulty of making arrangements in far-flung places, with problems of language, currency, and communication. Although the Internet has made self-packaging of holidays easier now, tour operators still have their competence in arranging tours for those who do not have the time to do so. They specialize in large group events and meetings, such as conferences or seminars. Also, tour operators still exercise contracting power with suppliers (airlines, hotels, other land arrangements, cruises, etc.) and influence over other entities (tourism boards and other government authorities) in

Fig. 1.8 National Theatre—a landmark created for the 2008 Beijing Olympics

order to create packages and special departures for destinations that are otherwise difficult and expensive to visit.

Tourist Destinations A tourist attraction is a place of interest for tourists, typically for its inherent or exhibited cultural value, historical significance, natural or built beauty, or amusement opportunities. Some examples include historical places, monuments, zoos, aquaria, museums, art galleries, botanical gardens, buildings and structures, which include castles, libraries, former prisons, skyscrapers, bridges, landmarks (Fig. 1.8), national parks and forests, theme parks and carnivals, ethnic enclave communities, historical trains, and cultural events. Tourist attractions are also created by capitalizing on unexplained phenomena such as a supposed UFO crash site near Roswell, New Mexico and the alleged Loch Ness monster sightings in Scotland. Ghost sightings also make popular tourist attractions. Ethnic communities, such as Chinatowns or the Jew community in Kochi (Kerala), are also popular among tourists.

Free promotional brochures and flyers of popular destinations are handed out in information centres, fast food restaurants, hotel and motel rooms or lobbies, and rest areas frequented by travellers. While some tourist attractions provide visitors a memorable experience for a reasonable admission charge or even free, others can be of low quality and may overprice their goods and services (such as admission, food, and souvenirs) in order to profit from tourists excessively. Such places are commonly referred to as tourist traps.

Cultural Industries Cultural or creative industries are responsible for the creation, production, and distribution of goods and services that are cultural in nature and usually protected by intellectual property rights. These include literary works, visual and performing arts, crafts, and other creative fields. Cultural industries are knowledge-based and labour-intensive, creating employment and wealth. By nurturing creativity and fostering innovation, societies develop a cultural heritage and enhance economic performance. As tourists like to visit places of cultural significance and soak in the culture of the area, the cultural industry is very important to travel and tourism (Fig. 1.9).

Fig. 1.9   Indian festivals   (a) Diwali   (b) Durga Puja   (c) Elephant Festival of Jaipur, Rajasthan
(d) Baisakhi, Punjab   (e) Boat Race, Kerala

Leisure, Recreation, and Sport   Leisure or free time is a period of time spent out of work and essential domestic activity. Recreation or fun is spending time in a manner designed for therapeutic refreshment of one's body or mind. While leisure is more like a form of entertainment or rest, recreation requires active participation in a refreshing and diverting manner. As people in the world's wealthier regions lead increasingly sedentary lifestyles, the need for recreation has increased. The rise of so-called active vacations exemplifies this.

The spread of mass media has led to a growing public interest in sports. This has turned popular sports into good business opportunities, where rules of the game are sometimes bent to make them more profitable and popular. The emergence of Twenty20 format in cricket is a case in point. Good marketing strategies and the promise of wholesome entertainment are attracting larger audiences, making sporting events popular among fans that are willing to travel to the games venues to get a first-hand experience of their favourite game. Thus, it is a little wonder that cities and countries across the world bid years in advance for hosting international sports events like Olympics.

Thus, we have seen that tourism today encompasses a wide range of products and services—travel, accommodation, catering, and recreation, among others—for its clients. We have also briefly read how the hospitality industry emerged from the man's need to travel and has evolved to into its present state today. The hotel industry is arguably the most significant part of the hospitality industry. In the succeeding sections, we will trace the origin and growth of this industry in the world, as also in India.

EVOLUTION AND GROWTH OF THE HOTEL INDUSTRY IN THE WORLD

The invention of currency and the wheel sometime in the fifth century BC are regarded as the two main factors that led to the emergence of inn-keeping and hospitality as a commercial activity. While Europe can safely be regarded as the cradle of organized hotel business, it is in the American continent that one sees the evolution of the modern hotel industry over the past century. From the rudimentary ancient inns to the present day state-of-the-art establishments that provide everything under the sun to the modern traveller, the hotel industry has come a long way. The origin and growth of the hotel industry in the world can be broadly studied under the following periods:

- Ancient Era
- Grand Tour
- Modern Era

Ancient Era

The earliest recorded evidence of the hospitality facilities in Europe dates back to 500 BC. Ancient cities, such as Corinth in Greece, had a substantial number of establishments that offered food and drink as well as beds to travellers. The inns of the biblical era were of primitive type, offering a cot or bench in the corner of a room and, at times, even a stable. Travellers used to stay in a large hall. Privacy and personal sanitation were non-existent. In the third century AD,

Fig. 1.10   A Swiss chalet

numerous lodging premises mushroomed along the extensive network of brick-paved roads throughout Europe and minor Asia (part of Asia adjoining Europe). The lodging houses were known as *mansionis* during that time.

These conditions prevailed for several hundred years, till the Industrial Revolution in England led to the development of railways and steamships, making travelling more efficient, comfortable, and faster. The Industrial Revolution also brought about a shift in the focus of travel that became more business-oriented than educational or social.

The lead in organized hotel keeping, as we see it today, was taken by the emerging nations of Europe, especially Switzerland. The early establishments were mainly patronized by the aristocracy, and took shape in chalets (small cottages) (Fig. 1.10) and small hotels that provided a variety of services. Between 1750 and 1825, inns in Britain gained the reputation of being the finest hospitality establishments.

Grand Tour

The second half of the eighteenth century, prior to the French Revolution (1789–99), is referred as the 'golden era of travel' as the popularity of the 'Grand Tour' gave a big push to the hotel industry. In those days, a Grand Tour of the European continent constituted an indispensable element of the education of scions of wealthy families in Britain. As this tour often lasted several years, it was a good business opportunity for people in the prominent cities of France, Italy, Germany, Austria, Switzerland, and Ireland to establish lodging, transportation, and recreation facilities. Far-sighted entrepreneurs, who smelt money in the exercise, developed the skills of hospitality and pioneered the modern hotel industry.

Fig 1.11 The Imperial, Vienna

Fig 1.12 The World's first tour operator—Thomas Cook

Prominent among the hotels that emerged during this period were Dolder Grand in Zurich, The Imperial in Vienna (Fig. 1.11), the Vier Jahreszeiten in Hamburg, and Des Bergues in Geneva. In 1841, a simple cabinet maker, Thomas Cook (Fig. 1.12), organized a rail tour from Leicester to Loughborough and immortalized himself as the world's first tour operator.

Modern Era

The improvisation in modes of transport made journeys safer, easier, and faster, enabling economical as well as frequent mass movement. The introduction of Funiculars (the ropeway) made high altitude mountains accessible, leading to the growth of many hotels in the Alpine ranges. Bürgenstock and Giessbach are among the hotels in Switzerland that owe their existence to the development of the ropeways.

The two world wars, especially the second (1939–45), took their toll on the hospitality industry. The massive destruction caused by the war and the resulting economic depression proved to be a major setback

Fig. 1.13   Tremont House, Boston

for the travel business. The 1950s witnessed slow and steady growth of travel in the European continent. The development of aircraft and commercial passenger flights across the Atlantic stimulated travel across the globe, and in the process accelerated the growth of the hotel industry.

But it is the American entrepreneurs who are credited with literally changing the face of the hospitality industry with their innovations and aggressive marketing. The inauguration of the City Hotel in New York in 1794 marked the beginning of the present-day hotel industry. It was a 'giant' building at that time, with 73 rooms, and it went on to become a favourite meeting ground for socialites.

Prior to the establishment of the City Hotel, lodging facilities in the American continent were patterned on European style taverns or inns. The City Hotel, however, triggered a race of sorts among American hoteliers, resulting in the construction of large hotels like the Exchange Coffee House in Boston, the second City Hotel in Baltimore, Mansion House in Philadelphia, etc. The opening of the Tremont House (Fig. 1.13) in Boston is another landmark in the evolution of the hotel industry. Regarded as a forerunner of luxury hotels, the 170-room hotel had many firsts to its credit. For example, it was the first to provide locks, indoor plumbing, running water, and bathing facilities, besides providing a bowl, pitcher, and free soaps in its rooms. It was also the first to provide front office services like bell boys and a reception. It was also the first hotel to serve French cuisine in the US.

Throughout the nineteenth century, the contest among hoteliers to build better, larger, and most luxurious hotels continued. Several luxury hotels, like the Grand Pacific, The Palmer House (Fig. 1.14), and The Sherman House in Chicago, as well as The Palace (with 800 rooms) in San Francisco were built. The year 1908 saw the emergence of the first business hotel, the Statler Hotel in Buffalo, New York (Fig. 1.15). This magnificent 450-room multi-storey building was a pioneer in many ways. Some of the innovations included an attached bathroom with hot and cold water in each room, an electric lamp on the desk, and a radio in each room.

The decade of the great depression in the 1930s witnessed the liquidity of most of the hotels in America. The hotel industry streamlined with slow and steady growth during the 1940s. The increase in automobile travel in the 1950s led to the rise of 'motor hotels' or *motels,* a new category in the hotel industry. The motels, which offered free parking facilities, served as rest houses for people travelling

Fig. 1.14 The Palmer House, Chicago   **Fig. 1.15** Statler Hotel, Buffalo

between two cities or tourist destinations. The following decades saw the growth of motels on a large scale, and also the introduction of budget hotels that offered basic facilities at half the rates. Gradually, with the passage of time, these evolved into countrywide and international chains. We shall learn about them in detail in the next chapter.

EVOLUTION AND GROWTH OF THE HOTEL INDUSTRY IN INDIA

Although the origin of the hotel industry in India cannot be traced to a definite point of time, there is evidence of its presence even during the Indus Valley Civilization and Vedic era. In olden days, travel was predominantly undertaken for pilgrimage and trade. The concept of *char dham* (i.e., visiting religious places located in the four corners of India) among the Hindu community is an important indicator of the significance accorded to pilgrimage by our ancestors. The country stands dotted with many such shrines, some of which are frequented by people of all faiths. Some such popular destinations are Vaishno Devi, Amarnath cave shrine in Kashmir, Tirupati Balaji, Shirdi Sai, Sikh Golden Temple in Amritsar (Fig. 1.16), Dilwara Jain temples at Mount Abu, Bodhgaya for Buddhists, Ajmer Sharif shrine in Rajasthan, Haji Ali Tomb in Mumbai, St Francis Church in Goa, etc. Ancient texts and literature, as also Hindu mythology, have many references to travel and the provision of accommodation facilities for travelling pilgrims and traders by the authorities of those days.

Ancient India was well known for its silk, spices, gold, and gemstones. Records of famous travellers of the yore speak of Indians trading with countries like

Fig. 1.16   Golden Temple, Amritsar

Greece, Italy, Indonesia, Malaysia, China, and Japan, among others. The main mode of transport were animals on land, and boats and ships that criss-crossed rivers and seas for connectivity with distant lands. That is why we find major trading cities in the world situated along the banks of rivers or on sea ports.

The origin and evolution of the hotel industry in the country can be broadly categorized in the following three periods:

- Ancient and Medieval Era (from Indus Valley Civilization to AD 1600)
- Colonial Era (AD 1601 to AD 1947)
- Modern Era (1947 onwards)

Ancient and Medieval Era (from Indus Valley Civilization to AD 1600)

The beginnings of the hospitality sector in India stand rooted in the Hindu philosophy of '*atithi devo bhava*', implying that an unannounced guest is to be accorded the status of God. While it is not clear when hospitality emerged as a commercial activity in ancient India, there is evidence of accommodation facilities for travellers and guests, though not as organized as we see them today. The lodging houses during those times were known as *dharamshalas* (*dharama* in Sanskrit means religion and *shala* school).

Fig. 1.17   Chaupals

Dharmashalas, the resting places for pilgrims, are believed to have their origins in village *chaupals* (Fig. 1.17), which served as a meeting ground for villagers to plan and discuss various social welfare and development measures. These became the places of lodging as travellers started putting up camps there due to safety reasons. Gradually, with the help of local residents and financial assistance from the rulers, *zamindars*, or other influential people, permanent structures (or *dharmashalas*) were built for travellers. Here they were provided with a safe place to relax and spend the night. Other words in literature that are indicative of according facilities to travellers are *anna-kshetras* (*anna* means food grains and *kshetra* area), *bhojnalaya* (*bhojana* means meal and *alaya* house), *paakshala* (*paak* means cooking and *shala* school), *panthagar* (*panth* means way or road and *agar* house), etc. Similarly, in the Ramayana and Mahabharata, there is a mention of the existence of *avasathagar* (the outer portion of the house) to accommodate people who were invited during festivals, *yagnas,* or other celebrations organized by kings.

Records of many foreign visitors and philosophers who came to India speak highly of the hospitality facilities. Famous Chinese scholars Fa Hien (AD 399–414) and Huein Tsang (AD 629–643), who came during the reigns of Chandragupta Vikramiditya and Harshvardhana respectively, have mentioned the existence of shelters for travellers. Huein Tsang has, in fact, referred to the wonderful arrangement of food for 10,000 students in Nalanda University, a famous seat of learning.

In the medieval era, between the eleventh and thirteenth centuries, many *sarais* and *musafirkhanas* were built, primarily as resting places for messengers of the postal system established by the Sultans of the Slave or Mamluk dynasty. The system was refined by Allauddin Khiljee, who established *dak chowkis* with horse runners and messengers to deliver post. According to the *Tarikh-i-Sher-Shahi* by Abbas Khan Sherwani, the postal service *Diwan-i-Insa* employed nearly 3,400 people to man 1,700 horse-relay stations at *sarais,* which also served as post offices. The Mughals continued the practice and built many such *sarais* to accommodate travellers. The *sarais* during those times fulfilled the basic necessities of a traveller—they provided water, a room, a stable for the livestock (like horse, elephant, or camel) along with fodder, and sometimes also a place for worship. There are several localities in Delhi, such as Katwaria Sarai, Lado Sarai, Sarai Kale Khan, that have retained their names till date, although the medieval constructions are hard to find.

Colonial Era (1601–1947)

The organized existence of the hotel industry in India started taking shape during the colonial period, with the advent of Europeans in the seventeenth century. The early hotels were mostly operated by people of foreign origin to cater to the needs of the European colonizers and later officials of the Raj. Among the first such properties were taverns like Portuguese Georges, Paddy Goose's, and Racquent Court, which opened in Bombay (now Mumbai) between 1837 and 1840. However, within a period of about ten years, most of the taverns disappeared and more respectable hotels like Hope Hall Family Hotel began to make an appearance. Other famous properties included the Victoria Hotel, more famous as British Hotel, by Pallanjee Pestonjee in 1840; Esplanade Hotel in 1871; Watson's, which was exclusively for Europeans; Auckland Hotel (1841) in Kolkata, which went

Fig. 1.18 Taj Mahal Palace and Tower in Mumbai

on to become the Great Eastern Hotel in post-independent India, and so on.

In December 1903, Jamshetji Nusserwanji Tata, inaugurated the Taj Mahal Palace and Tower hotel (Fig. 1.18), overlooking the Gateway of India in Mumbai, following a racial discrimination incident wherein he was refused entry into the Watson's Hotel for being an Indian. The hotel, which is an architectural marvel, is credited with being the first luxury hotel for Indians by an Indian. In 1923, Shapurji Sorabji built the Grand Hotel in Mumbai. A few years later, the Majestic Hotel was opened.

Until 1900, almost all hotels were constructed and run as per Western traditions. The first Indian style hotels were Sardar Griha, which opened in 1900, and Madhavashram in 1908. The two world wars brought a fresh lot of hotels to Mumbai, an important port city of the times. The Ritz, The Ambassador, West End, and Airlines, which opened during these years, are fondly referred to as 'war babies' by industry historians.

Modern Era (1947 onwards)

Post independence, there were big leaps in the hotel trade in the country. The Oberoi Group of Hotels (founded by Rai Bahadur Mohan Singh Oberoi) and the Taj Group took over several British properties, maintained high standards of service and quality, and expanded their business overseas. The later decades saw corporates like the ITC (Indian Tobacco Company) also join the hotel industry with properties under ITC WelcomGroup. The year 1949 saw the organization of four regional hotels and restaurants associations with head offices in Delhi, Mumbai, Calcutta (now Kolkata), and Madras (now Chennai). These four associations were linked in a federation, the Federation of Hotels and Restaurants in India (FHRAI), in 1955. The federation serves as an interface between the hospitality industry, political leadership, government, international associations, and other stake holders in the trade.

The Ashok Hotel in Delhi's diplomatic enclave has the distinction of being the first luxury hotel built by the government. It was founded in 1956 to host independent India's first ever international event, a United Nations Industrial Development Organization (UNIDO) conference. Realizing the importance and potential of the tourism and hospitality industry, the government constituted India Tourism Development Corporation (ITDC) in 1966, which opened many large and small hotels across the country. The most popular face of ITDC is the Ashoka group of hotels that provides a wide range of hospitality-related services.

Over the last few decades, various well-known international hotel chains have come to India. These include Hyatt Hotels and Resorts, InterContinental Hotels and Resorts, Marriott International, Hilton Hotels, Best Western International, Shangri-La Hotels and Resorts, Four Seasons Hotels and Resorts, Carlson Hotels Worldwide, and Aman Resorts.

Current Scenario   The liberalization of the Indian economy has provided a boost to the hotel industry in a big way, leading to a sharp rise in the number of the inbound and domestic tourists in the last two decades. While the main focus of the international traveller has shifted from seeing the Taj Mahal in Agra and sunbathing on Goan beaches to doing business with one of the world's fastest growing economies, the boom in the information technology and other service sectors has placed substantial disposable incomes in the hands of Indian people, spurring the travel urge in them.

According to the Union Ministry of Tourism, 5.08 million tourists visited India in 2007 (Table 1.1). Almost one third of the international arrivals were from the United States and the United Kingdom (Table 1.5). The foreign exchange earnings from them were US $10.7 million, which was 24.3 per cent more than the previous year (Table 1.2). As many as 526.57 million Indians travelled within the country (Table 1.3) to register an annual increase of about 14 per cent in the domestic as well as inbound tourism categories. Even in the outbound sector, 9.78 million Indians travelled abroad last year (Table 1.4). However, India's share in the global tourism business is only 1.25 per cent. It is projected that in 2008 earnings

Table 1.1   Foreign tourist arrivals (FTA) in India (1996–2008)

Year	FTA (in million)	Percentage change over the previous year
1996	2.29	7.7
1997	2.37	3.8
1998	2.36	-0.7
1999	2.48	5.2
2000	2.65	6.7
2001	2.54	-4.2
2002	2.38	-6.0
2003	2.73	14.3
2004	3.46	26.8
2005	3.92	13.3
2006	4.45	13.5
2007	5.08	14.3
2008 (Jan–June) (P)	2.72	11.1*

P: Provisional, * Growth rate over Jan–June, 2007

Source: (i) Bureau of Immigration, Government of India, for 1996–2007.
   (ii) Ministry of Tourism, Government of India, for 2008.

Table 1.2 Foreign exchange earnings (FEE) from FTA during 1996–2008

Year	FEE from tourism in India (in US$ million)	Percentage change over the previous year
1996	2832	9.6
1997	2889	2.0
1998	2948	2.0
1999	3009	2.1
2000	3460	15.0
2001	3198	−7.6
2002	3103	−3.0
2003	4463	43.8
2004	6170	38.2
2005	7493	21.4
2006*	8634	15.2
2007*	10729	24.3
2008# (Jan–June)	6382	25.5 @

* Revised estimates, # Advance estimates, @ Growth rate over Jan–June, 2007
Source: (i) Bureau of Immigration, Government of India, for 1996–2007.
(ii) Ministry of Tourism, Government of India, for 2008.

Table 1.3 Domestic tourism during 1996–2007

Year	No. of domestic tourist visits (in million)	Percentage change over the previous year
1996	140.12	2.5
1997	159.88	14.1
1998	168.20	5.2
1999	190.67	13.4
2000	220.11	15.4
2001	236.47	7.4
2002	269.60	14.0
2003	309.04	14.6
2004	366.27	18.5
2005	391.95	7.0
2006	461.76	17.8
2007*	526.57	14

* Provisional
Note: Figures for Maharashtra and Chhattisgarh have been estimated.
Source: State/UT Tourism Departments.

from tourism would make up 6.36 per cent of the national GDP and 10.17 per cent of the employed Indians would be working in this industry directly.

The revenue from the hotel and restaurant industry in India during the financial year 2006–07 was Rs 604.32 billion, a growth of 21.27 per cent over the previous year. The hospitality industry is poised to grow at a faster rate and is expected to reach Rs 826.76 billion by 2010. There are about 1,980 hotels approved and classified by the Ministry of Tourism, Government of India, with a total capacity of about 110,000 hotel rooms.

According to Tarun Thakaral, Chief Operating Officer, Le Meridien, a leading business hotel in Delhi, the gap between demand and supply of hotel rooms is also growing. There is currently a shortage of 1,50,000 rooms, fuelling hotel room rates across India. The industry estimates that the demand is going to exceed supply by at least 100 per cent over the next two years. Five-star hotels in metro cities allot the same room more than once a day to different guests, receiving almost twenty four

Table 1.4 Number of outbound visits of Indian nationals, 1996–2007

Year	No. of outbound visits (in million)	Percentage change over the previous year
1996	3.46	13.3
1997	3.73	7.6
1998	3.81	2.3
1999	4.11	8.0
2000	4.42	7.3
2001	4.56	3.4
2002	4.94	8.2
2003	5.35	8.3
2004	6.21	16.1
2005	7.18	15.6
2006	8.34	16.1
2007	9.78	17.3

Source: Bureau of Immigration, Government of India.

Table 1.5 Top ten source countries for FTA in 2007

S. No.	Source country	FTA (in million)	Percentage share
1	USA	0.799	15.73
2	UK	0.796	15.67
3	Bangladesh	0.480	9.45
4	Canada	0.208	4.10
5	France	0.205	4.03
6	Sri Lanka	0.204	4.02
7	Germany	0.184	3.62
8	Japan	0.146	2.86
9	Australia	0.136	2.67
10	Malaysia	0.113	2.22
Total of top 10 countries		3.271	64.37
Others		1.810	35.63
All countries		5.081	100.00

Source: Bureau of Immigration, Government of India.

hour rates from both guests against six to eight hours usage. With demand-supply disparity, hotel rates in India are likely to rise by 25 per cent annually and occupancy by 80 per cent over the next two years.

This growth is attributed to the country's 'Incredible India!' international marketing campaign, which mounted a concerted effort in international print and electronic media, besides Internet and outdoor advertising and road shows, to showcase the country's tourism-friendly aspects. India's open skies policy has also led to a massive growth in travel for business and pleasure. The upgrading of national highways connecting various parts of India has opened new avenues for the development of budget hotels here. All this has resulted in exciting opportunities for the hotel industry.

While the potential of the hotel business is great, there are several constraints for the industry to grow. The high cost of land in the country often discourages an investor to put money in the construction of new hotels. The construction of hotels is highly capital intensive—it is estimated that constructing a single five-star room costs around Rs 12.5 million (Rs 1.25 crore). This, according to hoteliers, is hardly an incentive to construct new hotel properties. So there is a mismatch between demand and supply, leading to higher occupancy rates and increasing prices. In fact, the average rate of hotel rooms in five-stars has gone up from Rs 4,000 five years ago to Rs 16,000 in 2008. Though this rate is affordable for business travellers, it is very difficult for leisure travellers to shell out so much money.

Let us now get an overall insight into hotel operations by understanding the definition and the core departments of a hotel.

HOTEL: DEFINITION AND CORE AREAS

The term hotel was used for the first time by the fifth Duke of Devonshire to name a lodging property in London sometime in AD 1760. The word hotel is derived from the French *hôtel,* which refers to a French version of townhouse. Historically in the United Kingdom, Ireland, and several other countries, a townhouse was the residence of a peer or an aristocrat in the capital or major cities. The word hotel could have also derived from *hostel,* which means 'a place to stay for travellers'.

A hotel or an inn is defined by the British Law as a 'place where a bonafide traveller can receive food and shelter, provided he is in a position to pay for it and is in a fit condition to be received'. Hence, a hotel must provide food (and beverage) and lodging to a traveller on payment, but the hotel has the right to refuse if the traveller is not presentable (either drunk, or disorderly, or unkempt) or is not in a position to pay for the services. Alternatively, a hotel may be defined as 'an establishment whose primary business is to provide lodging facilities to a genuine traveller along with food, beverage, and sometimes recreational facilities too on chargeable basis'. Though there are other establishments such as hospitals, college hostels, prisons, and sanatoriums, which offer accommodation, they do not qualify as hotels since they do not cater to the specific needs of a traveller.

A hotel is thus an establishment that provides paid accommodation, generally for a short duration of stay. Hotels often provide a number of additional guest services, such as restaurants, bar, swimming pool, healthcare, retail shops; business facilities like conference halls, banquet halls, board rooms; and space for private parties like birthdays, marriages, kitty parties, etc. Most of the modern hotels nowadays provide the basic facilities in a room—a bed, a cupboard, a small table, weather control (air conditioner or heater), and bathroom—along with other features like a telephone with STD/ISD facility, a television set with cable channel, and broadband Internet connectivity. There might also be a mini-bar containing snacks and drinks (the consumption of the same is added to the guest's bill), and tea and coffee making unit having an electric kettle, cups, spoons, and sachets containing instant coffee, tea bags, sugar, and creamer.

Core Areas of a Hotel: An Overview

The organization of a hotel today is very complex and comprises various departments. The number of departments varies from one establishment to another. All departments may have their own managers, reporting to the general manager and the assistant general manager. Figure 1.19 shows the various departments typically present in a large hotel. Hotel departments fall under the category of either revenue-earning departments or support departments.

Revenue-earning departments are operational departments that sell services or products to guests, thus, directly generating revenue for the hotel. These departments include front office, food and beverage, and hotel-operated shops.

Support departments are the ones which help to generate revenue indirectly by playing a supporting role to the hotel's revenue-earning departments. These include human resource, maintenance, purchase, housekeeping, and so on.

The various departments in a hotel are discussed below in brief (for details, please refer to Chapter 3).

Rooms Division Department   In a large hotel, the housekeeping, front office, and maintenance departments come under rooms division. These departments together are responsible for maintaining and selling the rooms in a hotel. In most hotels, these are the departments that directly or indirectly generate more revenue than any other department. This is because the sale of rooms constitutes a minimum of 50 per cent of the total revenue of a hotel. A hotel's largest margin of profit comes from room sales because a room, once made, can be sold over and over again. The rooms division is headed by the rooms division manager to whom the front office manager, executive housekeeper, and very often the chief engineer report.

Housekeeping department   The housekeeping department is responsible for the cleanliness and upkeep of the front of the house areas as well as back of the house areas, so that they appear as fresh and aesthetically appealing as on the first day when the hotel property opened for business. This department is headed by the executive housekeeper or, in chain hotels, the director of housekeeping.

Front office department   Headed by the front office manager, the front office department is the operational department that is responsible for welcoming and registering guests, allotting rooms, and helping guests check out. Uniformed services like concierge and bell desk, and EPBAX operators are part of the front office department.

Maintenance department   The maintenance department, also called the engineering and maintenance department, is headed by the chief engineer or the chief maintenance officer. The department is responsible for all kinds of maintenance, repair, and engineering work on equipment, machines, fixtures, and fittings.

Food and Beverage Department   The food and beverage (F&B) department includes restaurants, bars, coffee shops, banquets, room service, kitchen, and bakery. This department is headed by the F&B director. While the restaurants, bars, coffee shops, banquets, and room service may be grouped specifically under the F&B service department, headed by the F&B manager, the kitchen and bakery fall under the F&B production department, headed by the executive chef.

Human Resource Department The human resource (HR) department—or the personnel department, as it used to be called earlier—is headed by the human resource manager. Recruitments, orientation, training, employee welfare and compensation, labour laws, and safety norms for the hotel come under the purview of the HR department. The training department is an ancillary department of the HR department. This is headed by the training manager, who takes on the specific task of orientation and training of new employees as well as existing ones.

Sales and Marketing Department The sales and marketing department is headed by the sales and marketing manager. A large hotel may have three or more employees in this department, whereas a small hotel can do with just one employee. The function of this department is five-fold—sales, personal relations, advertising, getting MICE (meeting, incentive, conference, and exhibition) business, and market research. All these functions lead to the common goal of selling the product of the hotel—i.e. rooms—and the services of the hotel by 'creating' customers.

Purchase Department The purchase department is led by the purchase manager, who, in some properties, may report to the financial controller. The procurement of all departmental inventories is the responsibility of the purchase department. In most hotels, the central stores are part of the purchase department.

Financial Control Department Also called the controls department, the financial control department is headed by the financial controller, who is responsible for ratifying all the inventory items of the operational departments. Inventory control procedures are the responsibility of this department. The financial controller, along with the general manager, is responsible for finalizing the budgets prepared by the heads of other departments. The hotel's accounts are also maintained by the controls department. Accounting activities include making payments against invoices, billing, collecting payments, generating statements, handling bank transactions, processing employee payroll data, and preparing the hotel's financial statements.

Security Department Headed by the chief security officer, the security department is responsible for safeguarding the assets, guests, and employees of the hotel. Their functions include conducting fire drills, monitoring surveillance equipment, and patrolling the property.

Fig. 1.19 Departments of a large hotel

SUMMARY

Hospitality industry is an umbrella term for a broad variety of service industries, including, but not limited to, hotels, food service, casinos, and tourism. The industry is very diverse and global, and is greatly impacted by fluctuations within the economy as also by various happenings across the world.

Tourism and hospitality are among the major revenue earning enterprises in the world and also happen to be among the highest priority industries and employers. There has been an upmarket trend in tourism over the last few decades due to developments in technology and transport infrastructure as well as aggressive marketing of tour operators and travel agencies. Tourism contributes to the economic growth of a country by causing employment generation, foreign exchange earning, and infrastructure development. It also promotes a wide range of related industries, such as restaurants, retail and shopping, transportation, and cultural industries.

The origin of the global tourism industry can be traced to early lodging facilities in Europe. But the modern hotel industry took shape in the American continent, some landmarks being the City Hotel in New York, the Tremont House in Boston, and the Statler Hotel in Buffalo. Indian hotel industry has also risen by leaps and bounds from ancient times to modern era. Today, India is an important international tourist destination with 1.25 per cent share in the global business. In absolute terms, 5.08 million international tourists arrived in India in 2007 and spent US $10.7 million, marking a 24.3 per cent rise over the previous year. This growth is attributed to the country's 'Incredible India!' international marketing campaign and its open skies policy, which have led to a massive growth in travel for business and pleasure. All this has opened exciting opportunities for the hotel industry. The hospitality industry is poised to gross Rs 826.76 billion by 2010.

A hotel may be defined as an establishment whose primary business is to provide lodging facilities to a genuine traveller along with food, beverage, and sometimes recreational facilities too on chargeable basis. The organization of a hotel is complex and comprises various revenue-earning and support departments—rooms division, food and beverage, human resource, sales and marketing, purchase, financial control, and security.

KEY TERMS

Bureau de change *fr.* An office or part of a bank where foreign currency is exchanged.

Busboy An employee in a restaurant or café who clears away dishes, sets tables, and assists the servers.

Caravan A group of people, vehicles, or supervised animals that are travelling together for security.

Domestic tourism The tourism activity of people within their own country.

Hotel A place where a bonafide traveller can receive food and shelter, provided he is a position to pay for it and is in a fit condition to be received.

Inbound tourist This refers to tourists entering a particular country.

Itinerary A plan for a journey, listing different places in the order in which they are to be visited.

Memento An object given or kept as a reminder or in memory of somebody or something.

Motel A hotel for people who are travelling by car, with space for parking cars near the rooms.

Outbound tourist This refers to tourists travelling abroad for business or leisure.

Sommelier A wine steward in a restaurant, hotel, or other establishment, who supervises the ordering, storing, and serving of wine.

Souvenir Something bought or kept as a reminder of a place or occasion.

Tourism Movement of people from their normal place of residence to another place (with the intention to return) for a minimum period of twenty four hours to a maximum of six months for the sole purpose of leisure and pleasure.

REVIEW QUESTIONS

Multiple Choice Questions

1. What are the reasons for travelling?
   a) Trade
   b) Pilgrimage
   c) Social
   d) All of the above

2. The primitive lodging houses in Spain were known as:
   a) Dharamshala
   b) Pousadas
   c) Paradors
   d) Cabarets

3. The primitive lodging houses in Portugal were known as:
   a) Dharamshala
   b) Pousadas
   c) Paradors
   d) Cabarets

4. Which empire developed an extensive network of brick-paved roads?
   a) Roman
   b) French
   c) Czars of Russia
   d) Mughals

5. Which was the first building that was especially erected as a hotel?
   a) The Tremont house
   b) City Hotel
   c) Exchange Coffee House
   d) The Palace

6. Which hotel is regarded as the first business hotel in modern era?
   a) The Tremont house
   b) The Palmer house
   c) City Hotel
   d) Statler Hotel

Match the Following

Dharamshala	Japan
Ryokans	India
Relay houses	America
Taverns	China
Hospitia	Europe
Coffee houses	Switzerland

Discussion Questions

1. Define the term hotel.

2. Define tourism and enumerate the importance of tourism with respect to the hotel industry.

3. List the different types of lodging houses that existed in ancient Europe.

4. What facilities does a hotel provide to its guests?

5. Trace the origin and growth of the hotel industry in India.

6. What was the impact of the Grand Tour on the development of the hotel industry in Europe?

7. How does tourism affect the hotel industry?

8. Discuss the contribution of American hoteliers to the development of the hotel industry.

PROJECT WORK

Identify a leading hotel chain and find out the following:

1. When did the company start its operations?
2. Who is the owner of the chain?
3. Which is the chain's first property?
4. What are the innovations and contributions of the hotel chain?

5. Find the different brands operated by the chain.
6. Carry out a comparative analysis of the facilities and services with other hotel chains.

You may take help from the Internet for your assignment.

REFERENCES

Article

Thakaral Tarun (2008), 'Hotel Industry poised for a new growth phase', *Financial Express,* 20 March, http://www.financialexpress.com/news/hotel-industry-is-poised-for-a-new-growth-phase/286542/

Book

Raghubalan G. and Smritee Raghubalan (2007), *Hotel HouseKeeping*, Oxford University Press, New Delhi

Websites

www.buffaloah.com/h/statler/hotel/index.html: Website of the Statler Hotel, accessed on 6 November 2008.

www.fhrai.com: Website of the Federation of Hotels and Restaurants Association of India, accessed on 5 November 2008.

www.maharashtra.gov.in/english/gazetteer/greater_bombay/miscellanoues.html: For history of hotels during the colonial period, accessed on 4 November 2008.

www.nationmaster.com/encyclopedia/Indian-Postal-Service: For history of sarais in medieval India, accessed on 3 November 2008.

www.theashokgroup.com/itdc.html: Website of India Tourist Development Corporation, accessed on 5 November 2008.

http://tourism.gov.in: Website of the Ministry of Tourism, Government of India, for India-specific information and tourism statistics 2007, accessed on 7 November 2008.

www.unwto.org: Website of the United Nations World Travel Organization for current trends on tourism, accessed on 24 October 2008.

www.wttc.org: Official website of World Travel and Tourism Council, accessed between 24 October and 6 November 2008.

CHAPTER 2

Classification of Hotels

Learning Objectives:

After reading this chapter, you will be able to understand the following:
- The need and the criteria for the classification of hotels.
- Classification of hotels—on the basis of star rating, size, location, type of clientele, duration of stay, level of service, and ownership—and alternative accommodation.
- Various tariff plans in hotels.
- Types of guest rooms in hotels.

In the previous chapter we learnt how the hospitality industry has grown into a US $3.5 trillion industry worldwide, and hospitality establishments, specially hotels, are offering every imaginable service to make customers comfortable and to cater to all their needs. With competition getting tough and travellers demanding a wide range of services, hoteliers have come up with specialty products and services to carve out a niche for themselves. Hotels can be categorized on the basis of star rating, services on offer, location, number of rooms, types of rooms, target audience, or even the duration of guest stay, to provide customers an indication of their profile and what to expect from them. This chapter takes an account of the different methods used to classify hotels. As rooms are the most important accommodation product of the hotel industry, the chapter also discusses brief descriptions of various room types.

THE NEED FOR CLASSIFICATION

The hotel industry has grown to its present form by modifying itself with respect to services, architectural design, and care for its guests. The hotels/inns in the olden days only provided the basic need of shelter, and standards of hygiene and sanitation were almost non-existent. The modern hotel provides a clean, hygienic, and well-appointed room with excellent services to its guests. The industry is so diverse and specialized that each hotel has to have a unique selling proposition to survive in the business and also make a profit. Every hotel tries to establish itself as unique, offering the best service to its guests. The classification of hotels helps tourists select a hotel that meets their requirements.

The need for the classification of hotels was felt more with the advent of mass tourism. In order to provide travellers an idea of the type of accommodation they offered, many private clubs, agencies, and travel associations came up with descriptions of their lodging properties in specified regions. Gradually, the governments, national and state tourism organizations, and associations of industries with stakes in the hospitality business, realizing the significance of this, backed the idea and set the standards for various hotel categories. In a nutshell, hotel classification serves the following purposes:

- Lends uniformity in services and sets general standards of a hotel.
- Provides an idea regarding the range and type of hotels available within a geographical location.
- Acts as a measure of control over hotels with respect to the quality of services offered in each category.

CLASSIFICATION OF HOTELS AND OTHER TYPES OF LODGING

Hotels provide accommodation, along with services like food and beverages, and facilities like recreation, conference, and training arrangements, and organization of official or private parties. Each hotel has unique features associated with it. The features may be its location; number of guest rooms; special services such as concierge, travel assistance, and valet parking; facilities such as speciality restaurants, bars, business meeting venues, swimming pool, and so on. The diversity in services and facilities provided by each hotel makes it quite difficult to have any single basis of classification of hotels, and if we classify them on different criteria there will be some hotels which will fall into more than one group. The criteria on which hotels are classified are illustrated in Fig. 2.1 and a detailed classification of hotels is provided in Table 2.1.

Table 2.1 Classification of hotels and other types of lodging

CLASSIFICATION OF HOTELS AND OTHER TYPES OF LODGING							
Standard Classification (by the government committee)	Size	Location	Clientele	Duration of Guest Stay	Level of Services	Ownership	Alternative Accommodation
One star	Small	Downtown	Commercial	Commercial	Upmarket	Propriety ownership	Sarai
Two star	Medium	Suburban	Transient	Resort	Mid-market	Franchise	Dharamshala
Three star	Large	Airport	Suite	Semi-residential	Budget	Management contract	Dak bungalow
Four star	Very large	Resort	Residential	Residential		Time-share	Circuit house
Five star		Motel	B & B Hotel			Condominium	Lodge
Five star deluxe		Floatel	Time-share				Youth hostel
Heritage			Condominium				Yatri niwas
Heritage Classic			Casino				Forest lodge
Heritage Grand			Conference				
			Convention				
			Motel				

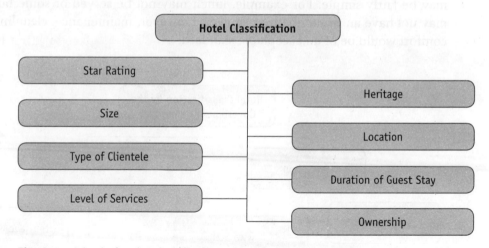

Fig. 2.1 Criteria for the classification of hotels

1. Standard Classification

The star classification system is among the most widely-accepted rating of hotels worldwide. Ratings of hotels in different countries are done by the government or quasi government sources, independent rating agencies, or sometime the hotel operators themselves. The Indian hotel industry follows the star rating system, which indicates the number and standard of facilities offered by the hotel. The classification of hotels is done by a central government committee called the Hotel Restaurant Approval and Classification Committee (HRACC), which inspects and assesses the hotels based on the facilities and services offered. The classification committee includes the Chairman (HRACC) and other members chosen from the government and industry associations such as Federation of Hotel and Restaurant Association of India (FHRAI), Hotel Association of India (HAI), Indian Association of Tour Operators (IATO), Travel Agents Association of India (TAAI), or Institute of Hotel Management Catering Technology and Applied Nutrition (IHM). In case of the Heritage category, a representative of the Indian Heritage Hotel Association (IHHA) is included in the committee. The committee visits the hotels and evaluates the facilities and services of the hotels before the grade is awarded. It classifies hotels as illustrated in Fig. 2.2.

A brief description of the various star categories is given below and Table 2.2 shows a detailed checklist for the classification of hotels in the star-rating system. The facilities that must be present in star category hotels are divided into mandatory (M) and desirable (D) facilities.

One-star Hotels These properties are generally small and independently owned, with a family atmosphere. There may be a limited range of facilities and the meals may be fairly simple. For example, lunch may not be served or some bedrooms may not have an *en suite* bath or shower. However, maintenance, cleanliness, and comfort would be of an acceptable standard.

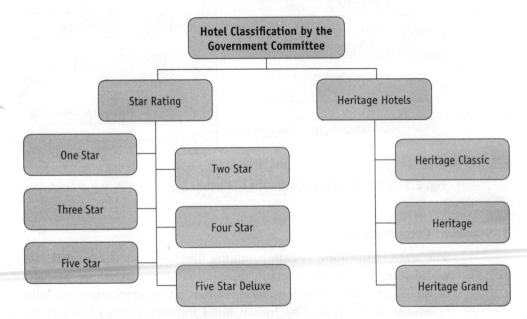

Fig. 2.2 Classification of hotels by the government committee

Table 2.2   Checklist for star classification of hotels in India

Facilities and services required for the classification of hotels in the star-rating system	One Star	Two Star	Three Star	Four Star	Five Star/ Five Star Deluxe	Remarks
GENERAL						
Full time operational	M	M	M	M	M	At least one room equipped for the physically challenged
Possession of necessary licenses	M	M	M	M	M	
Public Liability Insurance	M	M	M	M	M	
Elevator for buildings higher than ground plus two floors	M	M	M	M	M	
Bedrooms, bathrooms, public areas, and kitchens fully serviced daily	M	M	M	M	M	
Floor surfaces clean and in good repair	M	M	M	M	M	
GUEST ROOMS						
Minimum 10 guest rooms—all rooms with outside window or ventilation	M	M	M	M	M	
Minimum size of bedroom excluding bathroom (in sq. ft)	120	120	140	140	200	Single occupancy rooms may be 20 sq. ft less
Air-conditioning	25%	25%	50%	100%	100%	Room temperature should be between 20°C to 28°C for four star, five star, and five star deluxe
A clean change of bed and bath linen, daily and between check-ins	M	M	M	M	M	
Minimum bedding—two sheets, pillow and case, blanket, mattress protector or bed cover	M	M	M	M	M	Mattress protector is desirable in one star and two star, and necessary for all others
TV—cable or dish, whatever is available			M	M	M	Three star, four star, five star, and five star deluxe must have remotes
A writing surface with sufficient lighting			M	M	M	
Chairs	M	M	M	M	M	Preferable one per bedding
Drinking water and one glass tumbler per guest	M	M	M	M	M	Water treated with UV and filtration is necessary
A stationery folder containing stationery and envelopes	D	D	M	M	M	
Turndown service			M	M	M	
Suites				M	M	2% of room block with a minimum of one suite

contd

Table 2.2 *contd*

Facilities and services required for the classification of hotels in the star-rating system	One Star	Two Star	Three Star	Four Star	Five Star/ Five Star Deluxe	Remarks
BATHROOMS						
Percentage of rooms with attached bath	25%	75%	100%	100%	100%	
Minimum size of bathroom (in sq. ft)	30	30	36	36	45	25% of bathrooms in one star and two star to be Western style W.C.
One bath towel and one hand towel to be provided per guest	M	M	M	M	M	If no attached or dedicated bath, to provide in room
Guest toiletries to be provided—minimum one new soap per guest	M	M	M	M	M	Where bathroom is not attached, toiletries provided in room
Sanitary bin	M	M	M	M	M	
Hot and cold running water available 24 hours	D	D	M	M	M	
Bottled toiletry products	D	D	D	M	M	
PUBLIC AREAS						
A lounge or seating in the lobby area	M	M	M	M	M	
Reception facility	M	M	M	M	M	
Public restrooms to have low height urinal (24" max)	M	M	M	M	M	
Ramps with anti-slip floors and handrails at the entrance	D	D	D	M	M	For the physically challenged
Food and beverages						
Dining room serving breakfast and dinner	M	M	M	M	M	
Multi-cuisine restaurant on premises	D	D	M	M	M	
Speciality restaurant			D	M	M	
24-hour coffee shop			D	M	M	
Room service of full meals				M	M	
Room service of alcoholic beverages				M	M	If permitted by local law
Bar				M	M	If permitted by local law
KITCHENS						
Refrigerator with deep freeze	M	M	M	M	M	Capacity based on the size of food and beverages service
Segregated storage of meat, fish, and vegetables	M	M	M	M	M	Meat and fish in freezers; vegetables must be separate
Tiled walls, non-slip floors	M	M	M	M	M	

contd

Table 2.2 *contd*

Facilities and services required for the classification of hotels in the star-rating system	One Star	Two Star	Three Star	Four Star	Five Star/ Five Star Deluxe	Remarks
Head covering for production staff	M	M	M	M	M	
Daily germicidal cleaning of floors	M	M	M	M	M	
Clean utensils	M	M	M	M	M	
Ventilation system	M	M	M	M	M	
STAFF QUALITY						
Staff uniforms for front of the house	M	M	M	M	M	Uniforms to be clean and in good repair
English-speaking front office staff			M	M	M	May be relaxed outside the eight metros/submetros
Percentage of staff with minimum one year certificate course from government recognized catering or hotel institutes	10%	15%	20%	25%	30%	May be relaxed for hotels in rural, pilgrimage, and hill areas
GUEST SERVICES						
Valet service				M	M	
Laundry and dry-cleaning service			D	M	M	
Paid transportation on call			M	M	M	Guest should be able to travel from hotel
Acceptance of common credit cards			M	M	M	
Assistance with luggage on request	M	M	M	M	M	
A public telephone on premises, with unit charges made known			M	M	M	
Wake-up call service on request	M	M	M	M	M	
Messages for guests to be recorded and delivered	M	M	M	M	M	
Names, addresses, and telephone numbers of doctors with front desk	M	M	M	M	M	Doctors on call in three star, four star, five star, and five star deluxe
Stamps and mailing facilities			M	M	M	
Newspapers available	M	M	M	M	M	
Access to travel desk facilities	M	M	M	M	M	
Left luggage facilities			M	M	M	
Health/Fitness facilities					M	
Beauty salon and barber shop				D	M	

contd

Table 2.2 contd

Facilities and services required for the classification of hotels in the star-rating system	One Star	Two Star	Three Star	Four Star	Five Star/ Five Star Deluxe	Remarks
Florist				D	D	
Shop/kiosk			M	M	M	
Money changing facilities				M	M	
Bookshop			D	M	M	
Swimming pool					M	Can be relaxed for hill destinations
Safekeeping facilities available	M	M	M	M	M	
SAFETY AND SECURITY						
Smoke detectors	M	M	M	M	M	Can be battery operated
Fire and emergency procedure notices displayed behind doors in rooms	M	M	M	M	M	
Fire exit signs on guest floors with emergency power	M	M	M	M	M	
Staff trained in first aid	D	D	M	M	M	CPR/choking and regular first aid
First-aid kit with over-the-counter medicines with front desk	M	M	M	M	M	
M= Mandatory, **D**= Desirable						

Source: Adapted from Ministry of Tourism (India Tourism Statistics 2003).

Two-star Hotels   In this class, hotels will typically be small to medium-sized, and offer more extensive facilities than one-star hotels. Guests can expect comfortable, well-equipped overnight accommodation, usually with an *en suite* bath or shower. Reception and other staff will aim for a more professional presentation than at the one-star level and will offer a wider range of straightforward services, including food and beverages.

Three-star Hotels   At this level, hotels are usually of a size to support higher staffing levels as well as a significantly higher quality and range of facilities than at the lower star classifications. Reception and other public areas will be more spacious, and the restaurant will normally also cater to non-residents. All bedrooms will have an *en suite* bath and shower, and will offer a good standard of comfort and equipment, such as a direct-dial telephone and toiletries in the bathroom. Besides room service, some provisions for business travellers can be expected.

Four-star Hotels   Expectations at this level include a degree of luxury as well as quality in the furnishings, décor, and equipment in every area of the hotel. Bedrooms will also usually offer more space than at the lower star levels. They will be well-designed with coordinated furnishings and décor. The *en suite* bathrooms will have both a bath and shower. There will be a high staff to guest ratio, with provisions of porter service, twenty-four-hour room service, and laundry and dry-cleaning services. The restaurant will demonstrate a serious approach to its cuisine.

Five-star Hotels   Five star hotels offer spacious and luxurious accommodations throughout the hotel, matching the best international standards. The interior design should impress with its quality and attention to detail, comfort, and elegance. The furnishings should be immaculate. The service should be formal, well supervised, and flawless in its attention to guests' needs, without being intrusive. The restaurant will demonstrate a high level of technical skill. The staff will be knowledgeable, helpful, and well versed in all aspects of customer care, combining efficiency with courtesy.

Heritage Hotels

A recent addition to the hotel industry in the country, heritage hotels are properties set in small forts, palaces, or *havelis*, the mansions of erstwhile royal and aristocratic families. They have added a new dimension to cultural tourism. In a heritage hotel, a visitor is offered rooms that have their own history, is served traditional cuisine toned down to the requirements of internationals palates, is entertained by folk artistes, can participate in activities that allow a glimpse into the heritage of the region, and can bask in an atmosphere that lives and breathes of the past. Taj Lake Palace in Udaipur and The Oberoi Cecil in Shimla are examples of heritage hotels.

According to the Ministry of Tourism, the heritage hotels are further subdivided as follows:

Heritage   This category covers hotels in residences, *havelis*, hunting lodges, castles, or forts and palaces built between 1935 and 1950.

Heritage Classic   This category covers hotels in residences, *havelis*, hunting lodges, castles, or forts and palaces built prior to 1935 but after 1920.

Heritage Grand   This category covers hotels in residences, *havelis*, hunting lodges, castles, or forts and palaces built prior to 1920.

2. Classification on the Basis of Size

The number of guest rooms in a hotel is a criterion to classify hotels. Hotels can be grouped into the following categories (Fig. 2.3) on the basis of the number of rooms or the size of the hotel:

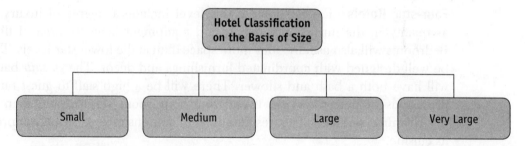

Fig. 2.3 Classification of hotels on the basis of size

Small Hotel In India, hotels with twenty-five rooms or less are classified as small hotels, e.g., Hotel Alka, New Delhi and The Oberoi Vanyavilas, Ranthambore. However, in the developed countries of Europe and America, hotels with less than 100 rooms are considered small. These hotels provide clean and comfortable accommodation but may not provide upmarket facilities, such as swimming pool, restaurant, bar, etc.

Medium Hotel Hotels with twenty-six to hundred rooms are called medium hotels, e.g., Hotel Taj View, Agra and Chola Sheraton Hotel, Chennai. However, in developed nations, hotels with up to 300 rooms are termed medium-sized.

Large Hotel In India, hotels with 101 to 300 guest rooms are regarded as large hotels, e.g., The Imperial, New Delhi and The Park, Kolkata. Whereas, hotels with 400–600 rooms are termed as large hotels in the developed world.

Very Large Hotel Hotels with more than 300 guest rooms are known as very large hotels in our country, e.g., Shangri-La Hotel, New Delhi and Leela Kempinski, Mumbai. In developed nations, hotels with 600–1,000 rooms may be considered very large.

3. Classification on the Basis of Location

The location of the hotel is one of the major criteria for a traveller to select and patronize a hotel. Hotels may be located in the city centre, sub-urban areas, natural locations such as hill stations and sea beaches, near the port of entry into a country, etc. They may be classified into the following categories on the basis of their location (Fig. 2.4):

Downtown Hotel A downtown hotel is located in the centre of the city or within a short distance from the business centre, shopping areas, theatres, public offices, etc. The centre of the city may not necessarily be the geographical centre, but it refers to an area that is considered to be the commercial hub of the city. The room rates in these hotels may be higher than similar hotels in other areas, so as to cover the huge investment made on the land. They are generally preferred

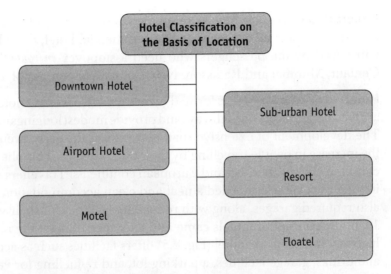

Fig. 2.4 Classification of hotels on the basis of location

by business clientele as they find it convenient to stay close to the place of their business activities. Hotel InterContinental, New Delhi and Hotel Le Meridien, Pune are examples of downtown hotels.

Sub-urban Hotel As the land cost in the city centre is higher and the space is limited, some entrepreneurs build their hotels near the outskirts of the city. Providing similar facilities as the downtown hotels, these hotels are set in sub-urban areas and have the advantage of quieter surroundings. Such hotels are ideal for people who prefer to stay away from the hustle and bustle of a city. The duration of the stay of guests in these hotels may be longer than at a hotel located in the city. The room rates in such hotels are moderate and may attract the budget travellers. Trident Hotel, Gurgaon and Uppal's Orchid, New Delhi are examples of sub-urban hotels.

Resort Hotel Hotels that are located at tourist destinations such as hill stations, sea beaches, and countryside are referred to as resort hotels. These hotels have a very calm and natural ambience. They are mostly away from cities and are located in pollution-free environs. The room rates in these hotels may range from moderate to high, depending on the additional services offered. These hotels combine stay facilities with leisure activities such as golf, summer and winter sports, etc. Some of these hotels are projected as dream destinations to guests who wish to enjoy the beauty of nature and have a memorable holiday. The occupancy in resorts is normally higher during the vacation time and weekends when guests want to take a break from their weekly routine. Taj Fort Aguada Beach Resort, Goa and Wildflower Hall in the Himalayas, Shimla are examples of resort hotels.

Airport Hotel   Airport hotels are situated in the vicinity of airports and other ports of entry. Offering all the services of a commercial hotel, these hotels are generally patronized by the passengers who need a stopover *en route* their journey. Hotel Centaur, Mumbai and Radisson, New Delhi are examples of airport hotels.

Motel   The word 'motel' is formed by merging two words 'motor' and 'hotel'. They are located primarily on highways and provide modest lodgings to highway travellers. The development of extensive road networks in the early twentieth century led to the increase in people travelling by their own vehicles. This phenomenon was quite common in the American and European continents. Travellers who were travelling in their own vehicles needed a neat and clean accommodation for the night. They also required garages, along with re-fuelling facilities for their vehicles. In the year 1950, the concept of motels came into existence to meet the requirements of such highway travellers. A motel (Fig. 2.5) offers facilities such as accommodation, food and drinks, garage facilities, a parking lot, and re-fuelling for vehicles.

Floatel   As the name suggests, floatels are types of lodging properties that float on the surface of water (Fig. 2.6). This category consists of all lodging properties that are built on the top of rafts or semi-submersible platforms, and includes cruise-liners and houseboats. Some of them provide luxurious accommodation, along with food and beverage facilities to guests. The houseboats of Dal Lake in Srinagar in Jammu and Kashmir and Kerala are some examples of floatels in India.

Fig. 2.5   A motel

Fig. 2.6 A floatel

4. Classification on the Basis of Clientele

Hotels cater to the needs of their guests. Every individual or a group of people who patronize a hotel has a different set of requirements. While some would prefer luxurious accommodation, others would like to stay in a simple and cheap room. Some would require facilities such as meeting rooms, business centres, and conference halls if their travel is business oriented. Being a capital-intensive industry, the diversities in guest requirements discourage hotels from catering to all types of travellers. As a result, hotels choose to carve out a niche for themselves by catering to the needs of specific guest segments. Hotels can be classified into the following categories on the basis of their clientele (Fig. 2.7):

Business or Commercial Hotel Designed to cater to the business traveller, commercial hotels are generally situated in the city centre. These hotels provide high-standard rooms and amenities, along with high speed Internet connectivity, business centres, and conference halls. They also provide in-house secretarial services, as well as facilities such as letter drafting, typing, fax, and photocopying of documents for the convenience of their guests. The guest amenities at commercial hotels may include complimentary newspapers, morning coffee, cable television, and access to channelled music and movies. The duration of guest stay is generally very short at these hotels. The occupancy level is higher during the weekdays and slightly lower during weekends. These hotels are also known as downtown hotels. The Park and Hotel InterContinental in New Delhi are examples of business or commercial hotels.

Transient Hotel Transient hotels cater to the needs of people who are on the move and need a stopover *en route* their journey. Located in the close proximity of ports of entry, such as sea port, airport, and major railway stations, these hotels are normally patronized by transient travellers. They have round-the-clock operational

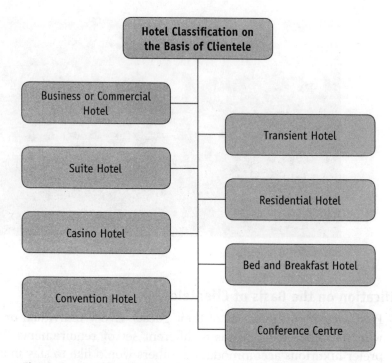

Fig. 2.7 Classification of hotels on the basis of clientele

room service and coffee shop, and offer all the facilities of a commercial hotel. Transient hotels are usually five-star, and their target market includes business clientele, airline passengers with overnight travel layovers or cancelled flights, and airline personnel. The occupancy rate is usually very high, sometimes more than 100 per cent, as rooms can be sold more than once on a given day. Hotel Centaur and Radisson in New Delhi are examples of transient hotels in India. Airport hotels fall under this category.

Suite Hotel   Suite hotels provide the highest level of personalized services to guests. The guest rooms generally comprise a living area, a compact kitchenette, complete with a refrigerator and a microwave, a bedroom attached with a bathroom, and sometimes even a dance floor. The facilities are highly customized and may include valet services, personalized guest stationery, high-speed Internet connection, and in-room safety locker facility. These hotels are patronized by affluent people and tourists who are fond of luxury. Burj Al Arab, Dubai and InterContinental The Lalit Goa Resort are examples of all suite hotels.

Residential Hotel   As the name suggests, residential hotels provide accommodation for a longer duration. These hotels are generally patronized by people who are on a temporary official deputation to a city where they do not have their own residential accommodation. Guests stay for a minimum period of one month and up to two years. The services offered by these hotels are modest. The room's configuration is usually similar to that of suite hotels. Guest rooms generally include a sitting room, bedroom, and small kitchenette. They are akin to small individual apartments. These hotels may have a fully operational restaurant or a dining room for the resident guests, and may provide services such as daily housekeeping, telephone, front desk, and uniformed services. The guest may choose to contract some or all of the services provided by the apartment hotel. The hotel signs a lease with the guest and the rent is paid either monthly or quarterly.

Bed and Breakfast Hotel A European concept, bed and breakfast (B&B) hotels are lodging establishments, generally operated in large family residences. These range from houses with few rooms converted into overnight facilities to small commercial buildings with twenty to thirty guest rooms. The owner usually lives on the premises and is responsible for serving breakfast to guests. Guests are accommodated in bedrooms and breakfast is served in the room or sometimes in the dining room. The bathrooms may be attached to the guest rooms or may be on a sharing basis. As the tariff is generally lower than a full-service hotel at these properties, they are suitable for budget travellers.

Casino Hotel Casino hotels provide gambling facilities, such as Luxor Hotel and Casino in Las Vegas. These hotels attract the clients by promoting gambling, arranging extravagant floor shows, and some may also provide charter flight services to its clients. They have state-of-the-art gambling facilities, along with speciality restaurants, bars, round-the-clock room service, well appointed and furnished rooms for its guests. Nowadays, these hotels are also attracting the MICE (meetings, incentives, conferences, and exhibitions) segment. The casinos of Las Vegas, USA are among the most famous casinos in the world.

Conference Centres The word conference means 'a meeting, sometimes lasting for several days, in which people with a common interest participate in discussions or listen to lectures to obtain information'. Thus, a conference centre is a hotel which caters to the needs of a conference delegation. These hotels provide rooms to delegates of conferences; a conference hall with the desired seating configuration for the meetings; food and beverage requirements during and after the conference; and other requirements, such as flip chart, white board with markers, overhead projector, television, VCR/VCD/DVD player, slide projector, LCD projector with screen, computer, and public address system. These are large hotels, having more than 400 guest rooms. The services provided are of the highest standard. Normally, conferences are charged as packages, which include accommodation and meeting facilities. Hotel Ashok, New Delhi is an example of conference centres.

Convention Hotels Convention is defined as 'a formal assembly or meeting of members, representatives, or delegates of a group for general agreement on or acceptance of certain practices or attitudes'. This type of meeting involves a large number of participants. The hotels catering to the needs of this segment are known as convention hotels. These hotels may have more than 2,000 rooms to accommodate the large number of delegates. They are equipped with state-of-the-art convention centre with all the required facilities, such as seating configuration (T-shaped, classroom-type, workshop-style, and theatre-style), audio-visual equipments, and public address system to meet the demands of a convention. Hotel Taj Palace, New Delhi and Hotel Jaypee Palace, Agra are examples of convention hotels in India. A convention hotel has a greater number of rooms to host the large number of attendees as compared to conference centers.

5. Classification on the Basis of Duration of Guest Stay

On the basis of the duration of guest stay, hotels may be classified into the following categories (Fig. 2.8):

Commercial Hotel   The duration of guest stay in these hotels is short, ranging from a few days to a week.

Transient Hotel   Mostly occupied by travellers as stopovers *en route* their journey, the duration of stay at transient hotels is very short, a day or even less.

Semi-residential Hotel   These hotels are generally patronized by people who are staying at a location while in transit to another place. The duration of stay may range from few weeks to some months. They incorporate the features of both transient and residential hotels.

Residential/Apartment Hotel   As the name suggests, residential hotels provide accommodation for long duration and are patronized by people who stay for a long time. The duration of stay may range from months to few years.

Extended Stay Hotel   In today's age of downsizing, outsourcing, and mobility, business executives are often away from their hometowns for extended periods of time and require more than a hotel room. These hotels are for those guests

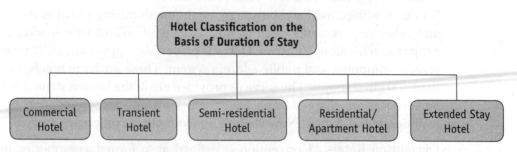

Fig. 2.8   Classification of hotels on the basis of the duration of guest stay

who wish to stay for a long period (from few days to weeks), and cater to their long-term needs with special services, amenities, and facilities, such as full-fledged kitchens with dishes and kitchenware, refrigerator, separate area to wash clothes, housekeeping services, grocery shopping services, and recreational facilities. The room rates of these hotels are determined by the length of stay.

6. Classification on the Basis of Level of Services

On the basis of services offered by a hotel, they may be classified into the following categories (Fig. 2.9):

Upmarket/Luxury/World Class Services Hotels Targeting the affluent segment of society, hotels in the up-market category offer world class products with personalized services of the highest standard. The emphasis is on excellence and class. These hotels provide upscale restaurants and lounges, exquisite décor, concierge service, opulent rooms, and abundant amenities. The design and interior decoration of the hotel itself reflects the standards maintained by the hotel. The guest rooms are large with exquisite decoration and furnishings. Generally, a valet is assigned to each guest room. These hotels have many speciality restaurants with full-assisted service. Top-end recreational facilities, such as golf course, tennis courts, designer swimming pools with trained life guards, and other sports facilities, shopping arcades, beauty salons, health spas with saunas and jacuzzi, are a regular feature. These hotels also offer the facility of health clubs with trainers and dieticians. The shopping arcade may have branded retails shops of books, gifts and souvenirs, jewellery, and handicrafts. These hotels are generally patronized by affluent people who care for quality and include business executives, celebrities, and high-ranking political figures. The Oberoi Udaivilas, Udaipur and ITC Hotel Grand Maratha Sheraton & Towers, Mumbai are few of the luxury hotels in India.

Mid-market/ Mid-range Services Hotels These hotels offer modest services without the frills and personalized attention of luxury hotels, and appeal to the largest segment of travellers. They may offer services such as room service, round-the-clock

Fig. 2.9 Classification of hotels on the basis of level of services

coffee shop, airport/railway station pick-up and drop facilities; and multi-cuisine restaurant with bar. A typical hotel offering mid-range service would be medium sized, having roughly 150 to 300 rooms. The room rent is much lower than the upmarket hotels. These hotels are patronized by business travellers, individual travellers, and groups. Since meeting rooms are usually found in mid-market hotels, people planning small conferences, group meetings, and conventions may also find these hotels attractive. Taj Residency, Lucknow and Trident Hotel, Jaipur are examples of mid-market hotels.

Budget/Economy Hotels   Budget hotels focus on meeting the most basic needs of guests by providing clean, comfortable, and inexpensive rooms. Also known as economy or limited services hotels, they appeal primarily to budget-minded travellers and groups. The clientele of budget hotels may also include families with children, bus tour groups, travelling business people, vacationers, retired persons, and groups of people travelling together. These hotels have clean and comfortable guest rooms, a coffee shop, a multi-cuisine restaurant, in-room telephone, and channelled music and movies. They may also have a swimming pool, a shopping arcade, and a beauty parlour.

7. Classification on the Basis of Ownership

On the basis of ownership of a hotel, they may be classified into the following categories (Fig. 2.10):

Proprietary Ownership   Proprietary ownership is the direct ownership of one or more properties by a person or company. Small lodging properties that are owned and operated by a couple or family are common examples of proprietary ownership.

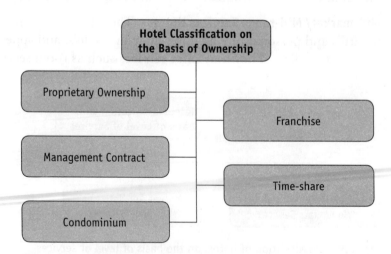

Fig. 2.10   Classification of hotels on the basis of ownership

Large properties that are owned by major international hotel companies, such as Marriott or Hilton, also belong to this category. A group of hotels that are owned or managed by one company is called a chain. In general, three or more units constitute a chain, but some major hotel chains have 300 to 500 properties. A proprietary chain is owned entirely by one company. In India, the Taj Hotels Resorts and Palaces and the Oberoi Hotels and Resorts fall under this category.

Hotel chains account for the majority of revenue in the hotel industry. Marriott ITT, Sheraton, Westin, Radisson, Sofitel, and InterContinental are examples of successful hotel chains in the world (refer Exhibit 2.1).

Franchise Let us understand the following terminologies related to franchise before we talk about it:

Franchise It is the authorization given by a company to another company or individual to sell its unique products/services and use its trademark according to the guidelines given by the former, for a specified time, and at a specified place.

Franchisor The franchisor is the company that owns the trademark, product/business format that is being franchised.

Franchisee The franchisee is the company or the individual to whom the franchisor confers the right to do business under its name as per the terms and conditions agreed upon.

Franchising A continuing relationship in which the franchisor provides a licensed privilege to do the business, plus assistance in organizing, training, merchandizing, and management in return for a consideration from the franchisee.

In the hospitality industry, we often come across many big chains that are operating on a franchise basis. In this kind of contract, which is mutually beneficial to both parties, the franchisor allows the franchisee to use the company's ideas,

---

Exhibit 2.1   List of some leading hotel chains of the world

Accor-Pullman	Best Western	Canadian Pacific
Choice International	Club Méditerranée	Conrad International
Dusit Thani	Forte Hotels	Four Seasons
Golden Tulip	Hilton International	Holiday Inn
Hyatt Hotels	InterContinental Hotels	Kempinski Hotels
Mandarin Oriental	Marriott Hotels	Meridien Hotels
New Otani Hotels	Nikko Hotels	Oberoi Hotels
Pentahotels	Radisson Hotels	Ramada Hotels
SAS International Hotels	Shangri-La Hotels	Sheraton Hotels
Steigenberger Hotels	Taj Hotels	Westin Hotels

methods, trademarks, as well as the brand logo to do the business. A private investor or franchisee can obtain the trademark license, architectural plans, blueprints, interior designs, training, and operating methods of the franchisor by paying a fee. The franchisee is generally responsible for financing the construction of the hotel, although some franchisors offer construction loans or may lease real estate to franchisees.

The franchisee must abide by the franchiser's quality standards and product specifications, but is the legal owner of the business. Thus, many hotels that are using the logo of Holiday Inn, Sheraton, or Hilton may actually be owned by local, independent investors.

The contract between the franchisor and franchisee spells out obligations of both sides. Subjects like accounting practices, maintenance procedure, sales and marketing, advertising, personnel hiring and training, and inventory control are described in detail in the agreement. A franchisee pays an initial fee upon signing the franchise agreement. Franchisees also pay ongoing royalties based on the total income of the hotel regardless of expenses. The franchisor may charge an additional fee for advertising, access to computer reservations systems, and other services. For example, Holiday Inn franchisees pay a percentage of room sales for the use of the company's computer reservations system (Holidex).

Uniform operating standards are important in a franchise organization. Travellers patronize a franchise hotel because they believe that the quality and service will be consistent from one location to another. The franchisees benefits immensely as they immediately get represented on the large chain of the franchisor. The central reservation systems of big franchisors provide leads to travellers worldwide about a franchised property. A franchisee who fails to conform to the franchisor's quality standards may lose the franchise and all of the associated rights and privileges.

Some of the well known franchise chains in the world include Holiday Inn, Days Inn, Ramada Inn, ITT Sheraton, Best Western, Accor and Choice Hotels International chain, which includes Quality Inns, Comfort Inns, and several other hospitality brands.

Management Contract Managing a hotel requires professional expertise. A new entrepreneur with little or no experience in the business may safely choose to become the franchisee of any well-established hotel chain. There could still be a problem in operating the business because the franchisor provides the well-established image, a tested and successful operating system, training programme, marketing, advertisement, and reservation system, but does not provide the cadre of experienced managers and employees necessary to run the business on a day-to-day basis. To bridge this gap, management contract companies came into existence.

These companies have the required expertise to manage hotels. They operate on the basis of management fee and sometimes on a percentage of the gross revenue.

Management contract, as the name suggests, is a contract between the owner of the property and a hotel operator (management contractor) by which the owner employs the operator as an agent to assume the full responsibility for operating and managing the hotel. The operator can be a hotel chain with reputed name and market image, such as Hilton, Sheraton, Best Western, Choice Hospitality, etc. (refer Exhibit 2.2)

Time-share Hotels   Time-share hotels, also referred to as vacation-interval hotels, are a new concept in the hospitality industry. As the name suggests, it entails purchasing a tourist accommodation at a popular destination for a particular time slot in a year. The buyers can then occupy the property for the appointed time or rent the unit to other vacationers if they cannot avail the facility. They have to make a one-time payment for the time slot and a yearly fee to cover the maintenance costs and related expenses, and take a share in the profit from the income generated if they are not utilizing their time slot. Club Mahindra holiday resorts are a popular example of time-share properties in India.

Time-share is an expanding segment in the industry today and is acquiring popularity among frequent vacationers. The following example will help us understand the concept of time-share. Let us suppose that there is a Hotel Beach Front in Goa with twenty apartments. The various apartments of the hotel can be sold to different people for different periods of time for a specific number of years. The total number of one week slots may be calculated as under:

No. of one week slot owners = No. of apartments (guest rooms) × No. of weeks in
$$\text{the year}$$
$$= 20 \times 52 = 1,040$$

Thus, the same property can be sold to 1,040 individual owners for specific time slots during the year. These individuals are the owners of the apartment for that time duration. They can either enjoy their time slots or can rent them out to a management company to run the hotel.

Exhibit 2.2   List of leading management companies of the world

Starwood Hotels & Resorts	Wyndham International	Meristar Hotel & Resorts
Westmont Hospitality	Interstate Hotels & Resorts	Prime Hospitality
Lodgian	Tharaldson Property Management	Boykin Hospitality
Sage Hospitality Resources	John Q. Hammons Hotels & Resorts	Columbia Sussex
Moa Hospitality	Sunburst Hospitality Corporation	Lane Hospitality

Condominium Hotels   Condominium hotels are similar to time-share hotels, except that condominium hotels have a single owner instead of multiple owners sharing the hotel. In a condominium hotel, the owner informs the management company when they would occupy the unit. The management company is free to rent the unit for the remainder of the year, and this revenue goes to the owner. Owners generally pay a monthly or annual maintenance fee to the management company that takes care of the premises, including landscaping, cleaning of common areas, water and power supply, etc. The RCI (Resorts and Condominiums & Inns) Group of Singapore are among the most popular examples of such properties.

Alternative Accommodation

Alternative accommodation can be simply defined as 'all those types of accom-modation that are available outside the formal or organized accommodation sector'. These establishments provide bed and breakfast and some basic services required by guests at a reasonable price. An alternative accommodation, thus, provides sleeping space and modest food to its users. There are certain properties that cater to the needs of a large group. The lodging houses constructed for the welfare of common travellers, such as *sarais, dharamshalas, dak* bungalows, circuit, houses, inspection bungalows, lodges, youth hostels, *yatri niwas*, and forest lodges, are examples of alternative accommodation (Fig. 2.11).

Fig. 2.11   Alternative accommodation

Sarai/Dharamshala These lodging properties are mostly found at popular pilgrimage places. They are generally constructed by welfare trusts, social organizations, or even the state, and provide basic security and sleeping facilities for a nominal fee.

Dak Bungalow/Circuit House/Inspection Bungalow/Forest Lodge A legacy of the British Raj, these were built as rest houses for colonial officials across the country as well as in remote areas and scenic locales. All these properties have an ageless charm and an old world style of hospitality as well as special cuisine, which forms a part of the attraction, apart from the low tariff. These are owned by the various state governments and can be accessed through the local district administration. Often these are the only lodging properties in remote areas.

Lodge/Boarding House Lodges are modest hotels situated away from the centre of the city or located at a remote destination. These are self-sufficient establishments that offer standard facilities, such as clean and comfortable rooms, food and beverage (F&B) services (bar facility may also feature sometime). Boarding houses are establishments that usually provide accommodation and meals at a specified period of time, such as weekends, or for a specified time of stay.

Youth Hostel The youth, from rural as well as urban areas, travel for various reasons, such as education, adventure, and recreation. Youth hostels were established to cater to the youth on the move, who couldn't afford steep hotel rents. A youth hostel generally provides low-cost dormitory accommodation with common bathing and cafeteria facilities. They may also provide kitchens for self-catering.

Yatri Niwas A yatri niwas provides low-cost, self-service accommodation to domestic tourists in cities. The emphasis is on modest comfort and affordability. These are generally frequented by people during brief stopovers while travelling between places, or by families with modest budgets. These properties are located at historical, cultural, and natural sites.

Camping Grounds/Tourists Camps Camping grounds are normally located within cities in open spaces. They provide parking spaces along with water, electricity, and toilets. Camps must follow certain regulations regarding the quality of services and cost, and are set up by municipalities.

Railway/Airport Retiring Rooms A retiring room is for the convenience of the transit travellers. These are situated at major railway stations and domestic and international airports. They provide a resting place to passengers with confirmed and current tickets. These retiring rooms are available at reasonable rates and are often air-conditioned. Booking for the same is made through the station superintendent or the airport manager. They are equipped with clean sanitation facilities and may include F&B facilities at a cost.

Paying Guest Accommodation   A paying guest (PG) accommodation is a non-institutional accommodation offered by individual households at various destinations. Besides tourist havens like Goa, this kind of accommodation is becoming popular in large metropolitan cities among outstation students and the employed youth migrants from other towns. Guests normally pay for accommodation, while the rules for F&B services may differ from host to host.

HOTEL TARIFF PLANS

The various tariff patterns followed by hotels have come to be identified with the areas where such patterns originated. Hotels charge their guests according to the European, Continental, American, Bed and Breakfast meal plans, etc. We shall briefly discuss these plans in this chapter and study them in greater detail in Chapter 6.

European Plan   The tariff consists of room rate only. All other expenses would be paid by the guest as per the actual use or consumption.

Continental Plan   The room tariff includes continental breakfast, along with the room rent. A continental breakfast includes a choice of fresh or canned juices; breads like croissant, toast, brioche, etc. with butter or preserves like jam, jellies, and marmalade; beverages like tea or coffee, with or without milk.

American Plan   It is also known as en-pension or full board. The tariff includes all meals (breakfast, lunch, and dinner) along with the room rent. The menu for the food and beverages is fixed.

Modified American Plan   It is also known as demi-pension or half board. The tariff consists of breakfast and one major meal (lunch or dinner) along with the room rent.

Bed & Breakfast (B&B) or Bermuda Plan   The room tariff includes American breakfast along with the room rent. American breakfast generally includes most or all of the following: two eggs (fried or poached), sliced bacon or sausages, sliced bread or toast with jam/jelly/butter, pancakes with syrup, cornflakes or other cereal, coffee/tea, and orange/grapefruit juice.

TYPES OF GUEST ROOMS

A hotel sells a combination of accommodation, food, drinks, and other services and facilities to its guests. The main accommodation product is the room, which is among the principal sources of revenue for the hotel. Other facilities and benefits, such as ambience, décor, in-room amenities, and security, are add-ons that play a significant role in the pricing of the services. In order to suit the profile and pocket of various kinds of guests, hotels offer different types of rooms that cater to the specific needs of guests. The rooms maybe categorized on the basis of the room size, layout, view, interior decoration, and services offered. The various types of rooms offered by a hotel are as follows (Fig. 2.12):

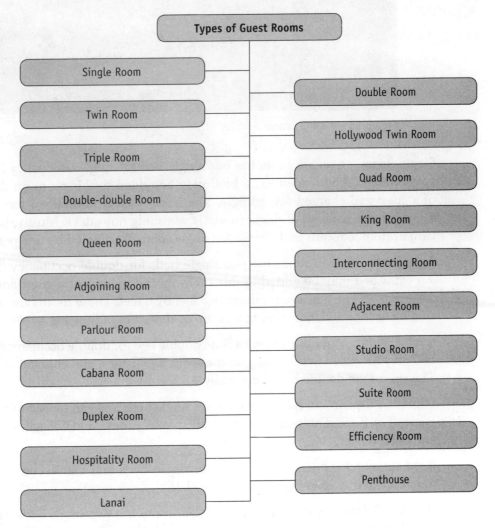

Fig. 2.12 Types of guest rooms

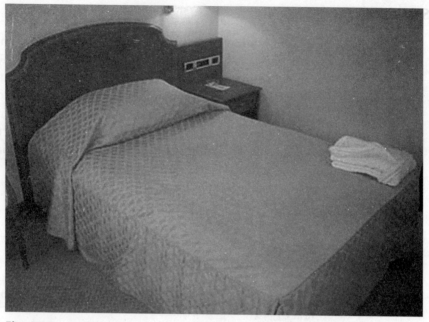

Fig. 2.13   A single room

Single Room   A single room has one single bed for single occupancy (Fig. 2.13). An additional bed (called extra bed) may be added to this room on the request of a guest and charged accordingly. The size of bed is normally 3 feet by 6 feet. However, the concept of single rooms is vanishing nowadays. Mostly, hotels have twin or double rooms and charge for single room if occupied by one person.

Twin Room   A twin room has two single beds for double occupancy (Fig. 2.14). An extra bed may be added to this room on the request of a guest and charged accordingly. The bed size is normally 3 feet by 6 feet. These rooms are suitable for sharing accommodation among a group or delegates of meeting.

Double Room   A double room has one double bed for double occupancy. An extra bed may be added to this room on the request of a guest and charged accordingly. The size of the double bed is generally 4.5 feet by 6 feet.

Triple   A triple room has three separate single beds and can be occupied by three guests (Fig. 2.15). This type of room is suitable for groups and delegates of meetings and conferences.

Quad   A quad room has four separate single beds and can accommodate four persons together in the same room (Fig. 2.16).

Hollywood Twin Room   A Hollywood twin room has two single beds with a common headboard (Fig. 2.17). This type of room is generally occupied by two guests.

Fig. 2.14   A twin room

Fig. 2.15   A triple room

Double-Double Room   A double-double room has two double beds (Fig. 2.18) and is normally preferred by a family or group as it can accommodate four persons together.

King Room   A king room has a king size bed. The size of the bed is 6 feet by 6 feet. An extra bed may be added to this room on the request of a guest and charged accordingly.

Fig. 2.16 A quad room

Fig. 2.17 A Hollywood twin room

Queen Room A queen room has a queen size bed. The size of the bed is 5 feet by 6 feet. An extra bed may be added to this room on the request of a guest and charged accordingly.

Fig. 2.18 A double-double room

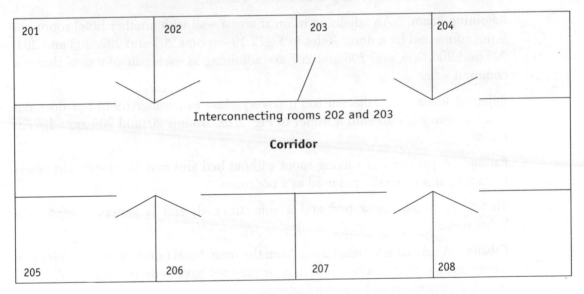

Fig. 2.19 Interconnecting, adjoining, and adjacent rooms

Interconnecting Room Interconnected rooms have a common wall and a door that connects the two rooms. This allows guests to access any of the two rooms without passing through a public area. This type of rooms is ideal for families and

Fig. 2.20 A suite

crew members. Refer to Fig. 2.19—rooms 202 and 203 are interconnecting rooms as there is an interconnecting door between them.

Adjoining Room   An adjoining room shares a wall with another hotel room but is not connected by a door. Refer to Fig. 2.19—rooms 201 and 202, 203 and 204, 205 and 206, 206, and 206 and 207 are adjoining as each pair of rooms shares a common wall.

Adjacent Room   An adjacent room is very close to another room but does not share a common wall with it. Refer to Fig. 2.19—rooms 201and 205 are adjacent rooms.

Parlour   A parlour has a living room without bed and may have sofa and chairs for sitting. It is generally not used as a bedroom.

Studio   A studio has a bed and a sofa-cum-bed, and is generally used as a living room.

Cabana   A cabana is situated away from the main hotel building, in the vicinity of a swimming pool or sea beach. It may or may not have beds and is generally used as a changing room and not as a bedroom.

Suite   A suite comprises more than one room; occasionally, it can also be a single large room with clearly defined sleeping and sitting areas (Fig. 2.20). The décor of such units is of very high standards, aimed to please the affluent guest who can afford the high tariffs of the room category.

Fig. 2.21 A duplex suite—lower level

Fig. 2.22 An efficiency room

Duplex A duplex suite comprises two rooms situated on different floors, which are connected by an internal staircase (Fig. 2.21). This suite is generally used by business guests who wish to use the lower level as an office and meeting place and the upper level room as a bedroom. This type of room is quite expensive.

Fig. 2.23   A hospitality room

Fig. 2.24   A penthouse

Fig. 2.25   A lanai

Efficiency Room   An efficiency room has an attached kitchenette for guests preferring longer duration of stay (Fig. 2.22). Generally, this type of room is found in holiday and health resorts where guests stay for a longer time.

Hospitality Room   A hospitality room is designed for hotel guests who would want to entertain their own guests outside their allotted rooms (Fig. 2.23). Such rooms are generally charged on an hourly basis.

Penthouse   A penthouse is generally located on the topmost floor of hotels and has an attached open terrace or open sky space (Fig. 2.24). It has very opulent décor and furnishings, and is among the costliest rooms in the hotels, preferred by celebrities and major political personalities.

Lanai   A lanai has a veranda or roofed patio, and is often furnished and used as a living room (Fig. 2.25). It generally has a view of a garden or sea beach.

SUMMARY

The hotel industry is so big and diverse that each hotel has come up with speciality products and services to carve out a niche for itself. Depending on the services on offer, or the clients they are targeting, or their location, hotels can be categorized variously to provide customers an indication of their profile and what to expect from them. The main advantage of classification is that it lends uniformity in services and sets the general standards of a hotel. Other benefits of the exercise include giving an idea about the range and type of hotels available within a geographical area, and protecting the users by ensuring the minimum quality available in each category.

The star-classification system is the most widely accepted form of rating, where hotels are rated as one star, two star, three star, four star, five star, and five star deluxe on the basis of services and facilities offered by them. Hotels in the heritage category, covering hotels in forts, palaces, *havelis*, and aristocratic residences, are classified into heritage classic and heritage grand categories. On the basis of their size, hotels are divided in small, medium, large, and very large categories. The location of a hotel decides whether it is a downtown hotel, suburban hotel, resort hotel,

airport hotel, motel, or floatel. Depending on the types of guests they cater to, hotels are classified as: business hotel, transient hotel, suite hotel, residential hotel, bed and breakfast hotel, casino hotel, conference centre, or convention hotel. The duration of guest stay determines whether a hotel is a commercial hotel, resort hotel, semi-residential hotel, residential/apartment hotel, and extended stay hotel. The level of services distinguishes a hotel as upmarket, mid-market, or budget hotel. On the basis of ownership, hotels are classified as proprietary ownership, franchise, management contract, time-share, and condominium.

Besides these hotels, alternative accommodation maybe found in sarai/dharamshala, dak bungalow/ circuit house, lodge/boarding house, youth hostel, yatri niwas, camping ground/tourist camp, railway/airport retiring room, or paying guest accommodation. Each hotel has a range of tariff plans, which include European plan, continental plan, American plan, modified American plan, and bed and breakfast plan. The types of guest rooms include single room, double room, twin room, Hollywood twin room, triple room, quad room, double-double room, king room, queen room, and many more.

KEY TERMS

Adjacent room It is a room that is very close to another room but does not share a common wall with the it.

Adjoining room It is a room that shares a wall with another hotel room but is not connected by a door.

Airport hotel A hotel situated in the vicinity of airport and other ports of entry.

B&B hotel It is generally a large family residence, where the owner lives on the premises and is responsible for serving breakfast to guests.

Cabana room It is a room situated away from the main hotel building, near a swimming pool or sea beach, and mostly used as a changing room.

Casino hotel A hotel that provides gambling facilities.

Commercial hotel A hotel situated in the city centre or business centre, catering to the business traveller.

Condominium A hotel owned by a single owner who might use it for some part of the year and rent it out for the remainder of the year.

Convention hotel A hotel with a convention centre and large number of rooms to accommodate all participants of a convention.

Double room This type of room has one double bed for double occupancy.

Double-double room It is a room with two double beds to accommodate four people.

Downtown hotel A hotel located in the city centre or within a short distance from the business centre, sopping areas, public offices, etc.

Duplex This type of suite has two rooms which are situated on two different floors and are connected by an internal staircase.

Efficiency room A room with an attached kitchenette for guests staying for a long duration.

Extended stay hotel A hotel where people, mainly business executives, stay for extended periods of time, providing facilities like kichens with dishes and kitchenware, washing area, and grocery shopping services.

Floatel A hotel that floats on water, like cruiseliners and houseboats.

Franchise An arrangement in which a private investor runs a hotel under a hotel chain on having signed a contract with the latter.

Heritage hotel A hotel set in a fort, palace, or *haveli*.

Hollywood twin room This type of room has two single beds with a common head board.

Hospitality room A room outside a guest room where the guest may entertain her visitors.

Interconnecting room These are rooms with a common wall and a door that connects the rooms. This allows guests to access rooms without passing through a public area.

King room A room with a king size bed (6 by 6 feet).

Lanai A veranda or roofed patio, furnished and used as a living room.

Management contract companies Companies having the expertise to manage hotels, operating on the basis of a management fee or a percentage of the gross revenue.

Motel A hotel located on a highway, providing moderate lodgings to highway travellers.

Parlour room A living room without a bed.

Penthouse A room with a terrace, located on the topmost floor of a hotel.

Proprietary ownership It is the direct ownership of one or more hotels by a person or company.

Residential hotel Also called apartment hotel, this type of hotel caters to people who stay for a duration of one month to two years.

Resort These are the hotels that are located at destinations of tourist attractions like hill stations, sea beaches, and countryside.

Quad room A room with four separate single beds to accommodate four people.

Queen room A room with a queen size bed (5 by 6 feet).

Semi-residential hotel A hotel catering to people in transit to another place, incorporating features of both transient and residential hotels.

Single room This type of room has one single bed for single occupancy.

Studio room A room with a bed and sofa-cum-bed, generally used as a living room.

Suite This type of room has a living room separated from bedroom area.

Sub-urban hotel These are hotels located in suburban areas, away from the city centres, and have the advantage of quieter surroundings.

Time-share hotel It is a hotel that is jointly owned by people who use it at different times.

Transient hotel These hotels cater to the needs of people who are on the move and need a stopover *en route* their journey.

Triple room A room with three single beds to accommodate three people.

Twin room This type of room has two single beds for double occupancy.

REVIEW QUESTIONS

Multiple Choice Questions

1. Hotels can be classified on the basis of:

   a) Location   b) Size

   c) Level of service   d) All of the above

2. On the basis of location, hotels are of the following types:

   a) Downtown hotel   b) Airport hotel

   c) Resort   d) All of the above

3. Which is not an example of alternative accommodation?

   a) Dharamshala   b) Dak bungalow

   c) Circuit house   d) Commercial hotel

4. Continental plan includes:

   a) Room rent only

   b) Room rent and lunch

   c) Only breakfast and dinner

   d) Room rent and continental breakfast

5. Which plan is also known as demi-pension?

   a) Continental plan

   b) American plan

   c) Modified American plan

   d) Bermuda plan

6. A room having separate living and bed room is known as:

   a) Double room   b) Suite

   c) Twin room   d) Hollywood twin room

7. Where are motels located?

   a) At sea port   b) At airport

   c) Along highways   d) At exotic location

Fill in the Blanks

1. Hotels located in the heart of the city are known as _____ hotels.

2. Hotels located at the port of entry are known as _____ hotels.

3. Boat houses floating on the surface of Dal lake in Kashmir are an example of _____ hotels.

4. _____ hotels generally provide accommodation for a longer duration.

5. _____ hotels provide gambling facilities to guests.

6. The room on the topmost floor of a hotel is called a _____

Discussion Questions

1. What are the different bases of the classification of hotels?

2. The classification of hotels is very important. Comment.

3. What are the factors that are considered to classify a hotel into star category?

4. Classify hotels in your area on the basis of location.

5. What is the difference between time-share and condominium hotels?

6. Explain the concept of time-share.

7. What is a residential hotel?

8. Explain a suite hotel and how it differs from other hotels.

9. What facilities does a casino hotel offer to its guests?

10. Explain B&B hotels.

11. Classify hotels on the basis of levels of services.

12. Describe the various types of rooms you will find in a hotel.

PROJECT WORK

Prepare a list of hotels in your area. Find out the information regarding the number of rooms, facilities, and services offered by them. Classify them on the basis of:

1. Star classification
2. Size
3. Location
4. Type of clientele
5. Duration of guest stay
6. Level of services
7. Ownership
8 Alternative accommodation

Assign reasons for the same.

REFERENCE

Book

Raghubalan G. and Smritee Raghubalan (2007), Hotel Housekeeping, Oxford University Press, New Delhi

Website

http://tourism.gov.in: Website of the Ministry of Tourism, Government of India, for guidelines on star classification of Indian hotels, accessed on 17 November 2008.

CHAPTER 3

Hotel Organization

Learning Objectives:

After reading this chapter, you will be able to understand:
- The need for organization in hotels.
- Corporate vision and mission.
- Hotel organization in various departments.
- Major departments of a hotel—their organization and functions.

When we stay in a hotel as a guest and enjoy its services and facilities, we seldom think how the hotel is able to provide us such flawless and streamlined services. Every hotel, irrespective of its size, type, and mode of operation, is an organization that utilizes all its resources in a definite way to realize its business objectives. The word organization can be defined as 'a group of people who form a business together in order to achieve a particular aim'.

In this chapter, we will study the need for organization and discuss the vision, mission, mission statement, objectives, goals—and strategies to achieve those objectives—of a business enterprise, especially in the context of the hotel industry. Then, we will study the departmental structure and organization charts of hotels.

THE NEED FOR ORGANIZATION

Peter Drucker, famous management guru, had posed three business questions, which are now classic:
- What is our *business*?
- Who is our *customer*?
- What does our customer consider *valuable*?

A hotel is a business organization with the main aim of providing clean, comfortable, and safe accommodation and meals (*business*) to travellers and tourists (*customer*) at a cost. Travellers consider various criteria *valuable* before finally selecting a hotel, such as cleanliness, safety, comfort, room rates, friendly staff, quality, service standards, distance from places of interest, and so on.

The hotel clients (called guests in the hospitality industry parlance) receive a wide variety of services and facilities from the hotel. To carry out all the functions effectively and efficiently, the hotel should have a well-organized structure. Such a structure has the following advantages:
- It facilitates managerial action.
- It encourages and improves efficiency.
- It makes communication easier, faster, and more effective.
- It ensures the optimal use of resources.
- It stimulates creativity and adherence to conformity.
- It creates job satisfaction in employees, thus motivating them to excel.
- It leads to quality services, nurturing brand loyalty in guests, which would ensure the growth of business.

Before a hotel begins its operations, it identifies its specific mission, keeping in mind its target market. This mission provides employees a shared sense of purpose, direction, and opportunity as they work independently towards the organization's overall goals and objectives. Let us understand the key concepts of vision, mission, mission statements, objectives, goals, and strategy, which would help us in understanding the organizational structure.

VISION

Corporate vision is a short, succinct, and inspiring statement of what the organization intends to become and to achieve at some point in the future, often stated in competitive terms. It concretely describes how a company sees itself in the future, and therefore must be realistic and attainable. Vision refers to the category of intentions that are broad, all-inclusive, and forward-thinking. It is the image that a business must have of its goals before it sets out to reach them. It describes aspirations for the future, without specifying the means that will be used to achieve those desired ends. This can be better understood by reading the corporate vision of the Oberoi Group of Hotels (Exhibit 3.1). The Oberoi hotels are known the world over for providing the right blend of service, luxury, and quiet efficiency. A distinctive feature of the group's hotels is their highly motivated and well-trained staff that provides attentive, personalized, and warm service.

MISSION

A business organization, like a hotel, is a deliberate and purposive creation, which strives for certain end results. It has a purpose for existence, which is known as its mission. Mission, which is an abstract idea, has an external orientation and relates the organization to the society in which it exists (refer Exhibit 3.2).

According to Vern McGinnis (1981), a mission should perform the following seven functions:

1. define what the organization is.
2. define what the organization aspires to be.
3. be limited to exclude some ventures.
4. be broad enough to allow for creative growth.
5. distinguish the firm from all others.
6. serve as framework to evaluate current activities.
7. be stated clearly so that it is understood by all.

Exhibit 3.1   Corporate Vision of The Oberoi Group

- We see an organization which aims at leadership in the hospitality industry by understanding its guests, and designing and delivering products and services which enable it to exceed their expectations. We will always demonstrate care for our customers through anticipation of their needs, attention to detail, distinctive excellence, warmth, and concern.
- We see a lean, responsive organization where decision making is encouraged at each level and which accepts change. It is committed and responsive to its guests and other stakeholders.
- We see a multi-skilled workforce, which consists of team players who have pride of ownership, translating organizational vision into reality.
- We see an organization where people are nurtured through permanent learning and skill improvement, and are respected, heard and encouraged to do their best. Oberoi is recognized as best practice for training and developing its people.
- We see a more multinational workforce which has been exposed to different cultures, problems and situations and can use its experiences to enrich the local employees whether in India or overseas.
- We see the world dotted with hotels of The Oberoi Group, in strategic commercial and resort locations.
- We see user-friendly technology enhancing value for our customers and helping our personnel by making information more accessible.
- We see an organization which is conscious of its role in the community, supporting social needs and ensuring employment from within the local community.
- We see an organization which is committed to the environment, using natural products and recycling items, thus ensuring proper use of diminishing natural resources.

Source: http://www.oberoihotels.com/Mission.aspx, last accessed on 28 November 2008.

Mission Statement

A mission statement is the statement of purpose that identifies the scope of a hotel's operations in product and market terms, and distinguishes the hotel from other competing hotels. A hotel develops a mission statement to indicate the activities that it intends to undertake in the present and the near future. The statement should suggest the uniqueness of the hotel from its competitors and should address the interest of guests, owners, employees, and society (refer Exhibit 3.3). It should be clear in terms of its intention, and should be feasible and achievable. A well-designed mission statement offers guidance to managers to develop sharply focused, result-oriented objectives, goals, and strategies to achieve the organization's mission.

The mission and vision statements provide the framework for developing the strategies and operations of an organization. The vision of a company complements the mission, so mission and vision statements of the company should be consistent and should be implemented properly to ensure the success of the organization.

Objective

As compared to mission, objectives are more precise—they are used to identify the end results that a hotel wants to achieve over varying periods of time (refer Exhibit 3.4). Objectives help to measure the progress of a hotel vis-à-vis its mission and vision.

Goals and Strategy

The words objectives and goals represent measurable end results. In this book, we will treat long-term measurable results as objectives and the short-term results as goals. The methods employed to achieve goals are known as strategy. The

---

Exhibit 3.2   Mission of Hotel Association of India

To secure for the hotel industry its due place in India's economy; project its role as a contributor to employment generation, and sustainable economic and social development; highlight its crucial role in the service to tourism industry as the largest net foreign exchange earner; help raise the standards of hoteliering and to build an image for this industry both within and outside the country.

Source: http://www.hotelassociationofindia.com/mission.htm, last accessed on 28 November 2008.

Exhibit 3.3   Mission statement of The Orchid Hotel, Mumbai

The Orchid, Asia's first 5 Star Ecotel ® Hotel, is committed to enhancing the guest's experience while setting a new standard of environmental responsibility, by conserving natural resources, educating, enlightening, and motivating our staff and cultivating community relationships.

Source: http://www.orchidhotel.com/mumbai_hotels/about_us.htm#mission, last accessed on 28 November 2008.

objectives, goals, and strategies should be planned in a way that they do not contradict and create conflict at departmental level.

Let us look at sample goal and strategies (Exhibit 3.5) and then at the goals of Four Seasons Hotels and Resorts (Exhibit 3.6), which is a five-star international luxury hotel chain based in Canada. Four Seasons is dedicated to perfecting the guests' travel experience through continuous innovation and the highest standards of hospitality. The game plan of the Taj group (Exhibit 3.7) shows the goals of the hotel chain.

HOTEL ORGANIZATION

To carry out its vision, mission, objectives, and goals, every hotel requires a formal structure, known as the organization structure. This structure defines the company's distribution of responsibility and authority among its management staff and employees. It establishes the manner and extent of roles, power, and responsibilities, and determines how information flows between different levels of management (for details on the flow of information, refer to Chapter 5). This structure depends entirely on the organization's objectives and the strategies chosen to achieve them. In a centralized structure, the decision-making power is concentrated in the top layer of the management and tight control is exercised over departments and divisions. In a decentralized structure, the decision-making power is distributed and the departments and divisions have varying degrees of autonomy. The most common way to represent the organization structure is by an organization chart.

Exhibit 3.4   Few measurable objectives

- Increase the average room revenue by 10 per cent above the previous year's level;
- Increase the group business above the previous year level by 5 per cent;
- Reduce the guest complaints by 15 per cent with respect to previous year;
- Increase domestic occupancy percentage by 10 per cent with respect to previous year level.

Exhibit 3.5   Sample goal and strategies

Goal: To reduce group check in time by ten minutes.
Strategy: To achieve the above goal, the following strategy may be used:
- Prepare the rooming list well in advance;
- Have enough number of bell boys to take the guest luggage to the rooms;
- Prepare luggage tags beforehand;
- Try to accommodate all the group members on one floor;
- Keep the welcome arrangements like garlands, aarti, tilak, etc. ready;
- Be in touch with the group leader to know the expected time of arrival of the group.

Exhibit 3.6 Goals of Four Seasons Hotels and Resorts

OUR GOALS, OUR BELIEFS, OUR PRINCIPLES

Who We Are

We have chosen to specialize within the hospitality industry, by offering only experiences of exceptional quality. Our objective is to be recognized as the company that manages the finest hotels, resorts and residence clubs wherever we locate.

We create properties of enduring value using superior design and finishes, and support them with a deeply instilled ethic of personal service. Doing so allows Four Seasons to satisfy the needs and tastes of our discriminating customers, and to maintain our position as the world's premier luxury hospitality company.

What We Believe

Our greatest asset, and the key to our success, is our people.

We believe that each of us needs a sense of dignity, pride and satisfaction in what we do. Because satisfying our guests depends on the united efforts of many, we are most effective when we work together cooperatively, respecting each other's contribution and importance.

How We Behave

We demonstrate our beliefs most meaningfully in the way we treat each other and by the example we set for one another. In all our interactions with our guests, customers, business associates and colleagues, we seek to deal with others as we would have them deal with us.

How We Succeed

We succeed when every decision is based on a clear understanding of and belief in what we do and when we couple this conviction with sound financial planning. We expect to achieve a fair and reasonable profit to ensure the prosperity of the company, and to offer long-term benefits to our hotel owners, our shareholders, our customers and our employees.

Source: http://www.fourseasons.com/about_us/company_information.html, last accessed on 28 November 2008.

Exhibit 3.7 Game Plan of Indian Hotels Company

The Indian Hotels Company Limited is the largest hotel, leisure, and hospitality company in south Asia. The company's hotel business emphasizes the global operation of hotels and resorts primarily in the luxury, premium, full service and value segments. The company's brand names include Taj Hotels Resorts & Palaces and Ginger.

Dedicated to the highest standards of hospitality, service and continuous innovation for over a hundred years, the Taj group includes owned, leased and managed hotels totaling 73 hotels in 15 countries on 5 continents with 9200 rooms. Our aim is to be recognized as one of the Top global hotel groups providing exceptional customer satisfaction in each of our hotels.

The growth strategy of our group is to operate 20,000 rooms, in 25 major destinations around the world and achieve a group turnover of US $2 billion, with 33% share from international operations, by 2010.

Courtesy: The Taj Mahal Hotel, New Delhi.

Organization Charts

An organization chart is a hierarchal, graphic representation of the the structure of an organization—a list of all positions and the relationship between them. It shows where each position fits in the overall organization, as well as where divisions of responsibility and lines of authority lie. It is a visual representation of how a firm intends authority, responsibility, and information to flow within its formal organizational structure. It usually depicts different management functions (accounting, finance, human resources, marketing, production, research and development, etc.) and their subdivisions as boxes, linked with lines along which decision-making power travels downwards and answerability travels upwards. The chart indicates direct reporting relationships as well as indirect relationships, which, though not connected directly, involve a high degree of cooperation and communication.

Each hotel is different and has its unique features, so the organization charts of hotels vary from each other. The organization structure depends on the size and functions of a hotel. Some hotels may lease their outlets to another company or may employ another agency to operate restaurant or housekeeping services. In such cases, those portions will not be a part of the organization chart of the hotel. A sample organization chart of a commercial hotel is shown in Fig. 3.1.

MAJOR DEPARTMENTS OF A HOTEL

We had gained an understanding of the various departments of a hotel in Chapter 1. We learnt that some of them are operated by the hotel, while some may be operated by an external agency. The departments like front office, housekeeping, kitchen, food and beverage (F&B) service, engineering and maintenance, accounts, etc. are operated by the hotel, and departments or sections like laundry, retails shops in shopping arcades, casino, and recreational services may be operated by an external agency on contract. The departments of a hotel can be classified as revenue-generating and support-providers. The major revenue-producing departments are front office and F&B service. There are certain minor revenue-producing services like telephones, membership charges from non-resident users of swimming pool and health club, and laundry services for resident guests. In this section, we will study about some of the major functional departments of a hotel (see Fig. 3.2).

Front Office

Front office is the first department of the hotel with which guests come in contact at the time of their arrival and is also the last department they interact with when they depart from the hotel. This department performs various functions like reservation, reception, registration, room assignment, and settlement of bills of a resident guest.

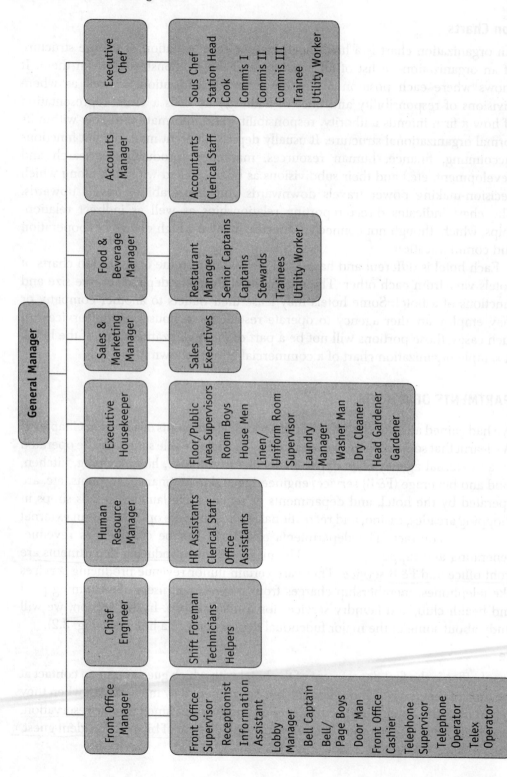

Fig. 3.1 Organization chart of a commercial hotel

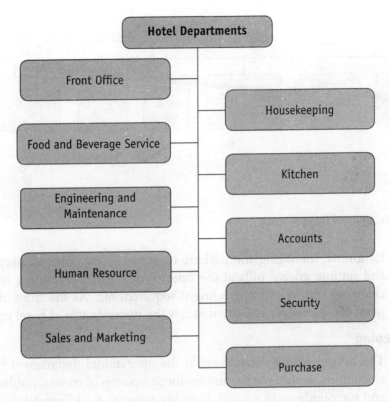

Fig. 3.2 Departments of a hotel

The guests remain in contact with the front desk throughout their stay for all kinds of information and help. The various sections of the front office department are illustrated in Fig. 3.3. For organization chart of front office department in a large hotel, please refer to Fig. 4.7 in Chapter 4.

The activities of the front office department include: processing the reservation requests of guests, which involves making room reservations, amendments, and cancellations; receiving guests at the time of their arrival; making arrangements for the traditional welcome of guests; registration of guests and the assignment of rooms; handling guests' luggage from the guest vehicle to the assigned room on arrival and from the guest room to the vehicle at the time of departure; accepting guests' valuables and cash for keeping in safety deposit lockers; delivering messages and mails of resident guests; handling guests' room keys; guest paging; posting and verifying the room charges and any other credit charges in the guest folio; providing information to guests about hotel products and services, and events or places of tourist interest; arranging postage and courier of mails and other documents; making travel arrangement like sightseeing tours or intercity travel

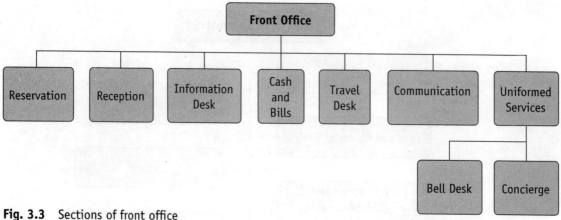

Fig. 3.3 Sections of front office

for guests; managing the parking of guests' own vehicles; preparing, presenting, and settling guests' bills at the time of departure; providing left luggage facility; changing rooms and upgrading if required, etc. As the front office is the contact point for guests, we can say that it is the nerve centre of hotel operations.

Housekeeping

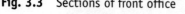

The housekeeping department is the operational department responsible for the cleanliness, maintenance, and aesthetic upkeep of rooms, public areas, back areas, and surroundings in a hotel. Keeping room status information up-to-date requires close coordination between the front desk and housekeeping departments. The housekeeping prepares a room status report, which is sent to the front office; the front office compares it with its records and the discrepancies are brought to the attention of the duty manager. This tallying is done after every shift. The various sections of the housekeeping department are illustrated in Fig. 3.4.

All the guest complaints and requests are noted at the *control desk*, which is manned round the clock. The person at the control desk interacts with the concerned section/person to resolve the complaints or to meet the requests. The progress is entered in a follow-up register, which maintains a record of all complaints.

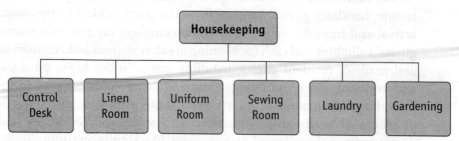

Fig. 3.4 Sections of housekeeping

Linen room, uniform room, and sewing room may be located separately or at one place depending upon the size of the hotel. Linen room maintains the supply of clean linen while the uniform room takes care of the uniform of employees. Sewing room looks after all the mending work and the utilization of discarded linen.

The hotel *laundry* is responsible for the cleaning and ironing of hotel linen, employees' uniform, and for the guest requirements of laundry. It may be located within the hotel or at a distant place. If present within the hotel premises, it is known as on-premises laundry, and if outside, it is called off-premises laundry.

The maintenance of *hotel gardens* is also done by the housekeeping department.

The organization chart of the housekeeping department is shown in Fig. 3.5.

Food and Beverage Service

The food and beverage (F&B) service department is among the major revenue producing departments of a hotel. This department looks after the service of food and drinks to guests. The sections of the department are illustrated in Fig. 3.6.

The *restaurants, coffee shops, bars, and other outlets like poolside barbeques and kiosks* take care of the food and beverage requirements of the hotel's resident and non-resident guests.

The *room service* section looks after the provision of food and drinks to guests in their rooms. Though restaurants and bars remain in operation during specific working hours, coffee shops and room service may be available round the clock.

Banquets and outdoor catering sections take care of functions and programmes both within the hotel premises and outside it.

The organization structure of the F&B service department is shown in Fig. 3.7.

Kitchen

The kitchen supplies cooked food to the F&B service department in hotels. The sections of the department are illustrated in Fig. 3.8.

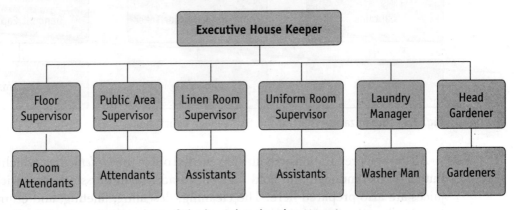

Fig. 3.5   Organization chart of the housekeeping department

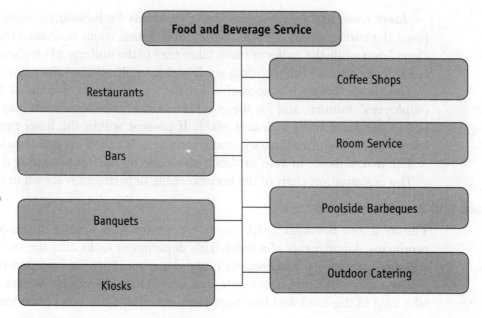

Fig. 3.6 Sections of food and beverage service

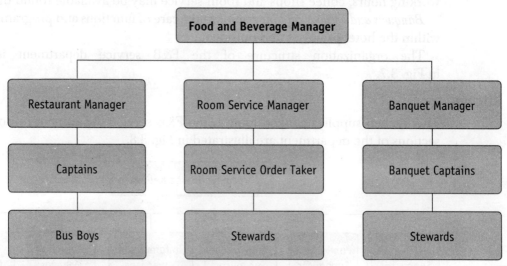

Fig. 3.7 Organization chart of the F&B service department

All the pre-preparation activities are carried out in the *larder section,* which includes butchery, fish monger, and cold kitchen. Salads, salad dressings, sandwiches, and juices are also prepared here. The cleaning, descaling, filleting, and crumbling of fishes is done by the fishmonger in the larder.

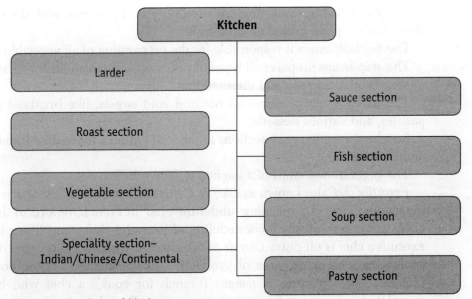

Fig. 3.8 Sections of kitchen

The *sauce section* is responsible for preparing sauces required for all meat, poultry, game dishes, with the exception of those that are plain roasted or grilled.

The *roast section* is responsible for providing all roast dishes of meat, poultry, and game.

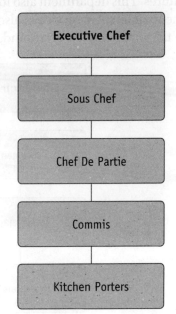

Fig. 3.9 Organization chart of the kitchen department

The *fish section* is responsible for supplying all fish dishes, with the exception of those that are plain grilled or deep fried.

The *vegetable section* is responsible for the preparation of all vegetable dishes.

The *soup section* prepares all types of soups such as consommés, creams, velouté, purees, broths, bisques, and international soups.

The *pastry section* prepares all hot and cold sweets, like breakfast rolls, cakes, pastries, and various desserts.

Besides these, there are sections for special kinds of foods, like Indian, Chinese, and Continental.

The organization chart of a kitchen is shown in Fig. 3.9.

Executive chef, also known as *Chef de Cuisine* or head of the kitchen, is the chief of the kitchen. *Sous chef,* meaning 'under the chef' in French, reports to the executive chef, and is responsible for scheduling of jobs and shifts, and filling in when the executive chef is off-duty. *Chef de partie,* also known as a station chef or line cook, supervises a particular area of production in the kitchen. At the bottom of the organizational structure is *commis* (French for cook), a chef who has recently completed a formal culinary training or is still undergoing training. Chefs are assisted by kitchen porters and apprentices.

Engineering and Maintenance

The engineering and maintenance department of a hotel is responsible for maintaining the property's structure, electrical and mechanical equipment, and all furniture and fixtures. This department also looks after landscaping and maintaining the grounds. The maintenance service is also referred to as facilities management, as it deals with the maintenance of ground, building, equipment, waste disposal

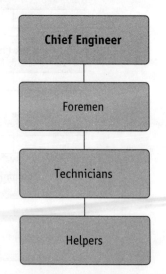

Fig. 3.10 Organization chart of the engineering and maintenance department

system, store and sanitary, pollution control equipments, gas distribution system, electrical energy supply system, fuel supply system, water supply system, ventilation, refrigeration and air conditioning, fire fighting, heating, telephone system, cable television, elevators, light, escalators, etc.

The maintenance department raises the level of equipment performance, life, and availability. Although it adds to the running costs, it raises more profits as it delays new purchases and investments. The department is headed by a *chief engineer*, who is responsible for the efficient working of the department. He takes care of planning, organizing, coordinating, delegating tasks, budgeting, etc., and all administrative functions. A *foreman* reports to the chief engineer and is in charge of the other workers, including electricians, carpenters, mechanics, plumbers, painters, lift-operators, masons, etc. All these skilled technicians are assisted by helpers, apprentices, or trainees.

The organization structure of the engineering and maintenance department is shown in Fig. 3.10.

Accounts

The accounts department monitors and records all the monetary transactions of the hotel. The accounting activities include paying outstanding invoices, distributing unpaid statements, chasing bills, processing payroll, accumulating operating data, and compiling financial reports. In addition, the accounting staff is responsible for making bank deposits, securing cash, and performing other control and processing functions required by the management of the hotel. In many hotels, the night audit and the F&B audit come under the purview of the accounting division. The department is headed by a chief accountant. The organization chart of the accounts department is illustrated in Fig. 3.11.

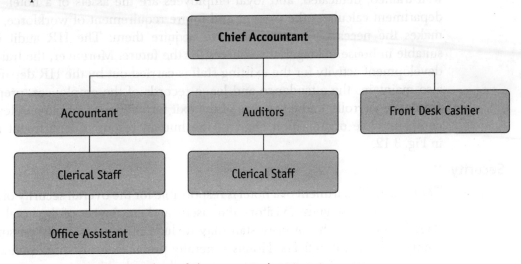

Fig. 3.11 Organization chart of the accounts department

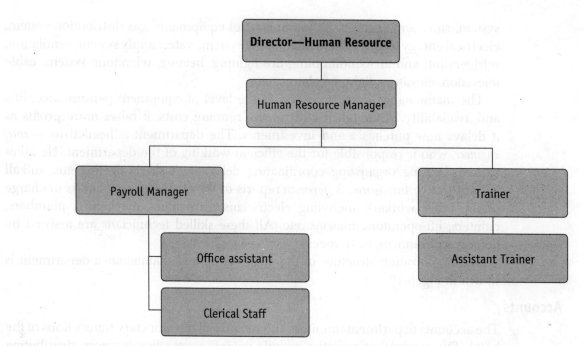

Fig. 3.12 Organization chart of the human resource department

Human Resource

The human resource (HR) department (earlier called personnel department) is responsible for the acquisition, utilization, training, and development of the human resources of the hotel. The hotel industry is people-oriented and service-oriented; well trained, dedicated, and loyal employees are the assets of a hotel. The HR department calculates the present and future requirement of workforce, and also makes the necessary arrangements to acquire them. The HR audit identifies suitable in-house managerial resources for the future. Moreover, the training and development activity for the existing staff is carried out by the HR department. It also maintains the attendance and leave records of the employees, prepares the employee payrolls, and takes care of the exit formalities of employees leaving the company. The organization chart of the human resource department is shown in Fig. 3.12.

Security

The security department of a hotel is responsible for the overall security of the hotel building, in-house guests, visitors, day users, and employees of the hotel, and also their belongings. The security staff may include in-house security personnel and contracted security officers. Hotels generally prefer ex-army or ex-police officials as their security officers because they are well versed with various security aspects.

Fig. 3.13 Organization chart of the security department

The responsibilities of security personnel include patrolling the property and its grounds; monitoring surveillance equipment; and, in general, ensuring that guests, visitors, and employees are safe and secure. To some extent, the effectiveness of the security department depends upon the cooperation and assistance of the local law enforcement officials. The security personnel should be trained to handle situations like vandalism, thefts, terrorist attacks, bomb threats, and also to prevent and fight fire. The front desk should report anything suspicious to the security staff. Figure 3.13 shows the organization chart of the security department.

Sales and Marketing

The sales and marketing department of a hotel has the responsibility of increasing the sales of the hotel's products and services. The major products are rooms, food and beverage, banquets, and outdoor catering. The sales and marketing staff of a hotel can vary from one part-time person to a dozen or more full-time employees, depending upon the size of the hotel. Their responsibilities can be divided into functions like sales, convention services, advertising, and public relations. To achieve their targets, the sales and marketing staff work in close cooperation with the front office, especially with the reservation section for an update on the reservation status. The sales and marketing department carries out market surveys and forecasts the future demand for various services provided by the hotel, based on past and present trends. On the basis of such forecasts, they develop strategies to capture the market and increase the revenue of the hotel.

Drucker said 'Because the purpose of business is to create and keep a customer, the business enterprise has two—and only two—basic functions: marketing and innovation. Marketing and innovation produce results; all the rest are costs. Marketing is the distinguishing, unique function of the business.' Hotels also strive to create brand loyalty in their guests in order to generate repeat business and positive word-of-mouth publicity. Hotels prepare marketing strategies especially

Fig. 3.14   Organization chart of the sales and marketing department of a medium-sized hotel

for their target market and constantly innovate in order to stand out against competition. Figure 3.14 shows the organization chart of the sales and marketing department of a medium-sized hotel.

Purchase

The purchase department is responsible for procuring the inventories of all departments of a hotel. The department is headed by the purchase manager. Hotels mostly make purchases from suppliers on contracted rates. In most hotels, the central stores is a part of the purchase department. The requisitions from all departments are sent to the stores, on the basis of which a consolidated purchase order is made and goods are purchased in bulk.

Apart from the above-mentioned departments, hotels provide the following facilities, which are operated and maintained by external agencies:

- *Retail outlets* like gift shops, art and craft shops, handloom and handicraft shops, beauty saloons, jewellery shops, and book shops.
- *Recreational activities* like swimming pools, golf courses, tennis courts, bowling alleys, snorkelling, and bicycle trips, etc.

In a hotel, a large number of employees work in the different departments. To provide flawless and streamlined services to guests, close cooperation and coordination between departments is needed. Front office, housekeeping, and food and beverage service and production staff must coordinate and share the information about the status of the room and other hotel services to ensure the satisfaction of guests.

SUMMARY

A business organization, like a hotel, is a deliberate and purposive creation, which strives for certain end results. It has a purpose for existence, which is known as its mission. Corporate vision is a short, succinct, and inspiring statement of what the organization intends to become and to achieve at some point in the future. The mission and vision of a hotel provide the framework for developing the mission statement, which indicates the activities that the hotel intends to undertake in the present and the near future. It suggests the uniqueness of the hotel from its competitors and addresses the interest of guests, owners, employees, and society. A well-designed mission statement offers guidance to managers to develop sharply focused, result-oriented objectives, goals, and strategies to achieve the organization's mission.

To carry out its vision, mission, objectives, and goals, every hotel requires a formal structure, known as the organization structure. This structure defines the company's distribution of responsibility and authority among its management staff and employees. It establishes the manner and extent of roles, power, and responsibilities, and determines how information flows between different levels of management. The organization structure is represented by an organization chart, which is a hierarchal, graphic representation of the structure of an organization, i.e., a list of all positions and the relationship between them.

In this chapter, we have also looked at the major departments in a hotel and gained an understanding about the sections and organization charts of each department.

KEY TERMS

Accounts This department monitors, records, and verifies all the monetary transactions of the hotel.

Bisque A thick cream soup made from shellfish.

Broth A clear soup made by cooking meat, poultry, fish, seafood, or vegetables in water, and then removing them.

Chef de partie Supervisor in the kitchen.

Commis A cook at the bottom of the kitchen organization structure.

Executive chef One who heads the kitchen.

Folio/guest folio It is the written record of a hotel guest's account, which shows the balance of her financial obligation to the hotel.

Food and beverage service This department of the hotel is responsible for serving food and drinks to guests.

Front office The department which takes care of reservation, reception, registration, and final settlement of guests' bills.

Goal It is a short-term, measurable end result.

Housekeeping This department is responsible for the proper upkeep and maintenance of the hotel.

Kitchen This department prepares the food for sale in all food outlets in the hotel.

Mission The reason or purpose for the existence of a hotel.

Mission statement The statement of purpose that identifies the scope of a hotel's operations in terms of product and market, and distinguishes it from competition.

Objective The end result that a hotel wants to achieve over varying periods of time.

Organization chart A graphic representation of the structure of an organization.

Organization structure The framework of a company defining the distribution of responsibility and authority among its management staff and employees.

Puree A thick soup made by cooking and then pureeing vegetables or ingredients used in the soup.

Sous chef The second highest authority in kitchen after the executive chef, responsible for the delegation of work among kitchen workers.

Strategy Plan of action for achieving the goals of a hotel.

Velouté A white sauce made of chicken, veal, or fish stock thickened with a roux of flour and butter.

Vision A statement that concretely describes how a hotel sees itself in the future.

Word-of-mouth publicity Oral or written recommendation of the services of a hotel by a satisfied customer to prospective customers.

REVIEW QUESTIONS

Discussion Questions

1. What is the need for organization?

2. What do you understand by the term 'mission'?

3. What is a mission statement?

4. Differentiate between objectives, goals, and strategies.

5. Explain hotel organization, with examples.

6. What are the various departments of a hotel?

7. Classify the departments of a hotel on the basis of revenue generation.

8. Why is inter-departmental coordination necessary in hotels?

PROJECT WORK

1. Design the vision, mission statement, and objective of a five-star deluxe resort with 50 cottages.

2. Prepare the mission statement for a hotel with 235 rooms and a conference centre, which can accommodate 1,000 people in theatre-style seating. The target audience of the hotel is the business traveller.

3. Compare the mission statements of three Indian and three international hotel chains, taking help from the Internet. Identify what customers in different parts of the world look for in a hotel.

REFERENCES

Drucker, Peter F., 1954, *The Practice of Management,* Harper & Row, New York.

McGinnis, Vern J., 1981, *The Mission Statement: A Key Step in Strategic Planning,* Business, November–December, pp. 39–43.

Part II

Front Office Operations

- Front Office Organization
- Front Office Communication
- Room Tariff
- Guest Cycle and Room Reservations
- Registration
- Guest Services
- Check-out and Settlement
- Front Office Accounting
- Night Auditing
- Safety and Security

CHAPTER 4
Front Office Organization

Learning Objectives:

After reading this chapter, you will be able to understand the following:
- The front office department and its function areas.
- Sections and layout of the front office—reservation, reception, information, cash and bills, communication, uniformed services.
- Organization of the front office staff—division of labour and span of control.
- Duties and responsibilities of some front office employees—front office manager, reservation assistant, receptionist, information assistant, telephone operator, bell boy, door attendant.
- Qualities of front office personnel.

Front office is the interface between a hotel and its guests. On their arrival at a hotel, guests first meet the front office staff and develop an impression about the level of services, standard, facilities, and hospitality of the hotel. They interact with the department throughout their stay for any kind of information and help. As they are responsible for services like reservation, reception of guests, assignment of rooms, and settlement of bills, the front desk personnel have the ability to multi-task and work in a fast-paced environment while maintaining a high level of guest service and professionalism.

This chapter is aimed at providing an understanding of the organization of the front office department. Here, we will study the various sections of the front office and their functions, the organization of the front office staff, and the qualities, attributes, duties and responsibilities of front office personnel.

FUNCTION AREAS

The front office personnel are mostly in direct contact with guests throughout their stay. Guests contact the front desk to book a room; check-in; inquire about hotel services, facilities, and about the city or surrounding areas; and finally, to settle bills and check out from the hotel. Apart from these services, the front desk also provides services like handling guest mails and messages, maintaining guest accounts, paging guests (locating guests within the hotel), arranging travel services, and various other services as per the guest's requirement.

The front office is the contact point between the guest, management, and other departments. It handles guests' complaints, dispatches housekeeping and engineering requests, prints and files reports, receives and answers phone calls, and sends and receives faxes. Thus, the front office personnel perform the following functions:

- Sell hotel rooms to guests, which may be standard or deluxe rooms, executive or presidential suites, etc.
- Accept advance booking of hotel rooms through telephone, fax, e-mail, websites, etc.
- Receive and register guests when they arrive at the hotel and assign them rooms according to their preferences—smoking/non smoking, pool view/ garden view/sea view, high floor/low floor, near the elevator/far from the elevator, etc.
- Maintain accurate room status information.
- Maintain guest accounts and monitor credit.
- Handle guests' demands and complaints.
- Prepare account statements of guests.
- Settle bills at the time of check-out.
- Coordinate guest services like handling of guest mails and messages, locating guests within the hotel premises, connecting guest telephone calls, keeping guests' valuables in safety deposit lockers, handling of room keys, making sundry payments on behalf of guests, and so on.
- Provide information about the hotel's facilities and services, the city, important events, festivals and shows, and places of tourist interest.

SECTIONS AND LAYOUT OF FRONT OFFICE

For the efficient and smooth functioning of a department, it is important to divide it in sections and delegate tasks accordingly. As discussed in Chapter 3 (see Fig. 3.3), the front office department is divided in these sections: reservation, reception, information desk, cash and bills, travel desk, communication, and uniformed services (which include bell desk and concierge).

Layout is the physical demarcation of the sections of a department. A well-designed layout should involve proper space utilization, aimed at improving the efficiency and control of the staff. The front desk should be located at a prominent place in the lobby. The front office layout (see Fig. 4.1) includes the following areas of the department: lobby, reservations, reception, information, cash and bills, travel desk, communication, and uniformed services like bell desk and concierge.

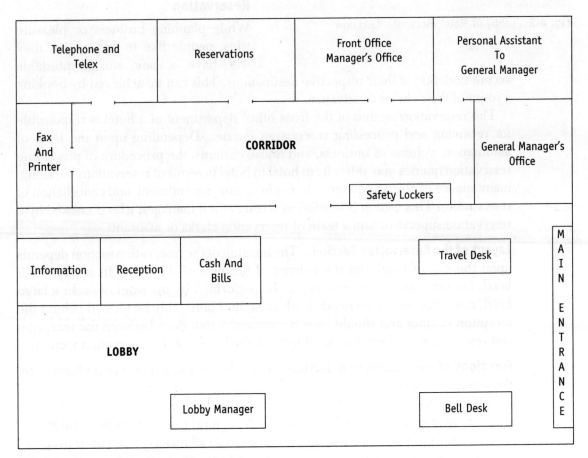

Fig. 4.1   Layout of the front office department

Fig. 4.2 Lobby of Hotel Piccadilly, Lucknow

The hotel lobby is an area furnished with seating arrangements just inside the hotel, where hotel guests and their visitors can meet and wait. Located just beyond the entrance to the hotel, the lobby is the first and last point of guest contact with the hotel. A well-appointed lobby (see Fig. 4.2) creates an impression about the overall standard of the hotel in the eyes of the guest. Hence, hotels spend a large amount of money to make the lobby aesthetically appealing to guests. The front office is strategically located in the lobby area.

Reservation

While planning business or pleasure trips, people like to ensure that they will have a safe and comfortable accommodation at their respective destinations. This can be achieved by booking a room of their choice in advance.

The reservation section of the front office department of a hotel is responsible for receiving and processing reservation queries. Depending upon the level of automation, volume of business, and house customs, the procedure of processing reservation queries may differ from hotel to hotel in terms of reservations handling, maintenance of reservation records, confirmation, amendment, and cancellation of reservations. This section is headed by a reservation manager, who is assisted by a reservation supervisor and a team of reservation clerks or assistants.

Layout of the Reservation Section The location of the reservation section depends upon the size of hotel and the volume of business of the hotel. In a very small hotel, the function of reservations can be performed by the front desk. In a large hotel, a separate section is needed, which should preferably be located behind the reception counter and should have a communication door between the reception and reservation sections. Fig. 4.3 illustrates the layout of the reservation section.

Functions of the Reservation Section The following functions are performed by the reservation section:

- Receiving reservation requests through various means like telephone, fax, e-mail, websites, sales representatives, or central reservations department.
- Processing reservation requests received from all means on the hotel property management system (PMS).

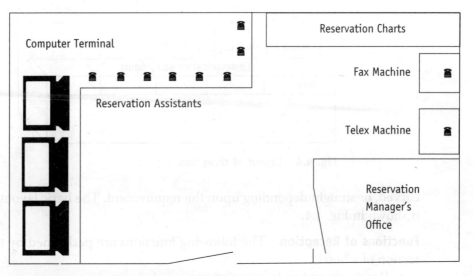

Fig. 4.3 Layout of the reservation section

- Depending upon the availability of desired room type and projected sales during and around the requested stay dates, the reservation request may be confirmed, waitlisted, or denied.
- Updating the room availability status after each reservation transaction, i.e., after each confirmation, amendment, and cancellation.
- Maintaining and updating reservation records to reflect accurate information about room status.
- Preparing reservation reports for the management.

Reception

This section of the front office receives and welcomes guests on their arrival in the hotel. It is headed by a supervisor and comprises a team of receptionists and front desk assistants. The personnel of this section procure all the necessary information about the guest to complete the registration process. After finishing the registration formalities, a room is assigned to the guest, and a bell boy carries the luggage and escorts the guest to her room. The entire process is carried out professionally in a warm and friendly atmosphere.

Layout of the Reception Section The reception section is located in close proximity to the entrance of the hotel. The layout of the section depends upon the size of the hotel and the volume of business generated by it. The front desk assistant carries out many tasks like receiving guests, registration, etc; hence, the reception area should be designed in such a way to assist the staff in performing their tasks efficiently and effectively. The front desk may be circular, L-shaped,

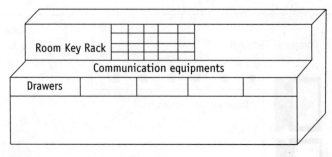

Fig. 4.4   Layout of reception

curved, or straight depending upon the requirement. The basic layout of reception is shown in Fig. 4.4.

Functions of Reception   The following functions are performed by the reception section of a hotel:
- Receiving and welcoming guests.
- Completing the registration formalities.
- Assigning the room.
- Sending arrival notification slips to the concerned departments.

Information Desk

As the name suggests, the information desk provides information to guests. It is manned by an information assistant. In a small hotel, the same function may be performed by the receptionist. The need of a separate information desk is felt in large hotels where the traffic of guests is higher. The information desk may be located next to the reception.

Functions of Information Desk   Some of the functions of the information desk are as under:
- Maintaining resident guest rack.
- Handling guest room keys.
- Coordinating guest mails, telegrams, faxes, couriers, parcels, etc.
- Providing information to guests regarding hotel facilities and services, city information, etc.
- Handling guests messages.
- Paging guests.

Cash and Bills

The cash and bills section records all the monetary transactions of guests. It maintains guest folios and prepares the guest bills to be settled by the guest at the time of departure. This section is headed by a cashier.

Functions of the Cash and Bills Section   This section performs the following tasks:
- Opening and maintaining of guest folios.
- Posting room charges in guest folios.
- Recording all credit charges in guest folios.
- Maintaining a record of the cash received from guests.
- Preparing bills at the time of check-out.
- Receiving cash/travellers cheques/demand draft for account settlement.
- Handling credit/debit/charge cards for the settlement of a guest account.
- Organizing foreign currency exchange for the settlement of a guest account.

Travel Desk

The travel desk takes care of travel arrangements of guests, like air-ticketing, railway reservations, sightseeing tours, airport or railway station pick up or drop, etc. The hotel may operate the travel desk or it may be outsourced to an external travel agency.

Functions of Travel Desk   The travel desk performs the following tasks:
- Arranging pick-up and drop services for guests at the time of their arrival and departure.
- Providing vehicles on request to guests at pre-determined rates (charged kilometre/hour wise and depend on the kind and size of vehicle used— premium cars, semi-luxury cars, coaches, mini vans, etc.)
- Making travel arrangements like railway reservations/cancellations/ amendments, or purchasing air-tickets for guests.
- Organizing half-day or full-day sightseeing tours in and around the city.
- Arranging for guides who can communicate in the guest's language.

Communication Section

The communication section maintains the communication network of the hotel, which is generally quite complex. The hotel may have its own private branch exchange (PBX), along with post and telegraph lines. Earlier all outgoing calls were routed through the telephone operator. This was done to ensure proper accounting of outgoing calls. Switchboard operators were required to place wake-up calls, monitor automated systems, and coordinate emergency communications. Recent technological advancement in telecommunications has revolutionized the way hotels operations are run. Now guests are able to make outgoing calls without routing them through the operator. There is a computerized call accounting system that charges the outgoing calls to the guest's account. Wake-up calls may also be registered on the system, which dials the guest's extension at the pre-registered time and plays a pre-recorded message when answered. So hotels can now manage with lesser number of telephone operators per shift. The telephone operators, who answer incoming calls, protect the guests' privacy and contribute to the hotel's security programme by not revealing guest room numbers to any unauthorized person. Many hotels also provide guest paging services over the public address system. These systems generally operate through the communications section.

Functions of Communication Desk   The duties of the telephone operator include:
- Answering incoming calls.
- Directing calls to guest rooms through the switchboard/PABX system.
- Providing information on guest services.
- Processing guest wake-up calls.
- Answering inquiries about hotel facilities and events.
- Protecting guests' privacy.
- Coordinating emergency communication.

Uniformed Services

The uniformed services in the hotel include the bell desk team and the concierge.

Bell Desk   The bell desk is located very close to the main entrance of the hotel. This section is headed by a bell captain, who leads a team of bell boys (also called bellhops) and page boys. They handle the guest luggage from the guest vehicle to the lobby and to guest rooms at the time of arrival and from their rooms to the guest vehicle at the time of departure. They escort guests to their rooms and familiarize them with hotel facilities, safety features, as well as in-room facilities.

The bell desk person is the last front desk employee who comes in contact with guests at the time of their departure.

Functions of bell desk   The bell desk is responsible for the following tasks:
- Handling guest luggage at the time of arrival and departure (see Fig. 4.5).
- Escorting guests to their rooms on arrival.
- Familiarizing guests about safety features and in-room facilities.
- Providing information to guests about hotel facilities and services when asked.
- Locating a guest in a specified area of the hotel.
- Posting guest mails.
- Making sundry purchases like postage stamps, medicines, etc. for the guest.
- Keeping guest luggage in the left luggage room if requested by the guest.

Fig. 4.5 Bell Boy carrying guest luggage on a trolley

- Checking if in-room amenities are in their original condition at the time of departure of guests.

Concierge A concierge is a hotel employee who provides information and personalized services to guests like dinner reservations, tour and travel arrangements, and obtaining tickets for special events in the city, etc. A concierge is often expected to achieve the impossible, dealing with any request a guest may have, relying on an extensive list of personal contacts with various local merchants and service providers. The concept of concierges came from the days of European royalty; the concierge was the castle doorkeeper in those times. His duty was to ensure that all castle occupants were safe in their rooms at night. When the royal families travelled, they often took their concierges with them for security and for making food and lodging arrangements. As the hotel industry grew, concierges became a part of the hotel staff to provide personalized services to hotel guests.

Functions of concierge The concierge provides the following services to guests:
- Making reservations for dining in famous restaurants.
- Obtaining tickets for theatres, musicals, sporting events, etc.
- Arranging for transportation by limousine, car, coaches, buses, airplanes, or trains.
- Providing information on cultural and social events like photo exhibitions, art shows, and local places of tourist interest.

ORGANIZATION OF FRONT OFFICE STAFF

The organization of front office staff is designed to achieve the objectives and goals of the hotel. The organization structure, which clearly defines all positions (each bearing a definite authority, responsibility, and accountability), is built upon the following criteria:
- Division of labour
- Span of control

Division of labour refers to narrow specialization of tasks within a process so that each employee can become a specialist in doing one thing. The process is divided into several separate tasks, each performed by one person. The specialization and division of labour defines each employee's 'sphere of competence' and ensures that employees perform their individual tasks without overlapping others.

The degree of division of labour depends on the degree to which the performance of particular tasks is measurable, the degree to which wages affect task performance, and the implementation of technology. Computerization has enabled organizations to increase the variety of tasks performed by employees, consequently reducing specialization and division of labour. The advance in information technology has also equipped individual employees or teams to combine different tasks more effectively to meet a guest's needs while enhancing productivity. For example, guest information gained from registration activities can be used to improve financial accounting practices, and employee information gained from training activities can be used to improve work practices.

Span of control in an organization is defined as the number of employees reporting directly to one supervisor. Traditionally, the span of control has been defined as four to seven subordinates under one manager. The average size of the span of control, together with the total number of employees, determines the number of levels in an organization structure.

For a rapidly-growing small hotel, it may be advantageous to create an organization structure that employs less than the maximum span of control agreed upon. Since growth usually requires adding personnel in many existing sections or units, keeping some positions free in each level allows for expansion without restructuring the whole organization. Also, it is only with experience that a new manager learns how to manage a section more effectively and allocate work to a large number of subordinates.

Using the minimum and maximum requirements of a hotel for the span of control, we can design the organization chart for a hotel. As we have seen, the organization of staff will depend upon the size of the hotel. The front office organization structure of a small hotel is depicted in Fig. 4.6.

As a large hotel will have a more complex hierarchy, its organization chart will show more lateral and vertical positions. The organization chart of the front office of a large hotel is illustrated in Fig. 4.7.

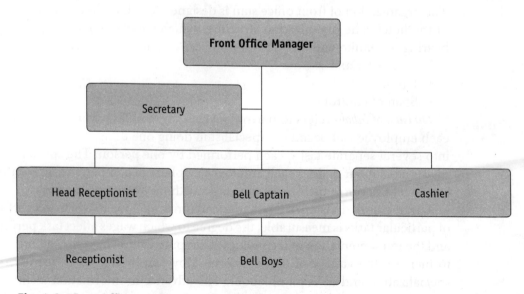

Fig. 4.6 Front office organization of a small hotel

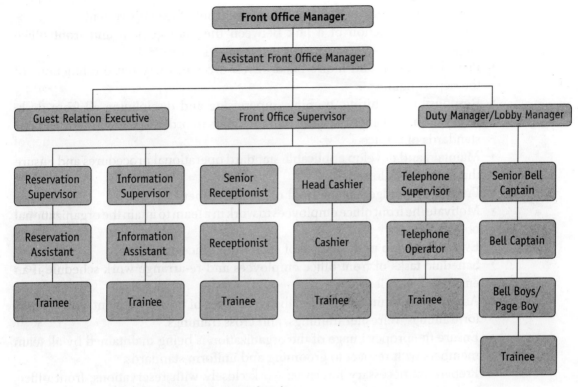

Fig. 4.7 Front office organization of a large hotel

DUTIES AND RESPONSIBILITIES OF SOME FRONT OFFICE PERSONNEL

As already seen, the organization structure of the front office depends on the size of the hotel. The organization charts of small and large hotels are given in Fig. 4.6 and Fig. 4.7. Now let us look at the duties and responsibilities of some key front office employees, like the front office manager, reservation assistant, receptionist, information assistant, cashier, telephone operator, bell boy, and door attendant.

Front Office Manager

Front office manager (FOM) is in charge of the front office department and allocates the available resources (men, machine, materials, and money) of the department to achieve the goals of the department and the organization. The basic function of the FOM is to directly supervise all the front office personnel and to ensure the proper and smooth operation of the department. FOM is often assisted by an assistant front office manager (AFOM). For a sample job description of FOM, please refer to Fig. 18.1 in Chapter 18.

Duties and Responsibilities of Front Office Manager   A front office manager has to perform the following duties:

- Direct and coordinate the activities of the front office department.
- Perform the function of a link between the management and front office employees.
- Plan the present and future need of resources to carry out the functions of the department.
- Responsible for hiring, training, supervising and disciplining all front desk, reservation, and guest services staff members in order to maintain the desired standards of service.
- Maintain and develop applicable standard operational procedures and ensure that they are followed.
- Prepare the budget for the front office department.
- Motivate the front office employees to work in a team to attain the organizational objectives.
- Evaluate the job performance of each front office employee.
- Schedule tasks of front office employees and re-arrange work schedule if an employee is on leave.
- Ascertain the training needs of the employees of the department, and arrange for trainings, refresher trainings, and cross trainings.
- Ensure the proper image of the organization is being maintained by all team members with respect to grooming and uniform standards.
- Prepare all necessary forecasts; work closely with reservations, front office, and sales to maximize occupancy, rate, and revenue. Keep all departments notified of any fluctuations in business levels, special guests, groups, etc.
- Review all reports generated by all the sections of the department.
- Hold regular meetings with staff members in order to keep them properly informed and trained.
- Maintain a good communication with other departments to ensure maximum cooperation, productivity, and guest satisfaction.
- Develop relationships with guests and clients by providing maximum personalized guest service.
- Resolve guest problems quickly, efficiently, and courteously.
- Arrange for private telephone line and other special services for guests.
- Conduct property checks.
- Be responsible for the cleanliness of the office area.
- Attend regular department heads' meetings and contribute ideas with regard to hotel operations in general.
- Manage online inventories.
- Keep abreast with the new trends and ideas in the hospitality industry.
- Assist staff with any concerns they have regarding housing, payroll, investment, and any other policy.

• Respond promptly and take a supervisory role in any hotel emergency or safety situation, and convey the required emergency procedures to the rooms division.

Reservation Assistant

Reservation assistants process the reservation requests that reach the hotel by any mode—telephonic, written, or online. Depending on the availability of a desired room type, they confirm, put on waitlist, or deny a reservation request. They are the sales persons of the hotel and may practice their skills of salesmanship by suggesting higher room categories, and also selling other hotel services like spa, speciality restaurants, etc. to guests at the time of receiving the reservation request. The reservation section generates the maximum revenue for a hotel, so the reservation assistants should understand, anticipate, and influence consumer behaviour in order to maximize revenue or profits from room reservations.

Duties and Responsibilities of Reservation Assistant The major duties and responsibilities of a reservation assistant are as under:

• To receive and process the reservation requests of future guests.
• To maintain reservation records by completing reservation forms, sending reservation confirmation or amendment letters, and updating the status of rooms after processing each reservation request (i.e., confirmation, amendment, and cancellation).
• To process reservations from the sales offices, other departments of the hotel, travel agents, tour operators, and corporate booking agents.
• To communicate the reservation information to the reception.
• To prepare the expected arrival list and the expected departure list every day.
• To fill the registration cards of guests that are expected to arrive each day (using the information available from reservation forms and guest history cards), and to send this information to front desk
• To prepare a guest folder and to keep the mails and messages of guests with reservation documents.
• To promote goodwill by being courteous, friendly, and helpful to guests, managers, and fellow employees.

Receptionist

A receptionist is the first person to come in contact with guests at the time of their arrival, so she is an important bearer of the hotel's image. The basic function of a receptionist is to receive guests and answer their queries.

Duties and Responsibilities of Receptionist   The major duties and responsibilities of a receptionist are as under:

- Greet guests on their arrival.
- Politely confirm the details of guests with confirmed reservation.
- Complete the registration formalities of guests with confirmed reservations.
- Check the availability of rooms in case of walk-in guests.
- Assign rooms and call the bell boy to escort guests to their rooms.
- Use up-selling techniques to sell higher category rooms and also to promote other services of the hotel.
- Coordinate room status updates with the housekeeping department.
- Notify housekeeping of all check-outs, late check-outs, early check-ins, and special requests.
- Process guests' check-out requests.
- Post all the credit charges to the guest folios.
- Process requests for safe deposit boxes according to the house policy.
- Process reservation requests of guests if directed by the reservation section.

Information Assistant

Information assistants provide information to guests about the hotel's products and services, nearby food and beverage outlets, places of tourist interest in the city and around, etc. They also handle guests' mails and messages, and provide other services.

Duties and Responsibilities of Information Assistant   The duties and responsibilities of an information assistant are as under:

- Provide desired information to guests.
- Update the guest rack after every arrival and departure.
- Maintain information rack.
- Handle guest mails and messages.
- Coordinate guest room maintenance work with the engineering and maintenance departments.
- Assist in guest paging.

Cashier

During their stay in a hotel, guests may perform various credit and debit transactions with the hotel. At the time of their departure, the hotel has to present them with a consolidated statement of their financial transactions, and raise the bill for the outstanding amount. It is the responsibility of a front desk cashier is to keep the guest folio updated by posting all credit and debit transactions.

Duties and Responsibilities of Cashier   The major duties and responsibilities of a cashier are as under:

- Prepare bills and present the same for settlement at the time of a guest's departure.
- Update guests' credit transactions on a daily basis.
- Maintain guests' weekly bills.
- Obtain the house bank (a fixed amount which comprises currency and coins of different denomination to carry out the day's work) and keep it balanced.
- Transfer guest balances to other accounts, as required.
- Handle paid-out vouchers of guests.
- Settle guest accounts by accepting cash, credit card, traveller's cheque, etc.
- Check the authenticity of the currency received.
- Exchange foreign currency according to daily exchange rate, in strict accordance with the rules and regulation of Reserve Bank of India.
- Balance the cash and close the shift.

Telephone Operator

Although telephone operators seldom come in direct contact with guests, they play an important role in creating the image of the hotel in the minds of guests. The basic skills of a good telephone operator include courteous tone of voice, attentiveness, clear and distinct speaking, and objective listening.

Duties and Responsibilities of Telephone Operator   The major duties and responsibilities of a telephone operator are as under:
- Answer all incoming calls.
- Direct incoming calls to the desired extension, which are routed through private branch exchange.
- Prepare bills of guests' outgoing calls and send them to the front desk to be posted in the guest folio.
- Provide paging services for guests and employees.
- Log all wake-up calls on the system.
- Answer questions about the hotel's services and products.
- Understand and follow the emergency procedure installed in the property.

Bell Boy

Bell boys transport the guest luggage at the time of check-in and check-out. They also escort guests to their rooms and familiarize them with the in-room facilities and services provided by the hotel. For a sample job specification of a bell boy, please refer to Fig. 18.2 in Chapter 18.

Duties and Responsibilities of Bell Boy   The major duties and responsibilities of a bell boy are as under:
- Handle the guest luggage, i.e., transport the guest luggage from lobby to the room at the time of check-in, and from the room to the vehicle at the time of departure.

- Put luggage tag at the time of the arrival of a guest.
- Escort guests to their rooms and familiarize them with the use of in-house telephone directory, weather control, and functions of all other equipment installed in the room.
- When collecting luggage at the time of check-out, take a cursory look inside the room to ensure that everything is intact.
- Keep the records of the left luggage rooms.
- Inform about the scanty baggage guest at the time of check-in.
- Perform sundry guest services like posting of guest mails, making purchases from outside the hotel premises like flowers, etc.
- Help in locating guests in a specified area within the hotel premises.
- Deliver mail, packages, and messages to guests in their rooms.

Door Attendant

A door attendant is among the first people to see and greet guests. A door attendant (see Fig. 4.8) is the person who opens the door of the guests' vehicles on their arrival in the hotel portico. He greets the guests and opens the hotel's main entrance for them.

Duties and Responsibilities of Door Attendant   Major duties and responsibilities of a door attendant are as under:

- Open the doors of guests' vehicles on their arrival in the hotel portico.
- Help bell boys in lifting luggage.
- Open the hotel's entrance door for guests.
- Coordinate with parking attendants for parking guests' vehicles in the hotel's parking area.

QUALITIES OF FRONT OFFICE PERSONNEL

Guests remain in direct contact with the front office staff throughout their stay at the hotel. As the front office personnel are the first and the last point of contact with the guests, they reflect the image of the hotel, and hence should carry themselves and behave in a way befitting the vision of the organization. The front office personnel must possess various qualities to discharge their duties efficiently, which are illustrated in Fig. 4.9.

Fig. 4.8 The Door Attendant

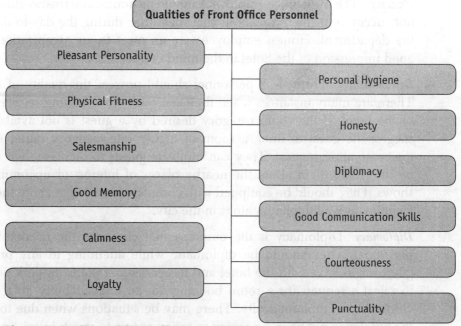

Fig. 4.9 Qualities of front office personnel

Pleasant personality   Most often, a front desk employee is the first person with whom a guest comes in contact. The guest starts building the image of the hotel from the physical appearance and personality of the front office personnel. The gestures, grooming, and personal presentation of a front desk employee are very important in leaving a good impression in the mind of the guest. The front desk personnel should be well turned out; they should have a pleasant personality, greeting guests with a smiling face and showing interest in their concerns.

Personal hygiene   The front desk employees should follow the highest standards of personal hygiene. They are in direct contact with guests throughout the day. A good sense of personal hygiene is imperative for front desk employees as their appearance influences the image of the hotel in the eyes of guests. As guests check into a hotel at all times and would be in touch with the front desk at any point of the day, the staff need to look their best at all times.

Physical fitness   It is important for front desk personnel to be physically fit as they have to be constantly on their feet during their long working hours. During peak business time or shortage of staff, they may have to work at long stretches. The bell desk personnel and sometimes the front desk staff too have to perform tasks like lifting and shifting guest luggage and parcels etc.

Honesty The front office employees should be honest and trustworthy. They should not succumb to the temptations that may arise during the day-to-day working of the department. Honest employees are an asset to an organization and leave a good impression of the hotel in the mind of guests.

Salesmanship Front desk personnel should possess the quality of salesmanship. There are many instances when they can push slow-moving services or products of the hotel. If the room category desired by a guest is not available, they can suggest the guest to book a room of higher rate category rather than rejecting the reservation request. They can motivate guests to increase their length of stay by informing them about the nearby places of interest or upcoming events and shows. They should be equipped with complete knowledge about the hotel and its facilities, as well the happenings in the city.

Diplomacy Diplomacy is the quintessential characteristic needed in front desk personnel. They should be diplomatic while attending to any problem that a guest might have with the hotel and its services. If the front desk personnel have to reject a request for a room booking due to unavailability, they should do so cordially and diplomatically. There may be situations when due to overbooking the hotel may not be in a position to assign rooms to guests in spite of them having a confirmed reservation; the front desk employees should deal with such situations diplomatically, without upsetting or offending the guests.

Good memory It is important for the front desk employees to have a good memory as guests like to be recognized by the hotel staff and addressed by their names on their repeat visits to the hotel. A sharp memory will help the front office staff remember and respond to the reservation requests and special preferences of guests. Guests appreciate it if their preferences are kept in mind while extending them various services, like allotting a room of their choice (in non-smoking area, away from elevator, on a quiet floor, etc.). This gives a personalized touch and establishes a lasting relationship with the guest.

Good communication skills The front office personnel must possess excellent communication skills as they interact with guests at the time of their arrival, stay, and departure. They should be confident and polite, and clear and precise in their communication. They should be proficient in English (or any other widely-spoken language); the knowledge of a foreign language is an added advantage.

Calmness The front office personnel should be able to remain calm and composed in high-pressure situations. There will be many situations when a guest might be unsatisfied and angry due to some problem in the services or products offered to the guest by the hotel, like the room rate confirmed to the guest at the time of reservation could be lower than the rate being charged at the time of check-out. The calmness and patience of the front desk personnel in such situations will help to diffuse the tension, resolve the problem, and win the guest's faith and loyalty.

Courteousness It is important that while interacting with guests the front desk personnel should be courteous and polite. They should never argue with a guest. In case they are unable to resolve any guest problem, they should involve their immediate supervisor. A smooth resolution of problems teamed with the courteous behaviour of the hotel staff will lead to goodwill among guests.

Loyalty The front desk personnel should be loyal to their job as well as to the management and the organization. Loyalty instils a sense of belongingness among employees, which reflects in their interactions with guests.

Punctuality The front desk employees should be punctual in reporting for their shifts, as well as in the discharge of their duties and responsibilities. The punctuality of employees reflects their commitment to their work.

In a nutshell, front office employees are pleasant, presentable, physically fit, honest, diplomatic, calm, courteous, loyal, punctual, and reliable. They are good communicators and salesmen, with a good memory, an eye for detail, good product knowledge, and general knowledge. They are the ambassadors of the hotel and need to be at their best at all times of the day.

SUMMARY

The front office department is the central point of the activities that take place between guests and a hotel. The employees of the department are among the first employees of the hotel to interact with the guest. This interaction starts with the processing of the reservation request and continues through the stages of arrival, stay, departure, and even after departure (when the hotel forwards mails received for the guest).

The department is organized on the principles of division of labour and span of control. It is organized into sections on the basis of the tasks performed by the employees of each section. Sections like reception, information, cash and bills, bell desk, travel desk etc. are located in the lobby in the close proximity of the entrance of the hotel. The sections which do not require direct access to the guest are located at the back of the department.

The organization structure of the front office department depends on the size of the hotel. A large hotel will have a complex structure of hierarchies and positions, while a small hotel will have a simple structure. For the efficient and smooth functioning of the department, it is important to list out the individual duties and responsibilities of the front office staff.

The front office personnel should be well turned out and at their best behaviour at all times. They should possess qualities like good communication skills, courteousness, salesmanship, honesty, and personal hygiene to carry out their duties effectively and efficiently.

KEY TERMS

Concierge A hotel employee who provides information and personalized services like dinner reservations, tour and travel arrangements.

Division of labour It refers to the narrow specialization of tasks within a process so that each employee can become a specialist in doing one thing.

Guest folio A statement showing the balance of the guest's financial obligation to the hotel.

Lobby It is an area just inside a large building, where people can meet and wait.

Paging Locating guests or employees within the hotel by a public address system.

Posting To enter information in an account.

Reservation section This section of the front office department receives and processes reservation queries.

Reception This is the front desk of the hotel, which greets guests and answers their queries on their arrival.

Span of control The number of employees reporting directly to one supervisor in an organization.

Walk-in guests Guests who arrive at a hotel without prior reservation.

REVIEW QUESTIONS

Discussion Questions

1. Discuss the role of the front office in a hotel.

2. Front office department is further divided into several sections. State the reasons for the same.

3. What role do reservations play in maximizing the revenue of the hotel?

4. What are the functions performed at the information desk?

5. What role does a cashier play in the front office department?

6. Explain the duties and responsibilities of the front office manager.

7. What are the duties and responsibilities of a reservation assistant?

8. Distinguish between the duties of a reservation assistant and a receptionist.

CRITICAL THINKING QUESTIONS

1. Bell boys are the image-builders of the hotel and also the protector of hotel properties. Discuss.

2. A concierge provides personalized guest services. Comment.

3. Telephone operators have to coordinate emergency communications. Discuss various situations in which emergency communications would be required.

PROJECT WORK

1. In groups of five, visit a lodge, a two-star hotel, a four-star hotel, and a five-star hotel, and study the following:
   a) Layout of the reception section.
   b) Layout of the reservation section.
   c) Different sections of front office.
   d) Hierarchy of the front office department.
   Try to find out the reasons for the difference in the above in each hotel visited by you. Discuss and analyse the differences. Do they vary according to the star rating?

2. Get to know more about concierges and their professional association—Les Clefs d'Or—on the Internet and by visiting five five-star hotels. 'A concierge is often expected to "achieve the impossible", dealing with any request a guest may have, no matter how strange, relying on an extensive list of personal contacts with various local merchants and service providers.'
   a) Do your research findings concur with the above statement?
   b) Prepare a description of the duties and responsibilities of a concierge.

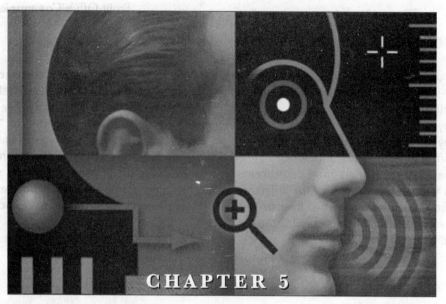

CHAPTER 5

Front Office Communication

Learning Objectives:

After reading this chapter, you will be able to understand:
- The definition of communication.
- The communication process.
- The seven Cs of communication.
- The importance of communication.
- Types of communication—oral, written, and non-verbal.
- The flow of communication.
- Barriers of communication—semantic, psychological, and personal.
- Inter-departmental communication.

People have been sharing ideas, views, feelings, information, knowledge, facts, and values with each other from the beginning of human civilization. In the ancient age, humans were communicating with each other by the use of symbols, actions, and gestures before they established languages for oral and written modes of communication. When they started travelling to other places, these ancient languages crossed borders. With the growth in human civilization, different languages came into existence. The use of a common language between two parties makes communication easier and clearer as both the parties are well versed with the language in which they are communicating and are able to understand the other.

Communication continues to play a vital role in modern life, especially in the hospitality industry. Communication is required for proper co-ordination between each section and division of the hotel for optimum performance and also for effective interaction with the guests. Each department of the hotel needs to exchange lots of information among themselves in order to carry out their day-to-day functions. Ambiguous and vague communication could lead to embarrassing situations; therefore, communication should be precise and clear.

The present chapter discusses the communication process, types of communication, importance of communication, oral and written communication, flow of communication, barriers of communication, and inter-departmental communication and coordination in hotels.

COMMUNICATION

The process of sharing views, ideas, and knowledge between two or more individuals or between groups is known as communication. The word communication is derived from the Latin *communicare*, meaning 'to impart, share, or make common.' According to Oxford Advanced Learner's Dictionary, communication means 'the activity or process of expressing ideas and feelings or of giving people information'. Newstrom and Davis (1997) define communication as 'the transfer of information from one person to another person. It is a way of reaching others by transmitting ideas, facts, thoughts, feelings, and values.'

Communication is the process of conveying information from a sender to a receiver with the use of a medium in which the communicated information is understood by both the sender and receiver. It is the exchange of information through various means like speaking, writing, or using a common system of signs or behaviour. The most important aspect in the process of communication is the interpretation of the message. The receiver of the message should interpret the message in the sense the sender intends it. So it is important to satisfy the following criteria for proper communication:

- There is something to transfer—ideas, feelings, knowledge, information, etc.
- There must be two parties for completing the communication process—sender and receiver.
- The message should be correctly interpreted.

THE COMMUNICATION PROCESS

Communication is as a process by which people convey information through the transmission of written, verbal, or symbolic messages. The term 'process' refers to an identifiable flow of information through inter-related stages of analysis, directed towards the achievement of an objective. The entire communication process may be broken into various stages of communication—sender/source, message, encoding, channel, receiver/target, decoding, and feedback—as shown in Fig. 5.1.

Let's take an example in the context of the hotel industry. Anjali Arora, a travel agent, calls up the reservations section of Hotel Crowne International to book a room for two nights for her British clients. The call reaches the reservation agent Anuj. He takes down the required details—like name of the guests (Mrs and Mr A.J. Smith), stay dates (10–12 November), arrival and departure details (BA 143 and BA 142), preferred room category (luxury suite)—assigns rate ($ 400 per night), confirms the reservation, recaps the reservation details, and gives Anjali the booking reference number (HCI-08-LS123).

Source The source or the sender of a message is an individual or a group, of people, who wish to share the given information, facts, or feelings with another person or group of people (the target audience of the message), and initiate the communication. A good communication primarily depends on the skills of the source, who should provide complete information in a proper manner. In the example, the source of the message is Anjali Arora, who, being a travel agent, is aware of the reservation process and the details required. She is thus an effective source of the communication process, who communicates her message effectively.

Message Message is the subject matter of the communication that is passed from the sender to the target audience. It may be views, ideas, feelings, orders, recommendations, facts, data, request, etc. In the example, the message is the request for a two nights' room reservation at Hotel Crowne International for a British couple from 10 to 12 November.

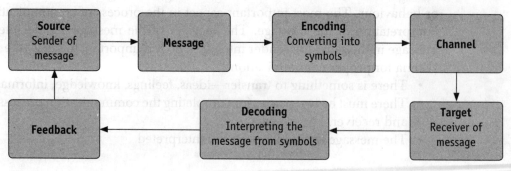

Fig. 5.1 The communication process

Encoding   In order to convey information, the sender must encode or translate the information into messages that others can understand. This encoding could be in the form of a letter, telephonic message, or e-mail. In the given example, Anjali uses a mutually understandable language (English) to give the details of the reservation request—guest names, stay dates, etc.

Channel   The medium through which the encoded message passes between the sender and the receiver is known as the channel of communication. It may be in a written form (like letter, e-mail, or fax), or telephonic conversation, or personal contact, etc. The channel of communication depends upon the communication options (like telephone, e-mail, etc.) available between the sender and the receiver. In the above-mentioned example, Anjali has called up the hotel. Hence, telephone is the channel of communication between Anjali (representing the travel agency) and Anuj (representing the hotel).

Target   The target or the receiver of the message is the individual or group of people to whom the message is sent by the sender or source. The extent to which the receiver comprehends the message will depend on a number of factors: the receiver's knowledge about the topic, their receptivity to the message, the relationship and trust between the sender and the receiver. In the example, Anuj (representing the hotel) is the target or receiver of the message and he comprehends the message properly as he is aware of the reservation process.

Decoding   Once the message reaches the receiver, the latter tries to interpret it. This process of interpretation constitutes decoding. A communication is successful if the receiver correctly interprets the sender's message. In the example, Anuj decodes the details provided by Anjali, like guest names (Mrs and Mr A.J. Smith), stay dates (10–12 November), etc.

Feedback   Feedback is the final link in the chain of the communication process. After receiving a message, the receiver responds in some way and signals that response to the sender. In this particular situation, the booking reference number is the feedback that Anjali receives from Anuj. It indicates that proper communication has taken place and the reservation has been booked in a luxury suite at Hotel Crowne International from 10–12 November in the name of Mrs and Mr A.J. Smith at a rate of $400 per suite per night.

In the above example, proper communication has taken place, as both the sender and receiver have encoded and decoded the message correctly. There are many times when it might not be so, for example:

Message sent	Missing information
One room for November.	No particular stay dates/year.
One room for family.	Number of members in the family.
The room rate is Rs 1,000 for four nights.	The room rate is Rs 1,000 per night, i.e., Rs 4,000 for four nights.
IC flight from Mumbai to Delhi.	Exact details of the flight—there are approximately twenty domestic flights between Mumbai and Delhi each day.

THE SEVEN Cs OF COMMUNICATION

The various aspects of effective communication are given below:

Completeness   The sender and the receiver should exchange all the relevant details. In the above example, the communication is complete as the details required for reservation—like the names of guests, the date of arrival, the date of departure, the type of room, the room rent—are exchanged between Anjali Arora, the travel agent (the sender of the message) and Anuj, the reservation assistant of the hotel (the receiver of the message).

Conciseness   The hotel representative should note down the required information in a concise, brisk, and professional manner, and not ask guests to repeat information that has already been given.

Consideration   The hotel staff should be considerate towards guests and their requirements, like guests could be allotted a room with a good view without having to ask for it.

Concreteness   The information gathered should be concrete or specific. It should not be vague like 'a room in December', which does not specify the stay dates.

Clarity   The message should be communicated clearly so that there are no communication gaps.

Courtesy   The hotel staff should be courteous towards all external (guests, vendors, etc.) and internal customers (colleagues) while conveying a message.

Correctness   While taking a message, the receiver should ensure that the message details, like the spellings of guests' names, the stay dates, arrival and departure details, etc., are correct so as not to create any problem at the time of guest arrival.

THE IMPORTANCE OF COMMUNICATION

Good communication is important for establishing a long-lasting relationship between a hotel and its guests. A guest's opinion of a hotel is formed on the basis of her overall experience at the hotel, which includes satisfaction with the hotel facilities and services like accommodation, food and beverage, recreation, etc., as well as treatment extended by the hotel staff. Let's suppose a guest walks into your hotel lobby, and you are busy speaking on the phone and ignore her. This behaviour would be considered rude by the guest, and from then on each negative experience, like late delivery of newspapers or meals ordered through room service, would add up and spoil the guest's overall experience at the hotel. The proper way to deal with this situation is to smile at guests as they walk in and convey to them that you would be with them in a minute. They should be seated in the lobby while the food and beverage department serves them a refreshing welcome drink and cold towels. This gesture would put the guests at ease while they wait to check into their room. Thus, effective external communication is very important to satisfy and please guests.

Internal communication is also very important for proper coordination among various departments. Every department of the hotel shares information with the other departments for the proper planning and execution of tasks. The front office communicates with other departments for all kinds of information, like with housekeeping for the status of rooms. At the same time, housekeeping will require information from the front office about the day's arrivals and their relevant details, e.g., the time of arrival,, whether the guest is a VIP, whether groups are expected (in order to schedule the availability of employees for the smooth operation of the department and also to have the rooms ready before the guests check-in), and the information about guests' special requests and preferences, if any (this maybe communicated to the front desk by the reservation assistant or could be known from the guest history). The importance of communication is illustrated in Fig. 5.2.

For Planning   Managers need information from all departments for planning and distributing work. For example, advance information about the day's arrivals and their relevant details would enable the manager or supervisor to prepare the roster and to plan out the day's work accordingly. Managers gather relevant information from each section or department through oral or written communication like arrival reports, staff briefings, reservation requests, etc. Good communication therefore leads to effective planning.

For Decision-making   On many occasions, managers are required to make important decisions on the basis of the information available to them. They should be able to study all the available options before choosing the most suitable alternative(s).

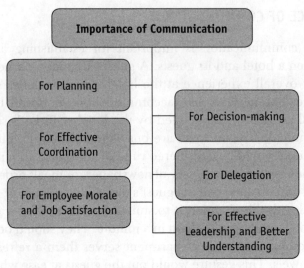

Fig. 5.2   Importance of communication

Effective communication generates all the necessary information and thus plays a vital role in the decision-making process.

For Effective Coordination   Effective inter- and intra-departmental coordination is important in providing flawless services to hotel guests. Such coordination is achieved though proper communication within the department and also with all the other departments of the hotel—housekeeping, food and beverage, kitchen, sales and marketing, IT, accounts, human resources, and so on.

For Delegation   Managers are responsible for planning work and delegating various tasks and duties. It is important that they communicate the delegation of authority to all the concerned persons. For example, if the front office manager (FOM) has delegated the task of making the duty roster to any shift supervisor, the same should be communicated to all concerned for better efficacy and implementation.

For Employee Morale and Job Satisfaction   Feedback and open communication between the FOM and his team members raises the morale of the team and leads to greater job satisfaction. When team members can discuss and resolve their problems, they are able to work and perform better.

For Effective Leadership and Better Understanding   Good leaders communicate effectively with their teams, leading to good understanding, cooperation, and coordination among team members.

All the above-mentioned benefits of good communication lead to increased productivity and revenue besides improved services.

TYPES OF COMMUNICATION

Oral Communication

Words are the most common symbols of communication. Oral communication describes any type of interaction that makes use of spoken words. It is a vital, integral part of the modern business world. In oral communication, both the sender and the receiver exchange their ideas through words either in face-to-face communication or through electronic devices like telephone, computers, etc. Oral communication is easy, effective, and produces instant feedback from the other party. However, oral communication is time consuming and has limitations like lack of proof and authenticity.

Importance of Oral Communication   Of all the language actions, listening and speaking are very important and are most often used in organizations, classrooms, or in the community. Speaking skills are universally recognized as a primary indicator of a person's knowledge, proficiency, and credibility. In any situation, be it a face-to-face talk, telephonic conversation, or video conference, good listening and speaking skills are essential for sending, receiving, and understanding messages. To understand the messages communicated by others, you should be able to listen carefully, taking special care to clarify what you have not understood. Listening and speaking play a very important role in the development of an individual. One should learn to express one's own ideas, feelings, and thoughts clearly as well as to respond to others appropriately, in both formal and informal situations. Listening can be defined as 'a process of receiving, interpreting, and reacting to a message received from the speaker'.

Hearing and listening are not the same, though people often use these two words interchangeably. In fact, hearing, which is solely dependent on the ears, is a physical act, and barring physically impaired persons, everyone can hear without deliberate effort. However, listening requires voluntary attention and then making sense of what was heard. It requires a conscious effort to interpret the sounds, grasp the meanings of the words, and then react to the message. The interpretation of sound signals is a cognitive act, which completely depends on the knowledge of the listener and also on their attitude towards the sender and the message. An untoward attitude towards the sender might affect the listening process to a great extent.

While working in a hotel, front office agents will use their listening skills in a variety of situations: while recording complaints of distressed and dissatisfied guests; during telephonic conversations with guests, travel agents, and corporate bookers; while taking instructions from the FOM or supervisors; while arranging for staff briefings; and many other instances. If you are effective in listening, you will be able to take right decisions. Listening patiently to employees enables the managers to feel the pulse of the organization. They can anticipate the employees' moods and reactions to the policies of the management. They will also be able to

Fig. 5.3 Grapevine—informal communication network

track rumours on the grapevine (see Fig. 5.3) that are liable to cause damage to the reputation of the organization. Effective listening and follow-up can suppress these rumours and control them from spreading further. Harmonious relationships can be created amongst employees, leading to a congenial working ambience.

On the other hand, lack of proper listening can lead to embarrassing situations because of gaps in coordination and understanding. Managers with closed minds do not like to discuss problems and their solutions with subordinates. They might simply refuse to listen to suggestions and solutions provided by their juniors. This type of dogmatic and inflexible approach eventually ruins the working environment, provoking bitterness, indignation, and misunderstanding among employees. Employees feel demoralized, which leads to a reduction in the productivity of the organization. Effective listening is a very important component of the open-door policy adopted by many organizations. When employees are encouraged to freely walk into the FOM's or General Manager's room and speak up, they do not harbour negative feelings. Effective listening, where both the management and the employees listen to each other patiently, will improve working conditions and nurture harmony and cohesion in the organization,. This will boost the morale of the employees, resulting in increased productivity. Refer to Table 5.1 for tips on effective listening and Table 5.2 for the globally-used phonetic alphabet list to have effective communication with guests.

Some letters sound alike when spoken and also over a telephone line, especially when two people have different accents. In these cases, the message might not be clear and the people might have a hard time understanding each other. In case you are not sure of the spelling of the guest name as per the booking agent's pronunciation, you can ask the booking agent to spell it phonetically. For example, the booking agent would like to make a reservation in the name of Mrs Suzanne Claude. You think it is spelt as 'Susan' and verify the exact spelling by repeating it phonetically,

Table 5.1 Tips for effective listening

Dos	Don'ts
• Be mentally prepared to listen. • Evaluate the speech, not the speaker. • Be unbiased to the speaker by depersonalizing your feelings. • Fight distractions by closing of sound sources. • Be open-minded. • Ask questions to clarify and corroborate thoughts. • Paraphrase from time to time. • Send appropriate non-verbal signals from time to time.	• Pay undue emphasis to the vocabulary as you can use the context to understand the meaning. • Pay too much attention to the accessories and clothing of the speaker. • Prepare your responses while the speaker is speaking. • Form preconceptions and prejudices. • Get distracted by outside influences. • Concentrate too hard. • Interrupt too often. • Show boredom even to an uninteresting speaker.

Table 5.2 Phonetic Alphabet List—Letters

Letter	Code word	Pronunciation
A	Alpha	Al Fah
B	Bravo	Brah Voh
C	Charlie	Char Lee
D	Delta	Dell Tah
E	Echo	Eck Oh
F	Foxtrot	Foks Trot
G	Golf	Golf
H	Hotel	Ho Tell
I	India	In Dee Ah
J	Juliet	Jew Lee Ett
K	Kilo	Key Loh
L	Lima	Lee Mah
M	Mike	Mike
N	November	No Vem Ber
O	Oscar	Oss Cah
P	Papa	Pah Pah
Q	Quebec	Keh Beck
R	Romeo	Row Me Oh
S	Sierra	See Air Rah
T	Tango	Tang Go
U	Uniform	You Nee Form
V	Victor	Vik Tah
W	Whiskey	Wiss Key
X	X-ray	Ecks Ray
Y	Yankee	Yang Key
Z	Zulu	Zoo Loo

'May I spell the guest name—S for sierra; U for uniform; S for sierra, ...,' and the booking agent would correct you and say, 'No, it's Z for zulu; A for alpha, ...' This eliminates the need for any clarification, avoids confusion at the time of registration, and also avoids duplicate bookings for the same guest under different spellings. The use of phonetic alphabet makes sure that you're heard correctly the first time. It is very useful in situations when the telephone lines have some disturbance or in the case of international calls where you cannot afford to go back and forth trying to figure out what the caller is saying, as the calls are expensive and the guest might get irritated at repeating the same information over and over again.

Written Communication

Written communication is communication by means of written symbols (either printed or handwritten). It may be in the form of letters, e-mails, reservation confirmations, hotel circulars, memos, reports, notes, manuals, in-house hotel magazines, etc. Messages that are not written properly create confusion and misunderstanding among readers. Thus it is important to understand the purpose, the audience, and the channel before composing a message. Written communication has several merits like authenticity, transparency, mass access, proof for future reference, legal defence, and permanent record. However, it also suffers from demerits like over-formalization, high cost factor, unnecessary paper work, no immediate response or feedback, lack of secrecy, and limited reach (to the literate world).

Importance of Written Communication   A hotel has to correspond in writing with its guests, other hotels, suppliers, bankers, and other partners and service providers. Business letters are an important tool of written communication, which serve as a means to reach out to people not only within the locality and neighbourhood but also in other cities and nations. Though there are many modern communication methods available these days, the traditional business letters still retain their importance in the business world for the following reasons:

- They assist you in sustaining your business relationships with other businesses and customers.
- They are an appropriate form of communication when the information you wish to convey is complex.
- They serve as permanent records and are a valuable repository of information, which you can refer to in the future.
- They help you reach a large and geographically diverse audience, thereby enabling the organization to save money on telephone calls.

The phenomenally rapid growth of the Internet and its widespread use in business has changed the way in which organizations communicate. Many hotels promote the use of e-mail for guest correspondence and also for other external and in-house correspondence. E-mail offers some tremendous advantages. It is fast (a message can be sent to many people instantaneously), inexpensive, and convenient (people can check their e-mail without leaving their desks).

While e-mail is an efficient way to communicate, it is also subject to limitations. In particular, one must recognize when e-mail is appropriate and when it is not. For example, when writing about emotionally-charged subjects (or when the person you are writing to may become angry, defensive, or otherwise upset about a subject), or when you are angry, a face-to-face conversation is generally more appropriate than e-mail. Similarly, discussing confidential matters or very complex issues is often better done in other ways than through e-mail. Refer to Exhibit 5.1 for details on e-mail etiquettes.

Exhibit 5.1   E-mail etiquettes

There are many etiquette rules that guide e-mail writing, which will differ according to the nature of the organization and its corporate culture. Here are some tips for effective e-mails that apply to nearly all formal communication situations:

1. **Respond promptly:** People send e-mails, rather than letters or faxes, as they wish to receive a quick response. Therefore, reply to an e-mail within twenty-four hours and preferably within the same working day. If an e-mail requires a detailed follow up and setting up a number of arrangements (like intercity travel itinerary, along with foreign language speaking guide, arrangements for dining, spa, etc.), send an acknowledgement e-mail to the client, stating that you have received their e-mail and would revert to them with all the necessary details.

2. **Write a meaningful subject line and be concise:** It is important to mention the subject correctly so that the guest reads your e-mail and does not delete it or move it to the spam folder. Also, do not make the e-mail longer than it needs to be. Avoid long sentences as e-mail is meant to be a quick medium.

3. **Use templates for frequently used responses:** When you receive similar queries about hotel facilities and services, distance of airport or railway station from the hotel, places of tourist interest in and around the city, etc., you can save your replies as response templates and paste these into your message as and when you need them. This would help save time and also maintain consistency when different reservation agents respond to the guest mails.

4. **Use attachments sparingly:** E-mails with attachments may become very heavy and may not get delivered to the guest. However, if the guest is coming to your hotel for the first time, you should send them pictures of the hotel, lobby, and places of tourist interest, though it would be better if you could send them a link to your hotel's photo gallery (if available on your hotel website). If you must send an attachment, try to compress it before sending.

5. **Answer all questions and pre-empt further questions:** The e-mail reply must answer all the guest's questions and also other relevant questions that the guest could have. If all the questions are not answered, the guest would send more e-mails, and you would be wasting the guest's and your time by the constant back and forth of e-mails. If you are able to anticipate relevant questions and answer them, the guest would be impressed with your efficiency and thoughtfulness.

6. **Maintain coherence:** When you reply to an e-mail, include the guest's original e-mail in your reply. As a hotel receives many e-mails throughout the day, one cannot keep track of individual e-mails. Thus a message without the previous correspondence will not provide all the information, and you (or your colleague) will have to spend a long time to find out the context of the mail. Also, it would save the guest much time and frustration if the earlier correspondence is included in the e-mail.

7. **Read the e-mail before you send it:** Read your e-mail to weed out the spelling and grammar mistakes. Also, reading the e-mail through the eyes of the recipient guest will help you send a more effective message and avoid misunderstandings and inappropriate comments.

Non-verbal Communication

When we communicate, we make use of spoken and written language to convey the content of a message to others. But we can also communicate without words. This kind of communication tells us something about the relationship between people and is often more important than conveying a message through words. We often find words inadequate to convey the proper meaning of a message. The meaning may be made clear by using body language (see Fig. 5.4). Body language does not employ words and is therefore called non-verbal communication. We use body language all the time, for instance looking someone in the eyes means something different than not looking the person in the eyes. When in contact with others, one is always communicating something or the other, verbally and non-verbally.

Non-verbal communication refers to the messages we give and receive through body language and facial expressions. Non-verbal messages often convey more meaning than the spoken word, as can be seen from the pie chart in Fig. 5.5.

Usually non-verbal communication occurs unconsciously. Our body language determines the meaning of communication to a large extent. Therefore, it would be good if we could learn to use our body language for a purpose and also learn to understand and interpret the body language of others. It is important to note that body language has different meanings in different cultures. How we interpret body language of a person depends on the situation, culture, our relationship with the person, as well as the gender of the person. There is not one signal that has the same meaning all over the world. Body language is also interlinked with spoken language and a whole pattern of behaviour. Moreover, various body language signs can complement each other to convey the meaning of what we communicate.

Fig. 5.4   Non-verbal expressions of relaxed, authoritative, and informal communication

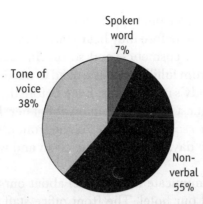

Fig. 5.5 Understanding gained from verbal and non-verbal communication

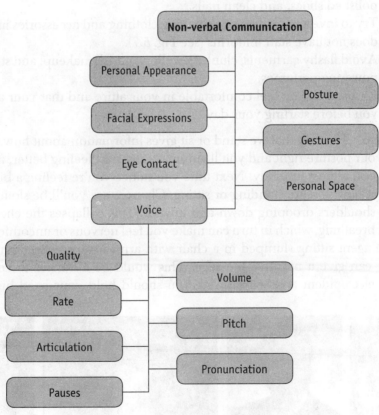

Fig. 5.6 Aspects of non-verbal communication

Other factors that play an important role in non-verbal communication include personal appearance, posture, facial expressions, gestures, eye contact, personal space, and voice (see Fig. 5.6).

Personal Appearance   Personal appearance plays a very important role in the hotel industry. Guests see you before they hear you. They assess you on the basis of your clothes, hair, jewellery, cosmetics, and so on. In today's society, the purpose of clothing has altered from fulfilling a basic need to making a statement about oneself. Clothes accent the body's movements. Even before the front office employee utters his first syllable, the guest forms an opinion about her. Her appearance may put the guest in a resistant or receptive mood. As the front office staff has to interact with guests throughout the day, they should be clean and well groomed, conforming to the hotel standards.

Appearances communicate how we feel about ourselves and how we want the guest to view us and our hotel. The front office staff should pay attention to the following points with regard to appearances:
- Be well turned out and well groomed; ensure a neat hairstyle, body hygiene, polished shoes, and clean nails.
- Try to invest in professional-looking clothing and accessories in case the hotel does not have staff uniforms (see Fig. 5.7).
- Avoid flashy garments, clunky jewellery, garish makeup, and strong and over-powering perfumes.
- Ensure that you feel comfortable in your attire and that your accessories suit you before starting your day.

Posture   The way that we stand or sit gives information about how we are feeling. Get your posture right and you'll automatically start feeling better, as it makes you feel good almost instantly. Next time you notice you're feeling a bit down, take a look at how you are standing or sitting. Chances are you'll be slouched over with your shoulders drooping down and inward. This collapses the chest and inhibits good breathing, which in turn can make you feel nervous or uncomfortable. A front office agent sitting slumped in a chair with arms firmly crossed and head turned away can give a negative message. This would be a barrier to communication. To feel confident and self-assured, you should hold your head high at all times

Fig. 5.7   Personal appearance—formal attire

(see Fig. 5.8). This posture would also help you in situations when you want to be authoritative and want your message to be taken seriously. However, when you want to be friendly and in the listening, receptive mode, tilt your head just a little to one side. You can shift the tilt from left to right at different points in your conversation with the guest.

A person's body posture is a strong indicator of the power equation in a one-to-one relationship. As a rule, the person in authority would be relaxed, while the supplicant would be watchful and on guard. While excessive tension is not good for either the superior or the subordinate, total relaxation is also inappropriate for a subordinate. For instance, a job candidate who matches the interviewer's casual sprawl creates a poor impression. In superior-subordinate interactions, the best posture for the subordinate is one that is slightly more tense and upright than that of the power-holder.

Given below is a list of some postures and the message they communicate:
1) Slumped posture: Low spirits
2) Erect posture: High spirits, energy, and confidence
3) Lean forward: Open and interested

4) Lean away: Defensive or disinterested
5) Crossed arms: Defensive
6) Uncrossed arms: Willingness to listen

Facial Expressions Our faces can display a myriad of expressions and feelings (see Fig. 5.9). As the receiver of a message, you can rely heavily on the facial expressions of the sender because their expressions are a better indicator of the meaning behind the message than their words. For example, a frown or a smile, depending on how and when it is used, determines the import of a message. The FOM's smile makes you feel happy while his frown leaves you discomfited; your subordinate's confused expression indicates the need to continue with an explanation; your guest's smile and nod signals the time to close a sale. It is believed that facial expressions also provide information

Fig. 5.8 Confident body posture

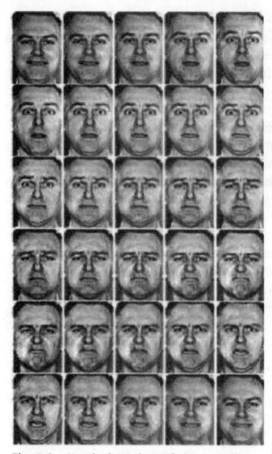

Fig. 5.9 Morphed continua of six expressions

about a communicator's thought process. For example, one can judge the confidence of the communicator in the information being given or the reliability of this information. Facial expressions also serve as a source of positive or negative feedback from the receiver. However, many believe that facial expressions are open to various interpretations of the receiver. Despite the element of subjectivity in interpreting facial expressions, they remain an important form of non-verbal communication.

Gestures Gesture is the use of actions to communicate something. By moving the parts of your body, you can express both specific and general messages, some voluntary and some spontaneous. Many gestures have a specific and intentional meaning; a wave of the hand, for example, means hello or good-bye. Most of us, when talking with our friends, use our hands and facial expressions to help us describe an event or object. We wave our arms about, turn our hands this way and that, roll our eyes, raise our eyebrows, and smile or frown. However, when presenting to people in a more formal setting, many of us become tongue-tied. We must understand that our business audience is no different from our friends—they all rely on our face and hands to 'see' the bigger, fuller picture.

Here are some of the gestures that people use to convey messages (see Fig. 5.10):

1) Folding hands: welcome or apology
2) Making a fist: you're angry
3) Thumbs up: okay or all the best
4) Pointing: showing something

Some gestures are not always understood properly and can cause misunderstandings. It is important to understand that many gestures mean different things in different cultures. For example, pointing at a person is considered very rude in some countries. Ideally, a person's gestures should complement verbal communication to enhance the content of a message. If the gestures do not agree with the vocal message, they can lead to confusion and misunderstanding. The hotel staff should make proper use of gestures to communicate effectively with guests.

Eye Contact Eye contact is a direct and powerful form of non-verbal communication. It can convey a wide range of emotions, signal messages, and indicate interest or boredom. During staff meetings, the superior generally maintains eye contact longer than the subordinates. The direct eye contact of the sender of a message conveys candour, openness, and elicits a feeling of trust. Downward glances are generally associated with modesty. Eyes rolled upward are associated with fatigue. When listening to subordinates, your eyes convey your attentiveness, your interest level, and even how you feel about what they are saying. Your eyes can also assert your authority over others. In fact, only physical force can challenge another person more than a direct stare. Thus such a look from you might reform a lazy employee more quickly than all the harsh words you could think of. You may recognize that your eyes can communicate a wide range of meanings, from a fleeting glance to a shifty gaze to a killer look. You might suspect the motives of your guests, employees, or customers who refuse to look at you directly. But again, the meaning might not be that simple because the facial expression may be combined with another non-verbal means of communication. For example, a firm handshake accompanied by an indirect gaze is harder to interpret than a simple glance. Eye contact also determines the credibility of the message to a large extent. As 'eyes are the window to your soul', maintaining eye contact during communication strengthens credibility, while averting eye contact is detrimental to credibility. It is important for front office employees to maintain eye contact with guests while communicating—this would lend credibility to their messages as well as display keenness on their part towards the guest's concerns.

Personal space Most people feel uncomfortable when somebody stands or sits either too close or too far away from them. This disturbs them and makes

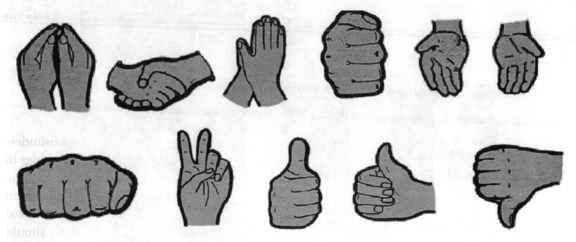

Fig. 5.10 Some hand gestures

communication difficult. Behavioural studies indicate that people set individual distance limits for different types of interactions. They have a comfortable distance zone for personal interaction and non-verbally define this as their personal space (see Fig. 5.11). The violation of this personal space can have serious adverse effects on communication. While communicating with guests, one must take care to respect their personal space.

Not only is a vocal message qualified and conditioned by the handling of distance, but the substance of a conversation can often demand special handling of space. Spatial changes give a tone to a communication, accent it, and at times even counteract the spoken word. There are certain thoughts that are difficult to share unless one is within the proper conversational zone. The telling of a secret at a distance of 20 feet, for example, is not only difficult but negates the confidentiality of the message itself.

In organizations, most people use space and distance to communicate important information about themselves. The proximity or distance we keep with others at workspace results from our sense of ownership of space or territory. You might have noticed how much closer you stand to a friendly colleague than to one you don't know too well. By becoming aware of the non-verbal cue of distance, you can also learn much about the guests you come in contact with.

Voice   The tone of a person's voice can communicate many important messages. Words can mean many different things, depending on the way they are said. We are able to tell if a guest is angry, happy, or nervous by their tone of her voice. Paralinguistic features are non-verbal vocal cues that help you give urgency to your voice. Your voice is your trademark; it is that part of yourself that adds human

Figure 5.11   Personal space communicates mental attitudes

touch to your words. The written word does not have that immediacy because it lacks emotion. Voice adds life to your message, so it is useful to understand the characteristic nuances of voice, namely *quality, volume, rate, pitch, articulation, pronunciation, modulation,* and *pauses.*

Quality Quality is a characteristic that distinguishes one voice from another. Each one of us has a unique voice and its quality depends upon its resonating mechanism. While the quality of one's voice cannot be changed, it can be trained for optimum impact.

Volume Volume is the loudness or the softness of the voice. If the place you are speaking in is large and open, the volume should be high, and if the place is small and enclosed, the volume should be low. If your volume is too high you may sound boorish and insensitive, whereas if it is too low you may convey an impression of timidity and lack of self-confidence. In all, you should vary your volume so as to make your voice audible and clear.

Pace/Rate Rate is the number of words which you speak per minute. It varies from person to person, from 80 to 250 words per minute. The normal rate is from 120 to 150 words. Cultivate your pace so as to fit in this reasonable limit. If a person speaks too slowly and monotonously, she is most likely to be considered a dull speaker even though the contents of her speech may be highly interesting. Similarly, a fast speaker also causes discomfort because the listeners do not get time to grasp the thoughts and switch from one thought to another. Under these circumstances, listeners may just stop listening and their attention may go astray.

Pitch Pitch refers to the number of vibrations per second of your voice. The rise and fall of the voice conveys various emotions. Inflections give warmth, lustre, vitality, and exuberance to your speech. Lowness of pitch can indicate sadness, shock, dullness, guilt, etc. If you are excited, joyous, ecstatic, triumphant, and even angry, then your pitch automatically becomes high. A well-balanced pitch results in a clear and effective tone. It helps you avoid being monotonous. Intonation refers to the rising and falling pitch of the voice when somebody says a word or syllable. By learning and adopting an appropriate intonation pattern, you will be able to express your intention very clearly.

Articulation Speakers should be careful not to slop, slur, chop, truncate, or omit sounds between words or sentences. If all the sounds are not uttered properly, the flow of understanding gets interrupted and deters the listener from grasping the meaning of the message. The result is similar to the negative impression that written errors leave with a reader. Lazy articulation, slurred sounds, or skipping over words will lower the credibility of the speaker. Develop the ability to speak distinctly; produce the sounds in a crisp and lucid manner without causing any confusion.

Pronunciation One should be careful to pronounce individual sounds along with word stress according to the set norms. As guests come from different parts of the nation and the world, they might pronounce words differently but we should follow our standards of pronunciation.

Voice modulation Modulation pertains to the way we regulate, vary, or adjust the tone, pitch, and volume of the sound or speaking voice. Modulation of voice brings flexibility and vitality to your voice, and you can express emotions, sentiments like impatience, careful planning, despondency, suspicion, etc. in the best possible way. If you do not pay special attention to the modulation of your voice, then your voice becomes flat and you emerge as a languid speaker with no command over your voice. Word stress and sentence stress also play an important role in voice modulation.

Pauses A pause is a brief moment of silence between words, sounds, or musical notes. A pause in speaking lets the listener reflect on the message and digest it accordingly. It helps you organize your thoughts and move smoothly from one thought to another. It enriches your speech because it is a natural process to give a break. A pause helps not only the listener but the speaker as well. Pauses automatically come in between the major points of your talk. You should use pauses thoughtfully and time them well as they exhibit assurance, confidence, and self-control. Also, use pauses at the end of certain thought units to let the listener fully absorb the information.

Excellent communication skills are the keys to success in your personal and professional life. Research shows that non-verbal communication is actually more important than verbal communication. Here are some tips for front office employees towards using non-verbal communication effectively in their interactions with guests and colleagues:

- Observe and understand the non verbal signals being sent your way on a moment-to-moment basis.
- Use good eye contact.
- Stop what you were doing when your listeners look glassy-eyed or bored.
- Use the tonality of your voice the way that a musician uses an instrument.
- Adopt the most appropriate posture that suits the occasion.
- Soak in the pats/hugs that others give to you.
- Understand the cultural nuances of the various forms of non-verbal communication.
- When there is a contradiction between the verbal and non-verbal messages of a person who you are listening to, try to assess the situation with the help of non-verbal cues.

Thus, effective communication involves an effective exchange of information with internal as well as external customers, through both verbal and non-verbal communication.

FLOW OF COMMUNICATION

Information flows in an organization both formally and informally. Formal communication refers to communication that follows the official hierarchy and is required to do one's job. Such information flows through formal channels—the main lines of organizational communication. Most of the communication that a hotel needs for its operations flows through these channels. For example, when an FOM instructs a front office assistant on some matter, or when an employee brings a problem to a supervisor's attention, or when two employees discuss a guest's reservation, it is formal communication. Moreover, information of various kinds flowing through formal channels, such as policy or procedural changes, orders, instructions, confidential reports, etc., is classified as formal communication. This type of communication can flow in various directions—downward, upward, lateral, or diagonal.

Downward Communication

Downward communication flows from a manager, down the chain of command. When front office managers inform, instruct, advise, or request their subordinates, the communication flows in a downward pattern. This is generally used to convey routine information, new policies or procedures, to seek clarification, to ask for an analysis, etc. Also, superiors send feedback about their subordinates' actions through this channel. Such communication increases awareness about the organization among subordinates and employees, and enables managers to evaluate the performance of their subordinates. Downward communication can be in the form of memos, notices, face-to-face interactions, or telephonic conversations. However, this should be adequately balanced by an upward flow of communication.

Upward Communication

Communication flows upward when subordinates send reports, or present their findings and recommendations to their superiors. This keeps the managers aware of how the employees feel about their jobs, colleagues, and the organization in general. Managers also rely on upward communication for making certain decisions or solving some problems which concern the organization. The extent of upward communication, especially that which is initiated at the lowest level, depends on the culture of the organization. In a hotel that has an open culture, i.e., not too many hierarchical levels, managers are able to create a climate of trust and respect, and implement participative decision-making or empowerment. In such a hotel, there is considerable upward communication as employees provide the input for managerial decisions. However, in a hotel which has a highly authoritative environment, where downward flow dominates, upward communication still takes place but it is limited to the managerial ranks. Suggestion boxes, employee attitude surveys, grievance procedures, review reports, statistical analyses, etc., provide restricted information to the top management.

Lateral or Horizontal Communication

Lateral or horizontal communication takes place among peer groups or employees at similar hierarchy levels. It is often required to facilitate coordination, save time, and bridge the communication gap among various departments. Generally, lateral communication is informal so as to bypass the formal hierarchical channels and expedite action. From the organization's point of view, lateral communication can be both advantageous and disadvantageous. As compared to vertical (downward or upward) communication, which can, at times, impede and delay timely and accurate transfer of information, lateral communication can be beneficial. However, it can also create conflicts when formal vertical channels are bypassed by employees in order to accomplish their goals, or when superiors find out that they had not been consulted before certain decisions were taken. Lateral communication enables the sharing of information and acquaints the peer group with the activities of a department. The vice president (Revenue) sending some forecast data in the form of a memo to the vice president (Corporate Communications) for further action is an example of lateral communication. This type of communication is very vital for the growth of an organization as it builds cooperation among the various branches. In such organizations where work is decentralized, it plays a greater role because there is a higher probability of communication gaps.

Diagonal or Cross-wise Communication

Diagonal or cross-wise communication flows in all directions and cuts across functions and levels in an organization. For example, when a sales manager communicates directly with the vice president (Rooms Division), who is not only in a different division, but also at a higher level in the organization, they are engaged in diagonal communication. Though this form of communication deviates from the normal chain of command, there is no doubt that it is quick and efficient. In some situations, ignoring vertical and horizontal channels expedites action and prevents other employees from being used merely as conduits between senders and receivers.

The increased use of e-mail also encourages cross-wise communication. Any employee can communicate via e-mail with another employee, regardless of the receiver's function or status. Since there is no specific line of command, diagonal communication is also referred to as cross-wise, radial, or circular communication, depending upon the structure of the organization. For instance, a hotel's general manager could directly call a housekeeping supervisor and give instructions.

BARRIERS OF COMMUNICATION

There are many obstacles that obstruct the free flow of communication. These obstacles, which may filter a part of a message, or convey incorrect meaning, or prevent a message from being communicated entirely, are known as barriers of communication. The barriers of communication may be classified as: semantic, psychological, and personal. Figure 5.12 depicts the various types of barriers of communication.

Semantic Barriers

Semantics is the study of how meaning in language is created by the use and interrelationships of words, phrases, and sentences. All communication symbols like words, pictures, actions, etc. suggest certain meanings. In verbal communication, a particular word may have several meanings; moreover, a particular word may have contradictory meanings in different parts of the world. There are several words which have similar pronunciations but differ in meaning, like 'assess' and 'access', which may create confusion. During communication, the sender might use jargon or overly complicated terms and sentences, which would be incomprehensible to the receiver. To understand the concept, let's go through the following telephonic conversation between a guest and a reservation assistant in Exhibit 5.2.

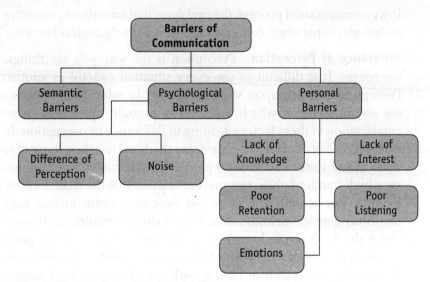

Fig. 5.12 Barriers of communication

Exhibit 5.2	Conversation between a guest and a reservation assistant
Reservation Assistant (RA) :	Good Morning! Reservations, Hotel ABC.
Guest	: Good Morning! I would like to book two good rooms for my family.
RA	: What would be your EDA and EDD?
Guest	: What is EDA/EDD?
RA	: EDA is the expected date of arrival and EDD is expected date of departure.
Guest	: We will arrive on 12th October and leave on 15th November.
RA	: For how many pax?
Guest	: What's that?
RA	: Number of persons.
Guest	: Five.
RA	: Which type of room do you prefer? We have executive rooms, deluxe rooms, and suites.
Guest	: Deluxe; what will be the room rent?
RA	: Rs 4500 ++ on EP
	Rs 5000 ++ on CP
	Rs 5500 ++ on MAP
	Rs 6500 ++ on AP

In the above conversation, the reservation assistant uses many industry terms like pax, EDA, EDD, deluxe room, executive room, ++, CP, AP, MAP, EP, which are not known to a person who is not from the hotel industry. Also, the person making the booking may think that a deluxe room will be of a higher standard than an executive room and vice-versa, which may not be correct. The communication problems created due to these reasons are known as semantic barriers.

Psychological Barriers

In a communication process, the problems that arise due to cognitive reasons (related to thought, experience, or senses) are called psychological barriers. These may be:

Difference of Perception   Perception is the way you see things, especially with the senses. It is difficult to see every situation exactly as another person sees it. Perception depends upon various factors like education, experience, culture, and the environment in which a person is brought up. Every person has a unique combination of these factors, leading to difference in perception. In Exhibit 5.2, the reservation assistant tells the guest that the hotel has three type of rooms–executive, deluxe, and suite. The general perception associated with the word 'deluxe' is of very high standard, thus, the guest may think that the deluxe room is more suitable for him, but actually the suite and executive room in that hotel may be more luxurious than the deluxe room. Unless the reservation assistant informs the guest about the facilities and services of each type of room, the guest may select the wrong type of room because of the nomenclature. This difference arises because the guest may have no or little knowledge about the hotel rooms and reservation assistant has not apprised him of the difference in the room categories. Thus the difference in perception prevents the smooth flow of communication.

Noise   Noise in the environment of communication is one of the major barriers in communication. It maybe the disturbance in a telephone line that prevents the receiver from hearing the sound properly. At the front desk, the noise level is higher at the time of arrival of groups or during peak check-in and check-out times, which makes it difficult for the front desk agent to have a proper verbal communication with the guest.

Personal Barriers

Personal factors that disrupt the flow of communication, like the attitude of the communicator, fear, lack of confidence, lack of awareness, inattentiveness, and poor retention, are known as personal barriers. Some of the personal barriers of communication are:

Lack of Knowledge   Lack of specialized knowledge about the basic and advanced principles of operations, technical terms, and house customs may pose a barrier while communicating with the different sections of a hotel. Such a situation arises when a new person, who has very little knowledge about the hospitality industry or the hotel, joins a hotel. For instance, Sumit has joined Hotel Surya in the information section. During the first week of his duty, a guest enquires about the depth of the hotel's swimming pool. As Sumit does not have that knowledge, he is not able to respond to the guest and this creates a barrier in their communication.

Lack of Interest   The lack of interest in the job may be one of the barriers of communication. The employee may lose interest in her job due to monotonous and long working hours, personal problems, work pressure, fatigue, physical illness, etc. A person who is not interested in her job, while interacting with guests, may mislead or even irritate them.

Poor Retention   The ability of retaining information differs from person to person. Some people have good retention power than others. Poor retention of facts may be a barrier in communication, especially in the case of verbal communication. For example, a front office agent with poor retention might annoy a guest by asking the same questions again and again.

Poor Listening   The front desk employees should be good listeners and should pay attention to the speaker. While processing a guest's reservation request, the reservation agent should listen carefully to the requirements of the guest. Poor listening skills of front desk employees, especially while handling guest complaints, may aggravate the problem.

Emotions   The encoding and decoding of a message is influenced by our emotions to a great deal. If we are not in a positive state of mind, we will communicate negative messages and interpret others' messages critically. For instance, an angry receptionist will not be able to welcome a guest cheerfully, which will harm the image of the hotel.

When you are communicating with someone and you do not receive the desired feedback, the following steps will help solve the problem:

- *Identify the problem:* When your communication fails to evoke the desired response, analyse the situation and identify the problem.

- *Find the cause:* Find the reason why your communication did not evoke the desired response.

- *Work out solutions:* Explore all possible solutions to the problem.

- *Opt for the best solution:* Apply the best solution that solves the problem and also that does not create any new problems and difficulties.

- *Follow up rigorously:* Implement the best solution relentlessly. Having once come across a particular communication barrier, make a conscious effort to never let it crop up again.

To enhance your communication skills, it is necessary to know the background of your audience and accordingly use that information to construct your message. For example, if you are aware that a guest is making a room booking for the first time, use jargon-free language and describe the rooms, rates, inclusions, etc. in a simple language and then analyse the guest's response. If she does not respond as desired, ask her if she wants the details to be explained again. Feedback is an effective way to know if the intended message has been understood by the receiver. Do not use words to impress; rather use them to express your ideas in a simple and clear manner.

INTERDEPARTMENTAL COMMUNICATION

The front office department plays a pivotal role in delivering quality services to guests. The front office communicates guests' requirements to other departments, which work in close coordination and cooperation to deliver required products and services. In order to maintain the desired level of service, the front office department communicates with the following departments of the hotel:

Housekeeping

The front office and housekeeping departments communicate with each other for the following information:

Room status As rooms generate maximum revenue for hotels, the information about the room status should be updated correctly and frequently. The front office and housekeeping departments must closely coordinate on the room status. The housekeeping department prepares an occupancy report, which is sent to the front office department, where it is tallied with room status records of front desk. This helps to:

- Update room status.
- Find sleepers (a room from which the guest has checked out but it is showing as occupied in front office room status records).
- Know as the exact house count.
- Charge the guest if an extra person has occupied the room.
- Coordinate in guest room change.

Security concerns The housekeeping personnel should inform the front office about any unusual circumstances that may indicate a violation of security for the hotel guests. For example, if a housekeeping personnel notices an act of violence, or a fire exit that has been propped open, or any other unusual event, he should inform the front desk immediately. The front desk personnel will in turn inform in-house or civil authorities to ensure the safety and security of guests.

Special arrangements Guests may request for additional or special amenities during their stay, like extra blanket, towel, soap, shampoo, iron, oil, etc. When such requests are received at the front desk, they should be immediately conveyed to the housekeeping department. For special guests, the front office may request the housekeeping department to put extra amenities in the guest room, like flower arrangement, bath robe etc. The front desk also informs the housekeeping department to make special arrangements for VIPs, groups, and crews.

Food and Beverage Department

The front office department informs the food and beverage (F&B) department about the arrival and departure of guests, which helps them to plan their work schedule and staff requirement. It also notifies the F&B department about special food arrangements and parties. The front desk sends the information about:

- the arrival and departure of guests.
- setting up bars in VIP rooms.
- special arrangements like cookies, fruit basket, and assorted dry fruits.
- in-house and expected VIPs, and corporate guests.
- in-house and expected groups.
- in-house and expected crews.
- the scanty baggage in-house guests; all points of sales are notified to receive all payment in cash from these guests.
- groups and guests with bookings of specific meal plans.

Sales and Marketing Department

The front office department coordinates with the sales and marketing department for the following information:

- Guest histories.
- Room reservation records.
- Current room availability status.
- Group, corporate, and crew bookings.
- Setting the transient and bulk room sales.

The front office staff must take every effort to keep the information on room availability status and guest histories current and accurate. The sales and marketing executives may have to check the availability of rooms three, six or even twelve months in future to devise marketing strategies for off season period. This information helps the sales and marketing department to sell hotel products by bundling two or more hospitality products, like rooms with meals; rooms, meals, and entertainment—all in one package. Thus a close cooperation and coordination between the front office and sales and marketing departments is important for hotel profitability.

Engineering and Maintenance

The front office communicates with the engineering and maintenance department for the proper upkeep of the equipments and systems installed in the hotel. The front office informs the maintenance department of any repair work required in guest rooms. In case the maintenance activity is required in a room which is occupied by a guest, the two departments work out a schedule so that the maintenance work is carried out in the absence of the guest. But if extensive work needs to be done, the guest may be requested to change rooms. The request from a guest to repair equipments and systems installed in her room may also be routed through the front desk. In case such a request is received at the front desk, it is communicated to the maintenance department, which in turn informs the front desk when it will carry out the repair so that the front desk can communicate the same to the guest.

Security

The front office is the link between guests and other departments of the hotel. When a guest has security concerns like fire, robbery, theft, and any other emergency, the front desk should explain the emergency procedure to the guest while calling on security personnel to resolve the problem.

Finance Controller

The front desk provides a daily summary of the financial transactions after night auditing to the finance controller. The information provided by the front desk helps the finance controller to make budgets and to allocate resources for the current financial period. The front desk provides the controller the financial data for billing and maintenance of credit card ledgers. High balance reports, etc. enable the controller to formulate policy guidelines and strategies to recover the money from guests and companies.

Human Resource

A close coordination and communication between the front desk and the human resource (HR) department help in the growth and development of front office employees. The front desk informs the HR department about its requirement of new staff, training requirement for the new staff, refresher training for the existing staff, and cross training requirements. On the basis of the guidelines provided by the front office department, the HR department develops the eligibility criteria for the initial screening of candidates. The guidelines for recruitment may include concerns about personal hygiene, completion of applications, education requirement, citizenship status, and experience. The HR department works in close coordination with the front office department to procure quality personnel for the front desk and to impart training to the employees to keep them up-to-date with the latest happenings in the hotel industry.

Banquets

The front office department coordinates with banquets for putting information on bulletin boards and placing directional signals for particular function areas. Non-resident guests, who come to the hotel to attend functions and are unfamiliar with the hotel layout, may ask for directions at the front desk. The banquet department sends function prospectus to the front desk, so that if any communication from the parties hosting the functions reaches the front desk, the same may be transferred or replied promptly. The preparation of marquee with messages of congratulations, welcome, sales promotion, or any other important message is handled by the front desk employees. If such an activity is required by the host of the party, it should be informed to the front desk through the banquet manager, so that the same can be handled efficiently.

Thus, besides communicating with guests and other external customers, the front office department also communicates with internal customers like housekeeping, food and beverage department, security, engineering and maintenance, accounts, banquets, sales and marketing, purchase, and control department for the efficient and smooth functioning of the hotel operations.

SUMMARY

Internal and external communication is very important for smooth hotel operations. The front office department is a vital link in both external and internal communication. In this chapter, we have understood the meaning of communication, the communication process between a sender and receiver, the importance of communication, and the types of communication. We have also seen the flow of communication in organizations and the barriers in communication.

Coordination among the various departments of a hotel is very important to provide flawless services and facilities to guests. As we have learnt, communication is the way information is gathered and transferred where it is needed. Thus, communication is important for effective coordination.

KEY TERMS

Chain of command Order in which authority and power in an organization is wielded and delegated from top management to every employee at every level of the organization. Instructions flow downward along the chain of command and accountability flows upward.

Channel The medium through which the encoded message passes from the sender to the receiver.

Communication The exchange of information between people, e.g., by means of speaking, writing, or using a common system of signs or behaviour.

Decoding Decoding is the converting the encoded symbols into abstract ideas. It is the reverse of encoding. By doing so, the target receives the original message.

Encoding The subject matter of communication is non-figurative and intangible; its transmission requires use of symbols like words, gestures, photo etc. The process of converting the abstract ideas into communication symbols is called encoding.

Grapevine The path of communication along which news, gossip, or rumour passes unofficially from person to person within a group, organization, or community.

Message The subject matter of the communication that is passed from the sender to the target audience. It may be a views, ideas, feelings, orders, recommendations, facts, data, request, etc.

Noise Anything that interferes with, slows down, or reduces the clarity or accuracy of a communication. The superfluous data or words in a message are noise because they detract from its meaning.

Personal barrier Personal factors, like the attitude of the communicator, fear, lack of confidence, lack of awareness, inattentiveness, and poor retention, that disrupt the flow of communication.

Psychological barrier The problems that arise in communication due to cognitive reasons (related to thought, experience, or senses).

Semantics The study of how meaning in language is created by the use and interrelationships of words, phrases, and sentences.

Source The person who wishes to share the information, facts, or feelings with another person or a group of people.

Target The person to whom the message is sent by the sender.

REVIEW QUESTIONS

Multiple Choice Questions

1. Front office department communicates with:
   a) F&B Service   b) Housekeeping
   c) Banquets   d) All of the above

2. Front office and housekeeping departments communicate with each other for the following information:
   a) Room statistics   b) Security concerns
   c) Special arrangements d) All of the above

3. The written form of communication includes:
   a) Letter   b) Fax
   c) E-mail   d) All of the above

4. Verbal form of communication includes:
   a) Telegram   b) Telex
   c) Telephonic conversation
   d) All of the above

5. Effective communication should be:
   a) Clear   b) Ambiguous
   c) Contradictory   d) All of the above

True/False

1. Communication plays a vital role in the efficient functioning of hotels.

2. Coordination between the different departments of the hotel can be maintained even without a proper system of communication.

3. Correct interpretation and understanding of a message is necessary for effective communication.

4. The source of a message is the individual, or group, or organization that wishes to share the information, facts, or feelings with another person or group of people, and initiates the communication.

5. Message is the subject matter of the communication.

Fill in the Blanks

1. The medium through which the encoded message passes between the sender and the receiver is known as _____.

2. _____ is the individual/group/organization to whom the message is sent by the sender/source.

3. _____ is the subject matter of the communication that is passed from a sender to the target audience.

4. _____ is converting the encoded symbols into abstract ideas.

5. Effective _____is essential for planning activity of managers.

Discussion Questions

1. Define communication and explain the communication process with examples.

2. Communication is essential for interdepartmental coordination. Discuss with examples.

3. Discuss the importance of communication for a hotel.

4. List the departments of the hotel with which the front office communicates.

5. 'Communication between front desk and sales and marketing is essential for total hospitality sales.' Comment.

CRITICAL THINKING QUESTIONS

1. Inter-departmental communication is the back-bone for efficient hotel operations. Discuss.

2. The proper functioning of front office depends upon its effective communication with house-keeping and food and beverage departments. Explain with suitable examples.

PROJECT WORK

Visit a hotel and find out the different types of equipments that are used for communication. Make a list of the same and compare them on the basis of the following:

1. Speed of communication.
2. Accuracy in effective communication.
3. Technical difficulties in using the equipment.
4. Do these equipment require some specialized skills in operation

CASE STUDIES

1. Hotel Plaza has 400 rooms and a convention centre. The maintenance head, Arjun, found that the rooms of the sixth and seventh floors needed repainting. He took the consent from the reservation manager, Suraj, for blocking 100 rooms covering east and west wing, with 50 rooms in each wing, for five days. The reservation manager consented because out of the 200 rooms reserved for the pollution control convention, only 150 were confirmed and there were no major check-ins. So rooms on the sixth and seventh floors were blocked for five days as out-of-order rooms. At 10.00 a.m., Arjun puts 25 people on the job, who start painting the rooms in the east wings.

At 12:30 p.m., the reservation manager calls Arjun and inquires if the painting activity in the 50 rooms may be postponed as occupants for all the 200 rooms in the pollution control convention have arrived. The lobby is flooded with guests waiting for rooms. Arjun informs Suraj that the painting work has not been started in the west wing rooms and asks for an hour's time to clear the area of the painting preparatory articles.

Suraj contacts the banquet manager, Sheela, to provide the lobby level banquet hall and to make tea and snack arrangements for the guests. Sheela checks and finds that the lobby level hall is vacant for the day and informs Suraj that the hall can be utilized. She also agrees to arrange for the tea and snacks after taking the consent of the pantry chef.

In the above case, discuss the following and find remedial measures for the same:

a) What went wrong?
b) How would you avoid such situations?
c) Is it advisable to block 100 rooms for maintenance, be it peak or off season?
d) How important is communication among departments in such cases?
e) What is the level of cooperation among the departments of Hotel Plaza?
f) What would be the reaction of guests who arrive at the hotel after a long, tiring journey and find that their rooms are not ready and it would take about an hour's time?

2. Mr Kevin Lane is the CEO of a multinational company who visits Mumbai twice a month for a week and always stays in Hotel Sea View in the

deluxe suite 405, which overlooks the Arabian Sea. He is a very important guest for the hotel and the hotel staff is always on its toes to keep him satisfied. His secretary calls up at 11 p.m. to amend the flight details for the next day's pick up in a Mercedes Benz. Mr Lane's flight was supposed to reach at 8 a.m. but due to change in his plans, he is now arriving by an earlier flight at 5 a.m. The front desk agent takes the arrival information and passes it on only to the concierge who is entangled in peak time check-ins and answering guest queries. By the time he sorts these out, he is exhausted and confirms Mr Lane's Merc pick up for the next day at 8 a.m. instead of 5 a.m.

Mr Lane arrives in the hotel at 7 a.m. in a taxi and his preferred suite is not ready (housekeeping was not aware of his early arrival). He is absolutely furious and icily gives the duty manager a piece of his mind.

In the above case, discuss the following:
a) How can the duty manager calm Mr Lane down?
b) Whose fault is it? Should the front office agent have passed on this information to housekeeping as well as to the night shift so that they could have followed up for the necessary arrangements?
c) Will Mr Lane continue to stay at Hotel Sea View henceforth? Why or why not?

REFERENCE

Newstrom, John W. and Keith Davis (1997), *Organizational Behaviour: Human Behaviour at Work*, New York: McGraw-Hill, p.48

Raman, Meenakshi and Prakash Singh (2006), *Business Communication*, Oxford University Press, New Delhi

Raman, Meenakshi and Sangeeta Sharma (2008), *Technical Communication: English Skills for Engineers*, Oxford University Press, New Delhi

CHAPTER 6

Room Tariff

Learning Objectives:

After reading this chapter, you will be able to understand:
- Bases for establishing room tariff—cost, competition, level of service, location, target market.
- Room rate designation, including standard rates and special discounted rates.
- Various meal plans offered by hotels—European Plan, Continental Plan, American Plan, Modified American Plan, Bed and Breakfast Plan.
- Room tariff card, including prices of rooms, meal plans, taxes, applicable policies, etc.
- Room tariff methodology—cost-based pricing and market-based pricing.

Room rate, which is the daily rate charged for the usage of a hotel room and services, is among a traveller's basic criteria for choosing a particular hotel for stay. The basis for charging room rate differs from hotel to hotel. Hotels display their room rent on tariff cards, which provide information about the room rate for different types of rooms available in the hotel.

Price is one of the major elements involved in the marketing and positioning of a product or service. The price of goods and services of a hotel should cover the cost of production, overheads, and a fair amount of profit, so that the hotel business remains sustainable and profitable. The price band of a hotel attracts a particular segment of clients, and thus decides the positioning of a hotel and ~~in~~ the market. In this chapter, we will learn about room rates, differe~~nt~~ designations, and how hotels arrive at a decision for charging a certain room tariff.

ROOM TARIFF

The room tariff of a hotel must generate optimum revenue for the hotel and give the hotel proprietors a return on their investment. The rate of a hotel room is decided by several factors, which are illustrated in Fig. 6.1.

Cost The total expenditure that is incurred in providing services and products to the ultimate consumer of the hotel services is the cost. The total cost can be divided into fixed cost, material cost, and labour cost. The higher the investment that has been made in a hotel property, the higher would be the room rent.

Level of Services The level of services offered by a hotel determines the room rent to a large extent. A hotel offering the best of services like spa, gymnasium, banquet halls, speciality restaurants, etc. will charge a higher room rent in comparison to other hotels offering limited services. As the star classification of hotels is based on the level of services, the hotels that are classified as five star or above have better services and higher room rents as compared to those classified as four star or below. The guest and staff ratio would be higher in five-star hotels as they provide more personalized guest services.

Competition Competition between similar hotels (i.e., hotels with similar standards and providing similar services and facilities in similar locations of the city) in the market also plays an important role in determining the rack rate of the hotel. The higher the competition, the lower will be the room rent. Similar hotels should have competitive rates.

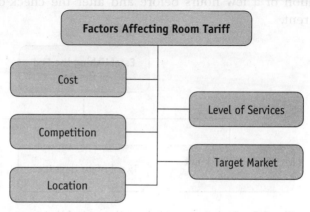

Fig. 6.1 Factors affecting room tariff

Target Market The target market also governs the rack rate of a hotel room. Hotels, while selecting their room rates, find out the disposable income of their target segment. Thus a budget or limited-service hotel quotes lower prices to attract guests with less disposable income and an upmarket hotel quotes higher prices for its products.

Location The location of the hotel also plays an important role in determining the room tariff. Hotels in a city centre or business centre (like Nariman Point, Mumbai), near places of tourist interest (like Taj Mahal, Agra), or on scenic locales (like beaches of Goa) would have a higher tariff. The location of the room also determines the room rate. Rooms with a better view (sea view/mountain view/ pool view) would have higher charges as compared to rooms facing a parking lot or a noisy commercial street.

We have seen that the room rate of a hotel is based on the competition, the standard of services and amenities offered by the hotel, the guests' profile, and the location of the hotel and the room. Once the room tariff has been decided, every hotel has to decide about the criteria for establishing the 'end of the day' to post the room charges into guest accounts (Fig. 6.2). The end of the day is an arbitrary time that is supposed to be the end of the financial transactions for a particular day. As hotels remain functional round the clock, it is very important to ascertain the time which will be treated as the end of the day and the beginning of a new day.

Fixed Check-in/Check-out Time Most of the hotels follow the fixed check-in/ check-out system for establishing the end of the day. In this system, a particular time is fixed to mark the end of the day. Generally, it is 12 noon. This means that a day begins in the hotel at 12 noon every day, regardless of the actual check-in time of the guest. The major advantage of this system of charging the room rent is that the same room can be sold more than once in a day. This system is normally adopted by commercial hotels. Most of the hotels following this system may allow relaxation of a few hours before and after the check-out time in charging the room rent.

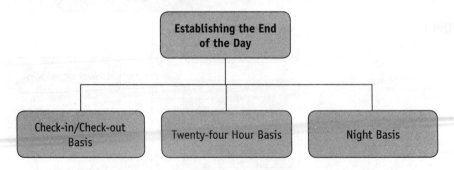

Fig. 6.2 Basis for establishing the end of the day

For example, Rajesh checks into a hotel at 12 noon on 15 July and meets a client at 4 p.m. He has to catch an international flight at 3.00 a.m. on 16 July. He finishes his dinner and checks out of the hotel at 11 p.m. (15 July) to catch the flight. Rajesh pays the room rent for one night (15 July).

Rita arrives into the hotel at 5.00 a.m. (16 July), and after a day's rest, she has to catch a train at 11 p.m. (16 July). She checks out of the hotel at 10 p.m. (16 July). Rita has to pay two nights' room charges, i.e., 15 July (12 p.m.) to 16 July (12 p.m.) and 16 July (12 p.m.) to 17 July (12 p.m.).

The hotel has given Rajesh and Rita the same room and has charged both of them for the night of 15 July as their stays overlapped. Thus, it has generated optimum revenue.

Twenty-four Hour Basis System In this system of charging the room rent, there is no fixed check-in/check-out time. A room is assigned to a guest for twenty-four hours from the time of her arrival. This system is generally followed in transit hotels and hotels that are located in the vicinity of railway stations, where guests normally stay for few hours. In this system, the hotel does not allow relaxation of time after the completion of twenty-four hours of stay.

In the above example, according to this system of charging room rent, Rajesh would be charged for the room from 12 noon of 15 July and Rita would be charged for the room from 5 a.m. of 16 July to 5 a.m. of 17 July. So the hotel would charge both Rajesh and Rita one night's room rent. This system is good for small hotels only.

Number of Nights This system of charging the room rent is a modification of the twenty-four hour system. Here, the room rent is charged on the basis of the number of nights spent in the hotel room. If a guest does not stay at night, a half day rent is charged from him. This system is now outdated and not so popular.

In such a hotel, both Rajesh and Rita would have paid only half a day's rent. Thus, the hotel would have earned a total of only a day's room rent from both of them.

ROOM RATE DESIGNATION

A hotel generally designates a standard rate for each category of rooms offered to guests. Apart from the standard rates, hotels also offer discounted rates to attract additional business from multiple market segments. Hotels may have various room rate designations as illustrated in Fig. 6.3.

Rack Rate Hotels generally designate a standard rate for each of the category of rooms offered for accommodation to guests. The standard rate of a particular type of room before any discount is called rack rate. Traditionally, a rate board

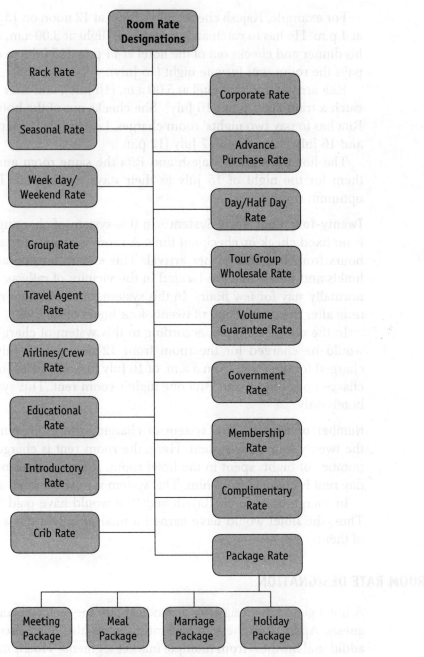

Fig. 6.3 Room rate designations

was placed near the room rack, hence the name rack rate. The tariff card of a hotel should mention the taxes applicable on room rents. For example, the rack rate for a standard room may be Rs 5,000 ++ ('++' means exclusive of taxes or taxes extra).

Corporate Rate   This is a promotional rate to attract the corporate market segment. The corporate rate is generally 10 to 20 per cent lower than the rack rate. For example, the corporate rate for a standard room may be Rs 4,000 ++.

Seasonal Rate   Depending on the desirability of a location at a particular time of the year, destinations may have high, low, and shoulder seasons. Destinations like hill stations, beaches, etc. receive heavy tourist traffic during particular period(s) of the year; the rest of the year is a lean period in terms of tourism. The duration when the tourist traffic (and so the demand for hotel rooms) at a particular place is high is known as the peak season; when the demand for hotel rooms drops down, it is known as the off-season. During peak season, hotels do not offer any discount; rather they may charge a higher room rate, known as the seasonal rate. To attract guests during low-demand periods, hotels offer a discounted rate known as the off-season rate. Hotels in these locations mention their seasonal and off-season rate clearly on the tariff card. For example, rainy season is off season in Shimla, while winters and summers are season time, as visitors go there to see snow in winters and to escape the heat during summers.

Advance Purchase Rate   Though popular in the airlines industry, the advance purchase rate is a relatively new concept in the hospitality industry. It entails heavy discounts on room rates when room bookings are done in advance. The rate of discount depends upon the advance period and the number of rooms available at the time of booking, i.e., a hotel may offer more discount for a room that is booked two months in advance as compared to a room that is booked fifteen days in advance. The advance booking of rooms ensures a certain amount of revenue at a given time and thus helps the management in planning a revenue management strategy.

Week Day/Weekend Rate   Some hotels observe a fluctuation in their occupancy levels with regard to the days of the week. The demand for rooms in a hotel maybe more on certain days in a week. Hotels analyse their demand levels over a period of time and fix a higher rate during high demand periods and a lower room rate during low demand periods. In vacation/resort hotels, the weekend rate would be higher than week day rate as the demand for rooms is higher on weekends. It would be reverse in the case of a commercial hotel.

Day and Half Day Rate   The day rate, charged from guests not staying overnight at a hotel, is lower than the rack rate. For instance, if a guest checks in at 10 a.m. and checks out the same evening at around 5 p.m., he may be charged the day rate. However, all hotels may not have day rates.

Sometimes a guest may wish to stay for a very short duration of time, not exceeding five hours. For example, a transit traveller, who has to catch a flight in few hours, might want to take rest in a hotel, or a person might want to rent a room for a short business meeting. In these cases, the half day rate, which is a bit higher than the numerical half of the rack rate, is charged from guests.

Group Rate   As a large group (more than 15 persons) provides bulk business to a hotel, hotels offer discounted rates to groups. The group rate depends upon the number of persons in the group and the frequency of their visits. The rates are negotiated by the sales team of the hotel and the representatives of the group.

Tour Group (Series Group) Wholesale Rate   These are heavily discounted rates for wholesalers who operate a series of tours for groups arriving and departing together. For example, a tour operator may conduct a week's tour of the Golden Triangle (Delhi–Agra–Jaipur–Delhi) on the 2nd, 12th, and 22nd of every month for groups of twenty persons. The tour operator guarantees the hotel that it would provide this series of business every month for a period of one year. In return, the hotel offers a heavy discount to the operator and allocates or 'blocks' rooms for the series for the entire year.

Travel Agent Rate   Travel agents sell travel products like hotel rooms, airlines bookings, etc. on a commission basis to the end users (guests). They provide a substantial volume of business to hotels, hence hotels offer them special discounts and commissions. Some major travel agencies include Cox & Kings, Thomas Cook, etc.

Volume Guarantee Rate   Hotels may offer a special rate (lower than the rack rate) in order to attract high volume of business from special market segments. A hotel may have a contractual agreement with a company, according to which the company's representatives are entitled to a special discounted rate when they reserve a room in the hotel. The percentage of discount will depend upon the volume of business promised and the mutual understanding between the hotel and company at the time of making the agreement. A frequent business customer might be offered a CP (Continental Plan) at the standard room rate.

Airlines/Crew Rate   It is a special discounted rate for the crew of one or more airlines that offer certain volume of business throughout the year on a consistent and continuous basis.

Government Rate   When government officials travel for official work, they are given a travel allowance to cover their hotel, meals, and other out-of-pocket expenses. Based on their designation, this amount is fixed and given in advance. A hotel interested in catering to this segment may quote room rates that match their travel allowances. The hotel may ask for proof of identity from guests before they can avail the government rates.

Educational Rate   Educational rates are special rates offered by hotels to students and educationists who have a limited travel budget. They are a significant source of business because of their large numbers and frequency of visits. They provide a large chunk of repeat business to hotels.

Membership Rate   Membership rates are offered to guests who are members of influential organizations that provide volumes of business to hotels. The membership rates are much lower than the rack rates and may also include discounts on food and beverage. Special discounted rates are given to FHRAI members, UN employees, travel writers, etc.

Introductory Rate   The introductory rate is offered by a hotel on the opening of a new property in town. It is a part of a new hotel's marketing strategy to make inroads into the existing market by offering a price lower than what is offered by competitors with the same standards. The introductory rate is generally offered till the hotel is established, or it may be revoked at the wish of the management.

Complimentary Rate   When a hotel does not charge the room rent from a guest, it is known as complimentary rate. Hotels generally offer complimentary rooms (also called comp rooms) to the tour/group leader. They may also offer comp rooms to tour operators, travel agencies, and local dignitaries who are vital to the public relations programme of the hotel. Hotels also provide complimentary rooms along with marriage packages and bulk bookings.

Crib Rate   This is the rate charged for children above five years and below of age 12 years who are accompanying their parents. The hotel provides a crib bed in the room for infants.

Package Rate   A package rate is quoted for a bouquet of products or services. The rate is generally lower that the sum total of the prices of individual products or services offered in the bouquet. These rates are tailor-made for specific guest requirements. A package rate may include room rent, meals, special arrangements (like marriage set-ups, banquet halls, meeting room, etc.), and may also include products and services offered by other services providers like transportation (rail, road, and air), sightseeing, and so on.

A package rate is more economical than the individual purchase of each of the products and services. It is a marketing strategy to sell the slow moving items along with the hot-selling products. Also, when products and services are sold in a bunch, the cost of individual advertisements is cut down. The money thus saved by the hotels is passed to the guest in the form of lower prices.

Hotels may offer the following packages:

Meeting package A complete meeting package includes the residential arrangement of the delegates, meeting room, food and beverage requirements (meals, tea/coffee, snacks), along with transportation facility, audio visual equipment like projectors, etc. to the meeting delegates.

Meal package A meal package is the combination of room rent and meals, which may be all meals or a combination of breakfast and lunch/dinner. The hotel may offer meal packages based on the requirement of guests and the suitability of the hotel's operations. The various meal plans offered by hotels are discussed at length in the subsequent section.

Marriage package A marriage package includes all the necessary arrangements for marriage, like *mandap*, priest, party hall/lawn, accommodation for the marriage party, arrangement of reception buffet, and even a complimentary room/suite for the newly-wedded couple.

Holiday package A holiday package may include transportation, accommodation, meals, guide, and sightseeing at the destination. Generally, this package includes non-hotel products from other service providers like airlines. Refer to Exhibit 6.1 for details of 'India in Luxury' offer from Oberoi Hotels and Resorts.

Exhibit 6.1   'India in Luxury' offer from Oberoi Hotels and Resorts

Welcome to India, a land of fantasy, mystique and colour.
Embark on a journey to explore 'India in Luxury'. One that takes you through the colourful state of Rajasthan, replete with palaces, forts and temples and the famous tiger reserve of Ranthambhore. And then to Agra to experience the timeless magic of the Taj Mahal. Thereafter to the majestic Himalayas. Choose from itineraries carefully crafted to ensure that your passage through India is luxurious, memorable and at a leisurely pace. Our experienced team will take care of every small detail from managing your travel within India to sightseeing to spa experiences and shopping. To ensure that you carry back memories to last a lifetime.

Offer includes
- Accommodation in the hotel or resort as specified in the itinerary selected
- Business class domestic airfare wherever available: (Delhi/Udaipur, Udaipur/Jaipur, Jaipur/Delhi)
- Economy class airfare from New Delhi to Shimla, Delhi to Jaipur, Jaipur to Agra and Delhi – Agra - Delhi
- All meals at the resort and outside as specified in the itinerary (excluding alcoholic beverages)
- All road transfers between cities, airports and hotels
- Spa treatments as specified in the itinerary.
- All road transfers within and between cities based on the itinerary using air-conditioned cars
- Entrance charges to places of interest and monuments
- Guide charges
- All currently applicable taxes as on 1st May 2008. (Any additional taxes imposed by the government would be extra)

Offer validity
From 1st October 2008 to 30th April 2009

Source: http://www.oberoihotels.com/Special Offers/Oberoi SOFF India In Luxury.aspx, last assured on 24 February 2009.

MEAL PLANS

The room tariff of a hotel may be based on the choice meal plans offered to guests. Depending on the needs of their target audience, hotels offer a variety of meal plans (Fig. 6.4). Table 6.1 explains each plan in a nutshell.

European Plan   European plan (EP) consists of room rate only and the meals are charged separately as per actuals. It is generally preferred in a commercial hotel where business executives have to socialize with their clients and do not take meals at the hotel.

Continental Plan   Continental plan (CP) consists of room rate and continental breakfast. Continental breakfast generally includes most or all of the following: sliced bread with butter/jam/honey, cheese, meat, croissants and Danish pastries, rolls, fruit juice and coffee/tea/hot chocolate/milk. This plan is generally found in hotels in Europe.

American Plan   American plan (AP) is also known as en-pension (full board). The tariff includes room rent and all meals (i.e., breakfast, lunch, and dinner). This tariff plan is popular in resort hotels located at remote places where guests do not have a choice of food outside the hotel premises, e.g., in a jungle or desert.

Modified American Plan   Modified American plan (MAP) is also known demi-pension (half board). The tariff consists of room rent, breakfast, and one major meal (either lunch or dinner). This tariff plan is popular in hotels located at tourist destinations, where the guest may want to go for sightseeing after breakfast, have lunch outside the hotel, and return to the hotel in the evening and have dinner. Alternately, they could have breakfast and pack lunch from the hotel, and then have dinner outside and come to the hotel late at night.

Bed & Breakfast (B&B) or Bermuda Plan   Bed and breakfast plan (B&B) or Bermuda plan consists of room rent and American breakfast. American breakfast generally includes most or all of the following: two eggs (fried or poached), sliced bacon or sausages, sliced bread or toast with jam/jelly/butter, pan cakes with syrup, cornflakes or other cereal, coffee/tea, orange/grapefruit juice.

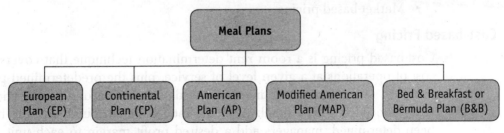

Fig. 6.4   Different meal plans

Table 6.1   Meal Plans

Plan	Plan includes				
	Room Rent	Morning Tea	Breakfast	Lunch	Dinner
European Plan (EP)	✓	✗	✗	✗	✗
Continental Plan (CP)	✓	✓	✓ Continental Breakfast	✗	✗
American Plan (AP)	✓	✓	✓	✓	✓
Modified American Plan (MAP)	✓	✓	✓	✓ Either Lunch or Dinner (One Major Meal)	
Bed & Breakfast (B&B) or Bermuda Plan	✓	✓	✓ American Breakfast	✗	✗

Note: ✓ means included in plan   ✗ means not included in plan

ROOM TARIFF CARD

Room tariff cards are published lists of the different tariffs offered by hotels for the use of the travel trade (travel agencies, tour operators), companies, and individual guests called FITs (free individual travellers). The document includes prices of rooms, meal plans, taxes, applicable policies, etc. Tariff cards of Ananda—In the Himalayas (Exhibit 6.2) and ITC Maurya, New Delhi (Exhibit 6.3) are given here.

ROOM TARIFF FIXATION

Fixing of room tariff is a difficult task for the management. If the management fixes a low room rent, the hotel operations might not be economical. However, if the rate is too high, guests may not patronize the property. Hence, an accurate and competitive room rent is one of the prerequisites for running a successful hospitality business. A hotel fixes the room tariff on the following two bases (Fig. 6.6):
- Cost-based pricing
- Market-based pricing

Cost-based Pricing

Cost-based pricing is a room rent determination technique that covers the basic cost of operations at a given level of service, plus the predetermined percentage of return on investment. It involves the determination of all fixed and variable costs associated with a hotel. After the total costs attributable to the hotel have been determined, managers add a desired profit margin to each unit, such as a

Exhibit 6.2   Tariffs and policies of The Ananda Spa

Rates & Packages (In Indian rupees)

Room Type	Occupancy	(INR)
Deluxe Palace View Room	Single/Double	14,500/15,500
Deluxe Valley View Room	Single/Double	15,500/16,500
Deluxe Suite	Single/Double	25,000/25,000
The Ananda Suite	Single/Double	32,000/32,000
Vice-regal Suite	Single/Double	36,000/36,000
One Bedroom Villa with Pool	Single/Double	55,000/55,000
Two Bedroom Villa with Pool	Single/Double	75,000/75,000

Please add 5% Government tax to this tariff. The taxes are subject to change.

The above-mentioned rates are inclusive of:
• Morning wake up signature tea
• Scheduled yoga or meditation classes
• Scheduled hiking trips in the Himalayan foothills
• Use of wet spa areas like sauna, steam bath, jacuzzi
• Complimentary use of the gymnasium
• Complimentary use of the swimming pool

Additional Suite & Villa Tariff Inclusions
• Ananda Breakfast for two—served in the room or restaurant.
• Choice of two Aromatic Baths in the suite.
• Complimentary two-way transfers from the Haridwar Railway Station or Dehradun Airport

Package valid from 1 December 2008 to 30 September 2009

Source: http://www.anandaspa.com/rates/rates9.asp, last accessed on 17April 2009.

5 or 10 per cent mark-up. The goal of the cost-oriented approach is to cover all costs incurred in producing or delivering the products or services and to achieve a targeted level of profit.

The traditional pricing policy can be summarized by the formula:

Cost + Fixed profit percentage = Selling price

By itself, this method is simple, requiring only the study of the hotel's financial and accounting records to determine prices. It does not involve examining the market or considering the competition and other factors that might have an impact on pricing. Cost-oriented pricing is also popular as it uses internal information that managers can obtain easily. In addition, hotels can justify their prices based on costs by demonstrating that their prices cover the costs plus a mark-up for profit.

Exhibit 6.3   Room Tariff of ITC Maurya, New Delhi

Room Type	INR	
	Single	Double
ITC One*	Rs 20,000	Rs 21,500
The Towers*	Rs 15,000	Rs 16,500
Executive Club	Rs 12,000	Rs 13,500
Executive Dynasty*	Rs 16,500	
Deluxe Suite*	Rs 30,000	
Luxury Suite*	Rs 65,000	
Presidential Suite*	Rs 1,75,000	

Note:
1. Rates mentioned above are all inclusive of taxes.
2. Above rates are valid until further advise.
3. Rates are subject to change without notice.

*Inclusive of Buffet Breakfast.
Rates effective 1st April 2009

Source: http://www.itcwelcomgroup.in/Hotels/itcmaurya.aspx?PT, last accessed on 17 April 2009.

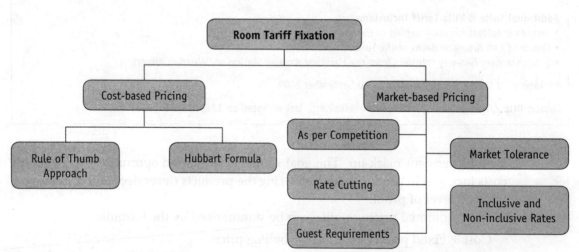

Fig. 6.5   Bases of tariff fixation

The following are the two widely used cost-based pricing techniques:
- Rule of Thumb Approach
- Hubbart Formula

Rule of Thumb Approach   Rule of thumb is the oldest method of determining the room rent of any hotel. According to this approach, the room rent should be fixed at the rate of Re 1 for each Rs 1,000 spent on the construction and furnishing of the room, assuming that the average occupancy is 70% for the year. If the hotel incurs a total expenditure of Rs 15,00,000 on a room, the room rent will be Rs 15,000 according to the rule of thumb approach.

This is a traditional approach considering only the cost that is incurred at the time of starting the operation. If we try to establish the room rent of a hotel after 10 years of its operation, the rate would be the same, though the cost of operation of the property would have increased manifold. There are several other drawbacks associated with the rule of thumb approach; some of them are as under:

- It only considers the cost incurred in constructing the room. It does not consider factors like inflation, competition, fixed expenses, etc.
- It considers the average occupancy to be 70 per cent, which might not be achieved by many hotels due to several reasons. Therefore, hotels expecting lower occupancy should set a higher rate to attain the same revenue.
- The return on investment (ROI) is not considered. If the money invested in constructing and furnishing the hotel room had been invested in the market for the duration of one year, it would have generated income for the investor.
- It does not consider the depreciation of fixed assets or the elevation of land costs.
- Establishing a hotel requires a large sum which is generated through borrowing from family, friends, financial institutions, and public through the sale of shares and debentures. The owner of the hotel has to pay the debt and interest on the sum received irrespective of the volume of the business generated by the hotel. This factor is not considered in this approach.
- The hotel business may incur some unexpected and unavoidable expenses, the provision for which is not made in this approach.
- The rule of thumb approach also fails to consider the contribution of other facilities and services (food and beverage service, laundry, health and fitness services, recreational services) to the profitability of the hotel while setting the price of a room.

Hubbart Formula The rule of thumb approach is an old traditional way of determining the room rent of a hotel. As seen, it is unscientific and suffers from many drawbacks. The Hubbart formula, which is a scientific way of determining the room rent, was developed by Roy Hubbart in America in the 1940s. It resolves all the problems of the rule of thumb approach. The following steps are involved in calculating the room rent according to the Hubbart formula:

1. Calculate the total investment including the owner's capital and loans, both secured and unsecured. Once the total investment has been calculated, calculate the fair rate of return on investment (ROI). ROI is the amount that would have been generated if the money invested in the hotel business had been invested in the open market.

2. Calculate the total expenses—like operating expenses, overheads, depreciation of fixed assets, interest paid, heating and lighting, etc.—that will be incurred during hotel operations.

3. Combine steps 1 and 2 to find out the gross operating income that is necessary to cover the operating cost, investment, and return on investment.

4. Calculate the income generated from other sources of income, like food and beverage sales, laundry, rent and lease of the hotel area, fitness centre, etc. Subtract the same from the amount calculated in step 3 to find out how much profit is expected from the room sales. This will be the total revenue generation by the room sales.

5. Calculate the total number of the guest rooms available for sale by multiplying the total number of rooms with the number of days in the year. Make the provision for expected average vacancy that is expected during the year. This step will provide the total number of rooms available for sale.

6. Divide the revenue generation (result from step 4) by the total number of rooms (result from step 5); the result obtained will be the average daily rate, which will cover the cost of operations and fair return on investment.

Now let's calculate the room rent for a hotel with the following details:

1. Hotel Aanchal has 300 rooms with an average occupancy of 75 per cent.
2. The owners' capital is Rs 15,00,00,000 and the total loan raised is Rs 10,00,00,000. Thus, the total investment is Rs 25,00,00,000.
3. Let the fair market return be 12 per cent.
4. The expenses are as under:

a. Operating expenses (in rupees)

Rooms division	45,00,000.00
Telephone expenses	75,000.00
Administrative expenses	25,00,000.00
Payroll and other expenses	35,00,000.00
Advertisement and promotion	15,00,000.00
Power and fuel	1,85,000.00
Repair and maintenance	70,000.00
Total operating expenses	**1,23,30,000.00**

b. Taxes and insurance

Real estate and property tax	45,000.00
Management fee	75,000.00
Corporate taxes	12,50,000.00
Insurance of building and other assets	8,00,000.00
Total taxes and insurance paid	**21,70,000.00**

c. Interest paid on loans

To financial institutions	1,45,000.00
To others	75,000.00
Total interest paid	**2,20,000.00**

d. Depreciation at book value

Building	1,85,000.00
Furniture, fixtures, and equipments	95,000.00
Total depreciation	**2,80,000.00**

5. Income generated from other sources is:

From food and beverage outlets	2,45,000.00
From lease of premises	75,000.00
Income from ancillary services (laundry, confectionary shop, beauty saloon, florist etc.) operated by hotel	65,000.00
Total income generated from other sources	**3,85,000.00**

6. The total area of the hotel that is covered by guest rooms is 85,000 sq. ft.
7. The area of a single room is 250 sq. ft and the area of a double room is 300 sq. ft. There are 100 single and 200 double rooms in the hotel.

Now calculate the room rent for the hotel, according to the Hubbart formula.

Step 1
Calculation of total investment

$$\text{Total investment} = \text{Owner's capital} + \text{Loans}$$
$$= \text{Rs } 15,00,00,000.00 + \text{Rs } 10,00,00,000.00$$
$$= \text{Rs } 25,00,00,000.00$$

Calculation of return on investment

The return on investment is the percentage of return that would have been generated had the amount been invested in the open market. In this case it is 12 per cent. Thus, fair return on investment will be:

$$\text{Return on Investment} = \text{Total investment} \times \text{Return percentage}$$
$$= \text{Rs } 25,00,00,000.00 \times 12/100$$
$$= \text{Rs } 3,00,00,000$$

Step 2

Calculation of total expenses

$$
\begin{aligned}
\text{Total expenses} \quad &= \quad \text{Operating expenses} + \text{Taxes and insurance} + \text{Interest paid} \\
&\quad\quad \text{on loans} + \text{Deprecation on book value} \\
&= \quad \text{Rs } 1{,}23{,}30{,}000.00 + \text{Rs } 21{,}70{,}000.00 + \text{Rs } 2{,}20{,}000.00 + \\
&\quad\quad \text{Rs } 2{,}80{,}000.00 \\
&= \quad \text{Rs } 1{,}50{,}00{,}000.00
\end{aligned}
$$

Step 3

Calculation of gross operating revenue

$$
\begin{aligned}
\text{Gross operating revenue} \quad &= \quad \text{Total expenses} + \text{ROI (Return on Investment)} \\
&= \quad \text{Rs } 1{,}50{,}00{,}000.00 + \text{Rs } 3{,}00{,}00{,}000.00 \\
&= \quad \text{Rs } 45{,}00{,}00{,}000.00
\end{aligned}
$$

Step 4

Find revenue generation from room sales only by subtracting revenue generated by all sources other than rooms from the gross operating revenue.

$$
\begin{aligned}
\text{Revenue to be generated by room} \quad &= \quad \text{Gross operating revenue} - \text{Revenue} \\
\text{sales to cover cost and fair ROI} \quad &\quad\quad \text{generated from other sources} \\
&= \quad \text{Rs } 4{,}50{,}00{,}000.00 - \text{Rs } 3{,}85{,}000.00 \\
&= \quad \text{Rs } 4{,}46{,}15{,}000.00
\end{aligned}
$$

Step 5

Calculation of the total number of rooms available during the year

$$
\begin{aligned}
\text{Total number of rooms} \quad &= \quad \text{Total number of rooms in the hotel} \times \text{Number} \\
\text{available during the year} \quad &\quad\quad \text{of days in the year} \\
&= \quad 300 \times 365 \\
&= \quad 1{,}09{,}500 \text{ rooms}
\end{aligned}
$$

The average occupancy is 75 per cent in this case; hence allowance for average vacancy of rooms in the year will be 25 per cent of total available rooms. Thus, total number of rooms after making provision for average vacancy will be:

$$
\begin{aligned}
\text{Total number of rooms available after} \quad &= \quad \text{Total number of rooms in the year} \\
\text{making the provision for vacancy} \quad &\quad\quad \times \text{Occupancy percentage} \\
&= \quad 1{,}09{,}500 \times 75 \\
&= \quad 82{,}125 \text{ rooms}
\end{aligned}
$$

Step 6
Calculation of Average Daily Rate

Average Daily Rate = Revenue to be generated by room sales to cover cost and fair ROI / Total number of rooms available after making the provision for vacancy

= Rs 4,46,15,000.00 / 82,125 rooms

= Rs 543.26 per room

Thus, the average daily rate of Hotel Aanchal in the above example is Rs 530.00. This is the average of the two room types available in the hotel—single and double. Further determination of room rent can be made by taking area of the room as one measure. The rent per square foot can be calculated by dividing the amount found in step 4 by the total area (in square feet) covered by the room (adjusting the average vacancy). In the above example, it will be:

Total area under the room = 85,000 sq. ft

Less adjustment (25%) = 85,000 sq. ft – 21,250 sq. ft

= 63,750 sq. ft

Rate per square foot (for a year) = Revenue to be generated by room sales to cover cost and fair ROI total area covered by rooms

= Rs 4,46,15,000.00/63,750 sq. ft

= Rs. 699.84 per sq. ft

Rate per square foot (per day) = Rate per square foot (for a year)/ Number of the days in a year

= Rs 699.84/365

= Rs 1.92 per sq. ft per day

Thus, the room rent for single room will be:

Rate for single room = Area of single room × Rate per sq. ft per day

= 250 × Rs 1.92

= Rs 480

And the rate for double room will be:

Rate for double room   =   Area of double room × Rate per sq. ft per day

                                  =   300 × Rs 1.82

                                  =   Rs 576

Market-based Pricing

Market-based pricing is setting a price based on the value of the product in the perception of the customer. The concept is based on an idea of what the ultimate consumer of goods and services, i.e. the guest, is prepared to pay and then use this as a starting point. In this case, the hotel works backwards as it first makes an accommodation product available at a price that a guest is willing to pay, then it tries to cut down on the cost to achieve a reasonable rate of return on that basis.

Some common methods of market-based pricing are:

- *As per competition*: Arriving at a pricing based on competing hotels' rates.
- *Market tolerance*: Checking competing hotels' best available rates for a room. These rates can be found out by hotels by calling up the competing hotels without disclosing their identity.
- *Rate cutting*: Lowering of rates to increase occupancy levels, especially during off season.
- *Inclusive and non-inclusive rates*: Charging room rates on the basis of meals, provided on a CP/ MAP/ AP basis.
- *Guest requirements*: Varying room tariff as per guest requirements, e.g., early check-in on CP basis or late check-out on MAP basis.

As compared to market-based pricing, cost-based pricing is more scientific and practical as it takes into account factors like the rate of return on investment, operating cost, overheads, fair profit, etc. In market-based pricing, one can get the advantage of selling the same product over a range of prices.

SUMMARY

Price is one of the major elements involved in the marketing and positioning of a product or service. The price of goods and services of a hotel should cover the cost of production and overheads, and include a fair amount of profit, so that the hotel business remains sustainable and profitable. The rooms of a hotel generate the maximum revenue, so an accurate and competitive room rent is one of the prerequisites for running a successful hospitality business. The rate of a hotel room is based on the competition, the standard of services and amenities offered by the hotel, the guests' profile, and the location of the hotel and the room. Once the room tariff has been decided, every hotel has to decide about the criteria for establishing the 'end of the day' to post the room charges into guest accounts. A hotel generally designates a standard rate for each category of rooms offered to guests. Apart from the standard rates, hotels also offer discounted rates to attract additional business from multiple market segments, e.g., advance purchase rate, volume guarantee rate, package rate. The room tariff of a hotel may be based on the choice of meal plans offered to guests. Depending on the needs of their target audience, hotels offer a variety of meal plans, such as European plan, American plan, Modified American plan, Bed and Breakfast plan.

There are two standard methods for establishing room tariffs: cost-based pricing and market-based pricing. As compared to market-based pricing, cost-based pricing is more scientific and practical as it takes into account factors like the rate of return on investment, operating cost, overheads, fair profit, etc.

KEY TERMS

++. Taxes would be extra

AI (all inclusive) Taxes are included in the rate.

American plan (AP) It is also known as en-pension (full board). The tariff includes room rent and all meals (i.e., breakfast, lunch, and dinner).

Bed & breakfast (B&B) plan or Bermuda plan: The room tariff consists of room rent and includes American breakfast.

Complimentary rate The room rent is not charged.

Continental plan (CP) The room tariff consists of room rate and continental breakfast.

Cost The total expenditure incurred by a hotel to provide services and products to the ultimate consumer of the hotel. The total cost can be divided into fixed cost, material cost, and labour cost.

Cost-based pricing A room rent determination technique that covers the basic cost of operation at a given level of service plus the predetermined percentage of return on investment.

End of the day It is an arbitrary time which is supposed to be the end of the financial transactions for a particular day.

European plan (EP) The room tariff consists of room rate only and the meals are charged as per actuals.

Hubbart Formula: A scientific method to determine the room rent. It is based on the principle of covering all the cost that is incurred in providing

the accommodation plus a reasonable return on investment.

Market-based pricing To make an accommodation product available at a price that a guest is willing to pay.

Meal plan The room tariff includes room rent and meals.

Modified American plan (MAP) It is also known demi-pension (half board). The tariff consists of room rent, breakfast, and one major meal (either lunch or dinner).

Occupancy rate The percentage of hotel rooms occupied during a specific time period, omitting rooms not available for one reason or another.

Package rate A package rate is quoted for a bouquet of products or services. The rate is generally lower that the sum total of the prices of the individual product/services offered in the bouquet.

Rack rate Rack rate is the published rate of a particular type of room before any discount.

Return on investment (ROI) It is the amount gained if a sum of money was invested in the open market rather than a commercial/industrial venture.

Room rate/tariff The rate charged daily for a hotel room.

Room tariff card These are published lists of the different tariffs offered by hotels for the use of the travel trade (travel agencies, tour operators), companies, and individual guests. They include prices of rooms, meal plans, taxes, applicable policies, etc.

Rule of thumb approach The room rent should be set at the rate of Re 1 for each Rs 1,000 spent on the construction and furnishing of a room,

assuming the average occupancy to be 70 per cent for the year.

Seasonal rate Rates fluctuating on the basis of the seasonal demand.

Volume guarantee rate A contractual room rate that is offered on guaranteed volume of business; it is much lower than rack rate.

REVIEW QUESTIONS

Multiple Choice Questions

1. The MAP plan is also known as:
   a) Half board   b) En-pension
   c) Full board   d) All of the above

2. American Plan is also known as:
   a) Demi-pension   b) Bread and Breakfast
   c) Full board   d) All of the above

3. Hubbart formula for computing room rent was developed by:
   a) Roy Hubbart   b) John F Hubbart
   c) McHarty Hubard   d) None of the above

4. Crib rate refers to:
   a) Rate charged for children below 5 years of age, accompanied by parents
   b) All children above 10 years of age
   c) All children aged between 15-18 years
   d) None of the above

5. A package rate may include:
   a) Room rent only
   b) Room rent and meals only
   c) Room rent and meals and others products and services like air transport, sightseeing, safari etc.
   d) None of the above

True/False

1. The rack rate is the highest rate that a hotel quotes for its particular room type.

2. Check in/check-out time is generally 12 noon in most of the commercial hotels.

3. European plan includes room rent and continental breakfast in tariff.

4. Seasonal rate is generally found in hotels that face seasonal fluctuation in occupancy.

5. Market-based pricing is the best way to set the room rent.

Fill in the Blanks

1. The discounted rate offered on booking a room in advance is known as _____.

2. _____ hotel generally follows twenty-four hour system for charging room rent.

3. _____ plan includes room rent and all meals in tariff.

4. _____ method of pricing is most accurate and scientific method of setting room rent.

5. When a hotel does not charge the room rent from the guest, such a room is called _____ room.

Discussion Questions

1. What are the different bases of charging the room rent?

2. Which criteria of charging room rent is suitable for a commercial hotel? Why?

3. What do you understand by a meal plan? Explain different meal plans offered by hotels.

4. What do you understand by the term 'room rate designation'? Explain.

5. A package rate is beneficial for guests as well as the hotel. Comment.

6. What do you understand by the rule of thumb approach of fixing the room rent? Explain.

7. What are the major drawbacks of the rule of thumb approach?

8. What are the cost-based room rent determining techniques? Explain.

9. Explain Hubbart formula for determining room rent and average daily rate, with examples.

CRITICAL THINKING QUESTIONS

1. Differentiate between:
   a) Rack rate and corporate rate
   b) Tour group rate and group rate
   c) Advance purchase rate and package rate.

2. Why does a hotel have different types of rates? Explain the advantages and disadvantages of having different types of room rates and room categories.

PROJECT WORK

Visit three hotels in your town and compare the following:
1. Number of guest rooms
2. Facilities and services offered by the hotel
3. Rack rates
4. Volume guarantee rate
5. Week day and weekend rates
6. Package rates

CASE STUDIES

1. Hotel Plaza is located in the heart of the city. The fact sheet of the hotel is as follows:
   - The hotel has 350 rooms (125 single, 200 double, and 25 suites)
   - The hotel has five speciality restaurants, seven banquet halls, and one convention centre with the capacity to accommodate 1,500 person in theatre style.
   - The hotel has its own travel agency with a fleet of 15 luxury cars and 10 luxury couches.
   - There is no seasonal variation in hotel occupancy but it suffers a lean occupancy during weekends.
   - The hotel tariff card has the following details:
     - Room rent on EP
     - Tariff structure as under:

S.No.	Room Type	Rate
1	Single	Rs 4,500.00
2	Double	Rs 6,000.00
3	Suite	Rs 14,500.00
Extra bed @ Rs 1,000.00		

As a front office manger, plan the following rates for your hotel and assign reason for the same.
a) Corporate rate
b) Volume guarantee rate
c) Government rate
d) Week day/Weekend rate
e) Group rate
f) Package rate

2. The following information is available from Hotel Aravali.

Hotel Aravali has 400 rooms with an average occupancy of 65%.
- The owner's capital is Rs 25,00,00,000 and the total loan raised is Rs 10,00,00,000. Thus, the total investment is Rs 35,00,00,000.
- Let the fair market return be 10%.
- The expenses are as under:
  - Operating expenses (in rupees)

Rooms division	85,00,000.00
Telephone expenses	75,000.00
Administrative expenses	35,00,000.00
Payroll and other expenses	55,00,000.00
Advertisement and promotion	25,00,000.00
Power and fuel	1,85,000.00
Repair and maintenance	70,000.00

  - Taxes and insurance (in rupees)

Real estate and property tax	75,000.00
Management fee	95,000.00
Corporate taxes	22,50,000.00
Insurance of building and other assets	18,00,000.00

- Interest paid on loans (in rupees)

To financial institutions	2,45,000.00
To others	65,000.00

- Depreciation at book value (in rupees)

Building	2,85,000.00
Furniture, fixtures, and equipments	1,25,000.00

- Income generated from other sources (in rupees)

From Food & Beverage outlets	5,45,000.00
From lease of premises	95,000.00
Income from ancillary services (laundry, confectionery shop, beauty saloon, florist etc.) operated by the hotel	85,000.00

- There are 150 single and 250 double rooms in the hotel. The area of a single room is 300 sq. ft and the area of a double room is 350 sq. ft.

Calculate the average daily rate and the room rent of the single and double room.

3. You are a travel agent who has guests planning to visit Goa in July (which is off season because of the rains). Based on the tariff cards given, select hotels and tariff plans that best match the following clients:
a) A honeymoon couple
b) Four backpacker friends
c) A family (a couple and two children below 12)
d) Ten corporate delegates

Option 1 – Ocean View Casa

Ocean View Casa

Room Category	Single Occupancy	Double Occupancy
Standard Room	Rs 2,500	Rs 4,000
Deluxe Room	Rs 4,000	Rs 5,500
Family Room	NA	Rs 7,000*

- Above rates are subject to change
- Rates are subject to taxes

* Room rate includes B/F and dinner

Facilities include play room, splash pool, outdoor games, and reading room.

Option 2 – Hotel Surf n Sand

Hotel Surf n Sand

Room Category	Single Occupancy	Double Occupancy
Standard Room	Rs 2,500	Rs 3,000
Deluxe Room	Rs 4,000	Rs 4,000

- Rates are subject to change
- Rates are subject to taxes

Facilities include discotheque, swimming pool, 24-hour bar and coffee shop.

Option 3 – Grand Mariner Resort

Grand Mariner Resort

Room category	Single occupancy	Double occupancy
Superior Room	Rs 3,500*	Rs 4,500*
Luxury Room	Rs 4,500**	Rs 5,500**
Deluxe Room	Rs 5,500***	Rs 6,500***

- Rates are subject to taxes
- Subject to change

* on room only

** with B/F

*** with B/F and airport/railway station transfers

Facilities include Indian and Chinese speciality restaurants, bar, swimming pool, gymnasium, boardroom, secretarial facilities.

Option 4 – All Suites Haven

All Suites Haven	
Room Category	**Room Tariff**
Deluxe Cottage	Rs 5,000 (with B/F)
Luxury Cottage	Rs 7,500 (with B/F and airport/railway station transfers)
Presidential Cottage	Rs 10,000 (with B/F, airport/railway station transfers, wine bottle on arrival, one complimentary spa treatment)

- Rates are subject to taxes
- Contact the hotel for customized packages

All Suites Haven is located on a secluded, one kilometre long, palm-lined beach front, which is maintained by the hotel. All suites have a beach view and have private patios, which can be set up for romantic candle light dinners after a long walk on the beach, under the cover of a star-studded sky. Light beams from the 100-year-old lighthouse add to the romance of an era long gone.

Hotel services include private butler and valet; facilities include Indian, Chinese and Goan speciality restaurants, bar, water sports, swimming pool, gymnasium, tennis courts, helipad and much much more...

CHAPTER 7

Guest Cycle and Room Reservations

Learning Objectives:

After reading this chapter, you will be able to understand the following:
- The stages of a guest cycle—pre-arrival, arrival, stay, departure, and post departure—and the role of the front office in taking the guest through each of these stages.
- The first stage of the guest cycle—reservations.
- The types of reservations—tentative, waitlisted, and confirmed.
- Modes of reservation inquiry—written and verbal.
- Various sources of reservations.
- Systems of reservations—manual and automated.
- Processing a reservation request—receiving inquiry, determining availability, and accepting or denying the request.
- Importance of reservation—for hotels and for guests.

The hotel industry provides food and lodging to people travelling to destinations away from their homes. It is the responsibility of hotels to ensure that their guests do not face any kind of problem during their entire stay at the hotel. There are various stages of interface between a guest and a hotel—pre-arrival, arrival, stay, and departure. The first interaction between a guest and a hotel is when the guest enquires about room availability and makes a room booking or reservation. As per *The American Heritage Dictionary*, reservation is 'an arrangement by which accommodations are secured in advance, as in a hotel or an airplane.' Reservation is a very important part of a guest's experience as it gives an assurance that the desired room will be available for the guest for the required dates and ensures a comfortable stay at the hotel. The reservation staff members need to keep themselves updated all the time about the status of the rooms for the current day (such as how many guest arrivals and guest departures are expected that day and how many rooms are available for walk-in guests). As rooms generate considerable revenue for the hotel, handling reservations demands a great deal of attentiveness and responsibility.

THE GUEST CYCLE

The guests of a hotel have four main stages of interaction with the hotel—at pre-arrival, arrival, stay, and departure. All guests go through the same procedure as they proceed from reservation to arrival and allotment of rooms, to their stay in the hotel, to the settlement of their bills and departure from the hotel. These various stages of activities constitute the guest cycle (Fig. 7.1).

Pre-arrival

The interaction between a guest and a hotel before the guest arrives at the hotel forms the pre-arrival phase of the guest cycle. Reservation is the most important pre-arrival activity. During this phase, the guest first selects a hotel for stay. The

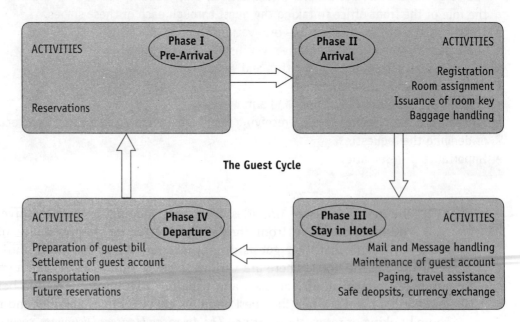

Fig. 7.1   The Guest Cycle

guest's choice about a particular hotel is affected by factors like advertisements, recommendations from family and friends, previous experience with the hotel, reputation, location, contractual agreement with the hotel, etc. Once a hotel has been chosen, the guest or a person designated by him (who could be his secretary or spouse or a travel agent) contacts the selected hotel through telephone, e-mail, or fax for reserving a room for the period of his proposed stay in town. The reservation request is received by the reservation staff, whose efficiency and competence in handling the request creates a good first impression of the hotel in the mind of the guest.

Before confirming a reservation, the hotel may ask for a credit card guarantee or an advance deposit from the guest. In case of high occupancy periods, guests are requested to pay retention charges. This is to ensure minimum loss to the hotel in case of any last moment cancellations or no shows. Once the retention charges have been paid, the room is reserved or 'blocked' for the guest for the required stay dates. The hotel also makes note of any special arrangements to be made, like a wheelchair and a barrier free room; airport or railway station transfers; an extra bed or crib in the room; etc.

Thus the functions of the front office in the pre-arrival phase include:

- Processing the reservation request of the guest.
- Creation of guest folio (in case the hotel has received any advance payment).
- Blocking the room for the guest.
- Making special arrangements for the guest (if required).

The data collected during the process of reservation can be utilized in future front office and sales activities. A well-managed reservation system can maximize the room sales and revenue by constantly monitoring the room status and forecasting the room revenue.

Arrival

Guests have their first face-to-face interaction with the hotel staff on their arrival at the hotel. This is a very critical stage as guests form an opinion about the standards and services that the hotel can provide to them. During this phase, guests are greeted by the front desk staff and the registration process begins. The guests are asked to verify the details printed in the registration card—these details are generated from the information received in the pre-arrival stage. The registration activity is an agreement between the hotel and the guest, whereby the hotel offers the accommodation product and services to the guest, and the guest agrees to pay for the services received. A hotel might pre-register guests (i.e., register guests before their arrival) like VIPs, groups, airline crews, and frequent guests.

Once the guest has registered with the hotel, she is assigned a room at the negotiated room rate. The guest is then shown to her room and her luggage is brought to the room by the bell desk. If any mails or messages have arrived at the hotel before the arrival of the guest, they are given to her.

Thus the functions of the front office on the arrival of a guest include:

- Reception and welcome of the guest (*aarti*, *tilak*, and garlanding, or offering welcome drink as per the policy of the hotel).
- Registration of the guest (see Chapter 8 for details).
- Room rate and room assignment to the guest.
- Handing over the room key to the guest.
- Luggage handling of the guest by bell desk.
- Delivering the mails and messages that the hotel has received on behalf of the guest.

The front office staff maintains lists of expected arrivals and departures (see sample in Chapter 8) on a daily, weekly, and monthly basis. They keep updating these lists, along with the arrival and departure details, and keep the other departments informed of any changes in the schedule of guests. This is very essential to provide a flawless service to guests and to avoid embarrassing situations like not arranging for the pick-up of a guest, or not having the room ready in time and making the guest wait for it.

Stay

During this stage the guest gets a first-hand experience of the facilities and services offered by the hotel. These services and facilities (discussed in detail in Chapter 9) are the most important part of a guest's overall experience at a hotel. An excellent level of services would lead to the satisfaction of the guest, which would make him come back to the hotel and give positive feedback to other potential customers. The front office is the interface between the guest and the other departments of the hotel, so it must coordinate well with other departments to ensure that the guest receives smooth and efficient services and facilities. The stay phase is the most important phase in the guest cycle for the hotel. During this phase, the guest would interact with the front office staff for various reasons, like asking for directions in and around the hotel, arranging for inter-city travel, wanting to know about the history of the city or hotel. The front office staff should handle the guests' queries politely and patiently, and provide satisfactory answers. In case of any lapse in services, the front office staff must be courteous and use all possible resources to satisfy the guest.

The functions of the front office during the stay of a guest include:

- *Handling guest accounts*: The creation and maintenance of guest accounts by the front desk cashier and the daily auditing of guest accounts by the night auditor.
- *Message coordination*: Receiving messages for guests when they are not in their rooms and ensuring the delivery of the same on their arrival by the information assistant.

- *Key handling*: Accepting the room key when the guest goes out of the hotel premises and returning the same to the guest when she comes back to the hotel. Some hotels also issue a key card to the guest at the time of accepting the key, and ask the guest to present the key card at the time of collecting the room key. This ensures that the room key is delivered to a genuine person.

- *Guest mail delivery*: Accepting mails of guests and delivering the same to them. When a guest is not in the room, the front desk receives her mail, keeps it in the room key rack, and delivers it when the guest comes back. If the guest is in her room, the bell boy delivers the mail to her. If the hotel receives mails for a guest who has a reservation in the future, the mails are sent to the reservation section and are kept in the reservation docket. The same is attached with the pre-filled guest registration card (GRC), which is given to the guest at the time of registration.

- *Guest paging*: Locating the guest in a specific area of the hotel when she is not in the room. If a guest is expecting a visitor, she may request for this service by filling a form.

- *Safety deposit locker*: Providing the locker facility to guests to keep their valuables like important documents and jewellery. The safety lockers are located in the back office of the front desk. Some hotels may have lockers in guest rooms.

- *Guest room change*: Changing the room of a guest, in case the guest's preference for view (garden facing, pool facing, etc.), type of room (single, double, suite, etc.), or location (ground floor, top floor, near elevator, no smoking zone, etc.) could not be fulfilled at the time of check-in due to unavailability of such a room. The room can also be changed if there is any defect in the room that requires extensive maintenance work or in case of upgrading, i.e., allotting a room of a higher price band without any extra charge from the guest.

- *Handling guest queries and complaints*: Responding to guests' queries and communicating guests' complaints to relevant departments.

- *Information about the hotel*: Providing information to guests about the products and services offered by the hotel.

- *Information about the city*: Providing information to guests about the city, like places of tourist interest, shopping malls, cinema halls, restaurants, bars, public offices, etc.

- *Travel arrangements*: Making intra- and inter-city travel arrangements for the guest if required.

Departure and Post Departure

The maxim goes that 'all's well that ends well'. The front office should try to cover up any unpleasant episodes during a guest's stay by ensuring a smooth and hassle-free departure of the guest. During the check-out, guests settle their account by making payment by a pre-established mode (like cash/credit card, travel agency voucher, bill to company) for the services rendered to them by the hotel. The hotel should take great care to present all unpaid bills for payment and carry out the whole procedure efficiently.

The functions of the front office at the departure stage are as follows:

- *Preparation and presentation of guest bills:* The front desk cashier prepares a guest's bill on the basis of financial transactions between the hotel and the guest recorded in the guest folio. The bill is presented to the guest for settlement.
- *Settlement of guest account:* A guest's account is settled by zeroing the guest folio balance. The folio balance may be in credit or debit. If the guest folio balance is in debit, then the required amount of money is received from the guest to make the balance zero. If the balance of guest folio is in credit, then the balance amount is returned to the guest to settle the guest account.
- *Luggage handling by the bell desk:* After the settlement of the guest account, a luggage pass is made and a bell boy carries the guest luggage from the hotel to the guest's vehicle.
- *Left luggage handling:* In case a guest wishes the hotel to keep her luggage for a short duration of time after checking out of the hotel, the hotel keeps the same in the left luggage room. The front office makes a luggage tag and hands over the guest copy to the guest, which the guest has to produce when she comes back to claim the luggage.
- *Sales and marketing activity (future reservation):* Giving promotional materials to guests, informing them about any upcoming offers, and making future bookings in the same hotel or sister concerns in other cities.
- *Farewell:* The guest is given a warm farewell at the point of departure.

It is important to keep in touch with guests even after their departure. This is generally taken care of by the sales and marketing team, which sends guests mailers or flyers with special offers or discounts, gift vouchers, and hotel updates like changes in room rates or room categories on a regular basis.

RESERVATIONS

Reservation in the hotel industry is defined as 'blocking a particular type of guest room (e.g., single room, double room, deluxe room, executive room, suite, etc.), for a definite duration of time (i.e., number of days of stay), for a particular guest'.

Due to globalization, advancement in the means of travel, and increase in the disposable income of people, more and more people are travelling to different cities. This increase in the traveller traffic has led to an increased demand for tourist accommodation at various destinations. To ensure a safe and secure place for stay during their visit to another town, people make advance reservations in hotels and other types of accommodation.

All hotels accept advance bookings of their rooms in order to achieve high occupancy and to maximize their revenue. When a person makes an advance reservation at a hotel, it is expected that the hotel will honour its commitment by providing the specified type of room when the guest arrives. A reservation is a bilateral contract between the hotel and the guest, according to which the hotel must provide the specified type of room to the guest and the guest should bear all relevant charges. However, the reservation assistant must inform the guest all relevant details about the booking, i.e., type of room, stay dates, room charges, government taxes, and VAT and service charges (if applicable) involved. If either the hotel or the guest wishes to alter or cancel the reservation, they can do so only by mutual agreement. If a guest does not notify the hotel of a cancellation, the hotel is entitled to charge the guest for the loss of accommodation revenue or may retain any deposit paid. Alternatively, if a hotel cancels the accommodation without prior notice to the guest, the hotel has to provide alternative accommodation of similar standard in another hotel and pay for any differences in room rates and additional expenses the guest may have to incur (e.g., taxi, telephones, etc.).

Hotels use a variety of methods to deal with reservation requests. The reservation department handles all the reservation requests for accommodation, interacts with guests and other external customers, and constantly monitors the status of rooms and reservations.

TYPES OF RESERVATION

Hotels accept reservations for their rooms and suites only after checking various factors, such as the availability of rooms and suites, sales forecast, room rates, profile of guests and their importance to the hotel, etc. The reservation made by a guest could be tentative, confirmed, or waitlisted (Fig. 7.2). Once a reservation request is confirmed by a guest, the hotel will make a guaranteed or non-guaranteed reservation as per the guest's requirement.

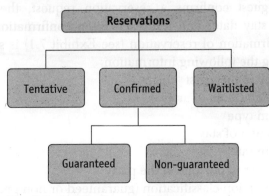

Fig. 7.2   Types of reservations

Reservations can be of the following types:
- Tentative reservation
- Confirmed reservation
- Waitlisted reservation

Tentative Reservation

It is a reservation request that a prospective guest makes on a tentative basis for particular stay dates. The hotel holds the room for the guest till a cut off date, by which the guest should confirm the reservation. Upon confirmation from the guest the hotel changes the tentative reservation to a confirmed reservation, otherwise it cancels the tentative reservation, and updates its records accordingly.

Waitlisted Reservation

A reservation is waitlisted when the requested category of room is not available for the requested dates. The waitlisted reservation is confirmed when the hotel receives a cancellation request for a room of the same category. This way the hotel ensures that its rooms will not remain vacant in case of cancellations. The hotel does not guarantee a room for waitlisted reservations; it is understood that the guest will be assigned a room only in the case of a cancellation or a no show. The hotel informs the guest at the time of processing the reservation that the reservation request of the guest is being put on waitlist and may be confirmed at a later date if some rooms are made available due to cancellation. This situation normally occurs in high occupancy periods like a long weekend, or festival/fair time, or season time. To avoid overbooking, when the total number of rooms reserved for a certain period of time exceeds the total number of rooms available for sale, the reservation department makes a waitlist on the basis of earlier records of reservations vis-à-vis actual arrivals. The hotel keeps clearing waitlists on a regular basis as per the cancellations received and the overbooking level for the day.

Confirmed Reservation

Once a guest confirms a reservation request, the hotel blocks a room for specified stay dates and sends a written confirmation of the same to the guest. The confirmation of reservation (see Exhibit 7.1) is sent through letter or e-mail containing the following information:
- Name of the guest
- Date and time of arrival
- Room type
- Duration of stay
- Room rate
- Number of persons in the party
- Reservation classification (guaranteed or non-guaranteed)

| Exhibit 7.1 | Sample confirmation letter |

Hotel Sun n Sand

Confirmation

217 Route 303
Valley Cottage, New Delhi
Tel: (011) 35829294
Fax: (011) 48035701

Dear Guest,

Thank you for your reservation. We look forward to your visit. Please note the information below for accuracy. Please review it and report any discrepancies.

Guest Name   - Mr John
Room Type   - Executive
Reserve Notes   - Room facing swimming pool
Guest Type   - Group
Rate Type   - Special
Confirmation No. - AC300150786
Arrival Date   - 15 November 2008
Departure Date - 15 January 2009
No. of Nights   - 61
Adult /Child   - 2 Adults, 0 Child

RESERVATION CHARGES
Room Rate   - Rs 4,500 ++
Misc. Total
Room Total   - Rs 2,74,500
Total Tax   - Rs 3,2,940
Total   - Rs 3,07,440

DEPOSIT RECEIVED Rs 2,74,500.00
BALANCE DUE Rs 32,940.00

Balance due upon arrival in cash, traveller's checks, or credit card. We cannot accept personal or business checks for payment of balance. If you have placed a deposit by credit card, you must bring your credit card with you along with a form of identification with signature. We cannot accept the use of another's credit card under any circumstances.

We must receive a notice from the guest of any cancellation or change in the number of rooms or nights reserved no later than 4 p.m., 14 calendar days prior to the guest's arrival in order for the guest to receive a refund of 90% of the amount deposited. If notice is not received 14 calendar days prior to date of arrival, the guest forfeits 100% of the deposit.

Check-in time: 3:00 p.m., Check-out time: 10:00 a.m. Please contact our office for late arrival information.

Thank you for your reservation!

SIGNATURE UPON ARRIVAL: DATE:

- Reservation confirmation number
- Special request made by the guest like airport pick-up, wheel chair, baby sitter, non-smoking room, barrier-free room, etc.

A confirmed reservation can be of the following two types:
- Guaranteed reservation
- Non-guaranteed reservation

Guaranteed Reservation A guaranteed reservation is a confirmation that the hotel will hold the reserved room for the guest and not release it to any other guest even if the guest doesn't arrive on time. This requires the guest to make an advance payment (part or full, depending on the hotel policy and the hotel occupancy for the requested stay dates), irrespective of whether the guest avails the reservation or not, unless the reservation is cancelled according to the hotel's cancellation procedures. Most hotels have their own guarantee and cancellation policies (Exhibit 7.2). In the case of guaranteed reservations, the hotel is indemnified from no-shows and holds the room for the guest beyond its cancellation hours. The guests can be sure of finding a room ready for them even if they arrive late without any prior information to the hotel. The guaranteed reservation can be obtained through one of the following ways:
- Pre-payment
- Contractual agreement
- Allotment

Pre-payment A guaranteed reservation requires the payment of the room rent or a specified amount in advance, known as pre-payment. As the hotel holds the room for the guest even after the cancellation hours, pre-payment protects the hotel from any loss of revenue in case of a last moment cancellation or a no-show. Pre-payment can be made by sending demand draft or depositing cash at the hotel. Cash deposit is the most preferred mode of accepting guaranteed reservation by most of the hotels. In case of deposits of high amounts, hotels might ask the guests for their PAN (Permanent Account Number) details.

Guests can alternatively choose to pay the full amount in advance through their credit/charge cards. A guest should send a letter authorizing the hotel to charge payment to their credit card account for obtaining guaranteed reservation, along

---

Exhibit 7.2 Sample Guarantee Policy

Guarantee Policy

Hotel Akbar Palace

All bookings must be guaranteed at the time of reservation by a Credit Card or Travel Agency. All major credit cards are accepted.

with a copy of the front and back of the credit card (photocopy if sending by letter or fax, and scan if sending by e-mail). These days credit card is the most preferred method of getting guaranteed reservation. The hotel staff must check the validity and authenticity of the card before using it as a guarantee. Reservations made online through hotel websites or travel websites, like Travelocity and Expedia, require valid credit card details before confirming a reservation. The booking amount is charged to the credit card account when the reservation is confirmed; a percentage of the charge might be reversed in case of reservation cancellation within the cancellation period.

Contractual Agreement A hotel may have a contract with an individual or a company for providing guaranteed reservations. According to such a contract, the hotel confirms the reservation for the individual or a person referred by the company on a guaranteed basis, and the person or the company agrees to pay for the reservation, even in the case of a no-show. A guaranteed reservation will turn into a non-guaranteed reservation if the payment is not made in full in advance, or the travel agency voucher or the bill to the company is not received by the cut off date specified by the hotel. Hotels may have contractual agreement with the following:

- Travel agencies/Tour operators
- Corporate houses

Travel Agencies/Tour Operators: Travel agencies and tour operators make bulk purchases of rooms at a relatively low contracted price. They guarantee the hotel a minimum number of room nights in a particular period and agree to pay the room charges even if they are unable to fill the number of rooms as per their agreement with the hotel. The hotels guarantee these reservations on the basis of vouchers issued by the travel agency or the tour operator, by which they agree to pay for the room and service charges mentioned on the voucher; the other services are charged from the guest.

Corporate Houses: In this case, a company or a corporate body may enter into a contract with a hotel, whereby the company guarantees payment for its employees or sponsored guests and accepts the financial responsibilities for any no-shows. The hotel, in turn, agrees to provide the mutually-agreed number of room nights to the clients or employees of the company during a certain period of time. Hotels guarantee these reservations on the basis of a letter from the company, called a bill to company or BTC letter, acknowledging the guest as its employee or client and agreeing to pay her bills as per the contract.

Allotment Allotment is a set of rooms booked for a particular period of time for a company or a group. This type of reservation is made for training courses, conferences or conventions, and private parties. A guest maybe asked for a booking reference or any other verification before she is provided a room in the allotment. Allotments are controlled by either the reservations manager or the group coordinator, and their operational issues are checked and assessed on a daily basis.

Non-guaranteed Reservation　When a guest confirms her reservation at a hotel but does not guarantee it with an advance deposit, it is treated as a non-guaranteed reservation. In this type of reservation, the hotel agrees to hold the room for the guest till the cancellation hour, unless the guest informs the hotel about her late arrival. The cancellation hour is the time fixed by a hotel after which a non-guaranteed reservation stands cancelled and the room is released to a walk-in guest—it is generally 6 p.m. If the guest does not arrive by the cancellation hour, the hotel is free to release the room to any other guest. This enables the hotel to cover the probable loss due to a no-show. Hotels nearing full occupancy might accept only guaranteed reservations once a specified number of expected arrivals is achieved.

MODES OF RESERVATION INQUIRY

The process of reservation begins with an inquiry. A guest may contact a hotel for reservation either in writing or verbally (Fig. 7.3).

Written Mode

When a reservation request reaches the hotel in writing, the mode is classified as a written mode of reservation. The different written modes of reservation request include letter, fax, telex, and e-mail. The advantages of the written mode of reservations are that they are clear, unambiguous, and provide a written record for the hotel, which can be referred to in case of any miscommunication or confusion. The correspondence with the guest is filed for future reference. The disadvantage of a letter is that it takes time to reach a hotel, and in case the information is not

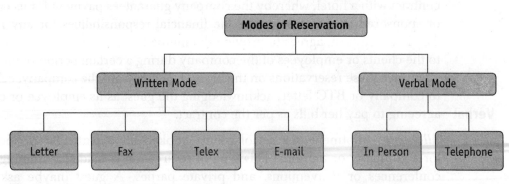

Fig. 7.3　Modes of reservation

complete, the communication of the same is not immediate, which may cause a delay in the reservation.

Letter   A letter is a good mode of making reservation requests if the guests send their letters to the hotel several months in advance (as the time taken for the delivery of a letter is more). This mode is commonly used by travel agents, tour operators, and corporate houses, which send reservation requests on their letterheads. Nowadays, though letter writing has largely gone out of fashion, a considerable number of holiday bookings are still made in this way. The hotel makes the reservation as per the details given in the letter and sends the confirmation letter to the guest. Figure 7.4 shows a sample reservation request by letter.

Fax   Fax, or facsimile transmission, uses electronic scanning technique to send copies of documents over an ordinary telephone line to a special machine that prints out an identical copy at the other end. It can be used to send memos, graphics, sketches, and letters. The machine can be run in auto mode, which makes it useful even if there is no one to answer the call. Fax makes it possible to send a written request instantaneously to a hotel in another part of the world. Hotels process the reservation as per the request and send the confirmation letter to the guest through fax. The guest might send the credit card authorization (front and back of the card) through fax to guarantee the reservation. The whole process is completed within a short span of time through fax.

Telex   Telex, or Tele Printer Exchange, involves the use of specialized telephone lines, where the message is communicated in the written form. As this is a written mode of reservation request, the information is clear and agreeable to the guest as well. Nowadays, this method is not used much because of the popularity of fax and computerized messaging or mailing system.

E-mail   E-mail is the mail sent by electronic means from one computer user to one or more recipients via a network from anywhere in the world. It is the electronic version of regular mails. The guest may send a reservation request to the hotel's e-mail address. The hotel will process the reservation request and send the confirmation letter through e-mail. Like other written modes of reservation, e-mail provides a written record for future reference. Besides that, it is fast (the delivery and response time is less) and convenient (guests can send an e-mail from the comforts of their home or office).

Verbal Mode

Reservation requests may also be made through oral communication, i.e., in person or on telephone. The advantage of oral communication is that it is fast, convenient, and generates immediate response or feedback; and one can get the complete information and clear any doubts through oral communication. The disadvantage is that it does not provide a permanent record.

TECHNO TRAILS LIMITED
ABC Road, Jaipur

Date: 15 September 2008

To
Reservation Manager,
Hotel Park International,
South Extension,
Bangalore.

Subject: Reservation of room for company representatives

Dear Sir,

Kindly book rooms for our executives as per details below:

Sr.	Name	Date of Arrival	Date of Departure	Type of room	Remarks
1	Mr A. Khanna	08/10/2008	10/10/2008	Executive	No smoking zone
2	Mr S.D. Bhatia	10/10/2008	12/10/2008	Deluxe	Near elevator
3	Mrs S. David	12/10/2008	25/11/2008	Single	Lower floor
4	Ms T. Alpna	25/11/2008	27/12/2008	Executive	Top floor
5	Mr S. Xavier	27/11/2008	25/12/2008	Deluxe	Garden facing
6	Mr M.C. Sharma	25/12/2008	07/01/2009	Suite	Pool facing

The room rent will be settled by the company and the food bills will be settled by the occupants.

Kindly send the confirmation as soon as possible.

Yours truly,

(Mr A.B. Yadav)
Catering Manager

Fig. 7.4   Reservation request by letter

In Person   If an individual or her representative goes to the hotel to book rooms for future, it is called in-person mode of reservation request. This is a good mode of processing reservation as the person is available to consider the various options and suggestions, in case the room, or its availability, or its rate does not match the guest's expectations. The hotel processes the reservation as per the details given by the guest and gives her the confirmation number and letter.

Telephone   Reservation requests generally come to a hotel through telephone calls. A lot of hotels have developed scripts for calls, whereby the reservation agent takes the required information sequentially as per the script. The telephone is fast and convenient, but it suffers from the major disadvantage that it does not provide a permanent record. These days hotels have high-end systems which record calls and these calls can be played back later as a proof of the guest's queries, or for the hotel records, or for training purposes (of reservation staff). This is the most popular mode of reservation request. The hotel processes the reservation request as per the given details and sends a confirmation letter.

As each of the above-mentioned modes of reservation requests suffers from some drawbacks—either in terms of speed, or convenience, or written record—there are no ideal means of making reservation. Guests choose their modes according to their personal preferences, so any hotel receives reservation requests through all modes.

SOURCES OF RESERVATION

A hotel receives reservation requests from different sources like direct guests, central reservation or global distribution system, travel agencies, companies, etc. Some of them are illustrated in Fig. 7.5.

Direct reservation A reservation request that a hotel receives directly from an individual or a group (without a mediator) is known as a direct reservation. The direct reservation request is processed by the reservation team. In most hotels, the staffing, equipment, location, and layout of the reservation section will depend upon the volume of the reservation requests received directly.

Central reservation system Central reservation system (CRS) is a computer-based reservation system, which enables guests to make reservations in any of the participating lodging properties at any destination in a single call. The central reservation office typically deals with direct guests, travel agents, corporate bookers, etc. by means of toll-free telephone numbers. The central reservation offices operate twenty-four hours a day, all round the year, and are equipped with the necessary communication equipment like computers, telephones, fax machine, etc. The systems at member hotels and CRS have accurate, up-to-date information on room availability. This is helpful for guests as they can check the availability and make reservations for more than one hotel at the CRS. In case rooms are not available, the itinerary can be reversed or re-planned, so as to accommodate the guests at the desired hotels. The reservation agents can be creative and can upsell room categories (e.g., suites and other high-category, low-moving rooms) in case the requested rooms are not available, or suggest alternative destinations. While making or revising the itinerary of guests, the agents should take care that the intercity travel arrangements should not tire the guests and spoil their experience of the various destinations.

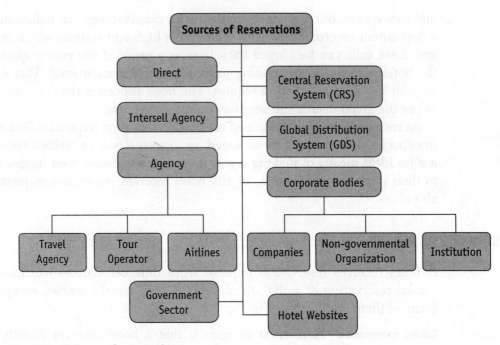

Fig. 7.5 Sources of reservations

For example, an American couple is travelling for eight nights, from 10–18 November, on the Golden Triangle (Delhi–Agra–Jaipur–Delhi). Their original plan is Delhi (10–12 Nov)–Agra (12–14 Nov)–Jaipur (14–17 Nov)–Delhi (17–18 Nov). However, rooms are not available in Agra for one of the requested dates, i.e., on 13 November. As per the room availability at the hotels, the itinerary can be reversed and the guests can go to Jaipur first (see Table 7.1 for more options):

1. Delhi (2N)–Jaipur (3N)–Agra (2N)–Delhi (1N)
2. Delhi (1N)–Jaipur (3N)–Agra (2N)–Delhi (2N)

Or, the guests can extend the stay in Jaipur or Delhi, and cut their stay in Agra:

3. Delhi (2N)–Agra (1N) –Jaipur (4N)–Delhi (1N)
4. Delhi (2N)–Agra (1N)–Jaipur (3N)–Delhi (2N)

Or, the guests can go directly to Agra or Jaipur from the airport without staying in Delhi.

5. Agra (2N)–Jaipur (3N)–Delhi (3N)
6. Jaipur (4N)–Agra (2N)–Delhi (2N)

Or, they can also go to other destinations like Udaipur.

7. Delhi (2N)–Agra (1N)–Jaipur (1N)–Udaipur (3N)–Delhi (1N)
8. Delhi (1N)–Udaipur (2N)–Jaipur (1N)–Agra (2N)–Delhi (1N)

Or, the guests can select a higher category room at Agra on 13 November.

9. Delhi (2N)–Agra (2N, Luxury Suite)– Jaipur (3N)–Delhi (1N).

These options ensure confirmed reservation at all cities for the guests. Without CRS, the guests would have had to call up the Delhi, Agra, and Jaipur hotels separately for room availability, then prepare their revised itinerary and call back the respective hotels. As the room rates and room availability status are dynamic, the rates quoted and rooms available at the time of inquiry might have sold out by the time the guests call back, and the guests would have to go through the entire process again. The central reservation offices help a guest get the information and room availability status for all the group hotels and to plan their itinerary in one toll-free call or e-mail and to make reservations.

Hotels are required to provide accurate and current room availability data to the central reservation office. They may pay a flat fee for obtaining the services of a CRS and an additional fee for each reservation received through the central reservation office. The CRS is of two types:

- Affiliated system
- Non-affiliated system

Table 7.1 Various itinerary options

Plan	10 Nov	11 Nov	12 Nov	13 Nov	14 Nov	15 Nov	16 Nov	17 Nov	Change
Original	DEL	DEL (car/train)	AGR	AGR (car/train)	JAI	JAI	JAI (car/train/flight)	DEL	
Option 1	DEL	DEL (car)	JAI	JAI	JAI (car)	AGR	AGR (car)	DEL	Interchange AGR and JAI
Option 2	DEL (flight)	JAI	JAI	JAI (car)	AGR	AGR (train)	DEL	DEL	Interchange DEL visits
Option 3	DEL	DEL (train)	AGR (train)	JAI	JAI	JAI	JAI (train)	DEL	Extend stay in JAI
Option 4	DEL	DEL (train)	AGR (car)	JAI	JAI	JAI (flight)	DEL	DEL	Extend stay in DEL
Option 5	AGR (car)	AGR (car)	JAI	JAI	JAI (car)	DEL	DEL	DEL	Go directly to AGR
Option 6	JAI (flight)	JAI	JAI	JAI (train)	AGR	AGR (car)	DEL	DEL	Go directly to JAI
Option 7	DEL	DEL (car)	AGR (car)	JAI (flight)	UDR	UDR	UDR (flight)	DEL	Go to UDR
Option 8	DEL (flight)	UDR	UDR (flight)	JAI	JAI (car)	AGR	AGR (train)	DEL	Go to UDR
Option 9	DEL	DEL (car)	AGR	AGR (car)	JAI	JAI	JAI (flight)	DEL	Higher category in AGR

Affiliated system   In affiliated reservation systems, all the participating hotel units belong to the same chain or group, like Welcome net by Welcome group of Hotels, Holidex by Holiday Inn Hotels, Image by Hyatt Hotels, and ITT by Sheraton Hotels.

Non-affiliated system   Non-affiliated system is a subscription-based system, designed to connect independent or non chain properties, like the Leading Hotels of the World (LHW), Small Luxury Hotels of the World (SLH). This enables non-chain properties to enjoy the benefits of CRS.

Intersell Agencies   An intersell agency is an agency that deals with many products such as hotel reservations, car rentals, travel arrangements, tour operations, airline reservations, railway bookings, etc. Such agencies as Expedia, Travelocity, Travelguru, MakeMyTrip, etc. are a rich source of reservations for hotels.

Global Distribution System   Global distribution system (GDS) is a worldwide computerized reservation network, which is used as a single point of access for reserving hotel rooms, airline seats, rental cars, and other travel-related items by travel agents, online reservation sites, and large corporations. GDS provides a bundle of products and services to the prospective user across geographical boundaries and is a link between the producers and end users of travel products and services. A number of hotel reservations are made through GDS. The premier GDS are Amadeus, Galileo, Sabre, and Worldspan, which are owned and operated as joint ventures by major airlines, car rental firms, and hotel groups.

Amadeus IT   Amadeus is one of the most commonly used GDS. Owned by the Amadeus IT Group, it was formed in 1987 out of an alliance between Air France, Lufthansa, Iberia Airlines, and Scandinavian Airlines. It specializes in the bookings of hotels, airlines, cruises, travel services, and car rentals.

Galileo CRS   Galileo International was founded in 1971 as Chicago-based United Airlines introduced the Apollo® computer reservation system for use in their own offices to automate seat reservation, booking, and tracking. This computer-based reservation system is owned by Travelport, and is used for the reservation of travel, tourism, and hospitality products and services. It allows a single record to be created for multiple airline bookings in one database.

SABRE   Semi-automated business research environment (SABRE) is a computer based reservation system used by airlines, hotels, travel agents, railways, and other travel-related companies for reservation of their products and services. It was first developed in the early 1960s to help American Airlines automate their reservation system. It is a unit of Sabre Holding's Sabre Travel Network division and is one of the largest electronic travel reservation systems.

Worldspan This is a GDS used by travel agents and tour operators for travel and hospitality-related bookings. Owned by Travelport, it was created in 1990 by Delta Airlines, Northwest Airlines, and Trans World Airlines to sell their GDS services to travel and hospitality operators worldwide.

Agencies Many guests make reservations through travel agents or tour operators. The agent will normally take a pre-payment from the guest, send a confirmation to the hotel, and issue an accommodation voucher on its behalf. Travel agents receive (or deduct) a commission for their services from the guest, or the hotel, or both. Many airlines also offer booking service to their passengers. As hotels receive bulk bookings and huge volume of business throughout the year from agencies like tour operators, travel agencies, and airlines, they offer very low rates to these agencies for various room categories.

Corporate Bodies Hotels also receive bookings from companies (FMCGs, pharmaceutical, etc.), non-governmental organizations (such as Care, Oxfam, Red Cross, WHO, etc.), and institutions (which may be educational, financial, banking, etc.). These companies also provide bulk reservations to hotels and get rooms at low rates.

Government Sector Hotels receive bookings from government sectors such as public sector undertakings, embassies, and consulates. As the government officials travel to different places on official work and need accommodation at the place of visit, they constitute a major source of reservation and revenue to the hotel.

Hotel Websites A hotel's website is another potential source for receiving reservations. The website contains a link for reservation requests. By clicking the link, guests can make a hotel reservation as per their requirements from the comforts of their house/office/cyber cafe. Most of the hotels provide photo galleries, descriptions of room categories and hotel facilities, and virtual tours of the hotel to aid the guest in selecting the hotel and the room category.

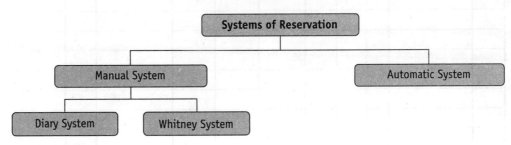

Fig. 7.6 Systems of reservations

SYSTEMS OF RESERVATION

Depending on the needs of the hotel and the volume of business, a hotel may adopt either manual or automatic system of reservation (Fig. 7.6).

Manual System of Reservation

In a manual system, all the reservation records are maintained manually. This old system of reservation is suitable for a small property, where the number of rooms is less and the volume of reservation requests is also low. The hotel may use one of the following systems of manual reservation: diary system of reservation or Whitney system of reservation.

Diary system of reservation   This is a manual system of reservation. As the name suggests, in this system a daily diary is kept, in which the reservation agent lists all arrivals due on a particular day. It is usually kept on a loose-leaf basis. The top page represents arrivals on the current date; this is removed and sent to the front desk for receiving the guests. A new blank sheet is added at the back of the diary to record the reservation on a new date. The hotel booking diary may be hard bound also. The format of a hotel diary is shown in Fig. 7.7. The diary system of reservation is only suitable for very small properties.

Room No.	Name	Pax	Arrival		Advance	Date of Departure	Booking Date	Booked by		Signature of Reservation Assistant	Remarks
			Time	Mode				Name	Con. No.		

Fig. 7.7   Sample hotel booking diary

The tools used in diary system of reservation are as under:
- Booking diary
- Room status board/ reservation journal
- Expected arrival list/ Movement list
- Cancellation register (if required, for taking cancellation)
- Black list (if required, to refuse reservations to undesirable or black-listed guests)

Whitney system of reservation This system of room reservation, developed by the American Whitney Duplicating Check Company, is suitable for small and medium properties–with up to 150 rooms. It is based on the use of standard size slips, known as Whitney slips or Shannon slips, which can be held on a metallic carrier on Whitney racks. A sample of a Whitney slip is shown in Fig. 7.8. The slips may be colour coded to identify the status of guests like FIT, group, crew, VIP, commercially important person, etc. The top line of the slip contains essential information (like dates of arrival and departure, name of the guest, room type, and rate) as this part remains visible after placing the slip in the metallic carrier.

The Whitney system uses racks that are vertically mounted on walls. It requires a total of forty-three racks, out of which thirty-one racks are kept for the current month (one for each day), eleven racks for the next eleven months of the year, and one rack for the next year. The thirty one racks are arranged as per the date of the month. As soon as a reservation request is received, the reservation is processed, Whitney slips are made in duplicate, and the original is placed in the Whitney rack. The Whitney slips can be arranged in alphabetical order on the Whitney rack.

The advantages of using Whitney system are as under:
- Bookings can be kept in order of the date of arrival.
- Booking records may be arranged in alphabetical order.
- The racks and carriers can be used over and over again. The running expense is only of the slips.
- The Whitney racks are placed vertically, saving storage space.

Date of Arrival	Name of Guest	Room Type	Rate	Date of Departure
Mode of Reservation	Reserved by	Date Received		
Agency (if any)				
Billing Instruction			Confirmation Date	

Fig. 7.8 Whitney Slip

Room Availability Records used in Manual System Processing a reservation request requires tools which can help ascertain the availability of rooms for the desired duration. The following room availability records are used in manual systems: bed room journal, conventional chart/advance letting chart, and standard density chart.

Bed room journal A bed room journal is very similar to the reservation diary. Tiled in a date-wise sequence, each page of the journal contains the occupancy details for that date–the name of the guest, the room number, and the type of room. If a guest has made a booking from 10–14 November, his/her name, room number, and room type will be entered on four pages of the journal, from 10 November to 14 November. The format of bed room journal is shown in Fig. 7.9. The major disadvantage in using this availability record is the requirement of data-entry staff.

Conventional chart Conventional chart, also known as advance letting chart, is an improved version of the bed room journal and is simple to understand. The format of a conventional chart is shown in Fig. 7.10. The chart is prepared for each month, so only twelve such charts are required for one year. The room number and the room category is mentioned in one column, and there are twenty-eight to thirty-one more columns, depending upon the number of days in the month. The name of the guest is written between the days of their stay—the arrival and departure indicated by the symbols < and > respectively.

Date			Date		
Name of Guest	**Room No.**	**Particular**	**Name of Guest**	**Room No.**	**Particular**

Fig. 7.9 Bed room journal

Month: April, 2009																		
Type and No. of Room	1	2	3	4	5	6	7	8	9	......	24	25	26	27	28	29	30	31
Double 201	<	-	-	-	>													
Double 202					< >													
Double 203																		
Double 204																		
Double 205																		
Single 101																		
Single 102																		
Single 103																		
Single 104																		
Single 105																		
Deluxe 501																		
Deluxe 502																		
Deluxe 503																		
Deluxe 504																		

Fig. 7.10   Conventional chart

The major disadvantages associated with the use of conventional charts are:
- There are problems in case of long guest names and short stays.
- The chart becomes untidy in the case of cancellations and amendments.

- Its use is limited to medium-sized hotels.
- Counting of available rooms is difficult.
- No overbooking can be taken.
- Specific rooms are pre-assigned to guests, which creates a problem in case of overstay or understay.

Month: January, 2010

Type of Room: Single

Date

No. of Rooms	1	2	3	4	5	6	7	8		20	21	22	23	24	25	26	27	28	29	30	31
20	/	/								/											
19	/	/								/											
18	/	/								/											
17	/	/	/	/	/	/	/	/		/	/	/	/	/	/		/	/	/		
16	/																				
15	/	/	/	/	/	/	/	/		/	/	/	/	/	/	/	/	/	/	/	/
14	/	/	/	/	/	/	/	/		/	/	/	/	/	/	/	/	/	/	/	/
13	/	/	/	/	/	/	/	/		/	/	/	/	/	/	/	/	/	/		
12	/			/	/					/	/	/									
11	/			/	/					/	/	/	/	/	/	/	/	/			
10	/			/	/					/	/	/	/	/	/	/	/	/			
09	/			/	/					/	/	/									
08	/			/	/					/	/	/									
07	/			/	/					/	/	/									
06	/			/	/					/	/	/									
05	/			/	/					/	/	/									
04	/			/	/					/	/	/									
03	/			/	/					/	/										
02	/			/	/					/											
01	/			/	/					/											
-1	/			/	/					/											
-2	/			/	/					/											
-3	/			/	/																
-4	/			/	/																
-5	/																				

Fig. 7.11   Standard density chart

Standard density chart Standard density charts were developed to overcome the problems and drawbacks of a conventional chart. A density chart is prepared for each category of rooms for the duration of one month. The vertical column indicates the date and the horizontal column represents individual rooms. An indicative mark (/) is put in appropriate boxes for indicating a reservation. The minus sign indicates that one can take overbooking using the density chart. The format of a standard density chart is shown in Fig. 7.11.

The density chart has the following advantages over the conventional chart:
- Long name and short stay problems are solved as one does not have to enter names.
- The chart remains tidy in case of cancellations and amendments.
- Large hotels may also use this system.
- Counting of available rooms is easy.
- Overbooking can be taken.

Automatic System

Automated reservation systems are computerized reservation systems that are used to store and retrieve room status information and conduct transactions. The information stored in the automatic system is the same as in a manual system. However, the processing of reservation request does not require manual study of bed room journals, density charts, or conventional charts. The reservation assistant can check the availability of rooms by clicking on a link on the computer. In this system, the reservation information is keyed into the electronic format of the reservation form, and this information is transferred to the central server where the room status is updated automatically. When a reservation assistant receives a reservation request, she checks whether the room is available or not using this system. If the request is accepted, the system automatically blocks the room for the desired duration of time and removes the room from the availability records. The automated system saves the trouble of manually updating the records. It also generates electronic confirmation letters that are sent to the guests' e-mail addresses or postal addresses. The system is also equipped to automatically generate reports like occupancy records or forecasts and lists like expected arrival lists, expected departure lists, etc. Central reservation system (CRS) and global distribution system (GDS) are examples of automated systems.

PROCESSING RESERVATION REQUESTS

Every hotel has its own standard operating procedure (SOP) to deal with a reservation request from a guest. The standard procedure of responding to a guest's reservation request is first receiving the reservation inquiries, then determining room availability, and then accepting or denying the request for reservation.

Receiving Reservation Inquiries

The request for a room reservation may reach a hotel from any one of the various modes discussed earlier. While receiving a reservation request, the reservation agent should ask for only that information which will help in processing the reservation request faster. The following information will help to determine the availability of the room requested by the guest:

- Date and time of arrival.
- Date and time of departure.
- Number and type of rooms required.
- Number of persons in the party.

Determining Room Availability

Using the information gathered at the time of receiving the reservation request, the reservation agent will ascertain whether the requested type of room is available in desired number for the required duration. The reservation agent will use one of the following records for determining the availability of the room: bed room journal, conventional/advance letting chart, standard density chart, or computerized system.

Accepting or Denying Request for Reservation

Once the reservation agent has established the availability of the room for the guest, she will either accept or deny the reservation request and conclude the processing of reservation request. The manner in which the reservation assistant interacts with the guest and handles the reservation request goes a long way in determining the guest's impressions of the hotel.

If rooms are available as per the guest's requirements, the reservation request is accepted. The following details are gathered from the guest while accepting the reservation:

- Name of the guest
- Designation and company, if corporate guest
- Address and contact details of the guest
- Time and mode of arrival
- Reservation classification (confirmed, guaranteed, etc.)
- Caller data (in case of third party reservation)
- Special requirements (baby sitter, no smoking room, garden/pool facing, sea facing, barrier free rooms for a physically challenged guest, interconnecting rooms, etc.)

The hotel should always honour the rate quoted and confirmed to the guest. The agent should be aware of the following:

- Supplementary charges for extra services or amenities
- Minimum stay requirements in effect for the dates requested

- Special promotions in effect for the dates requested
- Applicable currency exchange rates (for international tourists)
- Applicable room tax percentages
- Applicable service charges

Once the availability of the room has been ascertained, the hotel blocks a room for the guest and sends a confirmation letter to confirm the same. The reservation transaction is allotted a number, known as the confirmation number, which is mentioned in the confirmation letter. This alphanumeric code is used to identify and document the booking. A computerized reservation system automatically generates the confirmation letter and the same may be sent to the guest's mailing address or e-mail.

The reservation department using manual reservation system uses a specially designed form (Fig. 7.12) to record the reservation transactions. This helps prevent any ambiguity in the information generated during the reservation process. The reservation form contains information like the personal data of the guest, stay dates,

---

Hotel ABC
RESERVATION FORM
No. _____

Name of the Guest _____

Company _____ Designation _____

Address of the guest _____

_____ Tel. _____

Date of Arrival _____ Time of Arrival _____

Date of Departure _____ Expected time of departure

Time of Room   S [ ]   D [ ]   T [ ]   Others   Category _____

No. of Pax _____ Room Rate _____

Mode of Arrival _____ Discount _____

Flight No. _____

Mode of Payment/Settlement of Bills _____

Credit Card No. _____ Date of Expiry _____

Personal Details of the Person/Agency Making the Reservation _____

Special Request _____

Date & Time of booking _____

Remarks:

Reservation Assistant

Name _____

Signature _____

Fig. 7.12 Reservation form

mode and time of arrival and departure, number and type of rooms, mode of bill settlement, guarantee details, special request, etc. Using a reservation form has the following advantages: it provides a permanent record, it helps to summarize data generated while processing reservation request, and it enables the management to ascertain the person who handled the reservation request.

The reservation department may choose to turn down a reservation request in the following cases:

- The hotel is fully booked.
- The requested room is not available for the requested duration.
- The guest is blacklisted (i.e. the hotel does not want to accommodate the guest for various reasons).

When denying a specific request, the agent should always be polite and helpful, and should follow the procedure below:

- If the requested type of room is not available, apologize and explain to the guest that this particular room is not available. Try to offer alternative accommodation or dates at the hotel, and if this is unacceptable for the client, try to offer accommodation in a sister hotel, if applicable.
- If the hotel is fully booked, apologize and explain that the hotel is fully booked. Offer alternative dates or accommodation at the hotel, or in another hotel of the group, if applicable.

Amending Reservation

When guests with confirmed reservations change their travel plans, they convey the same to the hotel. This change–in the type of reservation (guaranteed or non-guaranteed), date of arrival, duration of stay, type of room, etc.–is termed as amendment. In case of amendments, the hotel has to check the availability of rooms again as per the fresh details given by the guest. The hotel might charge an amendment fee for making changes to the existing booking. The reservation agent should ascertain that the person requesting the amendment is the same as the one who has made the original booking. This is done to avoid any problem or confusion that may arise at the time of the arrival of the guest. The changes are recorded in a specialized form known as the reservation cancellation/amendment form.

Exhibit 7.3   Sample cancellation policy

Hotel GardenView   Cancellation policy

Reservation must be cancelled 30 days prior to the planned date of arrival. One night's stay will be levied for cancellations received upto 8 days prior to arrival. Full stay will be levied for cancellations received within 7 days prior to arrival.

Cancellation of Reservation

The cancellation of a reservation occurs when a guest with a confirmed reservation informs the hotel about her intention to cancel the reservation. As cancellation might lead to the loss of room revenue, hotels discourage cancellations by imposing retention charges (Exhibit 7.3). In case of a guaranteed reservation, if the cancellation is not made before a stipulated date and time, the hotel may charge retention charges, which may be equal to the rent of one night or more.

RESERVATION REPORTS

The reservation department compiles many reports for the use of all departments. Some of the most commonly used reservation reports include:

- *Reservation transaction report:* The reservation transaction report is the summary of the daily activities of the reservation department in terms of:
  - Creation of reservation records
  - Amendment request
  - Cancellation of reservation request

- *Commission agent report:* This report includes the amount payable by the hotel to the different commission agents (like travel agents, tour operators, CRS, GDS, etc.) that provide business to the hotel. This report is maintained alphabetically.

- *Turn away or refusal report:* At times hotels have to 'turn away' guests due to unavailability of rooms. The reservation department compiles a report of the total 'turn away' during a period of time. This report aids the management in planning the expansion and developing new properties in the city.

- *Revenue forecast report:* The revenue forecast report is a projection of the volume of business that the hotel will be generating in a specified duration. This is calculated by multiplying the reservations and the room rent offered to guests.

On a daily basis, the reservation team prepares the expected arrival, stayover, and departure lists, which help in maintaining a daily record of the room availability and thus maximizing room revenue.

- *Expected arrival list:* The list of names and surnames, along with the respective room types, of the guests who are expected to arrive the next day.

- *Stayover list:* The list of names and surnames, along with the respective room numbers, of the guests who are expected to continue to occupy their rooms the next day.

- *Expected departure list:* The list of names and surnames, along with the respective room numbers, of the guests who are expected to depart the next day.

IMPORTANCE OF RESERVATION

The role of the reservation department is not limited to making reservations. It maintains records of the hotel occupancy, which help in planning sales and marketing strategies and estimating manpower requirements. At the same time, properly executed reservations go a long way in ensuring a comfortable stay for guests. Thus, the reservation department is important for the hotel as well as for the guest.

Importance of Reservation for the Hotel

The reservation department plays a very important role in increasing the efficiency of the hotel. The data generated during the reservation process can be utilized to accelerate the facilitation of guest services and planning the activities of the sales and marketing department. The reservation process is of vital importance to a hotel as it:

- gives the first impression of the hotel to guests.
- sells the main product of a hotel (accommodation).
- generates customers for other departments.
- provides important management information to other departments.

The reservation department improves the efficiency of the hotel operations by providing the following services:

- It updates the room availability record and thus maximizes the revenue generated from room bookings.
- It prepares the housekeeping and front desk for arrivals by communicating the arrival details taken at the time of reservation.
- It helps in planning the distribution of staff at the front desk—the roster for the staff can be prepared according to the number of confirmed reservations for the day.
- It provides the reservation data to the finance department, which forecasts the volume of business on the basis of confirmed reservations. The sales forecast is compared to expenditure budget (e.g., money available for staff wages and purchases), on the basis of which cost is cut on materials, labour, and overheads.
- It generates customers for the hotel—first time customers as well as repeat customers—by handling reservation queries and requests politely.
- It maintains hotel occupancy records, which help the management to plan business strategies—change in room rates, renovation of rooms, expansion programmes, or the opening of a new unit in the city.

Importance of Reservation for the Guest

A person travelling to another city likes to book a room in advance in the hotel of her choice. This is to avoid any problem in securing a comfortable place to stay on arrival in the city. A confirmed reservation has the following advantages for the guest:

- *Assurance about accommodation*: The guest is sure that when she reaches the destination, she will have a place to stay.
- *Choice in the type of accommodation*: The guest can make the reservation as per her choice, like:
  - *Type of room or suite*: The guest might prefer a suite or a deluxe room.
  - *As per the guest's budget*: Hotels offer a variety of rooms at different charges; the guest can select from a room that matches her budget.
  - *Preference of floor, view, and personal choice*: The guest can request for a high-floor or low-floor room; sea view/pool view/garden view/monument view room; smoking/non-smoking room; etc.
- *Receive correspondence at the hotel address*: If the guest is travelling, she can use the address of the hotel to receive any urgent mails, couriers, messages, or calls.

SUMMARY

There are four main stages of interaction between a hotel and its guests–pre-arrival, arrival, stay, and departure. All guests go through the same procedure as they proceed from reservation to arrival and allotment of rooms, to their stay in the hotel, to the settlement of their bills and departure from the hotel. These various stages of activities constitute the guest cycle. At each of these stages, guests are assisted by the front office department, which provides services like processing reservations, receiving guests and allotting rooms, preparing guest folios, looking after guests' requirements during their stay, and settling guests' accounts.

There has been a tremendous increase in the number of people travelling for business or pleasure. This has led to a rise in the demand for hotel accommodation and the number of reservations. A reservation is a bilateral contract between the hotel and the guest, according to which the hotel must provide the specified room to the guest and the guest should bear all the relevant charges. The reservation made by a guest could be tentative, confirmed, or waitlisted. Once a reservation request is confirmed by a guest, the hotel will make a guaranteed or non-guaranteed reservation as per the guest's requirement.

Hotels receive reservation request from different modes (written and verbal) and different sources (direct guests, central reservations or global distribution system, travel agencies, companies, etc.). The standard procedure of responding to a guest's reservation request is first receiving the reservation inquiries, then determining room availability, and then accepting or denying the request for reservation. Depending on the needs of the hotel and the volume of business, a hotel may adopt either manual or automatic system of reservation. The reservation activities are important for the hotel as well as the guest as they help to maximize revenue and ensure a comfortable stay for guests.

KEY TERMS

Allotment: It is a set of rooms reserved by a company or a group for an event or training.

Cancellation hour: It is the time decided by a hotel (generally 6:00 p.m.) after which a non-guaranteed reservation stands cancelled and the room is released to a walk-in guest

Central reservation system: A computerized reservation system that enables guests to make a reservation in any of the participating lodging properties at any destination through a single call or mail.

Cut-off date: It is the date by which the payment for a confirmed reservation should be made in full, or it will be given the status of a non-guaranteed reservation.

Global distribution system (GDS): Worldwide computerized reservation network used as a single point of access for reserving hotel rooms, airline seats, rental cars, and other travel-related items by travel agents, online reservation sites, and large corporations.

Group reservation: Reservation for groups of fifteen or more members with a common itinerary.

Guaranteed reservation: A reservation for which the hotel has received an advance payment and confirmed to hold the room for the guest and not release it to any other guest, irrespective of whether the guest turns up or not.

Guest cycle: The four stages of a guest's interaction with the hotel—pre-arrival, arrival, stay, and departure—constitute the guest cycle.

Intersell agency: It is an agency that deals with many products such as hotel reservation, car rental, travel arrangements, tour operation, airline reservations, railway bookings etc.

No-show: It is a situation in which a guest with a room reservation does not arrive on the scheduled date and time and does not cancel the reservation as well.

Non-guaranteed reservation: A reservation in which the guest has agreed and confirmed her stay at the hotel but not guaranteed the reservation with advance payment or credit card. The hotel can cancel the reservation in case the guest does not arrive by the cancellation hour.

Overbooking: The practice of taking more reservations than the available number of rooms in the expectation that no-shows will bring the number of reservations actually used below the maximum occupancy.

Overstay: A situation in which a guest would like to stay for more days than her scheduled stay dates.

Standard operating procedure (SOP): Established procedure to be followed in carrying out a given operation.

Understay: A situation in which a guest would like to stay for lesser number of days than her scheduled stay dates.

Upselling: To try to persuade a customer to buy a more expensive item or to buy a related additional product at a discount.

REVIEW QUESTIONS

Multiple Choice Questions

1. The example of GDS is:

    a) Amadeus IT
    b) SABRE
    c) Galileo CRS
    d) All of the above

2. The Central Reservation System of Holiday Inn is known as:

    a) Wardspan
    b) Image
    c) Holidex
    d) Holiwex

3. Reservation is important for:

    a) Hotels
    b) Guests
    c) Both
    d) None of the two

4. Whitney Slips are also known as:

    a) Shannon Slips
    b) Whit slip
    c) Sher slips
    d) Kennon slip

5. In which manual system of reservation overbooking is possible?

    a) Diary system
    b) Whitney system
    c) Both
    d) None of the two

True/False

1. Reservation reports are useful for planning the expansion of the hotel.

2. Overbooking is possible in diary system of reservation.

3. GDS is among the good source for reservation request.

4. SABRE is a well-known central reservation system.

5. A hotel can refuse bookings.

Discussion Questions

1. What do you understand by guest cycle? Explain in detail.

2. Describe the four phases of the guest cycle.

3. What are the various modes of making a reservation?

4. Explain Whitney system of reservation and diary system of reservation.

5. What is a standard density chart? Give the importance of using this chart for reservation.

6. On what conditions can reservation be denied?

7. What do you understand by centralized reservation system?

8. Differentiate between guaranteed and non-guaranteed reservation.

9. Draw a neat diagram of guest reservation form.

10. What are the various sources of reservation?

Critical Thinking Questions

1. Discuss the various modes of reservation enquiry on the basis of:
    a) Speed
    b) Accuracy
    c) Economy

2. Discuss the various criteria for selecting a reservation system to be used for the hotel.

3. Discuss the importance of reservation details for:
    a) Hotels
    b) Guests

Project Work

1. You are a reservation agent of Hotel ABC. While attending a reservation call from Ms Chandni, you found that she has queries regarding whether she should guarantee her booking.
   a) Briefly explain about the benefits of guaranteed reservations.
   b) Explain the different modes of payments for guaranteed reservations.

2. Practice filling reservation forms by choosing a partner who acts as a guest for booking a room.

3. Practice telephone etiquettes and telephone booking with a partner who acts as a guest for booking a room.

Case Studies

1. The weather was bad in Bhopal on that day. The city was hit by a storm the previous night and the road conditions were unsafe. The room reservation department at Hotel Cityview found that there would be very low occupancy on that day. Two groups of 100 members each have cancelled their bookings. Due to bad weather conditions, it is expected that most of the expected arrivals will be no-shows. Mr L.K. Yadav arrives at front desk without any prior reservation. The front desk assistant recognizes him as a frequent guest.

   Discuss whether the front desk assistant should upgrade Mr L.K. Yadav. Why or why not?

2. Babloo is a reservation agent. While attending a reservation call, he found that the guest calling for reservation is a regular guest and is a member of the frequent flyer's club to whom the hotel offers 20 per cent discount on room rent and 15 per cent discount on food and beverage. The guest wants to book a room from 24 December to 26 December (Tuesday to Thursday) for the India-Pakistan test match, scheduled to be held in a stadium close to the hotel from 24 December. The hotel is expected to be full during the requested period due to Christmas celebrations on 25 December. The reservation manager has informed every reservation agent to be cautious while making bookings during the period 20 December to 7 January. Study the case and answer the following questions:
   a) Should Babloo accept the reservation request of the guest? Why or why not?
   b) Should Babloo deny the request of the guest as the hotel is expected to be sold out during the second half of December on rack rate?
   c) Suggest other alternatives to Babloo to process this reservation request.

3. Ruchi, a reservation agent, received a call from a guest for booking a single room for four days from 15 July. While checking the reservation status, she finds that on 18 July the lower category of rooms are sold out but an executive room is available (room rent of the same is Rs 850 more than the requested room type). While going through the guest history, she also finds that the guest is a frequent visitor to the hotel and a considerable amount of business is gained from him.
   a) What should Ruchi do?
   b) What alternatives can be suggested to the guest?
   c) Should Ruchi upgrade the guest for the night of 18 July on a complimentary basis? Why or why not?

CHAPTER 8

Registration

Learning Objectives:

After reading this chapter, you will be able to understand the following:
- Activities associated with the second stage of the guest cycle, i.e., arrival—pre-registration and registration.
- The various pre-registration activities, including preparing the arrival list, room availability status, and amenities vouchers.
- Formats of registration records—hard-bound register, loose-leaf register, and guest registration cards.
- Flow of the registration process—identifying guest status, completing registration records, assigning rooms and rates, establishing the payment mode, and issuing room keys.
- The check-in procedures for manual, semi automated, and fully automated hotels.

The first phase of the guest cycle deals with reservation, which we learnt in the previous chapter. The second stage–arrival–deals with the activities involved in the processes of pre-registration and registration. The activities carried out before the arrival of a guest to ensure a speedy check-in are termed as pre-registration activities. The registration process, which involves the formalization of a valid contract between a guest and a hotel, begins with the arrival of the guest at the hotel front desk. Here, we will also study how the registration activities can be hastened in order to avoid long queues at the front desk during the peak hours of guest arrivals and to enhance guests' experience.

Hotels follow different check-in procedures for different types of guests–individual, group, crew, VIP, walk-in, scanty baggage, and so on. In this chapter, we will study the steps involved in the check-in of different categories of guests.

PRE-REGISTRATION

The activities that are carried out by the front desk agents before the arrival of guests, which help accelerate the process of guest registration, are termed as pre-registration activities. The expected arrivals list is prepared on a daily basis to indicate the number and names of guests expected to arrive the next day, along with their time of arrival, date of departure, rooms requested, reservation status, special requests, and instructions. Then, the room position is calculated, i.e., the room availability status for the next day is arrived at, based on the expected arrivals and departures, and also including factors like overstays, understays, no-shows, and out-of-order rooms. Then, the amenities vouchers are prepared for the arriving guests, which are sent to the concerned departments like housekeeping and food and beverage (F&B). These vouchers instruct the departments to provide the mentioned amenities in the guest rooms, like cookies, fruits, flowers, etc., prior to the guest arrival. The front office agent then checks the condition of the vacant rooms to make sure that the rooms are ready to move in.

The front office agent next prepares the guest registration card (GRC). The information required to fill the GRC can be gathered from two sources: the reservation form and the guest history card. The information contained in these forms is used to complete the registration form. Guests can experience a quick check-in when they arrive at the registration desk, as they only have to verify the information already entered in the registration card and sign the card. The check-in of a walk-in guest takes comparatively longer as it is not supported by the pre-registration activity.

The pre-registration activity may also include room and rate assignment and the creation of guest folios (in case advance payment has been received by the hotel). Some front office managers prefer to assign the room and the rate on the arrival of a guest in order to adjust any changes in room availability. The pre-registration activity is carried out manually in manual and semi-automated systems, whereas in the case of fully-automated front office systems, the task is carried out by the system that transfers the guest's data from the reservation form and the guest history card onto the registration card. A sample registration card is shown in Fig. 8.1.

Thus, the pre-registration process informs the hotel staff about the expected arrivals and the room availability status. This allows the front desk to make necessary arrangements in advance. It also makes the check-in faster for guests.

Hotel ABC

Guest Registration Card

No.

Surname ______ First Name / Initials ______ Date of Birth ______

Company Name ______ Passport No. ______

Designation ______ Date of Issue ______

Nationality ______ Place of Issue ______

Permanent Address ______ Date of Arrival in India ______

Proposed duration of stay in India ______

Date of Arrival in Hotel ______ Time ______ Whether employed in India [ ] Yes [ ] No

Arrived from ______ Registration Certificate No. ______

Proceeding to ______ Date of Issue ______

Purpose of Visit ______ Place of Issue ______

Date of Departure from Hotel ______ Time ______

Credit Card No. ______ ***I agree to abide by the Hotel Rules & Regulations.***

 # Check-in / Check-out Time : 12 Noon

 # All valuables & cash should be deposited with the cashier. Guest's Signature Manager's Signature

FOR OFFICE USE ONLY

Nationality Code ______ Payment Code ______ Resv. No. ______

Room No.	No. of Persons		Room Rate	Billing Instructions Cash Voucher Cred. Card Company	Booked by	Initials of FOA
	Adult	Children				

Fig. 8.1 Sample guest registration card

REGISTRATION

On their arrival in a hotel, guests usually go to the reception area first. The reception area is manned by a receptionist who welcomes the guests and answers their queries. This is the first face-to-face interaction between the hotel and the guests. The reception remains a focal point of guest contact throughout their stay at the hotel. The registration activity takes place at the same desk. The guests have to fill the required details on a registration card or may have to make entries in a hotel register.

Registration is the process of gathering information from the guest that is mandatory as per the laws prevailing in the country. According to the Foreigner's Act, 1946 and the Registration of Foreigners' Rules, 1992, the innkeeper should keep the records of the guests staying in his premises as per Form F (of the Registration of Foreigners' Rules, 1992). Registration is the formalization of a valid contract between the guest and the hotel, in which the hotel offers safe and secure boarding and lodging facilities to the guest and the guest accepts to pay for the services and facilities received. In case of foreign visitors, the front desk staff should fill Form C and verify the passports and visas of guests.

Form C According to the Registration of Foreigners' Rules, 1992, Rule 14, it is obligatory on the part of the hotel owner to send information about foreigners registered at the hotel. Any person who is not an Indian national (i.e., a person holding a passport of any country other than India, except Nepal and Bhutan) is known as a foreigner. The hotel is liable to send the information in the format of Form C to the nearest Foreigner's Regional Registration Office (FRRO) or to the Local Intelligence Unit (LIU) within twenty-four hours of the arrival of a foreign national; in the case of Pakistani, Bangladeshi, and Chinese nationals, this information should reach within 12 hours to the nearest FRRO or LIU, and also to the local police station. Form C should be prepared in duplicate and serial numbered–the top copy is sent to the competent authority and the second copy is kept for permanent records for the duration as specified in the law related to the same. Figure 8.2 shows the format of Form C.

Passport The front office staff should verify the passport of foreign nationals. A passport is a document issued by a government to allow its citizens to travel abroad, and requests other governments to facilitate their passage and provide protection on a reciprocal basis. Without a valid passport a person is not permitted to move in the territory of a foreign country. Figure 8.3 provides the illustration of a passport.

The public authorities competent to issue passports and other identity documents vary from one country to another. The external affairs ministry issues passports to the citizens of India after verifying the details of the applicants from various quarters. To apply for a passport, the applicant has be a citizen of the issuing country. When a person is outside the country of her residence, the passport can be issued to her by the diplomatic or consular offices representing her country.

All passports generally bear the following information of the passport holder, though the format may vary from country to country:

- Family name/Surname
- Given name
- Nationality
- Date of birth
- Place of birth
- Gender
- Date of issue
- Holder's photograph
- Name of father/legal guardian
- Name of mother
- Name of spouse
- Address
- Validity period (expiry date)
- Children

```
┌─────────────────────────────────────────────────────────────────┐
│                          Hotel ABC                              │
│                           Form C                                │
│                          (Rule 14)                              │
│                     Hotel Arrival Report                        │
│                 (To be completed in duplicate)                  │
│                                                                 │
│                                          Sr. No.: ..............│
│                                          Date: ................ │
│ Name of the Hotel:_____                         │
│                                                                 │
│ Name of the Foreign Visitor:_____            │
│ (In full in block capitals, surname first)                      │
│ Nationality:_____                             │
│ Passport No.:_____                                │
│ Date of Issue:_____                                  │
│ Place of Issue:_____                                   │
│ Address in India: _____               │
│                                                                 │
│                                                                 │
│ Date of Arrival in India:_____                         │
│ Arrived From:_____                                 │
│ Whether Employed in India: Yes/No                               │
│ Proposed Duration of Stay in India:_____               │
│ Proposed Duration of Stay at Hotel:_____               │
│ Proceeding to:_____                           │
│ Registration Certificate No._____                   │
│ Date of Issue:_____                                   │
│ Place of Issue:_____                                   │
│                                                                 │
│                                          Manager's Signature    │
└─────────────────────────────────────────────────────────────────┘
```

Fig. 8.2   Format of Form C

- Place of issue
- Holder's signature
- Endorsement
- Emigration status
- Validity for certain countries as well as restrictions for travel to others

The terminology related to passports is generally standard around the world. There are different types of passports, some common types being:

- *Ordinary passport or tourist passport:* Issued to ordinary citizens.
- *Official passport or service passport:* Issued to government employees for work-related travel, and to accompanying dependents.
- *Diplomatic passport:* Issued to diplomats and consuls for work-related travel, and to accompanying dependents.
- *Emergency passport or temporary passport:* Issued to persons whose passports were lost or stolen, and who do not have the time to obtain replacement passports.

- *Collective passport:* Issued to defined groups for travel together to particular destinations, such as a group of school children going on a school trip to a specified country.
- *Family passport:* Issued to one member of the family, who may travel alone or with other family members. A family member who is not the passport holder can only travel with the passport holder.

In India, the following types of passport are issued under the provisions laid in the Passport Act 1967:
- *Ordinary passport:* It is dark blue in colour and is issued to any ordinary citizen of India.
- *Official passport:* It is white/grey in colour and is issued to government officials or persons on government missions.
- *Diplomatic passport:* It is red in colour and is issued to persons with a diplomatic or consular status as per international laws and customs.

Visa   Foreign nationals visiting India are required to possess a valid passport and a valid Indian visa. Visa is an endorsement on the passport, allowing the holder to enter the territory of the issuing country. It is a document or, more frequently, a stamp in a passport, authorizing the bearer to visit a country for specific purposes and for a specific length of time. However, the issuance of a visa may not be treated

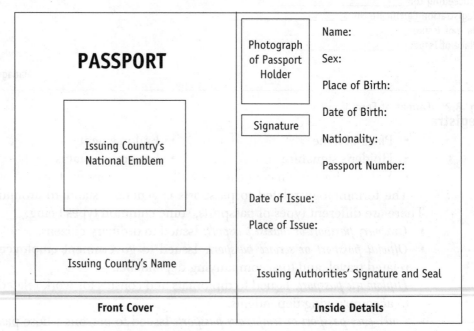

Fig. 8.3   Illustration of a passport

as a guarantee to enter into the foreign territory. The bearer may be subjected to inspection at the port of entry and may be asked to produce the documents presented at the time of the procurement of the visa.

The Consular Passport and Visa (CPV) Division of the Ministry of External Affairs issues Indian visas to foreign nationals through various Indian missions abroad. Depending upon the nature of visit, the following types of visa may be issued:

Immigrant/Permanent visa   It authorizes the holder of the visa to settle permanently in the county issuing the visa. This type of visa is rarely issued by countries and there are some countries that never issue such type of visa.

Temporary/Non-immigrant visa   This type of visa is issued for a specific duration only. The person holding such a visa will have to return back to the home country after the expiry of the term of the visa. Temporary visas are of the following types:

- *Tourist visa*: Issued for a limited period for leisure travel only, no business activities allowed.
- *Student visa*: Issued to students who have got admission in universities located in the issuing country. It is issued for the duration of the course of study.
- *Business visa*: Issued for business related activities, but precludes permanent employment.
- *Work visa*: Issued for approved employment in the host country, with longer validity than a business visa.
- *Transit visa*: Issued for passing through the countries that fall en route the final destination; valid for 15 days or less.

The front office staff should be able to identify different types of visas to complete the registration process and to verify the credentials of guests. This also helps to understand the guest's purpose of visit and to make arrangements for them accordingly.

Registration Records

The registration activity is carried out at the front desk. The first step in the guest registration process begins with acquiring basic information about the guest, like name, address, purpose of visit, duration of stay, special requests, affiliation, designation, etc. The information gathered during the process of registration is stored as the registration record, which is based on Form F of the Registration of Foreigners' Rule, 1992. Hotels have different ways of posting and storing registration records. Depending upon the requirements of a hotel, the registration records may be maintained in a hard-bound register, loose-leaf register, or guest registration card.

Hard-bound Register   Hard-bound registers are normally used by small hotels. In such a register, all the pages are bound into a thick book and it can be used for a long time. The format of the register is shown in Fig. 8.4. The major advantages of using hard-bound registers are:

- All the records for the duration are available in a single book.
- Wastage of paper is minimal.
- No filing is required.

There are certain disadvantages associated with the use of hard-bound registers for registration records. Some of the major disadvantages are:

- If the book is misplaced, all the records for that entire duration are lost.
- Only one guest can register at a time.
- During peak hours of guest arrival, guests will have to form a queue and wait for their turn for registration.
- Privacy of guests cannot be maintained.
- Pre-registration is not possible.
- Registration of groups/crews will take more time.
- As it is very bulky and is used for a long duration of time, the register might look shabby at the counter.

Loose-leaf Register   A loose-leaf register (refer to the format given in Fig. 8.4) contains the same data as a hard-bound register, with the difference that the pages are not bound. One new page is used everyday. The following are the major advantages of using a loose-leaf register:

- The privacy of the guest can be maintained to some extent.
- If a sheet is lost, only one day's records are lost.
- It's convenient to hand over to guests to fill their details.

The major disadvantages associated with the use of a loose-leaf register are:

- The pages may be lost easily.
- The space in the sheet goes waste if there is not enough number of guests on a particular day.
- Only one guest can register at a time.
- Pre-registration is not possible.
- The sheets have to be filed.

Guest Registration Card   To overcome problems of hard-bound and loose-leaf registers, most hotels use individual guest registration cards (GRC) for registration records. The format of a GRC is shown in Fig. 8.1. GRCs may be used in duplicate or triplicate as per the policy of the hotel. They are given to the guest at the time of arrival to complete the registration formality. The following advantages are associated with the use of individual GRCs:

- The efficiency of the front desk can be increased as many guests can register themselves at the same time using different cards.

S. No.	Name of Guest	Address	Pax	Nationality	Passport No.	Date of Arrival in India	Whether Employed in India	Registration Details	Proposed Duration of Stay in India	Date and Time of Arrival in Hotel	Purpose of Visit	Date and Time of Departure	Signature of Guest
						IN CASE OF FOREIGNER GUESTS							

Fig. 8.4   Format of a hotel register (hard-bound and loose-leaf)

- As each guest fills a separate card, the privacy of guests can be maintained.
- It is possible to pre-register guests.

The major disadvantages of using individual GRCs for registration activity are as follows.

- They are quite expensive.
- If not stored properly, they can be lost or misplaced.

Registration Process

The registration process involves many stages. The different stages of the registration process are shown in Fig. 8.5.

Identification of Guests   The identification of a guest's status is important as the hotel processes the registration of guests with confirmed reservations and walk-ins in a slightly different way. The front desk agents verify the status of guests with confirmed reservations by referring to the day's arrival list. As the pre-registration activity has been carried out for these guests, they have a speedy check-in. For walk-in guests, the front desk first refers to the room availability status. If the room

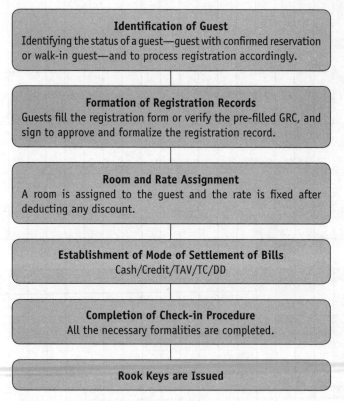

Fig. 8.5   The registration process

is available, the front office staff collects the relevant information from guests for filling the GRC. The check-in of these guests usually takes longer than the guests with confirmed reservations.

Formation of Registration Records A guest fills the registration form (or verifies the information in the pre-filled GRC) and signs it. The guest's signature completes and formalizes the registration record. On the basis of this record, the hotel develops other hotel records like guest folio, visitor's tabular ledger, arrival notification slip, guest history card, etc. The completed registration record is a legal requirement; this should be stored for a minimum period of three years or as required by the law prevailing in the state. The same records can be accessed by a competent local authority as and when required.

Room and Rate Assignment After completing the registration record, the next step is to allocate and assign a room of the specific category as requested by the guest. In case of a walk-in guest, the hotel may exercise the option of upselling. The details regarding the availability of the different types of rooms and their corresponding rates help the front office in deciding which room should be assigned to the guest. While assigning a room, the guest's preferences, like floor level, proximity to the elevator, view of the room, colour scheme, etc., should be kept in mind.

Establishment of the Mode of Settlement of Bills The determination of the guests' credibility and the mode by which they will be settling their accounts is very important for the hotel. Hotels prefer cash and cash equivalent modes (traveller's cheque, demand draft, and credit/charge card) of account settlement. Other modes include travel agent (TA) vouchers or bill to company. The credibility of a guest can be determined by:
- Asking the guest to produce her credit card at the time of arrival and by swiping the same for authorization from the credit card company.
- The guest may be asked to produce the TA voucher/authorization letter from the company, in case the bills would be settled by the TA or company.
- Advance deposit may also be asked at the time of check-in.

Completion of Check-in Procedure and Issuance of Room Keys After the front desk registers a guest, assigns her a room, and establishes the mode of account settlement, it issues the room keys to the guest. A bell boy is called to escort the guest and to take the guest luggage to the assigned room. The front desk agent carries out the following activities after every check-in:
- Updates room status report.
- Prepares arrival notification slips and sends them to the concerned departments in the hotel.

- Creates guest folio.
- Fills Form C (in case of foreign nationals) and sends the same to the concerned authority.

CHECK-IN PROCEDURES

The check-in procedure involves all stages from the arrival of a guest to the issuance of the room key to the guest. In case of manual or semi-automated operation systems, the process begins as the guests arrive at a hotel and are greeted by the front office staff, subsequent to which they complete the registration formalities, and finally the guests are assigned rooms and issued the room key by the front office personnel. In a fully automated system, the same activity is performed automatically by self-service terminals located in the hotel lobby, which look like ATM machines (refer Exhibit 8.1).

Check-in Procedures in Manual/Semi-automated Hotels

The check-in procedure varies for guests with confirmed reservation and walk-in guests. It may take a specialized form in case of VIPs, groups, crews, scanty

Exhibit 8.1   Self Service Terminals

Leading hoteliers such as Hilton, Marriott, Fairmont, and Starwood have self-service applications for guest check-in and check-out. A guest-operated front desk processing station is all contained in an upright stand alone housing (see Fig. 8.17). The housing contains a touch screen and keyboard for guests to input information, and a signature pad in an upper portion. The housing front face contains a credit card swipe device for scanning a credit, debit or brand card, a slot for dispensing a receipt from a printer inside the housing, and a key slot for dispensing a key card, generated by a key making device within the housing.

Some terminals also contain a slot for accepting various currency denominations and a slot for dispensing currency change. The processing station is connected by a network data cable to a property management system (PMS) at the hotel.

It caters to guests who want a fast, seamless transit through the hotel lobby. In one quick, efficient process, the machine assigns a room in accordance to the guest's preference, dispenses the room key, and provides the loyalty card numbers to guests. The guests just have to use their credit/debit/charge card.

Guests can review their reservation details—name, room type, bed type, smoking preference, check-out date, hotel loyalty card number, and payment card information—before accepting a transaction. If the requested room is not available, a list of alternative rooms is shown.

These rooms match the guest's requests as closely as possible and have the same room rate. At the end of their stay, guests can review their folio and check out promptly in the same way.

baggage guests, and foreigners. The check-in procedures of guests with different status are discussed as under:

- Guests with confirmed reservation
- Walk-in guests
- VIPs
- Groups/crews (domestic and international)
- Scanty baggage guests
- Foreign nationals

Guests with Confirmed Reservation   The procedure for the check-in of guests with confirmed reservation (refer Fig. 8.6) involves the following steps:

- As the guests arrive at the hotel, the front office staff should welcome them and ask them if they have confirmed reservation.

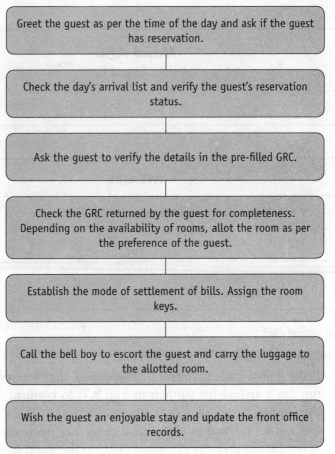

Greet the guest as per the time of the day and ask if the guest has reservation.

Check the day's arrival list and verify the guest's reservation status.

Ask the guest to verify the details in the pre-filled GRC.

Check the GRC returned by the guest for completeness. Depending on the availability of rooms, allot the room as per the preference of the guest.

Establish the mode of settlement of bills. Assign the room keys.

Call the bell boy to escort the guest and carry the luggage to the allotted room.

Wish the guest an enjoyable stay and update the front office records.

Fig. 8.6   Front office tasks for the check-in of guests with confirmed reservation

Hotel ABC

Date: 30 January 2008

Name	No. of Guests		Type of Room	No. of Room Nights	Arrival time	Remarks
	Adults	Child				
Mr Sanjay Singh	2	2	Duplex	3	10:15 a.m.	Baby sitter required
Mr M.S.K. Ahmed	1		Single	2	12:15 p.m.	Garden facing
Mr Vibas Sarkar	2		Double	5	09:00 a.m.	Honeymoon couple
Mr Hriday Nath Singh	2	1	One double, one single	2	11:25 a.m.	Interconnecting room
Ms Pooja	2		Double	2	02:30 p.m.	Sunset view

Fig. 8.7   Sample arrival list

Hotel ABC
Arrival Errand Card

Bell Boy Name:				Call Time:
Name of Guest:				Room No.:

Articles

Suitcase	Hand Bag	Package	Briefcase	Overcoat
Others				
Signature (Bell Captain)				Signature (Receptionist)

Fig. 8.8   Arrival errand card

- If the guests have confirmed reservation, the front office agent should check the day's arrival list (shown in Fig. 8.7) to confirm the reservation status of the guests.
- Once the reservation status of a guest has been confirmed, the front office agent should give the pre-filled GRC to the guest to verify the details.
- When the guest has signed the GRC, the front office agent should check if all the details have been filled in, including the billing instructions.

Hotel ABC

Bell Captain _____   Sheet No. _____

Shift _____   Date _____

Room No.	Bell Boy Name	Arrival Time	Departure Time	Service Call Time		Remarks
				From	To	

Bell Boy's Signature.: 1. _____   2. _____   3. _____   4. _____

Bell Captain Signature.: _____

Fig. 8.9 Sample lobby control sheet

- The front office agent should check the availability of rooms as per the guest's preference, and allot the room accordingly.
- The front office agent should issue the room keys to the guest and authorize a bell boy to escort the guest and carry the guest luggage to the room. The bell captain will fill the information in the arrival errand card (Fig. 8.8) and lobby control sheet (Fig. 8.9).
- The front office agent should wish the guest an enjoyable stay at the hotel.

Walk-in Guests   The check-in procedure for walk-in guests (refer Fig. 8.10) involves the following steps:

- As the guests arrive at the hotel, the front office staff should welcome them and ask them if they have confirmed reservation.
- If the guest does not have a reservation, the front office staff should check room availability status for the duration of stay requested by the guest. If rooms are available for the requested duration, the front office should process the reservation and proceed with the check-in activity of the walk-in guest. However, in case of undesirable or blacklisted guests, the font office should

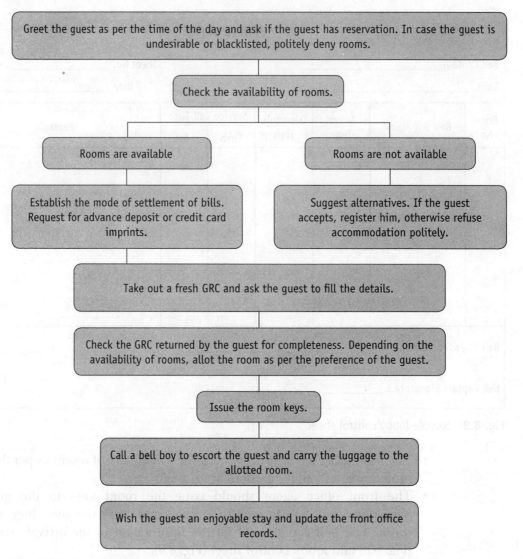

Fig. 8.10   Front office tasks for the check-in of walk-in guests

politely deny reservation even if the rooms are available. (It is essential to ascertain the credibility of a walk-in guest—the front office may request for credit card imprint or advance deposit.)

- The front office should request the guest to fill the GRC and assist the guest in doing so.
- Once the guest has filled and signed the GRC, the front office agent should check it for completeness.
- The front office agent should check the availability of rooms as per the guest's preference, and allot the room accordingly.

- The front office agent should issue the room keys to the guest and authorize the bell desk personnel to escort the guest and carry the guest luggage to the room. The bell captain will fill the information in the arrival errand card and lobby control sheet (as shown in Fig. 8.8 and 8.9).
- The front office agent should wish the guest an enjoyable stay at the hotel.

VIP Guests Very important persons (VIPs) include heads of states, ministers, senior media personnel, sports personnel, film stars, rock stars, travel writers, top executives of corporate houses, CEOs of large business houses, senior defence personnel, famous public figures, etc. They get special treatment and attention from the hotel staff due to their VIP status. The check-in process of VIPs may start with their arrival at the airport. The role of the hotel in welcoming political VIPs at airport is minimal due to security reasons. In the case of corporate heads of business houses, the hotel representative may receive them at the airport and escort them to the hotel room. The registration process may be carried out during the transfer the from the airport to the hotel or in the hotel room. The check-in procedure of VIP guests (refer Fig. 8.11) involves the following steps:

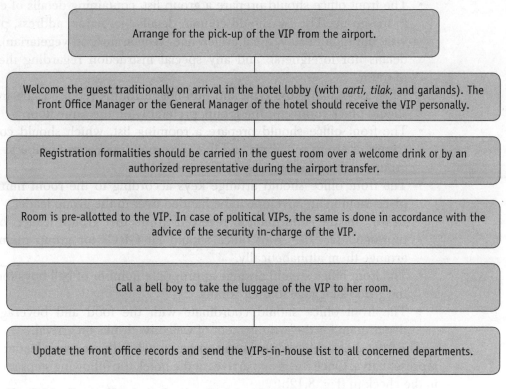

Arrange for the pick-up of the VIP from the airport.

Welcome the guest traditionally on arrival in the hotel lobby (with *aarti, tilak,* and garlands). The Front Office Manager or the General Manager of the hotel should receive the VIP personally.

Registration formalities should be carried in the guest room over a welcome drink or by an authorized representative during the airport transfer.

Room is pre-allotted to the VIP. In case of political VIPs, the same is done in accordance with the advice of the security in-charge of the VIP.

Call a bell boy to take the luggage of the VIP to her room.

Update the front office records and send the VIPs-in-house list to all concerned departments.

Fig. 8.11 Front office tasks for the check-in of VIP guests

- The hotel may arrange for the pick-up of a VIP guest from the airport. Depending upon the status the VIP, the pick-up vehicle may vary from a luxury car to a limousine.
- When the guest arrives at the hotel, the front office staff should give him a traditional welcome—*tilak*, garlanding, and *aarti*. The General Manager (GM) of the hotel and the Front Office Manager (FOM) should also be present to welcome the VIP.
- The registration formalities are mostly completed in advance by an authorized representative of the VIP. Otherwise, they can be completed in the guest room over a welcome drink.
- The GM or FOM should escort the VIP to his room.
- The front office should send the arrival notification slip and any special instruction of the VIP to all the concerned departments.

Domestic and International Groups or Crews The check-in procedure for a group or crew requires specialized pre-registration activity as a group contains a large number of people who have to be registered at the same time. The following pre-registration activities are required for the check-in of a group/crew (refer Fig. 8.12a):

- The front office should prepare a group list, containing details of each guest in the group. The list should contain details like name, address, purpose of visit, duration of stay, meal preference (vegetarian/non vegetarian), passport details (for foreigners), and any special instruction regarding the location of room.
- After ascertaining the type and number of rooms required, the front office should block rooms for the group, preferably on the same floor.
- The front office should prepare a rooming list, which should contain the names of group members and the corresponding room numbers. A sample group rooming list is shown in Fig. 8.13.
- The front office should arrange keys according to the room numbers and place them in an envelope to be handed over to the group leader.
- Based on the information received from the group leader or airport representative, the front office should fill GRCs for group members and arrange them alphabetically.
- The front office should arrange appropriate number of bell boys for carrying the group's luggage to their rooms.
- The front office should coordinate with the food and beverage service department for the arrangement of welcome drinks on arrival.

The front desk agent should be in constant touch with the group leader or airport representative. Once the group arrives at the hotel, the following steps are involved in the check-in (Fig. 8.12b):

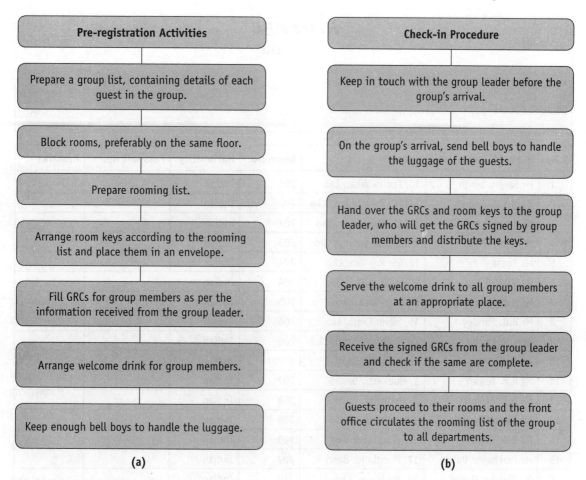

Pre-registration Activities	Check-in Procedure
Prepare a group list, containing details of each guest in the group.	Keep in touch with the group leader before the group's arrival.
Block rooms, preferably on the same floor.	On the group's arrival, send bell boys to handle the luggage of the guests.
Prepare rooming list.	Hand over the GRCs and room keys to the group leader, who will get the GRCs signed by group members and distribute the keys.
Arrange room keys according to the rooming list and place them in an envelope.	
Fill GRCs for group members as per the information received from the group leader.	Serve the welcome drink to all group members at an appropriate place.
Arrange welcome drink for group members.	Receive the signed GRCs from the group leader and check if the same are complete.
Keep enough bell boys to handle the luggage.	Guests proceed to their rooms and the front office circulates the rooming list of the group to all departments.
(a)	(b)

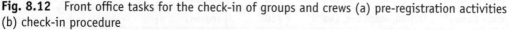

Fig. 8.12 Front office tasks for the check-in of groups and crews (a) pre-registration activities (b) check-in procedure

- When the guest vehicle arrives at the portico, bell boys should handle the guest luggage. They should identify the luggage of individual guests and put the luggage tags as per the rooming list. Then they should transfer the luggage to the respective rooms using luggage trolleys.
- The front office agent should escort the group leader to the reception desk to complete the registration formalities. The receptionist should hand over the room keys and the registration forms of all the members to the leader, who can get the GRCs signed by the group members and distribute room keys.
- Meanwhile, the front office staff should organize welcome drinks for the group members in a pre-scheduled area.
- Once the group leader hands over the signed registration cards at the front desk, the guests may proceed to their respective rooms.

Hotel ABC
Rooming List

S. No..............
Date:..............

Source of Booking:..
Name of Group Leader/Airport Representative:...................................

S.No.	Name of Guest	Address	Room No.	Nationality	Passport No.	Remarks
1	Mr Sanjay Singh	10, Indira Vihar, Lko	701	Indian		
2	Mr M.S.K. Ahmed	1/112, Preet Vihar, Lko	702	Indian		
3	Mr Vibas Sarkar	1/111, Ramnagar, Lko	702	Indian		
4	Mr Hriday Nath Singh	7/56, Star Colony, Lko	703	Indian		
5	Ms Pooja	12/45, Raj Vila, Lko	704	Indian		
6	Ms Kavita	2, Housing Plan, Lko	704	Indian		
7	Mr Neeraj Pandey	5, Gold Plaza, Lko	705	Indian		
8	Mr B.B. Pandey	15, Silver Cross, Lko	706	Indian		
9	Mr K.N. Pandey	14, Diamand Land, Lko	706	Indian		
10	Ms Maya	1, Mudkatti, Basti	707	Indian		
11	Mr R.P. Tewari	1, Mudkatti, Basti	707	Indian		
12	Mr H.R. Tewari	2, Mudkatti, Basti	708	Indian		
13	Mr Suresh Tewari	3, Mudkatti, Basti	708	Indian		
14	Mr B.P. Dewdi	17, Plantland, Basti	709	Indian		
15	Mr Prabhakar Dubey	17, Plantland, Basti	709	Indian		
16	Mr Diwakar Dubey	22, Mediland, Lko	710	Indian		
17	Mr Vikas Dubey	20, Mediland, Lko	710	Indian		
18	Mr S.P. Mishra	11, Gandhinagar	711	Indian		

Front Office Assistant

Fig. 8.13   Rooming list

- The office agent should ask the group leader about the group's activities, meal schedules, wake-up calls, and other requirements, and make a note of the same.
- The front office cashier should prepare a master folio for the group and individual folios for each member of the group after the mode of payment is settled.
- The front desk should distribute copies of the rooming list of the group to different departments—housekeeping, telephone exchange, and room service—in order to inform them about the arrival of the group.

Scanty Baggage Guests A guest who arrives at the front desk requesting for accommodation and is carrying very little or no baggage is known as a scanty baggage guest. The bell boy carrying the guest luggage should report the same at the front desk. The following steps are involved in the check-in procedure (refer Fig. 8.14) of scanty baggage guests:

- The bell boy should inform the front desk about the scanty baggage.
- For registering a scanty baggage guest, the front desk assistant should take the authorization from the duty manager (DM).
- The registration formalities should be completed as in the case of walk-in guests.
- An advance payment for the entire duration of stay may be asked from the guest.

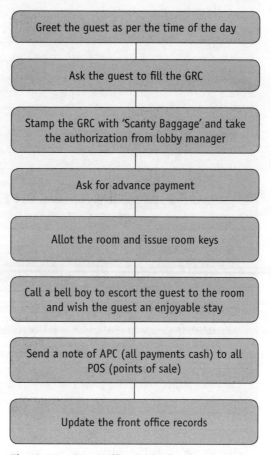

Greet the guest as per the time of the day

Ask the guest to fill the GRC

Stamp the GRC with 'Scanty Baggage' and take the authorization from lobby manager

Ask for advance payment

Allot the room and issue room keys

Call a bell boy to escort the guest to the room and wish the guest an enjoyable stay

Send a note of APC (all payments cash) to all POS (points of sale)

Update the front office records

Fig. 8.14 Front office tasks for the check-in of scanty baggage guest

- The front office assistant should imprint the 'Scanty Baggage' stamp on the guest registration card.
- The front office assistant should prepare APC (all payment cash) slips and send to all POS (points of sales).
- The front office assistant should allot a room and hand over the room key to the guest. A bell boy should escort the guest to the room.

Foreign Guests   The check-in procedure for foreigners (Fig. 8.15) is the same as that of domestic guests, with the exception that Form C has to be filled for registering a foreign guest. It is also called hotel arrival report. Diplomats and NRIs do not have to fill this form. The hotel staff should also check the validity of the guest's passport and visa.

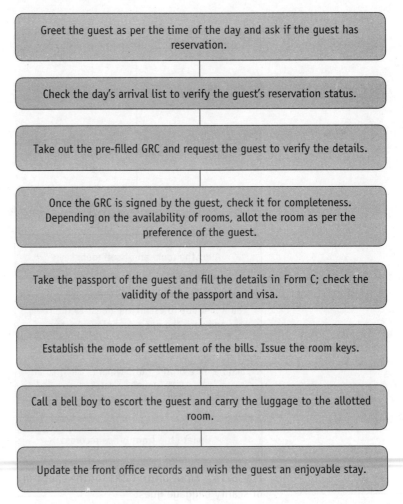

Fig. 8.15   Front office tasks for the check-in of foreign guests

Check-in Procedure in Fully Automated Hotels

In fully automated hotels, guests can register themselves at self check-in terminals without the intervention of hotel employees. By installing self-service terminals, hotels reduce the waiting time for check-in and thus offer a superior customer service experience to guests. This also gives the hotel staff more opportunity to look after the other hospitality needs of guests.

Self check-in terminals are an outcome of the advancement of technology and 'do-it-yourself' competency in guests. A self check-in terminal is like an interactive ATM machine, which may be located at the airport or at a convenient place in the hotel lobby. The use of such machines reduces manpower requirements. The check-in procedure is described in Fig. 8.16. Guests with confirmed reservations can check into the hotel without any assistance from the hotel staff, simply by operating the self check-in terminal and using their credit cards. They are assigned a room by the terminal and the room keys are also dispensed by the machine. It also sends arrival notifications to other departments instantaneously. The efficiency of the front desk is increased when such terminals are used as it reduces the load on front office agents. However, some customers may feel the lack of human touch in using self check-in terminals.

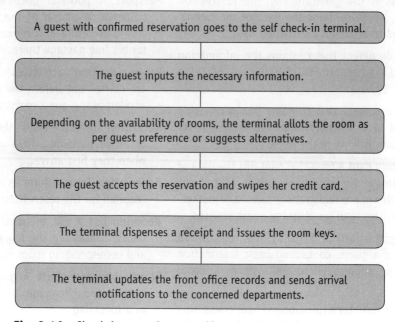

Fig. 8.16 Check-in procedure at self service terminals

SUMMARY

In the present chapter, we have studied the second phase of the guest cycle, i.e., arrival. The activities carried out before the guest arrival—that ensure the speedy check-in of the guest—are termed as pre-registration activities. These activities include the preparation of the guest arrival list, room availability status, amenities report, and GRCs.

The registration of a guest at the front desk involves legal implications for both the hotel and the guest, as a reservation is a valid contract between the two. According to the law, it is mandatory for hotels to maintain registration records of their guests, which they may do in hard-bound registers, loose-leaf registers, or guest registration cards. The registration process involves the identification of guest status, the formation of registration records, room and rate assignments, the establishment of the mode of settlement of bills, the completion of the check-in procedure, the issuance of room keys, and the generation of relevant documents during the registration process.

In manual or semi-automated operation systems, the check-in process involves the manual completion of registration formalities. In a fully automated system, the same activity is performed automatically by self-service terminals located at convenient places like the hotel lobby or the airport.

KEY TERMS

Arrival list A list generated by the reservation section, which contains the data of the guests' expected to arrive on a particular day.

Form C A document that contains the information required to be sent to FRRO/LIU in case of foreign guests.

Form F A document that contains the information required to be maintained by the innkeeper for all visitors arriving in the hotel.

Guest history card A form that contains the data of guests frequently visiting the property. This document helps in pre-registration, sales, and marketing activities, and for planning guest services.

Guest Registration Card (GRC) The registration record of a guest, containing basic information like name, address, purpose of visit, duration of stay, etc., as per Form F.

Hard-bound register A thick, bound book containing the registration records of a hotel.

Loose-leaf register The pages of this book, containing the registration records of a hotel, are not bound and one new page is used everyday.

Passport A political document recognizing the holder as a citizen of the country granting it, and is in nature of a request to other countries for his free passage there.

Pre-registration activities The activities that are carried out before the arrival of a guest to accelerate the guest registration.

Reception The place inside the entrance of a hotel or office building where guests or visitors go when they first arrive.

Reservation form A form used to gather the data required for the reservation of a specific guest.

Rooming list A list prepared for the groups and crews, containing the names of group members and corresponding room numbers.

Scanty baggage guest A guest who arrives at a hotel without luggage, or only with a briefcase or a hand bag.

Visa Visa is an endorsement on the passport, allowing the holder entry into the territory of the issuing country.

REVIEW QUESTIONS

Multiple Choice Questions

1. Data for pre-filling of guest registration card is obtained from:
   a) Reservation form   b) Guest history card
   c) Both   d) None of the above

2. In which of the following conditions can a hotel refuse accommodation to walk-in guests even though enough number of vacant rooms is available?
   a) Guests are disorderly dressed
   b) Guests are in drunken state
   c) Guests are suffering from contagious disease
   d) All of the above

3. Indian government issues the following types of passport:
   a) Ordinary   b) Official
   c) Diplomatic   d) All of the above

4. The non-immigrant visa may be of the following type:
   a) Student visa   b) Tourist visa
   c) Work visa   d) All of the above

5. After every check-in, front desk carries out which of the following activities?
   a) Updating room status
   b) Preparing arrival notification slip
   c) Creating guest folio
   d) All of the above

True/False

1. The hotel register is also known as red book.

2. Form F requires the necessary data to be taken from each and every hotel guest.

3. The check-in procedure of walk-in guests differs from the check-in procedure of guests with confirmed reservation.

4. The guest who arrives at a hotel with very little or no baggage is known as walk-in guest.

5. The registration activity of VIPs is carried out at the reception counter.

Fill in the blanks

1. The innkeeper should keep the records as contained in _____ of The Registration of Foreigners Rules, 1992.

2. The registration of a scanty baggage guest requires authorization from _____ manager.

3. Filling _____ is mandatory in case of the registration of a foreigner guest.

4. One must have _____ and _____ document for travelling to a foreign country.

5. _____ is a proof of nationality.

Discussion Questions

1. What do you understand by pre-registration activities? Explain the importance of pre-arrival activities.

2. What is registration? Explain the legal implications of registration, for the guest and for the hotel.

3. Explain the flow of registration process.

4. Explain Form F and Form C.

5. Explain the check-in procedure of guests with confirmed reservation.

6. Explain the check-in procedure of walk-in guests.

7. Explain the check-in procedure of VIPs.

8. Explain the check-in procedure of groups/crews—domestic and international.

9. Explain the check-in procedure of scanty baggage guests.

10. Explain the check-in procedure of foreign guests.

11. What is a self check-in terminal? What are the advantages and disadvantages of having the same?

CRITICAL THINKING QUESTIONS

1. Explain what the front desk agent should do if a guest wishes to check-in early at 6:30 in the morning when the hotel's check-in time is 12 noon.

2. Explain the reasons why a guest history card is useful to a hotel.

3. A walk-in guest can be harmful to the hotel as well as to the other resident guests. Comment.

PROJECT WORK

1. Study the details contained in reservation forms and guest history cards of different hotels and use them in filling GRCs for pre-registration of guests with confirmed reservations.

2. Visit a hotel and collect the formats that are used in the hotel during the check-in of a guest. Practise the check-in procedure by choosing a partner who acts as guest.

CASE STUDIES

1. Raghu is a receptionist in Hotel Shalom. One day a guest arrives at the front desk and enquires about the availability of a room for three nights. There are fifteen rooms available for the requested duration. However, while talking with the guest, Raghu notices that the guest is heavily drunk though he is behaving decently. What should Raghu do in such situation?
   a) Should he register the guest for the requested duration? Why or why not?
   b) Should he deny accommodation to the guest? Why or why not?
   c) Suggest alternatives to Raghu, along with reasons.

2. A walk-in guest requests for a room for a ten-day stay. The receptionist checks and finds that he could get a room. However, while processing the request of the guest, the receptionist finds out that the guest is blacklisted in the hotel. The receptionist also knows that it is a slack period for the hotel and that most of the hotel rooms are vacant. Should the receptionist accept or reject the reservation request? Give reasons.

3. Hotel Mountain View is a hill resort located at a remote place. During monsoon season, the hotel suffers from very lean occupancy. In the month of July, the room status shows that most of the hotel rooms are vacant. Kamal, a frequent visitor to the hotel, arrives at the hotel with a confirmed reservation for a standard room. The receptionist can see that most of the rooms are vacant, and as per the guest history, Kamal had been very upset during his peak season visit to the hotel when he was not provided a room with a view of the sunrise. Due to the availability of rooms, the receptionist sees a chance to build better business relations with Kamal and contemplates upgrading the guest. The hotel has standard rooms, executive rooms, suites, and cottages. The hotel tariff is as under:

S. No.	Type of Room	Rent
1.	Standard Room	Rs 2,500
2.	Executive Room	Rs 3,500
3.	Suite	Rs 5,500
4.	Cottage	Rs 6,500

a) Should the receptionist upgrade Kamal?
b) If the receptionist decides to upgrade Kamal, which higher category of room should be offered to the guest?

CHAPTER 9

Guest Services

Learning Objectives:

After reading this chapter, you will be able to understand the following:
- The importance of guest services.
- Handling of guest mails, messages, and keys.
- Procedures for guest paging, issuing safety deposit locker, and guest room change.
- Handling left luggage and wake-up calls.
- Resolving guest complaints.

In the previous chapter, we learnt about the pre-registration and registration activities and processes involved in the second stage of the guest cycle, i.e., arrival. We also learnt about various check-in procedures in manual, semi-automated, and fully automated hotels. Once guests check into a hotel, they avail the various services and facilities offered by the hotel during their stay. This is the third phase of the guest cycle. This stage is very important for the hotel as the guests' experience is crucial in generating repeat business and positive word-of-mouth publicity. A guest's experience is primarily based on the level of services and facilities offered by the hotel. So the hotel staff should provide various services to guests in a caring and personalized manner to ensure that they come back to the hotel and recommend it to their colleagues and friends.

VARIOUS GUEST SERVICES

During a guest's stay in a hotel, the front office staff provides various kinds of guest services. These services may vary from hotel to hotel and from guest to guest. Some guests require that the hotel attends to their messages, mails, telephone calls, and visitors when they are not in the hotel. They may also want to keep their valuables and important documents in safety lockers. They also might require to be woken up at particular times and to be reminded of certain tasks and meetings by reminder services. Depending on the guest's requirements, the front office takes care of the guest's mails, messages, keys, and left luggage. It also handles guest paging and guest complaints, as well as arranges safety deposit lockers, guest room changes, and wake-up calls.

Handling Guest Mail

When guests are away from their homes, they need a contact address where they can receive any urgent mails, calls, parcels, or faxes. During their stay in a hotel, guests may provide their family and clients the contact details of their hotel for any urgent communication. Thus, they may receive letters, parcels, and packets at the hotel address. All the mails addressed to the hotel are received by the front desk, bell desk, or information desk as per the house customs. Mails can be divided in two categories (Fig. 9.1): incoming mails (which are received by the hotel on behalf of its staff and guests) and outgoing mails (which are sent by the hotel staff and guests).

Incoming Mails   The person who receives the incoming mails at the hotel stamps them with the date and time of receipt. The mails are sorted as guest mails or hotel mails and then they are arranged in alphabetical order. The hotel mails are further divided into official mails and employee mails. The hotel mails are delivered to the concerned departments and the employee mails are sent to the time office to be placed in the mail display boards, from where the employees may collect their mails. The guest mails are delivered in the guest rooms by the bell boys. If a guest is not present in the room, the mails are placed in the key rack and delivered to the guest when she arrives at the front desk to collect the room key.

Incoming mails may be of two types: ordinary mail and registered mail.

Ordinary mail   The mails whose delivery record is not maintained by the delivering agency are known as ordinary mails. Hotels keep a record of all mails received at the mail receiving desk in a mail log book, as shown in Fig. 9.2.

Registered mail   The mails whose delivery record is maintained by the delivering agency are known as registered mails. The postman maintains the record of delivery by asking the addressee to sign the delivery report as a token of receipt of

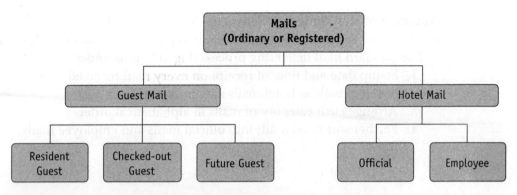

Fig. 9.1   Types of mails received by the hotel

Hotel ABC						
Incoming Mail Log Book						
S. No.	**Date and Time of Receipt**	**Name of addressee**	**Type of Mail**	**Delivered to**	**Signature**	**Remarks**
124786	25/01/2009 12:35 p.m.	Mr Dinesh Dubey	Registered	Time office		
124787	25/01/2009 01:15 p.m.	General Manager	Ordinary	GM office		
124788	25/01/2009 02:30 p.m.	Mr K.K. Shukla	Parcel	Front desk		
124789	26/01/2009 03:15 p.m.	Mr R.P. Tewari	Insured mail	Front desk		
124790	26/01/2009 03:20 p.m.	Mrs Kamla Tewari	Ordinary	Front desk		
124791	26/01/2009 03:25 p.m.	Ms Suman Tewari	Ordinary	Front desk		
124792	26/01/2009 03:25 p.m.	Mr Satish Chandra Pandey	Ordinary	Front desk		
124793	25/01/2009 04:35 p.m.	Mr Ramesh Dubey	Registered	Front desk		

Fig. 9.2   Mail log book

the mail. It is advisable not to accept tampered registered mails. When registered mails are received, they are recorded in the mail log book and the guest's signature is taken at the time of delivery (i.e., when they collect the mail from the front desk) as shown in Fig. 9.2.

Procedure of Mail Delivery   The mails received by a hotel on behalf of its guests are delivered according to the mail handling procedure followed by the hotel.

The standard mail delivering process (Fig. 9.3) is as under:

1. Stamp date and time of receipt on every mail received.
2. Sort the mails as hotel mails and guest mails.
3. Arrange each category of mails in alphabetical order.
4. Further sort hotel mails into official mails and employee mails.

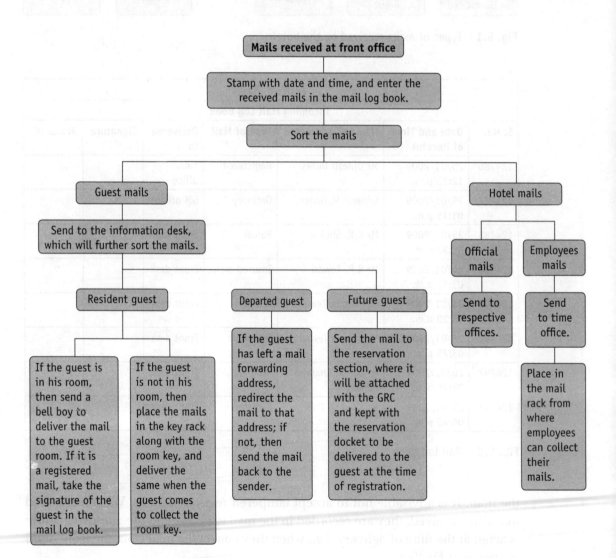

Fig. 9.3   Procedure of mail handling

5. Send employee mails to time office for delivering to the concerned employees.
6. Deliver the official mails to the concerned office.
7. Send guest mails to the information section.
8. The information section assistant will further sort the mails into the following categories:
   - Resident guest (staying in the hotel)
   - Checked-out guest (departed from the hotel)
   - Future guest (guest with a confirmed reservation for future dates)
9. The mails of resident guests are delivered in the guest rooms by the bell boys, if the guests are present in the rooms. If they are out of the hotel (and the room keys are in the key rack), the mails are placed in the key rack and delivered when they come to collect the room keys.
10. The mails of checked-out guests are sent to the back office, from where the mail forwarding address is taken and mails are re-directed to that address. The format of the mail forwarding address slip is shown in Fig. 9.4. In case there is no forwarding address, the mails are sent back to the sender.

Hotel ABC

Mail Forwarding Address Slip

This address will be in file for 10 days, unless otherwise requested. Please fill it and hand over at the reception.

Forwarding instructions: Forward until: _____

                                                  Hold until: _____

Forwarding Address: ....

....

....

....

                                                            Name & Signature of Guest

		Record of Forwarded Mails		
S. No.	Date	Type of mail	Forwarding address	Forwarded by

Fig. 9.4   Mail forwarding address slip

11. The mails of future guests are sent to the reservation section, where they are placed along with the reservation record. On the date of the arrival of the guest, the mails are attached with the pre-filled registration card and delivered to the guest at the time of registration.

Outgoing Mails   If a guest wants to send any personal mails, the hotel provides the service of collecting the mails from the guest room and posting them. The charges for the service are added to the guest account through a miscellaneous charge voucher (Fig. 9.5).

The miscellaneous voucher is authenticated by a competent authority and sent to the front desk cashier for posting into the guest master folio. A record of the same is maintained in the outgoing mail register, as shown in Fig. 9.6.

Message Handling

At times, there are telephone calls or visitors for a resident guest when she is not present in the hotel. In such situations, the front desk agents take the message for the guest and deliver the same as soon as the guest comes back. The process of receiving and delivering messages to resident guests is known as message handling. The prompt and timely delivery of messages to guests reflects the degree of professionalism of the front desk employees.

If a resident guest is expecting a call or a visitor during her absence, she may leave a location slip (which is similar to a message slip but is in a different colour) at the front desk. In such a case, the front desk assistant follows the instructions of the guest on receiving the telephone call or visitor for that guest. The format of a location form is shown in Fig. 9.7.

HOTEL ABC		
Miscellaneous Charge Voucher		
Name of Guest:_____	Room No.:_____	
Date:_____	Account No.:_____	
Explanation	Charge	
	Rs	Paisa
Total:		
	Signed by	

Fig. 9.5   Sample miscellaneous charge voucher

S. No.	Room No.	Name of Guest	Addressed to	Description of Mail	Charges	Received by	Date and Time of Receiving	Posted by	Date and Time of Posting	Remarks

Hotel ABC

Outgoing Mail Register

Fig. 9.6   Outgoing mail register

Hotel ABC

Location Form

Name of Guest: _____

Room No.: _____

While I am out of the hotel room I am expecting:

• Mr/Ms_____ to visit

• Telephone call

In an event if I am not in my room kindly locate me at:
• Café shop
• Gym
• Swimming pool area
• Restaurant
• Other (Specify) _____

Or convey my message to caller/visitor

Message:_____
_____
_____
_____

Signature of Guest

Fig. 9.7   Sample location form

Message Handling Procedure   Every hotel has its own standard operating procedure for handling guest messages. Most hotels follow the given procedure (refer Fig. 9.8), with some variations:

1. When there is a visitor or a telephone call for a guest, the front desk assistant should look at the information rack to see whether the guest is a resident guest, future guest, or checked-out guest.
2. In case of a resident guest, the agent must check whether she is present in the room or not. If the guest is not present in the room, then the agent must check the key rack for the location form (Fig. 9.7) or any instructions left by the guest. If the same is found, then act according to the instructions of the guest.
3. If guest has not left any instructions or the location form at the front desk, the front desk assistant should take down the message for the guest on a message slip (Fig. 9.9).
4. The message slip is prepared in duplicate—the original copy is placed in the key rack and the duplicate copy is placed in a message slip envelope

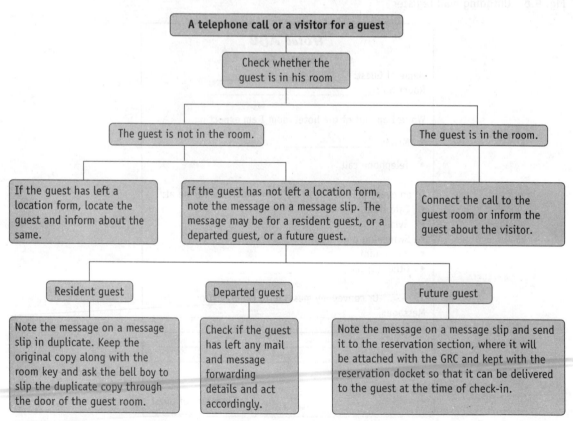

Fig. 9.8   Handling of messages

```
┌─────────────────────────────────────────────────────┐
│                   Hotel ABC                           │
│                  Message Slip                         │
│                                                       │
│   Date:_____        Time:_____       │
│   Name of Guest:_____                │
│   Room No:_____                 │
│                                                       │
│                  In your absence                      │
│                                                       │
│   Mr/Ms_____                │
│   From:_____                │
│                                                       │
│   ┌───┬────────────────┬───┬──────────────────┐       │
│   │ • │ Came in person │ • │ Will call again  │       │
│   ├───┼────────────────┼───┼──────────────────┤       │
│   │ • │ Telephoned     │ • │ Please call back │       │
│   ├───┼────────────────┼───┼──────────────────┤       │
│   │   │                │ • │ Waiting for you  │       │
│   ├───┼────────────────┼───┼──────────────────┤       │
│   │   │                │ • │ Please meet      │       │
│   │   │                │   │ him/her          │       │
│   └───┴────────────────┴───┴──────────────────┘       │
│                                                       │
│   Message:_____       │
│   _____       │
│   _____       │
│   _____       │
│   _____       │
│                                                       │
│                                                       │
│                                                       │
│            Signature of Information Assistant         │
└─────────────────────────────────────────────────────┘
```

Fig. 9.9 Sample message slip

and slipped through the door of the guest room by a bell boy. The purpose of preparing the message slip in duplicate is to ensure the delivery of the message to the guest.

5. If there is a visitor or a call for a guest who has checked out of the hotel, then the front office agent should give the information as per the instructions left by the guest.

6. If there is a call is for a future guest, then the agent should note the message on a message slip and send the slip to the back office, where it would be placed along with the reservation record. While printing the registration form on the date of arrival, the slip will be attached with the registration form so that the message can be delivered to the guest at the time of check-in.

7. Some hotels have automated systems for delivering messages to guests. The telephone in the guest room has a message indicator that can be switched on by the front desk agent in case any message is waiting for a guest. This

prompts the guest that there is a message for him and he may call the front desk to receive it. In some hotels, guests can read messages on the television screen by dialling a number.

Custody and Control of Keys

To ensure the safety and security of guests' belongings, the front desk must keep the room keys in safe custody. It is important for the front desk to exercise a strict control on room keys for the following reasons:

- It prevents unauthorized access to the guest room.
- It can be established who all entered the guest room.
- It ensure security of the guest and the guest's belongings.
- It prevents intrusion in the guest's privacy.

Key Control   Hotels may use conventional hard key system or computerized door locking system for securing the guest rooms. In case electronic locking system is used in the hotel, guests are issued card keys. A sample card key is shown in Fig. 9.10. Figure 9.11 illustrates the electronic door locking system installed in a hotel.

The room keys of unoccupied rooms should be placed in the mail and key rack (see Fig. 9.12) at the front desk. The keys of occupied rooms should be with the guests while they are in the hotel. When guests go out of the hotel, they should leave the keys with the receptionist, who should place them in the mail and key rack. To ensure that rooms keys are handed over to the right person, resident guests may be issued a key card (Fig. 9.13) when they deposit keys at the front desk. They are required to show the key card at the time of receiving the keys back from the front desk.

There are times when a room key may be lost or a guest may forget to return the key while checking out of the hotel. In such cases, the door lock should be immediately changed. In case of computerized door locking systems, the lock is recoded to prevent unauthorized access to the room (even by the guests who have just vacated the room).

Key control sheets (Fig. 9.14) are maintained by front desk employees in the night. The relevant details are entered in the appropriate columns of the key control sheet.

Guest Paging

Paging is the process of locating guests in a specified area of the hotel. When a guest is not in her room (though she is in the hotel premises) and is expecting a visitor, she may fill a location form (as shown in Fig. 9.7) and leave the same at the front desk. When the visitor comes to meet the guest, the front desk agent writes the name and room number of the guest on a page board (Fig. 9.15) and sends a

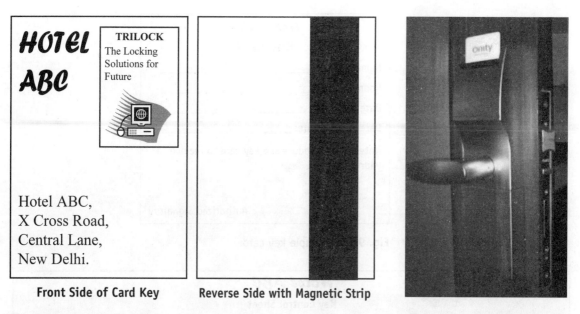

Front Side of Card Key   **Reverse Side with Magnetic Strip**

Fig. 9.10   Sample Card Key

Fig. 9.11   Electronic door lock
with card key

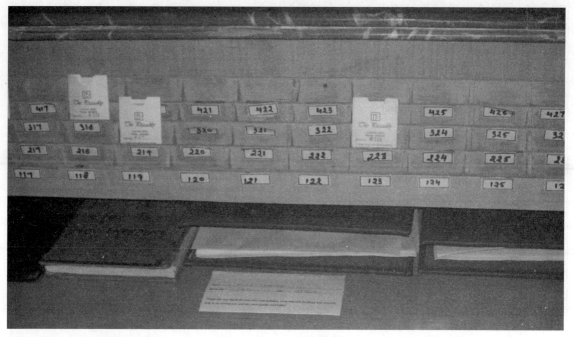

Fig. 9.12   Mail and key rack

Hotel ABC
Key Card

Name: _____

Room No.: _____

Date of Arrival: _____

Date of Departure: _____

Note: Please produce the key card to receive your room keys.

Authorized Signatory

Fig. 9.13   Sample key card

Hotel ABC
Key Control Sheet

Date:_____

Time:_____

Keys of occupied rooms at front desk

S. No.	Room No.	Name of Guest	Baggage Position	Bill Amount	Remarks

Vacant room whose keys are missing

101, 110, 305, 701

Details of Missing Keys

Room No.	Name of the Guest Who Stayed Last	Check-out Date and Time	Bell Boy at the Time of Departure	Front Desk Agent on Duty at the Time of Departure
101	Mr Dinesh Tiwari	25/1/2009 12:15 p.m.	Raja	Mr Salil
110	Mr John Alexander	25/1/2009 12:25 p.m.	Vijay	Mr S.S. Das
305	Ms Altarine	25/1/2009 12:15 p.m.	Tejpal	Mr S.S. Das
701	Mr Ashish Srivastava	25/1/2009 12:35 p.m.	Kishore	Mr Salil

Signature of front desk agent

Fig. 9.14   Sample key control sheet

Fig. 9.15 Page board

bell boy to the area mentioned by the guest on the location form. The bell boy holds the page board above his head and shakes it so that the bells attached to it ring and attract people's attention. The guest contacts the bell boy, who escorts her to the front desk to meet the visitor. Figure 9.16 explains the process of guest paging. In some hotels, guest paging is done through public address system.

Safe Deposit Locker

A key concern for guests is the safety of their belongings, especially cash, jewellery, and important documents. Hotels provide safe deposit lockers for the same. At the time of check-in, guests are advised to keep their valuables in the safe deposit lockers available at the front desk. Some hotels may also provide in-room safe deposit lockers, depending on the room category. These safe deposit lockers have a single key, so only the guest can operate the locker.

Some hotels have lockers which open by the simultaneous use of two keys—one is issued to the guest and the other is with the front desk agent. This means that the locker can only be opened when both the keys are used. Whenever a guest wishes to operate the locker, the front desk agent and the guest use their respective keys to open the lock. The hotel may provide this facility for a nominal charge or no charge, depending upon the house policy. Guests who wish to use this facility have to sign in the safe deposit locker register (Fig. 9.17) to get the keys of the safe deposit box.

Procedure for Using Safe Deposit Locker Every hotel has its own operating procedure for the allotment of safe deposit lockers. The standard procedure (Fig. 9.18) has two stages:
1. Issue of locker
2. Surrender of locker

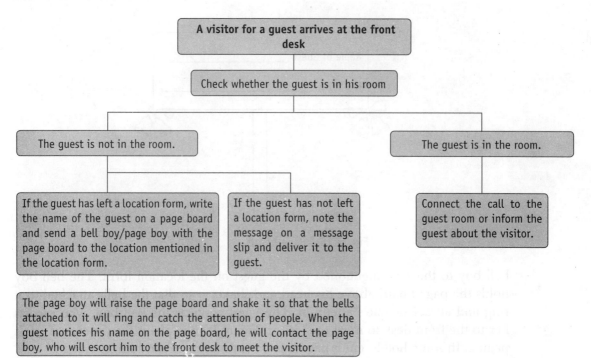

Fig. 9.16 Procedure of guest paging

			Hotel ABC						
			Safe Deposit Locker Register						
S. No.	**Date**	**Name of the Guest**	**Room No.**	**Locker No.**	**Key Issued**	**Guest Signature**		**Guest Signature**	**Remarks**

Fig. 9.17 Safe deposit locker register

Issue of locker When a guest wishes to use the locker facility extended by the hotel, the following procedure is followed:

1. An empty safe deposit locker is allocated to the guest with the locker number.
2. A safe deposit box registration card (Fig. 9.19) is handed over to the guest and the guest is requested to fill the necessary information.
3. The locker is assigned and the locker key is handed over to the guest.
4. The guest keeps his valuables and documents in the locker, locks the box, and carries the key.
5. The guest can use the safe deposit box as and when required; he is required to make an entry in the safe deposit locker register for each use.

Surrender of locker When the guest surrenders the safe deposit box, the following procedure is followed:

1. The guest is requested to withdraw the articles placed in the locker.
2. The guest is requested to sign an acknowledgement that he has received all the articles that had been placed in the safe deposit box (Fig. 9.19).
3. The guest surrenders the locker key to the front office agent.

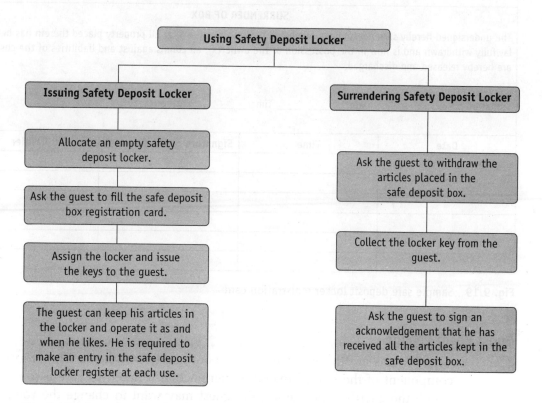

Fig. 9.18 Procedure for the allotment and surrender of safety deposit locker

Hotel ABC			
SAFE DEPOSIT LOCKER/BOX			
Box. No.	**Date Issued**	**Issued by**	**Room No.**

Terms and Conditions:

1. I/we shall not hold the hotel liable for any loss of, theft of, or shortage in the contents of the safe deposit locker which is being used by me/us exclusively.

2. In the event of the loss of the keys of the safe deposit locker, I/we shall reimburse the hotel Rs 2,000 only towards replacements.

Signature:_____

Address:_____

_____

_____

SURRENDER OF BOX

The undersigned hereby surrenders above numbered box and certifies that all property placed therein has been lawfully withdrawn and is now in the possession of the owner(s); all claims against and liabilities of the custodian are hereby released and discharged.

Signature :_____ Date:_____ Time:_____ Cashier:_____

Date	Time	Signature of the Guest(s)	Cashier

Fig. 9.19 Sample safe deposit locker registration card

Guest Room Change

Guest rooms are the most important commodity of a hotel. They form a large component of the guests' overall experience at a hotel. In case a room doesn't match the guest's expectations, the guest may want to change the room. There are times when the hotel may wish to change the room of a resident guest. If the change of room is done in the presence of the guest, it is called a live move, and if it is carried out in the absence of the guest, it is known as a dead move.

A guest may want to change his room in the following circumstances:

1. If the room assigned to the guest is not as per his choice.
2. If one or more equipments or facilities in the room are not working satisfactorily.
3. If the number of occupants in the room changes.

The hotel may wish to change the guest's room for the following reasons:

1. If the guest was upgraded due to the non-availability of the requested category of rooms.
2. If the guest overstays and the hotel does not have a room of the same type to allot to the next guest.
3. If the hotel has scheduled a spring cleaning for the room.
4. If the room requires maintenance work.

It is important for the hotel and the guest to mutually agree on the change of room to avoid any discord or unpleasantness.

Procedure for Changing the Guest Room To change the room of a resident guest, the following procedure (Fig. 9.20) is followed:

1. The front office informs the guest about the room change in advance so that the guest packs his luggage properly.
2. The front office agent fills six copies of the guest room change slip (Fig. 9.21)—for reception, bell captain, front desk cashier, telephone exchange, housekeeping, and room service—and takes authorization from a competent authority.
3. A bell boy is called and given the keys of the new room. He proceeds to the guest room to shift the guest's luggage.
4. In case of dead move, the bell boy asks the room boy/floor boy to open the guest room. If it is a live move, he goes to the room and requests the guest to allow him to shift the luggage.
5. The bell boy removes all the guest's belongings from the room and locks the room. He then carries all the belongings to the new room and hands over the new room keys to the guest. He collects the keys of the room being vacated from the guest and deposits the same at the front desk.

Left Luggage Handling

There are times when guests check out of their rooms but would like to leave their luggage in the hotel and collect it later. For example, a guest, who has to take an evening flight, may vacate the room at the check-out time to save the room charges for another day. In such a case, the guest luggage may be brought down and stored

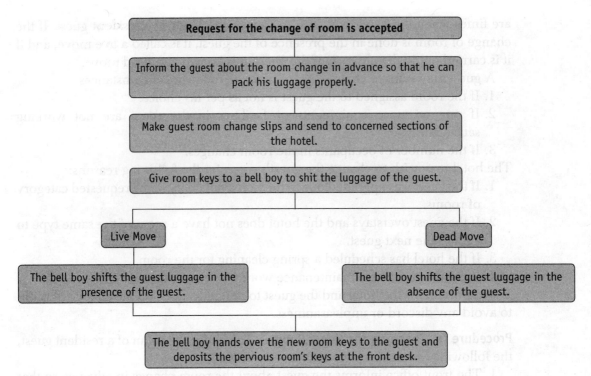

Fig. 9.20   Procedure of room change

Fig. 9.21   Room change slip

in the left luggage room. The same facility may be extended to a guest who would return to the hotel after a short visit to another city. Thus, the left luggage facility helps guests keep their luggage in the hotel for a short time, even though they have settled their bills and checked out of the rooms. Some hotels may charge for the left luggage facility while others may not.

Procedure for Left Luggage Handling Hotels normally follow the following procedure (Fig. 9.22) while accepting the luggage to be stored in the left luggage room:

1. The agent makes sure that the guest wishing to keep his luggage in the left luggage room has cleared his bills.
2. The luggage tag (Fig. 9.23) is filled and tied to each luggage.
3. The details of the luggage are entered in the left luggage register (Fig. 9.24).
4. The counterfoil of the luggage tag is torn and handed over to the guest. The guest is required to present the same for the collection of his luggage.
5. The luggage is kept in the left luggage room.

While delivering the luggage to the guest, the following procedure is followed:

1. The front office agent requests the guest is to show the luggage tag counterfoil.
2. The front office agent tallies the counterfoil with the tag attached to the baggage.

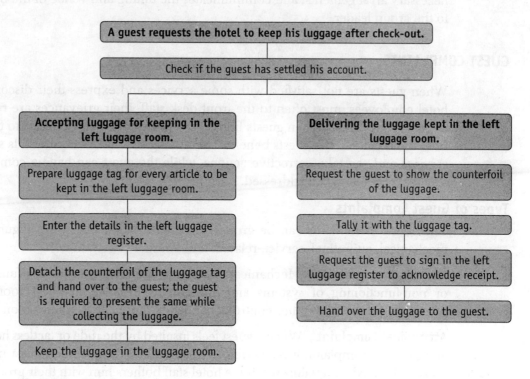

Fig. 9.22 Procedure for left luggage

3. The front office agent makes an entry in the left luggage register and requests the guest to sign for the delivery of the luggage.

4. The front office agent hands over the luggage to the guest.

Wake-up Call

Hotels also offer wake-up call services, wherein the hotel staff makes a telephone call at a requested time to awaken a guest. The guest who wishes to be given a wake-up call by the hotel personnel may place a request with the front desk, bell desk, information section, or telephone operator. The wake-up call request is entered in the wake-up call register (Fig. 9.25). The telephone operator gives the wake-up call to the guest at the time specified by the guest.

Hotels also give wake-up calls to groups or crews staying in the hotel at the time registered by the group leader or by the airline operation office. In such cases, the person registering the wake-up call informs the hotel about the pick-up timings for the group or crew. The front desk notes the details in the wake-up call sheet (Fig. 9.26) and the operator gives the wake-up call at the specified time. The front desk also arranges adequate staff to shift the luggage of the group members from their rooms to the pick-up vehicle. If the breakfast is to be provided to the group, the front office informs the food and beverage department and kitchen to make the necessary arrangements, and communicates the timing and venue of the breakfast to the group leader.

GUEST COMPLAINTS

When guests are not satisfied with some services and express their discontent to hotel employees, most often to the front desk staff, their grievances are recorded as guest complaints. When guests find it easy to express their opinions to the staff, both the hotel and the guests benefit. The hotel gets a feedback about its staff and services and can take corrective actions, while the guest can have a comfortable stay if his problems are addressed.

Types of Guest Complaints

The guests' complaints can be grouped into four major categories (figure 9.27): mechanical, attitudinal, service-related, and unusual complaints.

Mechanical Complaint Mechanical complaints are related to the malfunctioning or non-functioning of systems and equipments installed in guest rooms, like television, mini-bar, weather control, channelled music, geyser, and so on.

Attitudinal Complaint When a guest feels insulted by the rude or tactless hotel staff and lodges a complaint, it is referred to as attitudinal complaint. A guest may also make attitudinal complaints when the hotel staff bothers him with their problems.

Hotel ABC

_____

Guest Signature

....
LUGGAGE TAG

_____

Guest Signature

Front view of luggage tag

S. No. 786
Name:_____
Room No.:_____
No. of Items:_____
Date of Deposit:_____
Date of Collection:_____
Actual date of Collection:_____

•	Suitcase	•	Briefcase
•	Travelling Bag	•	Others

....
Sl. No. 786
Name:_____
Room No.:_____
No. of Items:_____
Date of Deposit:_____
Date of Collection:_____
Actual date of collection:_____

•	Suitcase	•	Briefcase
•	Travelling Bag	•	Others

Terms & Conditions
1. This ticket is required at the time of collection of baggage.
2. We take utmost care of your belongings but no responsibility can be expected.
3. No responsibility after 30 days.

GUEST COPY

Back view of luggage tag

Fig. 9.23   Luggage tag

Hotel ABC

Left Luggage Register

Date	Room No.	Name of Guest	Bell Boy's Name	Luggage Tag No.	Description of Luggage	Delivered on	Remarks

Fig. 9.24   Left luggage register

Hotel ABC				
Wake-up Call Register				
Date	Name of Guest	Wake-up Call Time	Call Given By	Remarks

Fig. 9.25   Wake-up call register

Service-related Complaint   Service-related complaints are about the problems in services provided by the hotel, like delay in the room service of lunch, or delay in the clearance of soiled crockery from the room after meals, etc.

Unusual Complaint   Unusual complaints are those over which the hotel does not have any control. For example, a guest may complain about the lack of golf course in the hotel, or the lack of central heating facility, etc.

Handling Guest Complaints

The front office should handle guests' complaints tactfully, exercising patience, empathy, and decision-making skills. As hospitality is a service-oriented industry, the hotel staff should always try to resolve the customer's problems immediately and thus appease him. If a front office agent is unable to handle a guest's complaint, she should call her superior before the situation gets out of control or becomes worse. The following guidelines may be followed while handling guest complaints:

1. Listen silently without interruption, with empathy.
2. Show concern and take complaints seriously.
3. Never argue. Remember the guest is always right.
4. Never try to win an argument—you may win the argument but lose the guest forever. (Remember it takes a lot to attract fresh customers but only a little to retain existing customers).
5. If possible, isolate the guest so that other guests may not overhear.
6. Offer choices and never make a false promise.
7. Monitor the corrective measures.
8. Follow up and inform the guest about the solution.
9. If unable to resolve the guest problem, consult your superiors.

In the hotel industry, service standards are very important. The services should be of exemplary standard so as to ensure guest satisfaction and delight. This would lead to repeat business and positive word-of-mouth publicity.

Hotel ABC

Wake-up Call Sheet

Crew/Group:			Group RV No.
Flight No.:			
Capt/Grp Leader:			Wake-up Call time
Name:			..........................hrs

S No.	Room No.		
01	102	Assistant Manager	
02	123		
03	124	Airline/Tel	
04	101		
05	110	Wake-up Call Confirmed by	
06	203	Bell Captain	
07	121	Telephone Supervisor	
08		Housekeeping	
09			
10			
11			
12		Baggage Down Time ....hrs	
13		Pick-up Time: ....hrs	
14			
15			
Remarks			
Department	Name		Amended Wake-up Call: ....hrs
Housekeeping			
Reception			
Telephone			Airport Service No.:
Coach No.:			

Fig. 9.26   Wake-up call sheet

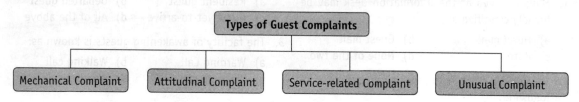

Fig. 9.27   Types of guest complaints

SUMMARY

In this chapter, we learnt about the front office services provided to guests during the third phase of the guest cycle, i.e., their stay in the hotel. The services include handling mails, messages, telephone calls, and visitors for guests in their absence. The front office also handles room keys and facilitates guest paging if required. Guests contact the front office for safety deposit lockers, left luggage, or wake up facilities. In case a guest or the hotel requires a room change, the front office ensures that it is carried out smoothly and efficiently. If guests have any complaints, the front office staff should take immediate measures to resolve them. All these services contribute to guest satisfaction, which ensures repeat business and positive word-of-mouth publicity.

KEY TERMS

Attitudinal complaint Complaint about the behaviour of hotel staff.

Card key A plastic card with a magnetic strip that has the code to open a guest room in an electronic locking system.

Guest paging Locating guests in a specified area of the hotel.

Left luggage room A room where the luggage of guests, who have checked out of their rooms and settled their bills, is stored.

Location form A form in which a guest gives information about her whereabouts and provides instructions to follow if someone visits or calls in her absence.

Mail log book A book in which a record of all received mails is maintained by the hotel.

Mechanical complaint Complaint regarding the malfunctioning of equipments in guest rooms.

Message slip The slip on which messages for guests are taken and delivered to the guest.

Ordinary mail The mails whose delivery record is not maintained by the delivering agency.

Registered mail The mails whose delivery record is maintained by the delivering agency.

Service-related complaint Complaint about hotel services.

REVIEW QUESTIONS

Multiple Choice Questions

1. Mails received at the information desk may be broadly classified as:
   a) Hotel mail
   b) Guest mail
   c) Both
   d) None of the two

2. The guest mails may further be grouped into the following:
   a) Resident guest
   b) Departed guest
   c) Guest yet-to-arrive
   d) All of the above

3. The facility of awakening guests is known as:
   a) Warning Call
   b) Walking call
   c) Wake-up call
   d) Worship call

4. The process of locating a guest in a specific location in hotel is known as:

   a) Searching   b) Paging
   c) Gazing   d) Wake-up call

5. Where should one place the message received for the guest who is out of the premises for prompt and ensured delivery?

   a) In the pocket of the front desk agent
   b) Anywhere
   c) In the key and mail rack along with room keys
   d) With the housekeeping floor boy

True/False

1. Mails are sorted as hotel mails or guest mails after they are received at the front desk.

2. The mails received for a future guest having confirmed reservation are sent to the reservation office to be kept with the reservation docket.

3. The person who does the job of locating a guest in a specified location in the hotel is known as a page boy.

4. The locker facility is provided to guests so that they can keep their valuables in safe condition.

5. Hotels provide the facility of keeping the luggage of a guest after the departure of the guest.

Fill in the Blanks

1. The facility of awakening guests at a time requested by them is known as _____ facility.

2. Hotel mails may be classified into _____ mails and _____ mails.

3. A _____ tag is attached to every article that is kept in the left luggage room.

4. The message slip is kept in the _____ rack with room keys for prompt delivery to guests.

5. If a guest is not in his room and wishes to be informed in case there is a visitor for him, he fills a _____ form.

Discussion Questions

1. What are the different types of mails received by the hotel?

2. Explain the procedure of distributing guest mails in hotels.

3. Explain the use of a location form in handling telephone calls in the absence of guests.

4. Explain the procedure by which a hotel ensures the delivery of guest messages.

5. What do you understand by paging? Explain the paging process.

6. What role does a page board play in guest paging?

7. Explain the procedure of allotment and surrendering of safe deposit box.

8. What are the possible reasons for changing guest rooms? Explain the room change procedure.

9. Explain the procedure for handling left luggage.

10. Explain the procedure for wake-up calls.

11. What are the possible causes of complaints by guests? How should a front office assistant handle the complaints?

CRITICAL THINKING QUESTIONS

1. The services provided to a guest—like mail and message delivery, paging, safety deposit lockers, left luggage handling, etc.—add to the guest satisfaction. Discuss in detail and support your answer with reasons.

2. It is important to exercise strict key control. Comment.
3. Wake-up call service is very important in case of groups. Comment.
4. Guest complaints lead to a high standard of services in hotels. Discuss.

PROJECT WORK

1. Find out the format of wake-up call sheet for groups and individuals, and practise filling the same.

2. Visit a hotel and watch how the bell desk handles luggage. Identify the steps that are followed by the bell desk.

CHAPTER 10

Check-out And Settlement

Learning Objectives:

After reading this chapter, you will be able to understand the following:
- The fourth stage of the guest cycle—check-out and settlement of bills.
- Departure procedures in manual, semi-automated, and fully automated systems.
- Modes of bill settlement—cash or credit settlement.
- Potential check-out problems—late check-out, long queues at the cashier counter, improper posting of charges in the guest folio—and solutions.

We have studied about the first three phases of the guest cycle—pre-arrival, arrival, and stay. This chapter deals with the fourth phase—departure and settlement of guest accounts. For repeat business, it is very important that the guest departs at a good note. So the hotel should take care to carry out the check-out procedure efficiently and smoothly. This chapter describes the departure procedures in manual, semi-automated, and fully automated systems. The modes of bill settlement—cash and credit—are discussed in detail with illustrations. The chapter ends with a discussion on the potential check-out problems and how they can be resolved.

DEPARTURE PROCEDURE

The last interaction of the guest with the hotel staff takes place during the final phase of the guest cycle—check-out. During check-out, guests formally vacate their rooms, settle their bills, and leave the hotel. This phase is very crucial as guests settle their financial transactions with the hotel, and any dispute at this stage can ruin their entire experience. On the other hand, a smooth settlement of bills and check-out would enhance the guests' experience. As every hotel endeavours to achieve high levels of guest satisfaction, the activities of the various departments should be coordinated to ensure a smooth check-out. The speed and accuracy in the preparation and presentation of bills will lead to the maximization of guest satisfaction. Error-free billing and speedy processing of check-out requests reflects the professionalism of the hotel and imparts a lasting good impression to the guest.

The departure procedure may vary slightly from hotel to hotel according to the degree of automation of the organization. The following steps are involved in the departure procedure (Fig. 10.1) in manual or semi-automated systems:
- The check-out request is received at the front desk or bell desk.
- The front desk sends a bell boy to transfer the guest's luggage from the room to the lobby.
- The bell boy fills the departure errand card.
- The front desk sends departure notification slips (DNS) to all concerned departments (Fig. 10.2).
- The front desk alerts all points of sale to rush last-minute credit transactions to the front desk.
- The front desk cashier updates the guest folio on the basis of recent bills received from the points of sales.
- The guest arrives at the front desk for check-out and hands over the room keys.
- The cashier prepares the master bill and presents it to the guest, along with supporting vouchers and bills, for review.
- The payment is received from the guest as per the pre-determined mode of payment.
- The front desk makes the 'luggage out' pass (Fig. 10.3).
- Marketing activities are carried out—the front desk communicates special offers, gives out brochures, takes future bookings, etc.
- The front desk communicates the check-out information to housekeeping and all the other concerned departments.
- The front office assistant updates the following front office records:
  - Current room status—by removing name slip from the room rack at the information desk.

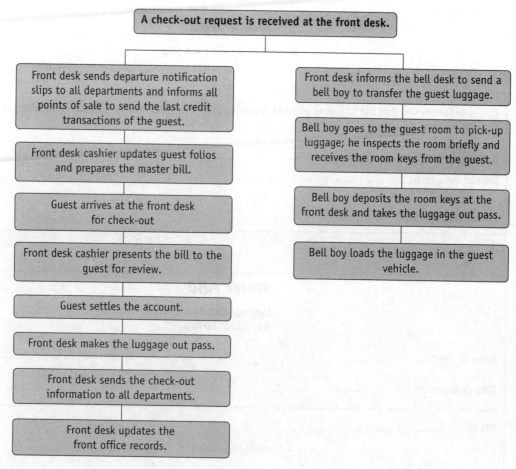

Fig. 10.1 Departure procedure

- Guest history card.
- Arrival/Departure register.

Check-out Request A request for check-out is received from the guest either at the front desk or at the bell desk. This information is communicated to all the concerned departments and points of sales. While processing the check-out request, the front desk agent should confirm the guest's details like name, room number, etc. and check the departure date. In case of early departure (i.e., the guest would like to leave before the departure date mentioned at the time of registration), other departments should be informed.

Luggage Handling The front desk requests the bell captain to send a bell boy to transfer the guest luggage to the lobby. The bell boy fills the departure errand card

Hotel ABC

Departure Notification Slip

Reception:................

Department:...

This is to inform you that the following guest is departing from the hotel. Kindly rush the credit charges to the front desk.

Name of Guest   :...   Room No. :...............................

Date of Departure :.......................................   Time :...............................

Authorized Signatory

Fig. 10.2   Departure notification slip

Hotel ABC

Luggage Out Pass
No. 0024500786

Name of Guest: ....   Room No.: ....

Date of Departure: ....   Time: ....

Bill No.: ....

Billing Settlement

☐ Complete   ☐ Partial   ☐ Corporate Settlement   ☐ Other......................

....

_____   _____
Authorized Signatory   Date

Fig. 10.3   Luggage out pass

(Fig. 10.4) and the bell captain makes an entry in the bell captain control sheet. The bell boy goes to the guest room, knocks on the door, and announces himself. After getting due permission from the guest, he enters the room and carries the guest luggage to the lobby.

Hotel ABC				
Departure Errand Card				
Reception	**Cashier**	**Information**	**Departure Date and Time**	**Room No.**
Bell Boy Name:				Call Time :
Name of Guest:				Room No.:
Articles				
Suitcase	Hand Bag	Package	Briefcase	Overcoat
Others				
Baggage brought down by			Baggage loaded by	
		Signature		Signature

Fig. 10.4   Departure errand card

Apart from carrying the luggage of the guest, the bell boy is also expected to do the following:

- Look around the room for signs of any damage to the hotel property.
- Draw the curtains and lock the balcony and windows.
- Check for any guest belongings left behind by mistake.
- Collect the room keys from the guest.
- Check the mini-bar consumption or politely enquire from the guest about the same.
- Lock the room and hang 'clean my room' tag on the door knob, so that the housekeeping department can quickly clean the room for the next occupant.

Accounting All Transactions   The front desk informs housekeeping and all points of sale to rush the latest credit transactions to the front desk, so that the cashier can add them to the guest account. It is very difficult to get payment for unpaid bills after the guest has checked out, unless she has gone to another hotel in the same chain or is going to return to the hotel later. As the guest might refuse to pay any charges after she has checked out, the hotel should ensure that all transactions have been billed to the guest at the time of account settlement.

Updating Guest Folio   The front desk cashier updates the guest folio (Fig. 10.5) by:

- Adding the latest credit transactions received from the points of sale.
- Checking if any late check-out charges are applicable; i.e., if the check-out time is 12 noon and the guest checks out at 6 p.m., he will be charged for late check-out.
- Checking for any late charges, i.e., if there are any latest bills that have not been added to the guest account.
- Examining the current entries in the guest account.

Hotel ABC				
Guest Folio				

Name of the Guest: Mr Dinesh Dubey
Date of Arrival: 10 March 2009
Date of Departure: 11 March 2009
Number of Pax: One
Rom No.: 2010
Rate: Rs 5,000
Folio No.: 21786

Date	Item	Description	Debit	Credit
10/3/2009	1	Cash		6,500
10/3/2009	2	Room	5,000	
10/3/2009	3	Dinner	500	
10/3/2009	4	Gazal Bar	800	
10/3/2009	5	Breakfast	300	
10/3/2009	6	Cash		100
Amount to be settled by the guest: Nil				
Balance: Rs 00.00				

Fig. 10.5   Sample guest folio

Bill   Guest bills are prepared on the basis of guest folios (explained in detail in Chapter 11). While preparing the bill, the front desk staff should check if late check-out charges are applicable. If so, they should be added in the master bill. The check-out time is the time fixed by the hotel to mark the end of the day. A departing guest should vacate the room by the check-out time, which is generally 12 noon, else he would incur late check-out charges. Late check-out charges are normally a point of contention between the hotel and the guest. In order to avoid such a situation, guests are often asked about their expected departure time at the reservation stage itself. At the time of registration, they are again informed about the extra charges in case of late check-out.

The front desk cashier should also pay special care to late charges while preparing the bills for settlement. A late charge is an outstanding payment from the guest, the bill for which reaches the front desk cashier after the master bill has been prepared. Some common examples of late charges are:

- Laundry bills
- Telephone bills
- Breakfast bills
- Mini-bar consumption

If the late charges reach the front desk after the guest has settled his bill and checked out, the hotel will have to bear the loss. In order to reduce the losses due to the late arrival of charges, the cashier should confirm from all the points of sale about any outstanding charges for the departing guest and also enquire about the mini-bar consumption from the guest before preparing the master bill.

In manual hotel operation, the front office follows the given procedure to prepare a guest's bill:

- Prepare bills in duplicate.
- Check the room number.
- Take out the guest folio.
- Calculate the correct number of room nights and establish whether a late check-out charge is to be added.
- Enter the guest's credit transactions in the master bill in the order of their occurrence.
- Enter the method of payment (cash, credit card, bill to company, etc.).
- Present the bills, along with supporting vouchers, to the guest for review.
- Once the guest has verified the charges and made the payment, give the top copy of the bill to the guest.
- File the second copy in the night auditor's file.

Determination of Mode of Payment   The method of settlement of bills is generally established during registration or even before, at the reservation stage. The methods of payment of bills may be cash—in local and foreign currency; cash equivalents like demand draft, traveller's cheque, and debit card; or through credit modes like charge card, credit card, travel agent vouchers, and corporate billings. The front desk is generally aware about the mode of settlement of bills. This information helps the front desk cashier to do necessary verification in case of credit payments or take authorization from superiors in case the bill is to be settled by personal cheque, which is normally not entertained by most of the hotels.

Receiving Payment   The guest reviews the bill and makes the payment in the pre-decided mode. The payment may be made through currency notes, traveller's cheque, personal cheque, demand draft, debit card, credit card, charge card, travel agent voucher, and bill to the company. The front desk cashier follows the house policy in collecting the payment from the guest.

Marketing Activity   As the guest and the hotel staff come face-to-face for the last time at the check-out stage, the front office should use this opportunity for marketing efforts in the following ways:

- The front desk should ask guests about their experience at the hotel and ask them to fill a feedback form.
- If guests have any complaints, the front desk should note the same and assure the guests of a quick resolution.
- The front desk agent should inform the guest about upcoming special offers.
- The front desk agent may suggest making future reservation for the guest's return trip or for a hotel in the same chain at the guest's next destination.

Communicating Departure to All Departments The front desk informs all departments about the departure of a guest to ensure smooth operation of the hotel. The points of sale will not offer credit facility to guests who have already settled their bills and politely ask them to make a direct payment. The housekeeping department will do the following:

- Prepare the room for the next guest.
- Block the room for special cleaning processes, like spring cleaning.
- Look for maintenance requirements in the room.
- Re-furnish the room for future sales.

To ensure proper room management, both front office and housekeeping must inform each other of the change in room status. As soon as a guest checks out, the front office must inform the housekeeping, so that the latter cleans the room and makes it available for sale. A flow of information in the reverse direction is equally necessary. The housekeeping prepares the 'housekeeping report' at the end of a shift, which indicates the housekeeping status of each room—whether rooms are ready for occupation, under repair, or out of order. The housekeeping department uses room status codes (Exhibit 10.1) to indicate the status of rooms. This report is sent to the front office, where it is compared to the front office occupancy report and discrepancies are sorted out. The close coordination between the front office and housekeeping keeps the room status information up-to-date, leading to maximum benefit to the hotel.

Updating Front Office Records When some guests depart from a hotel, the rooms they had been occupying become vacant. The front desk agent should update the

---

Exhibit 10.1   Room status codes

Check-in: A guest has registered at the front desk and been allotted this room.

Check-out: The guest has vacated the room, settled her bills and left the hotel; this room is to be serviced by housekeeping for a new guest.

Complimentary: The room is assigned to a guest but the hotel is not charging any room rent from the guest.

Do not disturb (DND): A DND knob-card displayed on the door knob of the room indicates that the guest does not want to be disturbed.

Occupied: A guest is residing in the room.

Out-of-Order (OOO): The room has been blocked for maintenance and repair, and cannot be allotted to a guest.

Skipper: The guest who leaves the hotel without settling his dues.

Sleeper: The guest has settled her bills and checked out, but the front desk has not updated the room status, i.e., the room is shown as occupied but it is vacant.

Sleep-out: A guest has registered but not used the room.

Stayover: The guest is staying in the hotel and is expected to stay at least one more night (beyond his date of departure).

Vacant and Ready: A room which has been serviced by the housekeeping department and is ready for sale again.

hotel records related to room status at the earliest so that the rooms can be sold again. The front office should also update guest history cards for marketing and research purposes.

Room status records As soon as a guest checks out, the front desk agent updates the following records related to the status of the room:

- The front office removes the name of the guest from the room rack at the information desk, so that the room shows as vacant and can be given to another guest.
- The front desk changes the status of the room in the front office occupancy report from occupied to vacant/dirty, so that the room can be cleaned and made ready for another guest.

Guest history card   Generally, most hotels maintain a record of their guests, with details like previous arrival and departure dates, type of room and rate charged, likes and dislikes of guests, the amount spent by them, any special requests. This record is known as the guest history card or GHC (Fig. 10.6). Hotels prepare the GHCs of corporate clients also. A GHC serves the following purposes:

- It provides current marketing data.
- The demographical data of the guest—age, sex, income, occupation, marital status, etc.—helps to develop new marketing strategies.
- The knowledge of the guest's personal likes and dislikes help in serving the guest better.

Hotel ABC
Guest History Card

S.No. 000786

Name... Company...

Designation.. Address...

Credit.. Date of Birth.......................................

Marriage Anniversary.................. ....

S. No.	Arrived	Room	Rate	Departed	Amount	Special Instructions	Remarks
1							
2							
3							
4							
5							

Fig. 10.6   Sample guest history card

- The information in GHC reveals the frequency of a guest's visits. If the guest is a frequent user of the hotel, her name may be entered in the frequent users' list and promotional offers and special rates may be offered to her.

Departure Procedure in Fully Automated System

The departure procedure in a hotel running on a fully automated system is smoother and more efficient. It involves the following steps:

- The check-out request is received at the front desk or bell desk.
- The front desk sends a bell boy to transfer luggage from the guest room to the lobby.
- The front desk informs all points of sale and other departments of the hotel about the departing guest through the interlinked computer network.
- Since all the points of sale terminals are interlinked, any credit transaction of the guest will instantaneously get added in the guest folio.
- The front desk prepares the master bill by selecting the bill option of the cashier module.
- The front office presents the master bill, along with supporting vouchers, to the guest for review.
- The payment is received from the guest as per the pre-determined mode of payment.
- The front office makes the luggage out pass.
- The front desk communicates the departure of the guest to housekeeping and all the other concerned departments.
- The front office records are updated automatically. These include:
  - The auto removal of the name of the departed guest from the in-house guest name list.
  - The automatic updating of the current room status—from occupied to vacant/dirty.
  - The automatic updating of the guest history card.

MODE OF SETTLEMENT OF BILLS

Generally hotels determine the mode of settling the guest accounts at the time of registration or sometimes even at the time of receiving the reservation request. This makes it very convenient for the front desk employee to prepare the guest bill at the time of check-out. There are several acceptable modes of payment—foreign currency, traveller's cheque, demand draft, debit card, credit card, and so on.

Foreign Exchange

The tourism and hospitality industry is among the major foreign exchange earners for any nation. All the foreign visitors in a hotel can settle their accounts in the currency of their country—dollar, Euro, Pound, etc.—except guests who are employed with the UN and its agencies, embassies, consulates, and high commissions. Even if the guests have already converted their currency into Indian currency, they still have to pay the room rent in foreign currency.

Hotels have to take a valid licence from the Reserve Bank of India (RBI) to deal with foreign exchange. RBI issues two types of licences to deal with foreign exchange—one for the purchase and one for the sale of the foreign currency. A hotel with the purchase licence can only purchase foreign currency, which means that the hotel can accept foreign currency from the guest, but the refund amount exceeding the billing amount will only be made in Indian currency. Hotels generally obtain the purchase licence; but if a hotel has obtained the licence for buying and selling foreign currency, it can buy and sell foreign currency, i.e., accept foreign currency and give the balance amount also in foreign currency.

Currency Exchange Procedure   To deal in foreign exchange, a hotel has to take a valid licence from RBI. The front office cashier is the hotel's authorized representative for foreign exchange dealing. When guests wish to exchange the currency of their country into Indian currency, the following procedure is followed:

1. The guest contacts the front desk cashier for foreign exchange.
2. The cashier requests the guest to produce his passport to verify his identity.
3. The cashier asks the guest for the amount of foreign currency to be exchanged and determines whether the amount is exchangeable as per the RBI guidelines.
4. The cashier checks the exchange rate from RBI or a leading nationalized bank of the town.
5. The cashier prepares the currency exchange certificate (as shown in Fig. 10.7).
6. The cashier requests the guest to sign the currency exchange certificate.
7. The guest gives the foreign currency to the cashier in cash or as traveller's cheques.
8. The cashier calculates the total amount to be paid in local currency as per the exchange rate.
9. The cashier dispenses the amount to the guest along with the original currency encashment certificate. He attaches the second copy with the foreign currency or traveller's cheques and leaves the stationary copy in the booklet.
10. The cashier fills the details of the daily currency exchange transactions in the foreign currency control sheet as shown in Fig. 10.8.

Hotel ABC
Foreign Currency Encashment Certificate

S. No.: 0786786
RBI License No. Hot/ABC/0786

We hereby certify that we have purchased today foreign currency from Mr/Ms.............. ....
Holder of passport No. .... Nationality .... and paid net amount in Indian currency after adjusting the amount towards the settlement of bills for goods supplied/services rendered as per the details given below.

A. Details of foreign currency notes/coins/traveller's cheques purchased

Currency Purchased (Notes and TC Separately)	Amount	Exchange Rate	Rupees Equivalent

Total:.........................

B. Details of adjustment made towards settlement of bills for goods supplied/services rendered

Bill No.	Date	Amount

Total:...................................

C. Net Amount Paid in Rupees................................Amount in Words...
   (Total under A–Total under B) ....

....
(Authorized Signatory)

Name:.................................
Designation:.............................

Note: This certificate should be preserved by the holder to facilitate the re-conversion of the rupees balance from the amount dispensed in column C, at the time of departure from India, or to make payment in Indian currency for the services received.

Fig. 10.7   Foreign currency exchange certificate

11. If the cashier receives the foreign currency at the time of settlement of bills, the same procedure is applied, and balance, if any, is returned to the guest in local currency.

The above-mentioned procedure is followed by hotels with licence for purchasing foreign currency. In case the hotel also has the licence to sell foreign currency, then in step 11, the cashier returns the balance amount in the foreign currency.

					Foreign Currency					Rupee Equivalent
S. No.	Date	Name of Guest	Nationality	Passport No.	Pound Sterling	US Dollar	Euro	Others	Rate	

Hotel ABC
Foreign Currency Control Sheet

Fig. 10.8 Foreign currency control sheet

Cash Settlement

The cash payment option is one of the most preferred modes of settlement of guest accounts. At the time of settlement, the cashier zeroes the balance in the guest account. If there is a credit balance in the guest folio, the hotel will pay back the balance amount to the guest to make the balance zero. Whereas, if there is a debit balance in the guest folio, the hotel will collect the balance amount from the guest to make the folio balance zero. The various modes of account settlement by cash are illustrated in Fig. 10.9.

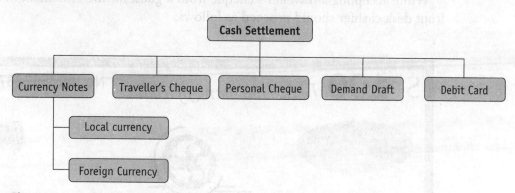

Fig. 10.9 Modes of cash settlement

Currency Notes Guests can settle their accounts by paying through currency notes. This is one of the most widely accepted modes of account settlement. While accepting currency notes, the cashier should check if the currency notes are genuine.

The following procedure is generally adopted for accepting cash payments:
- If accepting foreign currency from the guest, the cashier checks the daily currency conversion rate.
- To avoid any disputes, the cashier should retain the cash amount outside the cash drawer till the transaction is completed.
- The cashier should count the value of the currency in front of the guest.
- If accepting foreign currency from the guest, the cashier makes the currency encashment certificate.
- The cashier issues a receipt for the transaction.
- As per government regulations, the cashier should accept foreign currency only from foreigners and return the balance amount, if any, in local currency.

Traveller's Cheque   A traveller's cheque or TC (Fig. 10.10) is an internationally accepted cheque for a sum in a specific currency that can be exchanged elsewhere for local currency or goods. It is also among the most widely accepted mode of account settlement. Issued by a financial institution, it functions as cash but is protected against loss or theft. The value of the traveller's cheque is written on it. Traveller's cheques are useful when travelling, especially in the case of overseas travel when all the credit and debit cards are not accepted. When a person exchanges traveller's cheques for cash, she usually incurs a charge or commission, though some banks wave off this charge.

The purchaser of the traveller's cheque puts two signatures—one in front of the issuing authority and the second in front of the encashing authority. To prevent misuse, the loss of a traveller's cheque should be immediately reported to the issuing bank and local police authority.

While accepting a traveller's cheque from a guest for the settlement of bills, the front desk cashier should proceed as follows:

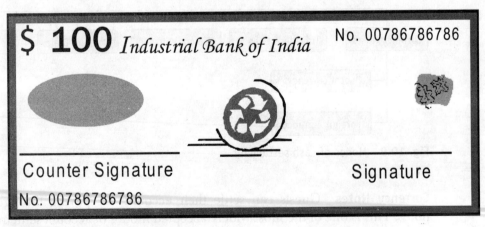

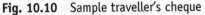

Fig. 10.10   Sample traveller's cheque

- Ensure that the second signature is put in front of him.
- Check the guest's passport to establish identity.
- Note down the passport number at the back of the traveller's cheque.
- If the traveller's cheque is in foreign currency, calculate the correct exchange value as per the daily rate.
- Return the balance to the guest in local currency.

Personal Cheque   Personal cheques (Fig. 10.11) are cheques drawn against funds deposited in an individual's personal bank account. It takes some time before the payment for the cheque is received from the issuing bank. There is also a chance of the bank refusing a payment—if there is insufficient amount in the account or if the guest has 'stopped' the cheque. Hence, it is normally not an accepted mode of account settlement. However, hotels may accept personal cheques from frequent guests or guests from companies that give a high volume of business to the hotel.

In case a guest insists on settling his bill by personal cheque, the front desk agent may politely request him to get an authorization from the lobby manager. On receiving authorization from the lobby manager, the guest has to submit an application for making payment by personal cheque. The front office agent needs to check the following details:

- The signatures in the application form and the cheque match.
- The cheque is crossed as 'A/c Payee only'.
- The amount in figures and words is the same.
- The date on the cheque is valid.
- Accept only MICR (Magnetic Ink Character Reader) cheques.
- Do not accept second or third party cheques.

Date:......................

Pay .... or Bearer

Rs ....

....   Rs ....

A/c No.	045888	Initials

Industrial Bank of India   Dinesh Pratap Singh
H-Block, Red Squire,
Lucknow

" 024 649"   "2000 0000 45"

Fig. 10.11   Sample of personal cheque

Demand Draft   A demand draft is a written order from the bank for the payment of money upon presentation of the same. A person may obtain a demand draft from a bank by filling the required form and paying the draft amount and the bank's commission. It is a secure and widely accepted mode of payment.

The major differences between the personal cheque, traveller's cheque, and demand draft are enumerated in Table 10.1.

Debit Card   A debit card (Fig. 10.12) is a card (usually plastic) that allows customers to access their funds immediately, electronically. It enables the holder to withdraw money or to have the cost of purchases charged directly to the her bank account without paying by cash or writing a cheque. In many countries, it also acts as an ATM card, which is used to withdraw money from ATMs (automated teller machines). It is a safe mode of account settlement as the amount is instantly transferred to the hotel's account. When the card is swiped, the electronic fund

Table 10.1   Differences between a personal cheque, traveller's cheque, and demand draft

S. No.	Features	Personal Cheque	Traveller's Cheque	Demand Draft
1	Issuing authority	Individual	Bank	Bank
2	Face value	Written by the account holder	Pre-printed	Endorsed by bank
3	Acceptance at merchant establishment	Generally not accepted by hotels for settlement of bills.	Widely accepted	Widely accepted
4	Need of bank account	Mandatory	No need	No need
5	Number of signatures	Only one	Two signatures—one at the time of issue and the other in front of the encashing authority.	Signed by the authorized signatory of the issuing bank.
6	Validity	Six months from the date of issue	Unlimited validity	Six months from the date of issue
7	Crossing facility	Yes	No	Yes
8	Payment may not be honoured	Yes, if insufficient balance in the account.	No, because the amount has been deposited.	No, because the amount has been deposited.
9	Issuance of lost/stolen/ damaged list	No	Yes	Yes
10	Collection charges	Applicable, in case of outstation cheques (except multi-city or at par cheques).	None, as the commission has already been paid.	None, as the commission has already been paid.

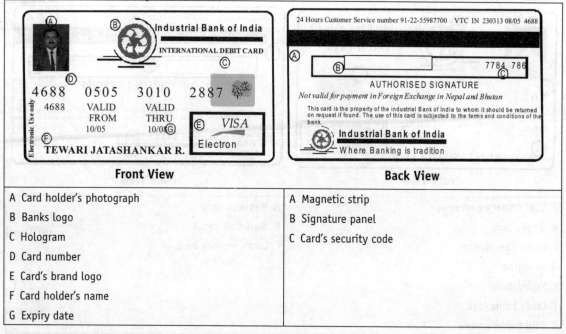

A Card holder's photograph	A Magnetic strip
B Banks logo	B Signature panel
C Hologram	C Card's security code
D Card number	
E Card's brand logo	
F Card holder's name	
G Expiry date	

Fig. 10.12   Sample debit card

transfer point of sale (EFTPOS) terminal contacts the computer network of the bank to verify and authorize the transaction. Once the authorization is received from the bank, the amount is debited from the guest's bank account and instantly credited to the hotel's bank account. In case of insufficient funds, the bank does not authorize the transaction and the guest is requested for an alternative mode of payment.

Credit Settlement

A credit settlement is an arrangement for the deferred payment of goods and services, i.e., a settlement in which the hotel does not receive any payment on the day of departure of the guest but would receive it later. The various credit modes are illustrated in Fig. 10.13.

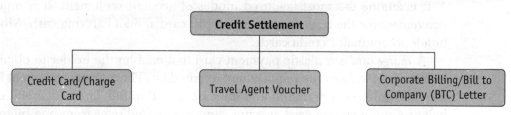

Fig. 10.13   Modes of credit settlement

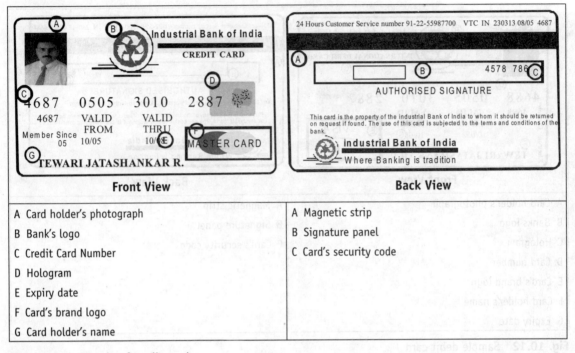

Fig. 10.14   Sample of credit card

Credit Card/Charge Card Payments   A credit card (Fig. 10.14) is a payment card (usually plastic) that allows the owner to obtain goods and services on credit terms, without paying cash. It may be used repeatedly to borrow money or buy goods and services on credit. In addition to obtaining goods, credit cards can also be used to obtain cash. The issuer (bank) assures the seller (hotel) that the owner (guest) has a satisfactory credit rating and that the bank will see to it that the hotel receives payment for the merchandise delivered. Transactions during a month are totalled and presented to the card holder for settlement on a monthly basis. Alternatively, a percentage of the outstanding amount can be paid and the balance extended to the next month and so on. This will normally incur a much higher annual rate of interest than usual; for example, 2 per cent monthly interest rate is equivalent to an annual percentage rate of 26.82 per cent.

It is among the most favoured modes of account settlement. It is much more convenient for the traveller to carry credit card(s) than carrying cash. Most of the hotels accept major credit cards.

A *charge card* is a plastic payment card that enables the holder to obtain goods and services without the requirement to pay cash. The account statement is sent to the card holder every month and must be settled in full. Unlike a credit card, the balance in the charge card account cannot be rolled over from one billing to the next. In addition to obtaining goods, the charge card can be used to obtain cash. Some examples of charge cards are American Express, Diners Club, and a number of gold cards.

While processing payment through credit cards, the front desk cashier follows the following procedure:

- Checks the card holder's name on the card.
- Checks the expiry date of the card.
- Checks if the card is a stolen card.
- Checks the credit limit of the card; if the amount of the bill exceeds the limit of the credit card, the cashier requests the guest to pay the balance amount by cash.
- Swipes the card through the EFTPOS terminal for verification and authorization from the issuer of the credit card.
- Asks the guest to sign on the transaction slip.
- Verifies the guest signature on the transaction slip with the signature on the signature panel at the reverse of the card.
- Returns the credit card and the carbon copy of the transaction slip to the guest.
- Follows the standard operation procedure to process the payment of the guest folio as per the house customs.

The major differences between a credit card, charge card, and debit card are enumerated in Table 10.2.

Travel Agent Vouchers Tour operators and travel agencies selling packages or customized tours make bookings for a guest's accommodation, food and beverage, and other services. Mostly, they receive advance payment from travellers at the

Table 10.2 Differences between a credit card, charge card, and debit card

S. No.	Features	Credit Card	Charge Card	Debit Card
1	Issuing Authority	Bank	Private organization	Bank
2	Need of bank account	No	No	Yes
3	Credit limit	As per the type of card	As per the type of card	Limited to the amount present in that account.
4	Acceptance	Accepted at most of the merchant establishments.	Accepted only at member merchant establishments.	Accepted at most of the merchant establishments.
5	Grace period	From twenty to fifty-five days	Normally, one month	No grace period; amount is instantly transferred to the merchant's account.
6	Provision of minimum payment	Yes	No, the card holder should pay the transaction amount in full.	No, the amount is debited instantaneously from the card holder's account.

time of selling the tour package itself. The travel agency (TA) sends a voucher (Fig. 10.15) to the service provider (hotel) with the details of the billing procedure (direct payment by the guest or bill to TA) and the services (room and meal plan) to be provided to the traveller. Apart from travel agencies and tour operators, airlines (that have contracts with hotels) also send meals and accommodation order (MAO) or passenger service order (PSO) to layover passengers in case of flight delays and cancellations. In such cases, the hotel obtains payments from the TA or the airline.

While processing the TA voucher/MAO/PSO, the front desk cashier should proceed as follows:

- Read the vouchers carefully.
- Refer to the list of approved TAs to whom the hotel offers credit.
- Check the billing instructions carefully.
- In the case of a foreign travel agency's voucher, get an authorization from the lobby manager.

Suman Travel Corporation (India) Pvt. Ltd.
सुमन Shubh Avash, Mahuli Road,
Mahson, Basti.
Uttar Pradesh

Voucher No.:............................

Date:......................................

To
The Manager
Hotel Sun Star
Lucknow

Dear Sir,
In exchange for this voucher, please provide the following services to our valued client

1. ....
2. ....
3. ....
4. ....
5. ....

Client's Details
Name of guest: ....
Arrival date: .... Arrival Time: ....
Departure Date: .... Departure Time: ....

Note: The bills for the above services may be:
         ( ) Presented to Guest for Direct settlement
         ( ) Forwarded to us for settlement

Signature of Issuing Authority   Seal

Fig. 10.15 Sample travel agent voucher

- Check the expenses covered by the voucher.
- Collect payment from the guest for the services not covered or included in the voucher; for example, bills for spa treatments.
- Attach all the vouchers signed by the guest with the master bill, and ask the guest to verify and sign the bill.
- Do not give the copies of signed bills to guest (as these have to be presented to the travel agent, who will make the payment to the hotel in this case).
- Send the guest bill and vouchers to the accounts department for the collection of the amount from the travel agent.

Corporate Billing or Bill to Company letter   Some companies, whose executives travel at the expense of the company, make a deal with hotels, whereby they determine the rates for different types of rooms and meal plans to be offered to their executives. The terms and conditions of the payment are also pre-determined. The reservations are made by the company on behalf of the travelling executives. The executives carry a letter from their company, which is called a bill to company (BTC) letter, as a proof of their identity.

The front desk cashier proceeds as follows while processing BTC letters:

- Establishes the identity of the guest by asking him to show his identity card or/and the BTC letter, which is prepared on the company letterhead.
- Checks and verifies that the company is listed in the company volume guarantee rate (CVGR) list of the hotel.
- Checks the services that are included in the agreement with the company; any service or facility utilized by the guest that is not covered by the company should be charged separately from the guest.
- Prepares the guest bill, along with all the supporting vouchers, and asks the guest to verify and sign the bill.
- Does not give the bill to the guest (as these have to be given to the company, which will make the payment to the hotel).
- Sends the duly signed bill to the accounts department for collection from the company.

Sometimes guests utilize facilities and services, like telephone, laundry, and drinks, that are not covered by the TA voucher or company agreement. In such cases, the guests should settle these sundry transactions by making direct payment to the hotel.

POTENTIAL CHECK-OUT PROBLEMS AND SOLUTIONS

As we have discussed, check-out is a very critical step of the guest cycle. The departure procedure should be simple and short. The guests who are checking out of the hotel are often in a hurry to catch a flight or a train. Hotels should take measures to avoid the formation of long queues at the front desk during peak check-out periods. A speedy check-out procedure and an error-free billing leave a lasting good impression on the guest. A guest who leaves the hotel with a good impression will return to the hotel/chain and will also recommend the hotel/chain to her friends and relatives. Despite measures taken by hotels to avoid problems during the check-out process, the following problems may occur during the departure of a guest:

- Late check out
- Long queues at the cashier counter
- Improper posting of charges in the guest folio

These problems can be rectified by informing the guests about check-in and check-out times at the time of registration, installing self check-out terminals, and implementing accurate guest accounting system.

Late Check-outs

Most hotels have a fixed check-out time—generally 12 noon—at which the departing guests must vacate their rooms and settle their bills. If a guest vacates his room after the check-out time, it is considered late check-out. This may create a problem, especially during high occupancy periods, as the guests with confirmed reservations will be required to wait for the room to be vacated and cleaned. A hotel may take the following preventive measures to minimize late check-outs:

- Inform the guest about the check-out time and late check-out charges at the time of reservation and also at registration.
- Have the information regarding the check-out timings printed on the key card and displayed at the back of the room doors.
- Add the late check-out charges in the guest bill.
- Request the guests to vacate the room as per the check-out time and offer to keep their luggage in the left luggage room at no extra cost.
- In case of groups, provide hospitality rooms without any extra charges.

Long Queues at the Cashier

The standard check-out procedure, involving number of steps dealing with the presentation and settlement of bills, takes some time. As more and more guests now want a speedy and queue-free check-out, hotels are coming up with alternatives to the standard check-out. These alternative methods are express check-out and self check-out terminals.

Express Check-out (ECO)   The front desk is flooded with check-out requests at the hotel check-out time. As the preparation and settlement of bills is a time consuming process, it leads to the formation of a long queue at the front office cashier's desk.

To avoid this situation, some hotels have developed a speedier check-out procedure known as express check-out (Fig. 10.16).

The express check-out procedure requires the guest to fill the express check-out (ECO) form and a pre-departure folio. The ECO form is an authorization by the guest to the hotel authorities to charge the outstanding balance to his credit card. By signing the ECO form, the guest agrees to pay the amount finalized by the front desk cashier after his departure. These forms are available at the front desk or are sent to the guest on the morning of the date of departure. The ECO form (see Fig. 10.17) is accompanied by a copy of the guest's folio, indicating the approximate total bill.

By signing the ECO, the guest transfers his outstanding folio balance to the credit card voucher (created at the time of registration). Some hotels have a policy to take the imprint of the credit cards of the guest to avoid any problems or disputes in the future. In case the final amount varies considerably from the approximate total amount—due to the use of any chargeable facility by the guest after signing the ECO form—the guest may be informed about the same. The variance may also be there in case of any late charges received by the front desk cashier. After signing the ECO form, the guest can leave the hotel at his convenience without having to go to the front desk or cashier's desk for the standard check-out procedure.

Once the guest has departed from the hotel, the front desk cashier finalizes his account, including any late charges, and completes the imprinted credit card

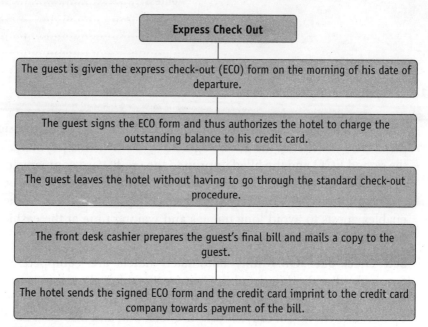

Fig. 10.16 Express check-out procedure

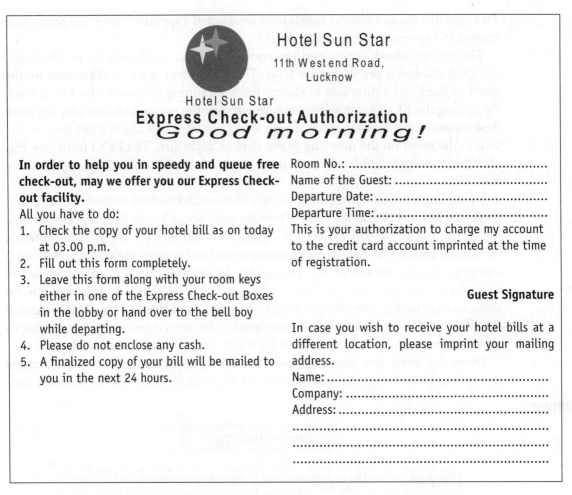

Fig. 10.17 Sample express check-out form

voucher. The guest's signature on the ECO form replaces the signature on the credit card voucher as the guest's agreement to make the payment. The hotel sends the signed ECO and the filled imprint to the credit card company for the settlement of the final bill and mails a copy of the bill to the guest's mailing address.

The express check-out service reduces the pressure at the cashier's desk. It also enables guests to avoid long queues and waiting time at the cashier's desk during peak check-out times and leave at their convenience.

Self Check-out Only fully automated hotels are equipped with self service terminals (discussed in detail in Chapter 8), which allow guests to check-in/check-out promptly by operating these interactive machines. They are available with options like check-out only, check-in/check-out, and also cash acceptor. Generally located in the hotel lobby, the self check-out terminals are interfaced with the property management system (PMs) of the hotel. They are also designed to be compatible with a system that allows air travellers to print boarding passes while checking out of the hotel.

Self check-in and check-out kiosks identify guests by their rooms' card keys or their credit cards, as in some cases the guests' credit cards may be coded like their room keys. At self check-out terminals, guests can access and review their folios and settle their accounts using credit cards. The check-out is completed when the guest's outstanding balance is posted to his credit card account. The terminal dispenses a printed statement of the account settlement. Simultaneously, the system communicates the room status to the front desk computer. The front office module of the PMS automatically updates the room status and other records like guest history card.

The self check-out terminals have the following benefits:

- They minimize the guests' waiting time as the guests can check-out themselves by operating the check-out kiosk and can settle their outstanding bills through credit card without having to go to the front desk cashier.
- They simplify the check-in and check-out procedure as the guests can easily follow the interactive instructions on the screen.
- They eliminate the scope of human error as they are integrated with the hotel PMS and thus track all the financial transactions between a guest and the hotel's points of sale and other sections.

Improper Posting of Charges

There are occasions when a guest's financial transactions are not properly posted in the guest folio and the final bill is inaccurate. This might be due to human error or system error. The front desk is flooded with check-out requests at peak check-out times and the cashier might make some mistake in the posting of charges or the calculation of bills. This could lead to a dispute with the guest and delay other guests in the queue. The whole experience can be quite damaging for the hotel. To avoid this, hotels should install guest accounting systems, which are more accurate and faster, leading to higher guest satisfaction.

SUMMARY

In this chapter, we have studied the issues relating to the final phase of the guest cycle—departure and settlement of guest accounts. The guests who are checking out of the hotel are often in a hurry to catch a flight or a train, so the departure procedure should be simple and short. A speedy check-out procedure and an error-free billing leave a lasting good impression on the guest. A guest who leaves the hotel with a good impression will return to the hotel/chain and will also recommend the hotel/chain to her friends and relatives. The chapter discusses the departure procedures in manual, semi-automated, and fully automated hotels. The modes of bill settlement—cash and credit—are also explained in detail.

Despite measures taken by hotels to avoid problems during check-out, problems like late check-out, long queues at the cashier counter, and improper posting of charges in the guest folio may occur during the departure of a guest. These problems can be rectified by informing the guests about check-in and check-out times at the time of registration, installing self check-out terminals, and implementing accurate guest accounting system.

KEY TERMS

Check-out The procedure of vacating the hotel room, settling bills, and leaving the hotel.

Departure errand card A card filled by the bell boy who brings the departing guest's luggage from his room.

Early departure The departure of a guest before his expected date of departure.

Guest folio A statement showing the balance of the guest's financial obligation towards the hotel.

Late check-out charge The charge levied to a guest in case she wants to retain the room after the check-out time.

Late charge A charge (for services or facilities utilized by the guest) that reaches the front desk cashier after the guest bills are prepared.

Personal cheque A cheque drawn against funds deposited in an individual's personal bank account.

Travel agent voucher A voucher made by a travel agency (that has an agreement with the hotel) with the details of the billing procedure and the services (room and meal plan) to be provided to the traveller.

REVIEW QUESTIONS

Multiple Choice Questions

1. Which of the following activities are carried out at the time of check-out?

   a) Settlement of guest account
   b) Updating front office records
   c) Creating long-lasting impression on the guest
   d) All of the above

2. The request for check-out from the guest may land at:

   a) Reception Desk   b) Information desk
   c) Bell Desk   d) All

3. The cashier prepares the guest bill by extracting information from:

   a) City ledger   b) City folio
   c) Guest folio   d) Employee folio

4. A guest may choose the following mode of settlement of bill:

   a) Cash   b) Credit card
   c) Traveller's cheque   d) All

5. Which one of the following is generally not accepted as a mode of settlement of guest account?

   a) Traveller's cheques b) Cash
   c) Travel agent vouchers d) Personal cheques

True/False

1. Master cards and visa cards are examples of credit cards.

2. American Express is an example of a charge card.

3. Traveller's cheques and personal cheques are the same.

4. One should have a saving account in the bank to get a credit card.

5. Settlement of accounts means zeroing the credit and debit balances in the guest folio.

Fill in the blanks

1. _____ check-out may not require queuing at the front desk.

2. Guests can check-out promptly by operating _____ terminals.

3. Hotel should obtain licence from _____ to deal with foreign currency.

4. _____ and _____ are cash equivalents.

5. Travel agent issues _____ to their clients for the settlement of hotel bills.

Discussion Questions

1. Explain the departure procedure.

2. What do you understand by late charges? How can late charges be avoided?

3. What role does a bell boy play in the departure of a guest apart from carrying the guest luggage?

4. What precautions will you take while preparing guest bills?

5. Draw foreign currency exchange certificate and foreign currency control sheet.

6. Discuss the difference between cash and credit settlement.

7. Updating front office records after a guest's departure is very important. Comment.

8. Guest history card is a tool for marketing the hotel. Discuss.

9. Explain the advantages of express check-out facility offered to guests.

10. What are the advantages of a self check-out unit?

11. What precautions should the front desk cashier take while accepting currency notes, credit cards, and travel agent vouchers for settling guest accounts?

CRITICAL THINKING QUESTIONS

1. A long waiting time at the front desk for check-out may spoil the overall experience of a guest. Comment.

2. Foreign currency encashment requires special attention. Comment.

3. Cash payment is the best mode of bill settlement. Explain with reasons.

4. A faulty bill, prepared by the front desk cashier, leads to loss for the hotel. Comment.

CASE STUDIES

1. Arvind, the front office manager of Hotel Sun Star, while reviewing the guest comment cards, found that many of the guests had complained about a long wait time at the front desk for check-out. He investigated the matter and found that the front desk was flooded with guests at peak departure time. He also found that the guests' bills were not ready because the front desk had not received the credit charges from the various points of sale.

   Arvind want to implement the following correction measures:

   - Automation of the front office.
   - Distribution of express check-out forms in the guest rooms on the eve of the guest departure.
   - Establishing proper coordination with points of sale for prompt transfer of transactions for recording in the guest folio.

   Discuss the following about each corrective measure that Arvind wants to implement:
   a) Expenditure incurred
   b) Employee responsiveness

2. Assume you are a front desk cashier. Mr Sunil, a regular guest, is checking out of the hotel. He wishes to settle his bill by paying some amount by cash, a part of the amount by his credit card, and the remaining part by a personal cheque.
   a) How you will proceed?
   b) Will you accept credit cards and personal cheques for settlement?
   c) What are the conditions for accepting personal cheques and credit cards for the settlement of guest accounts?
   d) Do you need authorization from someone to accept personal cheques and credit cards?

CHAPTER 11

Front Office Accounting

Learning Objectives:

After reading this chapter, you will be able to understand the following:

- Front office accounting and its functions.
- Types of accounts maintained by the front desk—guest account and non-guest account.
- Different kinds of vouchers—visitor's paid out, miscellaneous charge voucher, cash receipt voucher, telephone call voucher, travel agent voucher, commission voucher, guest allowances, restaurant or bar check.
- Various folios—master folio, guest folio, non-guest/city folio, and employee folio.
- Types of ledgers—guest ledger and city ledger.
- Front office accounting cycle—creation, maintenance, and settlement of accounts.

The aim of the hotel business is to generate profit by providing services like accommodation, food and beverage, and the use of facilities such as fitness centre, sauna and steam, jacuzzi, etc. on payment basis. The timely and accurate posting of a guest's financial transactions in the guest account is very important for the successful running of the hotel business—it enables the hotel to make an accurate bill and receive the payment from the guest. An efficient and error-free billing also leads to higher guest satisfaction. So it is of utmost importance that the hotel maintains its guest accounts properly and accurately, and keeps them up to date.

We have understood the four stages of the guest cycle in the earlier chapters. In this chapter, we will get an overview of how a hotel maintains guest accounts and ensures the settlement of the same. The chapter begins with discussing the different types of accounts, followed by a detailed study of folios, vouchers, and ledgers. The front office accounting cycle—the process of creating, maintaining, and settling guest accounts—is discussed in the later part of the chapter.

FRONT OFFICE ACCOUNTING

Accounting may be defined as the process of collecting, recording, summarizing, and analysing financial transactions of a business. According to the American Institute of Certified Public Accountants (AICPA), 'Accounting is an art of recording, classifying, and summarizing in a significant manner and in terms of money, transactions, and events which are, in part at least, of a financial character, and interpreting the results thereof.' In hotels, the front desk cashier maintains the guests' accounts and ensures the settlement of the same.

The resident or in-house guests of a hotel are those who are staying in the hotel. They seldom pay on the spot for the use of hotel services and facilities like restaurants, laundry, fitness centre, spa, salon, and so on. They sign the bills to verify their use of the services and the amount incurred. The bills are posted in their folio, and a final consolidated bill is made at the time of their departure. In other words, the hotel provides credit facility at the time of the utilization of the hotel services to the resident guests. An accurate posting of the guest accounts is very essential to ensure the guest's goodwill and the recovery of all the charges incurred by the guest.

In order to maximize revenue, hotels offer some services and facilities to non-resident guests as well. These may include the use of the fitness and health centre, swimming pool, club facilities, food and beverage outlets, and so on. When these services and facilities are offered to non- resident guests on credit, the account of the same is maintained by the front office cashier. As the number of financial transactions that take place between a hotel and its guests (resident and non-resident) is very high, the front desk cashier should maintain the guest accounts accurately and properly.

However, the collection of a non-resident account is not the responsibility of the front desk; it is collected by the accounts department. Also, when a resident guest, whose account is to be settled by his company, checks out from the hotel after signing the bills, his account turns into a non-guest account, and the collection responsibility shifts from the front desk to the accounts section.

The major functions of front office accounting system are as under:
- Creation and maintenance of guest and non-guest accounts accurately.
- Tracking financial transactions of guests throughout the guest cycle.
- Monitoring the credit limit of guests, and asking for a deposit from guests in case of high outstanding balance.
- Preparing a high balance report for collection and informing the management about the same.
- Providing an efficient management information system (MIS) to the management for departmental revenue generation.
- Maintaining effective control over cash and credit transactions.

Types of Accounts

The front desk maintains two types of accounts:
- Guest accounts
- Non-guest accounts

Guest Account   A guest account is the record of financial transactions between and a resident guest and the hotel. This account is created either during the registration of the guest (at the time of check-in) or during reservation, if the guest makes an advance payment. The front office creates an individual folio for each guest—for maintaining a record of all the financial transactions that take place during the stay of the guest. On the basis of a guest's folio, the final bill is prepared and presented to the guest for collection.

Hotels generally extend credit facility to guests for the use of the services and products provided by them. They fix an upper limit to the credit facility, which is known as the house limit. When the credit balance of the guest exceeds the house limit, the front desk cashier may ask the guest to make a part or full payment of the outstanding balance.

Non-guest Account   A non-guest account is the record of the financial transactions that take place between a non-resident guest and the hotel. This is also known as a city account. The front desk cashier maintains records of financial transactions between the hotel and a local resident to whom the hotel has extended the credit facility for the use of hotel facilities and services. Besides local guests, the front desk cashier also maintains other types of non-guest accounts, which include:
- Guests who leave the hotel without the settlement of their accounts are known as skippers; their accounts are also treated as non-resident guest accounts. The account is transferred to the city ledger awaiting eventual payment, and after a stipulated wait time, the same is written off as a bad debt.
- The status of guests, whose accounts are not settled by them (in case of bills to company), changes from resident to non-resident guests when they leave the

hotel. The front desk cashier transfers the balance to the city ledger and the payment is collected by the accounts department.

• When advance payment has been received for a guaranteed reservation and it is subsequently a no-show, the account is normally recorded in the city sales ledger.

Vouchers

The front desk cashier is required to present supporting documents of all the financial transactions recorded in the guest folio. A voucher—which entitles the bearer to certain goods, services, or discounts upon presentation—is a documentary evidence of a financial transaction. For every purchase, the point of sale presents the bill to the guest, receives cash from the guest, and gives a cash receipt to the guest. In case a charge purchase is made, the guest signs the bill and the same is sent to the front desk for posting it into the guest account; the same is given to the guest at the time of check-out.

The types of vouchers used in hotels are illustrated in Fig. 11.1.

Visitors Paid-out   The money paid by the hotel on behalf of guests is known as visitors paid-out (VPO). A VPO is generally made for the following charges:
• Payment for taxi, travel agency services
• Porter charges
• Florist charges
• Postage and courier charges
• Emergency medical expenses

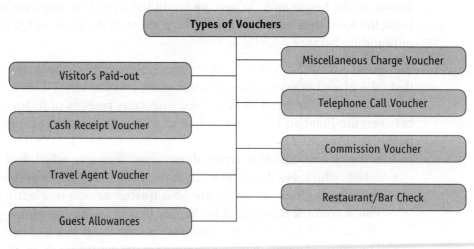

Fig. 11.1   Types of vouchers

Hotel ABC
Visitors Paid-out Voucher

Date:................

Room No.:...........

Name of Guest:_____   Room Account No.:_____

Explanation	Charge	
	Rs	Paisa
Rupees (in words)	Total:	
Signature of Recipient Approved by		Signature of Cashier

Fig. 11.2   Visitors paid-out voucher

The paid-outs are made from the cash bank that is maintained by the front office cashier. A proper authorization should be taken from the lobby manager before making the VPO. To make a paid-out, one should:

- Confirm the name, room number, and identity of the guest.
- Fill the paid-out voucher properly, mentioning the details of services paid for (as shown in Fig. 11.2).
- Get the VPO authorized by the lobby manager.
- Make the payment.
- Post the entry in the guest folio and place the voucher in the folio docket.

Miscellaneous Charge Voucher   A miscellaneous charge voucher is prepared for the payment of miscellaneous services and facilities, like laundry, health club, fitness centre, beauty salon, etc. The guest verifies and signs the miscellaneous charge voucher, which is sent to the front desk cashier for posting the charges into the guest folio. The format of a miscellaneous charge voucher is shown in Fig. 11.3.

Cash Receipt Voucher   A receipt is an acknowledgment that a payment has been made. A cash receipt voucher is prepared and issued to the person depositing cash as a proof of remittance of the deposited cash. A sample cash receipt voucher is shown in Fig. 11.4.

Telephone Call Voucher   Nowadays a lot of hotels use computerized systems, where, whenever a guest makes a call, the call accounting module automatically transfers the call charges to the guest folio. In small hotels, where outgoing calls are routed through the operator, the responsibility of billing the call charges lies with the telephone operator, who puts down the call details on a telephone charge

Hotel ABC
Miscellaneous Charge Voucher

Date:................

Room No.:...........

Name of Guest:_____   Room Account No.:_____

Explanation		Charge	
		Rs	Paisa
Rupees (in words)		Total:	
Prepared by	Approved by		Checked by

Fig. 11.3   Sample miscellaneous charge voucher

Hotel ABC
Cash Receipt Voucher

S. No........................

Date:................

Received from: ....

Address: ....

....

Amount in figure: ....

Amount in words: ....

On account of ....

Signature of Cashier

Fig. 11.4   Sample cash receipt voucher

voucher (Fig. 11.5) and sends it to the front desk cashier for posting into the guest account.

Travel Agent Voucher   Most tour operators and travel agencies receive advance payment from their clients for making travel arrangements like accommodation,

Hotel ABC

Telephone Call Voucher

Date:..................

Room No.:...........

Name of Guest:_____   Account No.:_____

Explanation			Charge	
			Rs	Paisa
Rupees (in words)		Total:		
			Signature of Telephone Operator	

Fig. 11.5   Sample telephone call voucher

food and beverage, and other services. The travel agency then makes the reservation in a hotel on behalf of the guest. It sends a voucher, known as a travel agent voucher, containing the details of the billing procedure and services to be provided to the guest (discussed in detail in Chapter 10). Airlines that have contracts with hotels also send meals and accommodation order (MAO) or passenger service order (PSO) for layover passengers due to delay or cancellation of flights. In these cases, the hotel obtains payments from the travel agency or airline.

Commission Voucher   Hotels offer commission to persons who provide regular business to them. Whenever a commission is paid by the cashier, a commission voucher is made. The commission voucher (Fig. 11.6) should be authorized by a competent authority of the hotel. Generally, it is authorized by the lobby manager. More commonly, commission vouchers are made for the following:
- A taxi driver who brings a walk-in guest to the hotel. In case the guest stays at the hotel, the hotel pays a commission to the taxi driver.
- A travel agent/tour operator working on commission basis (generally, the commission is 10 per cent on the room rates, excluding taxes).
- Any agency working on a commission basis.

Guest Allowances   An allowance is an amount deducted from an invoice to compensate the buyer for an expense or mistake. The guest allowance is the cash paid to the guest by the hotel, especially in the following circumstances:
- If there is a wrong posting of a charge in the guest folio, an allowance is given and the voucher is made to nullify the guest folio balance due to the wrong posting.

Hotel ABC
Commission Voucher

Date:................

Name of Recipient:_____

Explanation			Charge	
			Rs	Paisa
Rupees (in words):		Total:		

Prepared by	Approved by	Signature of Cashier

Fig. 11.6   Commission voucher

Hotel ABC
Allowance/Rebate voucher

Date:................
Room No.:...........

Name of Guest:_____   Room Account No.:_____

Explanation			Charge	
			Rs	Paisa
Rupees (in words):		Total:		

Prepared by	Approved by	Checked by

Fig. 11.7   Allowance voucher

- If a guest has deposited a large sum as advance and that amount exceeds the hotel bill.
- If an airline or a tour operator sends a crew or a group and guarantees the reimbursement of their bills.

Guest allowances are strictly controlled. The front desk cashier requires an authorization from a competent authority before making such a payment. Figure 11.7 shows the format of an allowance voucher.

Restaurant/Bar Check   Resident guests may enjoy their meals in any of the food and beverage outlets in a hotel. Whenever a guest consumes food or beverage in a restaurant, a bill is raised; in case a resident guest wishes to utilize the credit facility offered by the hotel, he should sign the bill. The signed bills serve as the proof of financial transactions at the food and beverage outlets and are treated as vouchers for posting the charges to the guest folio. A sample of a restaurant/bar check is shown in Fig. 11.8.

Folios

The front desk cashier transfers the financial transactions that are recorded in the vouchers to individual guest records or the concerned account folio. A folio is a written record of a guest's account and is created at the time of starting a book of account in the name of a guest. It is a statement of all the transactions that take place between a hotel and a guest. The initial balance at the time of opening a folio is zero. It changes with the credit (Cr) and debit (Dr) transactions. The credit or debit balance can be known at any point of time. The folio balance should be zeroed at the time of closing the folio, i.e., neither party (hotel or guest) should have any outstanding payments. Different types of folios are illustrated in Fig. 11.9.

Hotel ABC
Ghazal Bar

Name of Guest:_____   Room No._____   S. No._____
Date:...................   Table No.......................   No. of Pax...............................
Served by....................

S. No.	Description	Quantity	Rate/unit	Amount
			Total	

Please do not sign if paying by cash or credit card

Cashier POS

Fig. 11.8 Sample bar check

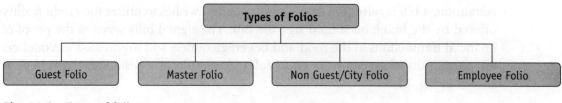

Fig. 11.9   Types of folios

Hotel ABC

Guest Folio

Name of the Guest: Mr Surya Prakash Mishra

Date of Arrival: 10 April 2009

Date of Departure: 11 April 2009

Number of Pax: One

Room No.: 210

Rate: Rs 5,000

Folio No.: 21786

Date	Item	Description	Debit	Credit
10/04/2009	1	Cash		6,500
10/04/2009	2	Room	5,000	
10/04/2009	3	Dinner	500	
10/04/2009	4	Ghazal Bar	800	
10/04/2009	5	Breakfast	300	
10/04/2009	6	Cash		100

Fig. 11.10   Sample guest folio

Guest Folio   A guest folio is created for each guest as soon as the first financial transaction takes place between the hotel and the guest. Generally, a folio is created at the time of the guest registration. In case a guest makes an advance payment at the time of reservation, his folio is created at that time, with the posting of the advance amount in the credit side. A sample guest folio is shown in Fig. 11.10.

Master Folio   A master folio contains accounts of more than one guest. In small hotels, a master folio contains the record of all the guests staying in the hotel. By glancing through the master folio, one can find the net credit or debit balance on a particular day.

Non-guest/City Folio   A city folio contains the financial transactions between a hotel and its non-resident guests. A hotel may offer credit facility to local businessmen to attract additional business for the hotel. A city folio is created for credit services, like the use of club facilities, fitness centre, health centre, sport facilities, etc., offered to guests who are not staying at the hotel.

Employee Folio   An employee folio contains the credit transactions between a hotel and its employees. This folio is created and maintained for employees to whom the hotel has permitted credit/charge purchases. The amount is later collected from the employees or deducted from their salaries, depending upon the hotel policy.

Ledger

A ledger is a collection of the same type of accounts. The front office ledger has a collection of folios. There are normally two ledgers maintained by the front office. One of them, designated as guest ledger, contains all the folio entries of resident guests; the other contains the folio entries of non-resident guest accounts and is known as city ledger.

Guest Ledger   A guest ledger contains the details of all the financial transactions between a resident guest and the hotel, including charge purchases and the payments received from the guest. It has two parts—debit and credit. By taking a look at the guest ledger, one can find the credit or debit balance of an individual guest as well as the total credit or debit balance on date. In a manual system, the financial transactions are recorded in a tabular ledger, or tab ledger, which is of two types:
- Horizontal tabular ledger
- Vertical tabular ledger

Horizontal tabular ledger   In a horizontal tabular ledger, all the credit expenses of the guest are recorded in one horizontal row, and at the end of the row, the guests' credit or debit balance is shown. The vertical row of the table contains the room numbers. At the end of vertical column, the daily sales balance can be seen. A format of the horizontal tabular ledger is shown in Fig. 11.11.

Visitors/Vertical tabular ledger   A vertical tabular ledger is a variation of the horizontal tabular ledger. It is also called visitors tabular ledger. The rows depict the room numbers, and in the columns, the details of the guests and their credit expenses as well as payments are recorded. At the end of every column, one can find the account balance of individual guests staying in a particular room. It is a loose sheet and is prepared on a daily basis by the front desk cashier. A format of visitors/vertical tabular ledger (VTL) is shown in Fig. 11.12.

City Ledger   A city ledger contains the collective accounts of all the non-resident individuals/agencies to whom the hotel extends credit facility. It is also called non-guest account. City ledgers also contain the accounts of resident guests who have left the hotel without settling their accounts, which would be settled at a later date

Day:.................								Date:....................					
Room No.	Name of Guest	No. Of Pax	Rate	B/ fwd	Room Rent	B'fast	Lunch	Dinner	Phone	Misc. Expense	VPOs Total	Credit	C/ fwd
201	Shivansh Tripathi	02	1500.00										

Fig. 11.11 Horizontal tabular ledger

by a third party (may be a credit card company, an airline, a travel agency, or a corporate house). This account would be closed at the time of receiving the complete payment. The account of skippers is also maintained in the city ledger for a specific period (as per the hotel policy); at the expiry of this period the same is written off as bad debt and the account is closed. This ledger also includes bad cheque accounts (cheques that have bounced), disputed bills account (bills that are in dispute), late charges accounts (bills that could not be posted in the guest bill at the time of check-out), and retention charges accounts (reservation was guaranteed but the same was cancelled or guest did not show up).

FRONT OFFICE ACCOUNTING CYCLE

An important function of the front office accounting system is to maintain an accurate and up-to-date record of all the financial transactions (credit and debit) between the hotel and each guest, so that all the outstanding accounts are settled

Room No.	101	102	201	202	301	303	Total
Name	Mr S. Shukla	Mr S.P. Mishra	Ms Pooja	Ms Poonam	Mr K.K. Shukla		
No. of Persons							
GR No.							
Plan							
Room Rate							
Tea							
Breakfast							
Lunch							
Dinner							
Beverages							
Room Service							
Telephone							
Laundry							
Tobacco							
VPO							
Others							
Beer							
Wine							
Miscellaneous							
Daily Total							
Cash Deposit							
Allowance							
Balance C/fwd							
Total Dr. Cr.							

Hotel ABC

Visitors Tabular Ledger

Fig. 11.12 Visitors/Vertical tabular ledger

and the hotel does not lose any revenue. The front office accounting cycle (Fig. 11.13) has three distinct phases:

- Creation of accounts
- Maintenance of accounts
- Settlement of accounts

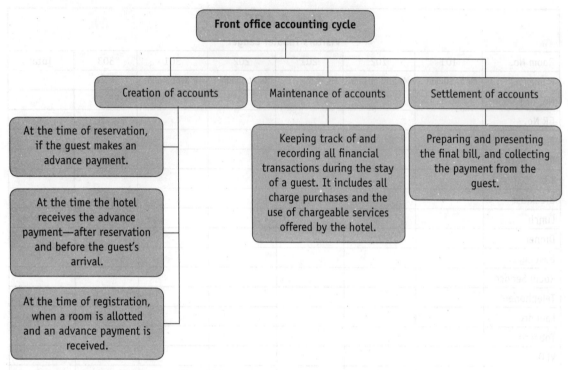

Fig. 11.13   Front office accounting cycle

Creation of Accounts

A guest account is created when the first financial transaction between the hotel and a guest takes place. It may happen at one of the following stages:

- At the time of reservation, if the guest pays an advance amount (may be part or full). For example, Shreya is reserving a room for 25 to 28 December on 25 October. The dates fall under the black-out period, and hence, all reservations have to be guaranteed by full advance payment. She deposits Rs 18,000 towards the room rent for three nights, which is entered as the first transaction in her account.
- At the time the hotel receives the advance payment for a booking–after the reservation has been made and before the arrival of the guest. For example, Kiran has made a reservation for a room from 14 to 17 September on 1 July. She makes an advance payment of Rs 10,000 on 14 August; her guest account is created immediately and the transaction is entered in the same.
- At the time of guest registration, when a room is allotted to the guest. For example, Vijay from Microsoft India has made a reservation from 1 to 3 August. He submits the bill to company letter for the room rent at the time of

registration on 1 August. His guest account is created and the day's room rent is posted in that. His sister, Anuja, also has a reservation for the same nights and she deposits a payment of Rs 5,000 for the same. Her account is also created on the same day with debit and credit information.

A guest folio is created on the day the hotel receives a payment from the guest and the transactions are recorded in the order of their occurrence. The hotel sets a credit limit, known as floor limit, for each guest, which is the maximum amount of credit that the hotel will extend to the guest.

Maintenance of Accounts

All the monetary transactions that take place between the hotel and a guest are recorded in the guest folio in the order of their occurrence. An entry in the guest folio may be either debit or credit.

The most common debit entries in a guest account include the following:

- Room charges
- Food and beverage charges (restaurant, bar, coffee shop, room service, etc.)
- Telephone and fax charges
- Health centre, business centre, fitness centre charges
- Laundry charges
- Postage charges
- Transportation charges
- Visitors paid-out

Credit entries in a guest account may include the following:

- Pre-payment, in part or in full (at the time of reservation or between reservation and arrival).
- Part payment during the stay.
- Allowances given to the guest.
- Adjustments made in case of any error in posting in the guest folio.
- Final payment for the settlement of accounts at the time of check-out.

Settlement of Accounts

This is the final and concluding phase of the front office accounting cycle. The settlement of account means zeroing the balance in a guest folio. The formula for calculating the outstanding balance is:

Opening balance + Debit entries – Credit entries = Outstanding amount

The guest account may have a credit or debit balance during the stay of the guest. At the time of departure, the final bill of the guest is prepared and settled in such a way that the outstanding balance is brought to zero. If the advance paid by the guest is less than the total billing amount, the guest should pay the balance amount. For example, Shreya had made an advance payment of Rs 18,000 at the time of reservation. Her total bill at the time of check-out is 21,000, so she pays the balance of Rs 3,000 to the cashier. In case the amount paid in advance exceeds the billing amount, the balance is refunded to the guest to settle the guest account. For example, Kiran paid Rs 10,000 for her stay, but due to an emergency, she had to leave in a day and her bill came to Rs 4,500. The balance amount of Rs 5,500 is refunded to Kiran.

The settlement of the guest account may be by cash or credit. In case of credit settlement, the account balance is transferred to the city ledger and the responsibility of collecting the balance is transferred to the accounts department. For example, Vijay's room bill is sent to Microsoft India for settlement as per the billing instructions while the other bills are settled directly by him at the hotel as per actuals. Anuja's bills came to a total of Rs 5,000. As she had deposited the same amount as advance, she does not need to make any additional payment nor does the hotel need to give a refund.

SUMMARY

The timely and accurate posting of a guest's financial transactions in the guest account is very important for the successful running of the hotel business—it prevents the loss of revenue for the hotel and leads to higher guest satisfaction. To ensure an efficient and error-free billing, the front desk cashier should record the financial transactions properly in different types of accounts, vouchers, folios, and ledgers. The front office accounting cycle deals with the creation, maintenance, and settlement of accounts.

KEY TERMS

Accounting The process of collecting, recording, summarizing, and analysing financial transactions of a business.

Cash receipt voucher A voucher prepared and issued to the person depositing cash as proof of remittance of the cash.

City ledger A ledger that contains the collective accounts of all non-resident individuals/agencies to whom hotel provides the credit facility.

Folio A statement of all the transactions that takes place between a hotel and its guests.

Guest account The record of financial transactions that take place between a hotel and a resident guest.

Guest allowance Cash paid to the guest by the hotel, especially in the case of a mistake in the posting of charges.

Guest ledger A ledger that contains the details of financial transactions between a hotel and a resident guest.

House limit/Floor limit The upper limit of the credit extended by a hotel to a guest.

Ledger A collection of a similar type of accounts.

Miscellaneous charge voucher A voucher for miscellaneous charges, like laundry, health club, fitness centre, beauty saloon, etc.

Master folio A folio that contains the accounts of more than one guest.

Non-guest account The record of the financial transactions between a hotel and a non-resident guest.

Non-guest/city folio A folio that contains the record of financial transactions between a hotel and non-resident guests.

Telephone voucher A voucher prepared by the tele-

phone operator for local and long distance calls made by a resident guest to be posted in the guest folio.

Voucher A written statement or a documentary evidence of a financial transaction.

Visitors paid-out The cash payments made by a hotel on behalf of guests.

REVIEW QUESTIONS

Multiple Choice Questions

1. Which of the following expenses may qualify as visitors paid-out?
   a) Florist charges
   b) Payment of taxi bill
   c) Emergency medical expenses on behalf of the guest
   d) All

2. Who prepares the telephone call voucher?
   a) Front desk agent   b) Front office cashier
   c) Receptionist   d) Telephone operator

3. What is a written record of all the transactions between a hotel and its guests called?
   a) Folio   b) Ledger
   c) Voucher   d) Guest account

4. Which of the following is not a part of the front office accounting cycle?
   a) Settlement of accounts
   b) Maintenance of accounts
   c) Registration of guests
   d) Creation of accounts

5. What is the maximum amount of credit that a hotel will extend to a guest called?
   a) Allowance   b) Floor limit
   c) Guest ledger   d) Folio

True/False

1. A folio is a document that entitles the bearer to certain goods, services, or discounts upon presentation.

2. The money paid by the hotel on behalf of a guest is known as visitors paid-out.

3. The vouchers for the call charges of guests, made by the telephone operator, are known as travel agent vouchers.

4. A commission voucher is prepared if the hotel pays commission to any person or agency that provides business to the hotel.

5. The folio in which a resident guest's transactions are maintained is known as city folio.

Fill in the Blanks

1. Cash paid to the guest by the hotel is called _____.

2. An airlines issues _____ to its crew to be accommodated in a hotel.

3. The _____ guest folio contains the financial transactions between the hotel and a guest.

4. The front desk accounting cycle begins with the creation of _____ folio.

5. The guest folio may be created at the time of reservation if the guest pays an _____ to the hotel during booking.

Discussion Questions

1. What is the front office accounting system? Describe its purpose.

2. Explain the different types of vouchers prepared by the front office.

3. What is visitors tabular ledger? Explain.

4. Discuss guest folio. Give the detailed process of preparing it.

5. What is city ledger?

6. What are bar checks, allowance vouchers, and miscellaneous charge vouchers?

CRITICAL THINKING QUESTIONS

1. Differentiate between:
   a) Folio and ledger
   b) Guest allowance and cash receipt voucher
   c) Guest ledger and city ledger

2. An accurate recording of the financial transactions between a hotel and its guests is among one of the major factors leading to guest satisfaction. Discuss in detail.

3. The front desk cashier is the image builder of the hotel and the protector of the financial interests of the hotel. Comment.

PROJECT WORK

Visit a hotel and learn the basic posting of guest accounts by obtaining the format of the guest folio and supporting vouchers.

CASE STUDIES

The following financial transactions take place at Hotel Starview on 20 July 2009:

- Xavier checks in at Hotel Starview at 12:30 p.m. on 20 July. He is offered a 25 per cent discount on room rent (rent Rs 2,500). He deposits an advance of Rs 5,000.
- Yash checked in on 18 July in an executive room on an MAP basis (rent Rs 4,500). He had paid an advance of Rs 10,000 at the time of reservation.
- Bindu has an early check-in on 20 July (room rent Rs 2,000). She pays Rs 750 in cash for buffet breakfast.

- Charu arrived on 12 July. Her company has a rate contract with the hotel for an executive room—40 per cent discount on room rent (of Rs 4,500) and 25 per cent discount on food and beverage. She has taken buffet breakfast (Rs 500) and buffet dinner (Rs 950) in the hotel every day till date.
- Kaushal arrives late in the evening on 20 July. His room rent is Rs 3,500. He orders for the following:
   i. Dinner   Rs 675
   ii. Drinks   Rs 450
   iii. Snacks   Rs 200

Post the above entries in the visitors tabular ledger given below. And find out the following:

a) Balance carried forward for Yash and Charu.

b) Credit/debit balance of Xavier, Yash, Bindu, Charu, and Kaushal.

c) Total credit/debit balance of each guest.

Hotel ABC							
Visitors Tabular Ledger							
Room No.	101	102	201	202	301	303	Total
Name	Mr Xavier	Mr Yash	Ms Bindu	Ms Charu	Mr Kaushal		
No. of Persons							
GR No.							
Plan							
Room Rate							
Tea							
Breakfast							
Lunch							
Dinner							
Beverages							
Room Service							
Telephone							
Laundry							
Tobacco							
VPO							
Others							
Beer							
Wine							
Miscellaneous							
Daily Total							
Cash Deposit							
Allowance							
Balance C/fwd							
Total Dr. Cr.							

CHAPTER 12

Night Auditing

Learning Objectives:

After reading this chapter, you will be able to understand the following:
- Night audit—its purpose and usefulness.
- Night auditor—duties and responsibilities.
- The process of night audit—establishing the end of the day, completing outstanding postings and verifying transactions, reconciling transactions, verifying no-shows, preparing reports, updating the system.

A hotel remains operational round the clock, 365 days a year. The guests staying in a hotel include regular guests as well as occasional guests, and their duration of stay may vary from a few hours to several weeks. A transaction, especially a financial one, should be reviewed on a daily basis, as guests might depart from the hotel anytime and it may be too late to recover an unpaid bill or a loss due to any mistake in the posting of charges in the guest account. In order to safeguard the interests of the hotel, a systematic examination of the financial transactions of guests is carried out by competent people at the end of every day. This chapter provides a detailed discussion on the process of night audit carried out by hotels.

NIGHT AUDIT

According to Oxford Advanced Learner's Dictionary, audit is 'an official examination of business and financial records to see that they are true and correct'. An audit is generally carried out at the end of every financial year in most businesses. Since hotels operate on $24 \times 7 \times 365$ pattern, continuous auditing is a pre-requisite to safeguard the loss of revenue that may occur due to any error in the posting of charges in the folios. One of the most important tasks in hotel operations is to establish the time when a day is considered to be over as hotels remain operational round the clock. The daily audit is carried out in hotels during slack time; normally this time is between midnight and early morning, hence the audit is known as night audit. The auditors check and confirm that the financial transactions that occurred during the day were correct and complete. The mistakes, if any, are corrected and the account is balanced. The main purpose of night auditing is to keep a track of the total revenue generated during the day and to keep the guest accounts correct and up-to-date. This leads to customer satisfaction as the guests are given accurate and up-to-date bills at the time of check-out. The night auditor also verifies the entries posted in non-guest accounts, monitors guest credit limits, balances all accounts, and sorts out any discrepancies in room status.

NIGHT AUDITOR

A night auditor is the person who audits the hotel accounts daily at night or at a time when the business is relatively slow. The audit team generally comprises members of the accounts department. The number of people in the audit team depends upon the size, location, and products of the hotel. Since most of the activities of the night auditor are concentrated in the front office, the front office manager (FOM) may provide the necessary inputs for the night audit process. So the members of the night audit team generally report to the accounts department as well as the FOM. As a night auditor has to work in the night, the position doesn't find many takers, so most of the hotels do not have a permanent team of night auditors.

A night auditor should be a skilled bookkeeper as he is required to track all the financial transactions between the hotel and its guests and to calculate the total revenue generated during the day. A night auditor should also possess the skills of a receptionist, as in many small and medium hotels, he may be required to carry out the check-in/check-out function at night.

Night auditors monitor the current status of guest accounts vis-à-vis the credit limits, and verify discounts, allowances, and promotional programmes that are offered to guests. They prepare reports about the front office operation for the management. Fully automated hotels may not require a team of night auditors as most of the functions (known as system updates) that a night auditor performs are carried out automatically by the computerized system, but a person is still required to physically verify the accounts and vouchers.

Duties and Responsibilities of a Night Auditor

A night auditor performs the following duties and responsibilities:

- Establishes the end of the day.
- Ensures the accuracy of front office accounting records and balances them.
- Reconciles all the financial transactions between a hotel and its guests.
- Calculates the total revenue generated during the day.
- Verifies and validates the cashier's posting of charges in the guest accounts.
- Posts the room charges in the guest folio.
- Transfers the unpaid guest accounts—i.e., accounts of guests who have left the hotel without settling their bills—to city ledger.
- Monitors the house limit of guests.
- Prepares a high balance report of guest accounts that are nearing or have crossed the house limit.
- Monitors the current status of discounts, meal coupons, and other promotional activities that are carried out by the front desk employees.
- Prepares reports for the management.
- Tracks the room occupancy percentage.

NIGHT AUDIT PROCESS

The night audit is conducted in every hotel to maintain an accurate and efficient accounting system that keeps proper records of all the transactions. This prevents the loss of revenue as well as leads to higher levels of guest satisfaction (as guests are presented error-free and up-to-date bills). The night audit is conducted on a daily basis as the creditors (hotel guests to whom the hotel extends credit facility) are mostly unknown and if their accounts remain unsettled due to some error in bookkeeping, the hotel will lose that revenue. The daily authentication of accounts, by verifying support documents and the posting of charges in the guest accounts, is necessary to prevent any possible loss of revenue. The flowchart shown in Fig. 12.1 explains the night audit process. The steps that are commonly involved in night audit process are as under:

- Establishing the end of the day.
- Completing outstanding postings and verifying transactions.
- Reconciling transactions in guest accounts, city accounts, and points of sale.
- Verifying no-shows.
- Preparing high balance report and occupancy reports.
- Updating the system.

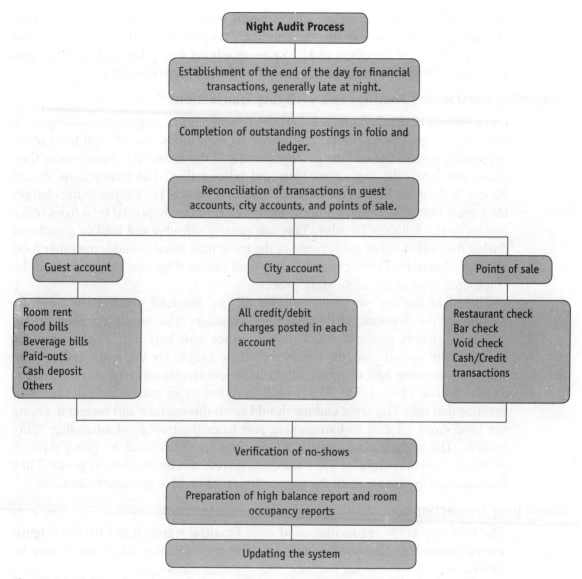

Fig. 12.1 Night audit process

Establishing the End of the Day

The end of the day is the arbitrary time that is supposed to be the end of the financial transactions for a particular day. As hotels remain operational round the clock, it is very necessary to ascertain the time that will be treated as the end of the day and the beginning of a new day in a hotel. This time is generally established by the night auditor. The time when the process of night auditing begins is usually taken to be the end of the day, which means that all transactions that take place after the commencement of the night audit are taken in the next day's business. For example, if a guest checks-in at 11.15 p.m. at a hotel where the night audit begins at 11 p.m., the guest's account is included in the next day's business.

Completing Outstanding Postings and Verifying Transactions

Once the end of the day is established, the first step is to complete the posting of all pending charges (room and tax) in proper account folios. An efficient front office accounting system ensures the prompt posting of the financial transactions as they occur and reach the front desk cash and bills section. The transactions should appear in the guest folio in the order of their occurrence. Let's suppose the charges for a meal that was consumed on Monday are mistakenly posted by a front office cashier in the folio on Tuesday. This can cause confusion and lead to a problem during the settlement of the account as the guest may have visited some other food outlet on Tuesday. The night auditor posts all outstanding charges properly at the commencement of the night audit process.

The night auditor physically verifies all the financial transactions by cross examining the account with supporting vouchers like credit vouchers, debit vouchers, visitors paid-out vouchers, allowance vouchers, etc. There might be errors in the posted charges, which should be caught by the night auditor. For example, the front office cashier might have incorrectly posted the room rent as $4,000 instead of Rs 4,000. This would have led to an inaccurate calculation of revenue that day. The night auditor should catch this mistake and correct it, saving the hotel from a lot of embarrassment and from the trouble of amending many records. The night auditors verify the postings in all accounts by going through all the documents carefully. They also validate the discounts given to guests. They examine and authenticate all the transactions that involve monetary elements.

Reconciling Transactions

The next step is the reconciliation of each financial transaction with the original source documents (generally vouchers). The reconciliation of accounts may be carried out in the following sections:

- Guest accounts
- City accounts
- Points of sale

Guest Accounts   All the financial transactions that occur between a hotel and its guests are examined by the night audit team. The folio of each guest is matched with the original documents of transactions for the verification of the account. The night auditor also checks for any discrepancy in room status reports of the front office and housekeeping departments. For example, the housekeeping occupancy report may show 104 occupied rooms while the front office occupancy report shows 105 occupied rooms. There is a discrepancy of one room, which means that one room is shown as occupied, though it is ready and could have been sold.

The reconciliation of charges in guest accounts is done in the following order:
- Room charges
- Food and beverage charges
- Other charges

Room charges The night auditor posts the room rent in the guest folio at the beginning of the night audit process. The basis of posting of the room charges may be as under, depending upon the house customs:
- *Check-in/Check-out basis*: It is generally followed in commercial hotels. The tariff cards of such hotels mention the check-in and check-out times (generally 12 noon).
- *Twenty-four hour basis*: It is generally followed by transient hotels where the duration of guest stay is very short. At times it may range from two to four hours for guests who have to catch connecting flights.

Food and beverage charges The food and beverage charges posted in the guest folio by the front desk cashier are verified by the night auditor against the restaurant checks, which bear the guest's signature as a token of the guest's acceptance that the services were availed by her and that the amount is correct. Every such entry in the guest folio is reconciled by the night auditor. Complimentary kitchen order tickets (KOTs) are also verified and reconciled by the night auditor.

Other charges The night auditor also reconciles other financial transactions that take place between the hotel and its guests. Transactions like visitors paid-out, miscellaneous expenses, discounts, etc. are verified by night auditors.

City Accounts Night auditors also examine the entries in non-resident guest accounts or city accounts. They check these accounts for completeness and accuracy. If any instance of high outstanding balance is found during the night audit process, the night auditors prepare the report of high balance (Fig. 12.2), which is presented to the management, and the responsibility of collecting payment (part/full) shifts to the accounts department.

Points of Sale The cashiers of all the points of sale (POS) prepare a summary sheet of financial transactions that occur at their POS and keep the same in an envelope, along with the second copy of bills. The same envelope, along with the cash and credit transactions, is generally deposited with the cashier at the front desk cash and bills section. The night auditor pulls out all the checks/vouchers (including void checks, paid-outs, allowances, foreign exchange transactions, miscellaneous charge vouchers, etc.) of individual POS and reconciles them with the POS cashiers' sales summary sheets.

Verifying No-shows

The night auditor also verifies no-shows. A no-show is a situation when a guest with a confirmed reservation does not arrive at the hotel on the date of arrival without any prior intimation about the cancellation. The night auditor verifies all such no-shows, and in the case of guaranteed reservations, posts the no-show in the guests' folios. Usually, hotels charge one night's retention for no-shows. The night auditor should verify carefully that the reservation was guaranteed, that the guest has not registered, and that it was not a duplicate reservation. For example, if there is a no-show in the name of John Adam, and a guest called Adam Johns has registered at the hotel, it should be checked if the two are the same.

Preparing Reports

The next step in the night audit process is to prepare daily reports for managerial use, which help the management to review the profitability of the hotel operations and plan future goals. In manual system, this is one of the typical tasks carried out by the night auditor. In fully automated hotels, these reports are automatically prepared by the system. The night auditor generally prepares the following reports for the management:

- High balance report
- Occupancy reports

High Balance Report   A night auditor monitors the credit limit of individual resident guest accounts as well as city accounts. The formula to calculate the outstanding balance is:

$$\text{Outstanding balance} = \text{Previous balance} + \text{Debit entries (purchases)} - \text{Credit entries (payments)}$$

The credit limit of a guest account depends upon the credibility of the guest and the floor limit of the guest credit card. The night auditor checks every account against the relevant credit limit of that account. A high balance report is made in case the account balance reaches or crosses the house limit. For example, the house limit might be Rs 10,000 and the guest might have paid Rs 7,000 earlier, but the total bill after room rent and meals for four days is coming to Rs 18,500, i.e., the outstanding is Rs 9,500. The night auditor generates a high balance report that indicates the guest account has crossed the house limit (Fig. 12.2). On receiving this report, the management may seek a partial or full settlement of the outstanding balance before the guest can avail further credit facility from the hotel. This protects the hotel from the loss of revenue in case the guest leaves without settling her bills.

```
                           Hotel ABC
                  Guest Ledger High Balance Report

                                               Date:_____
Name of Auditor:_____


Reviewed by:_____
```

Room No.	Name of Guest	Amount	Action Taken
101	Mr Michael	Rs 8,500	Holds a valid American Express credit card
214	Mr H.N. Singh	Rs 10,500	Contacted and received a draft of Rs 7,500
312	Mr S. Singhla	Rs 9,500	Left message for guest to contact
411	Ms Ketki	Rs 7,800	She wishes to pay by personal cheque. Request has been forwarded for approval.
421	Dr D.P. Singh	Rs 11,000	Left five messages for the guest but could not be contacted. Action necessary.
502	Dr A.K. Parashar	Rs 12,500	Guest informed the front desk that he will be giving cash next evening.

Fig. 12.2 High balance report

Occupancy Reports The night auditor also generates the following occupancy-related reports:

- Occupancy percentage
- House count
- Bed occupancy percentage
- Domestic occupancy percentage
- Foreigner's occupancy percentage

Occupancy percentage The occupancy percentage is the ratio of the number of rooms sold to the total number of saleable rooms. It determines the level of revenue that will be generated by the hotel and is an indicator of the performance of the hotel. The formula to calculate occupancy percentage is as under:

$$\text{Occupancy percentage} = \frac{\text{Number of rooms sold}}{\text{Total number of saleable rooms}} \times 100$$

For example, a hotel has 200 rooms, and on a certain day, 90 rooms are occupied. Then, the occupancy percentage is 90/200 × 100, i.e., 45 per cent. In case some rooms are under renovation, repair, or are out of order, the same are not included in the total number of saleable rooms. Let us suppose 40 rooms are blocked for spring cleaning at the same example, then the occupancy percentage will be calculated as under:

$$
\begin{aligned}
\text{Occupancy percentage} \quad &= \quad 90/(200 - 40) \times 100 \\
&= \quad 90/160 \times 100 \\
&= \quad 37.5\%
\end{aligned}
$$

House count   The house count is the total number of resident guests present in the hotel, i.e., the total number of rooms sold. It is used to determine the average room rate per person (see Chapter 15). The formula to calculate the house count is as under:

$$
\text{House count} = \text{House count of previous day brought forward} - \text{Today's departures} + \text{Today's arrivals}
$$

Let us suppose that there are ten departures and sixteen arrivals, then the house count is $90 - 10 + 16$, i.e., 96.

Bed occupancy percentage   It is the ratio of the number of beds occupied to the total number of available beds in the property. The formula to calculate bed occupancy percentage is as under:

$$
\text{Bed occupancy percentage} = \frac{\text{Number of beds occupied}}{\text{Total number of beds available for guests}} \times 100
$$

In our example, the number of beds occupied is 90 and the number of available beds is 200, so the bed occupancy percentage is $90/200 \times 100$, i.e., 45 per cent.

Domestic occupancy percentage   It is the ratio of the total number of domestic guests to the house count. This is the indicator of the type of clients visiting the hotel. The formula to calculate domestic occupancy percentage is as under:

$$
\text{Domestic occupancy percentage} = \frac{\text{Total number of domestic guests}}{\text{House count}} \times 100
$$

Suppose in our example, 60 rooms are occupied by domestic guests, then the domestic occupancy percentage is $60/90 \times 100$, i.e., 66.67 per cent.

Alternately, it may be calculated by subtracting the foreigners' occupancy percentage from 100.

$$
\text{Domestic occupancy percentage} = 100 - \text{Foreigners' occupancy percentage}
$$

Foreigner's occupancy percentage   It is the ratio of the total number of foreign nationals to the house count. This is an indicator of the type of clients visiting the property. The formula to calculate foreigners' occupancy percentage is as under:

$$\text{Foreigners' occupancy percentage} = \frac{\text{Total number of foreigner guests}}{\text{House count}} \times 100$$

As 60 rooms are occupied by domestic guests, 30 rooms are occupied by foreign guests, the foreigner's occupancy percentage is $30/90 \times 100$, i.e., 33.33 per cent.

Alternatively, it may be calculated by subtracting the domestic occupancy percentage from 100.

$$\text{Foreigners' occupancy percentage} = 100 - \text{Domestic occupancy percentage}$$
$$= 100 - 66.67 = 33.33\%$$

Updating the System

Once the outstanding charges have been posted and reconciled, no-shows have been verified, and reports and summaries for the management have been prepared, the night auditor updates the system and ends the night audit process. In fully automated hotels, the computerized system automatically carries out system updates.

Thus, a night auditor establishes the end of the day, takes stock, checks if charges have been posted properly, and reconciles all the financial transactions of the day between a hotel and its guests. The night auditor is also known as the in-house auditor who is responsible for conducting audit and generating reports for the management, which include the high balance report and occupancy percentage reports like house count, bed occupancy percentage, domestic occupancy percentage, and foreigners' occupancy percentage. The job of a night auditor is a very responsible position and requires basic accounting skills, and computer and hotel management knowledge and background.

SUMMARY

Audit is the official authentication of records, especially financial ones. Since hotels remain operational round the clock, 365 days a year, continuous auditing is important to safeguard the loss of revenue. The daily audit is carried out in hotels at night, which is a lean period for guest activities like arrival and departure. The main purpose of night audit is to verify the accuracy and completeness of the financial transactions between the hotel and its guests so that total revenue for that day can be known.

The night audit process involves establishing the end of the day, completing outstanding postings and verifying transactions, reconciling transactions (in guest accounts, city accounts, and points of sale summaries), verifying no-shows, preparing reports for the management (high balance report and occupancy reports), and updating the system at the end of the process.

KEY TERMS

Bed occupancy percentage It is the ratio of the number of beds occupied to the total number of available beds in the property.

End of the day The arbitrary time that is supposed to be the end of the financial transactions for a particular day.

High balance report A report prepared by the night auditor if a guest's account balance reaches or crosses the house limit.

House count Total number of resident guests present in the hotel.

Night audit The daily audit that is carried out in hotels during the slack time; normally this time is between midnight and early morning.

Occupancy percentage It is the ratio of the number of rooms sold to the total number of saleable rooms.

REVIEW QUESTIONS

Multiple Choice Questions

1. A night auditor carries out the following functions:
   a) Ensures the accuracy of various accounts
   b) Reconciles all financial transactions with supporting vouchers
   c) Monitors house limit
   d) All of the above

2. The night audit process includes:
   a) Establishment of the end of the day
   b) Verification of all accounts
   c) Posting of room charges in guest folio
   d) All of the above

3. The financial transactions that occur after the commencement of night audit process are posted in:
   a) Same day's business
   b) Next day's business
   c) Depends on monetary value
   d) None of the above

4. Occupancy percentage is the ratio of the number of rooms sold to:
   a) Total number of saleable rooms
   b) Total number of rooms

   c) Total number of occupied rooms
   d) None of the above

5. Which of the following reports are generated by the night auditor?
   a) High balance report
   b) Occupancy percentage report
   c) Both
   d) None

True/False

1. Daily audit is carried out in hotels during slack time; normally this time is between midnight and early morning, hence it is known as night auditing.

2. The night auditor does not monitor the house limit.

3. All the financial transactions between the hotel and its guests are authenticated by the front office manager.

4. Occupancy data is not so useful for the management.

5. Domestic occupancy percentage is the ratio of domestic guests to foreigner guests.

Fill in the blanks

1. A _____ audits the hotel accounts daily at a time when the business is relatively slow.

2. In case of high outstanding balance, the night auditor prepares the _____ report.

3. The _____ is the total number of resident guests in the hotel.

4. The ratio of the number of rooms sold to the total number of saleable rooms is called _____.

5. _____ percentage is the ratio of beds occupied to the total number of beds in the hotel.

Discussion Questions

1. What do you understand by the term night audit? Why is it known as 'night' audit?

2. What are the duties and responsibilities of a night auditor?

3. Explain the night audit process in detail.

4. Which reports does a night auditor prepare? What is the significance of these reports?

5. How does the night auditor reconcile the financial transactions?

6. Explain the following:
   a) City account
   b) Occupancy reports
   c) High balance report
   d) Reconciliation of financial transactions

CRITICAL THINKING QUESTIONS

1. A night auditor protects the financial interest of the hotel. Discuss.

2. Why do we need daily night audit in hotel? Explain in detail.

CASE STUDIES

1. Hotel Himalayan Retreat is located in the beautiful surroundings of Himalayan foothills. It has 200 rooms, which include standard rooms, deluxe rooms, holiday cottages, and deluxe cottages. The hotel also has facilities of adventure sports like trekking, rock climbing, river rafting, etc. There is a big banquet hall to accommodate 700 persons in theatre-style seating. The hotel has good occupancy percentage. It targets business clientele, tourists, and conference delegates. The area also receives a fair percentage of foreign tourists and nature loving people.

   However, things changed when Hotel Mountain Haven opened last year. The facilities at Hotel Mountain Haven were almost the same as Hotel Himalayan Retreat, but it also had a golf course, convention centre with a capacity of 1,500 persons in theatre-style seating, and a water park. After the opening of Hotel Mountain Haven, there has been a considerable fall in the business of Hotel Himalayan Retreat. The general manager, Mr Bakshi, tried to find out the reasons for the fall in business of the hotel.

   There were only three persons in the hotel's sales and marketing department. He appointed six more persons with Anand as the sales manager. Anand and Mr Bakshi asked the night auditor of the hotel to provide the financial details of the hotel and reports on the present status of the hotel business, so that they can formulate the marketing plan to re-capture their market share.

Assume you are the night auditor of the hotel and respond to the following questions:

a) List the sources of information that is available to you to procure the required information for Mr Bakshi.

b) Develop a daily report of the hotel, showing all the information requested by the general manager.

c) List the reports that will be prepared by you.

d) Discuss the role of the night auditor in connection with the vital information generated by him to help the management formulate future strategies to combat any business problem that may arise, as in the given case.

2. Hotel Lake View has 400 rooms (300 double and 100 single), out of which 50 double rooms are blocked for painting. Of the remaining, 10 single rooms are blocked for spring cleaning for seven days from 15 September 2008. The total number of rooms sold on 16 September 2008 is 275 rooms (200 double and 75 single) and the total number of resident guests are 475, out of which 155 are Indians. On 17 September 2008, there are a total of 15 arrivals and 10 departures, all in single rooms. All the arrivals and departures were of Indian nationals. Calculate:

a) Occupancy percentage on 16 and 17 September 2008.

b) House count on 16 and 17 September 2008.

c) Bed occupancy percentage on 16 September 2008.

d) Foreigners' occupancy percentage on 16 September 2008.

e) Domestic occupancy percentage on 16 September 2008.

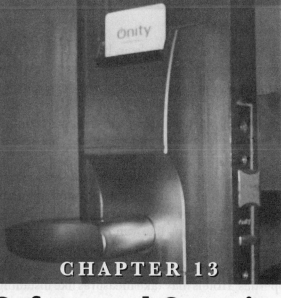

CHAPTER 13

Safety and Security

Learning Objectives:

After reading this chapter, you will be able to understand the following:
- The role of hotel staff in ensuring the safety and security of guests.
- The security of guest rooms—maintaining strict control on room keys.
- Fighting fire.
- Preventing accidents and providing first aid.
- Dealing with unusual events and emergency situations like terrorist activities, bomb threats, robbery, theft, and drunken guests.

It is the moral and legal responsibility of a hotel to protect its guests and their property against threats posed by human beings with a conscious intent to harm them. The security department of the hotel is responsible for the overall security of the building, in-house guests, visitors, day users, and employees of the hotel. Guests hold the hotel responsible for their safety and can file for compensations in case of a security lapse in the hotel's security measures.

Hotel Security Staff and System

A hotel's security staff may include in-house security personnel and contracted security officers. Hotels generally prefer ex-army or ex-police officials as their security officers because they are already well versed with various security aspects and have a lot of experience in the field. Security responsibilities may include patrolling the property, monitoring surveillance equipment, and, in general, ensuring that the guests, visitors, and employees are safe and secure. The security department is responsible for establishing the details of room keys security, fire safety systems, emergency evacuation plans, and emergency communication plans. The effectiveness of the security department depends upon the cooperation and assistance of the local law enforcement officials. The security personnel should be trained to handle situations like vandalism, terrorist attacks, and bomb threat. They may also be trained to prevent and fight fire.

Every hotel should have a proper security system to protect its guests, employees, and their properties. Hotels may take measures like installing close circuit televisions in public areas for proper surveillance, ensuring proper lighting of public areas, fencing of the hotel property, and positioning security guards at entry gates for the safety and security of their guests and their belongings. Hiring an independent security agency to routinely check the security systems also helps in ensuring the safety and security of guests.

Role of Front Office

A front desk professional is required to assume a variety of roles during a workday—chief among them being a gatekeeper, communications expert, phone whiz, trouble-shooter, and receptionist. As a hotel's first contact with guests, vendors, visitors, and delivery people, the front office staff is the eyes and ears of the organization. It is up to them to spot potential troublemakers, identify red-flag behaviours, prevent breaches of security, and act with confidence and authority when situations threaten to get out of hand.

A security programme would be more effective if all the hotel employees participate in the hotel's security efforts. The front office personnel play a vital role in assisting the hotel's security personnel to carry out their tasks efficiently. The front office employees like door attendants, parking attendants, bell boys, and receptionists should observe all the people who are entering or leaving the hotel premises, and if they notice any suspicious activity or circumstances, they should immediately report the same to the security personnel.

SECURITY AND CONTROL OF ROOM KEYS

A guest room is the most important hospitality product. One of the chief concerns of the hotel staff is to ensure the security of guest rooms, which is done by controlling the access to guest rooms by maintaining a strict control over room keys. Hotels may have a hard key system or an electronic key system. In case the hotel uses the hard key system, the following security measures can be followed:

- Request guests to deposit the room keys at the reception while leaving the hotel premises.
- Discourage guests to carry room keys with them while going out of the hotel premises. This is mostly done by putting heavy and large key tags, which are inconvenient to carry.
- In an event of loss of keys, the lock should be replaced immediately.

An electronic key system is an investment in guest safety and security. For each new guest registering at a hotel, a fresh plastic, metallic, or hard-pressed paper key is produced each time. The room door lock combination can be changed as and when required by options available through the master computer. Hence if a guest carries away the electronic key with her, it will not pose any security threat.

Hotels, for security reasons, use three types of room keys:

- Emergency/Grand master key
- Master key
- Guest room key

Emergency Key/Grand Master Key   An emergency/grand master key opens door locks of all guest rooms, even if they are double locked. (Double lock is an internal safety locking device, in which, if the door is locked from inside the room, it cannot be opened from the outside by its own keys or master key). The emergency key should be highly protected and should only be used in the event of an emergency. It should not be taken out of the premises, and a strict key control should be maintained for the same. Generally, the emergency key is under the control of the head of the property.

Master Key   A master key opens all those guest room door locks that are not double locked. This key may be such that it can unlock all guest room locks or may open only specific floor's guest room locks. The master key is under the control of the executive housekeeper of the hotel. There may be several floor master keys, which are used by room attendants for cleaning the guest rooms. These keys are strictly controlled and issued only to the staff on duty, who have to sign before taking the key and at the time of submitting it.

Guest Room Key   A guest room key opens the lock of an individual guest room. These keys are under the control of the front desk and are issued to guests who have registered in the hotel. Guests are required to deposit their room keys when they check-out and depart from the hotel.

Fig. 13.1 Fire extinguishers

FIRE SAFETY

Fire is among the major potential hazards associated with hotels. It could take place due to cigarette smoking in rooms, faulty electrical wiring, or faulty equipment. Hotels must be equipped to safeguard guests and their property from fire by installing smoke detectors and by conducting routine checks to see that the wiring and equipments are not defective. All the employees must be aware of specific procedures laid down by the establishment and must be ready to comply with them at any time. There should be fire drills during low occupancy periods to check how the employees put their knowledge of laid down procedures into practice. Generally, fire extinguishers (see Fig. 13.1) are installed in hotels at strategic locations and fire exits are earmarked for use in the event of fire. Guests should be made aware of the same.

The presence of three basic components—fuel (a combustible substance), oxygen (necessary as fire is an oxidation reaction), and heat (ignition temperature)—results in the outbreak of fire. If any one of them is absent, fire cannot break out. Fire can be extinguished by starving, smothering, and cooling

Starving Starving is the removal of fuel from the vicinity of fire so that it doesn't spread. In case fire breaks out in an area where wood is stored, it can be extinguished by removing all the wood (fuel) from that area. This way one of the major components of fire will be eliminated.

Smothering Smothering is the removal of air. Fire can be extinguished by cutting off the supply of air (oxygen), which is necessary for the existence of fire. Throwing a blanket over fire smothers the air and extinguishes the fire.

Cooling Heat (ignition temperature) is also essential for the existence of fire. Cooling—by adding water—brings down the temperature and puts out fire.

Classification of Fire

Depending upon the combustible material that has caught fire, fire is classified in the following five groups:

Class A: Wood, paper, textile, grass, garbage, and materials composed of cellulose.

Class B: Oil, petroleum products, varnishes, paints, non-ionic solvents.

Class C: Electrical equipment involving electrical short-circuits.

Class D: Metals such as magnesium, aluminium, zinc, potassium, etc.

Class E: Gases such as liquefied petroleum gas (LPG), methane, compressed natural gases (CNG), etc.

Procedure in the Event of Fire

The guidelines for the front office staff in the event of fire are as follows:

- When fire is detected, inform the concerned people immediately.
- Do not panic.
- Warn other people in the vicinity and sound the fire alarm.
- Do not jeopardize your own safety or that of others.
- Follow the procedure laid down by your establishment.
- Call the fire brigade immediately.
- Dot not try to extinguish fire if you are not trained for the same; fire may spread if not handled properly.
- If you are trained for fire fighting, use the appropriate fire extinguisher to put out the fire.
- Close the doors and windows; turn off the supply of electricity and gas.

It is important that all the passageways are kept clear and the doors and windows are opened. Fire exits should be marked properly and should be visible in dark too. The fire extinguishers should be placed at proper places and should be in working condition. Fire drills should be carried out periodically. Fire detecting systems (see Fig. 13.2), sprinkling system, smoke detecting system, fire fighting equipments, like fire hoses, etc. should be inspected and tested at regular intervals to ensure that they remain functional in the event of fire.

Fig. 13.2   Fire detection and alarm system

ACCIDENTS

According to Oxford Advanced Learner's Dictionary, an accident is 'an unpleasant event that happens unexpectedly and causes injury or damage'. Accidents may occur due to any one of the following reasons:

Excessive Haste   Excessive haste is among the prime causes of accident because a person in haste may overlook the safety rules or obstacles in the way. Therefore, to avoid accidents, one must not be in a hurry or run while on the job. For example, bell boys, when in a hurry to carry the luggage of a group, may overlook objects in blind corners and may meet with an accident.

Carelessness   Carelessness is also a common cause of accidents. The careless handling of goods and equipment may lead to accidents. For example, if a bell boy is careless with the luggage, he may trip and fall.

Anxiety   Anxiety is a feeling of worry or fear about something. An anxious person will not be able to concentrate on the task at hand and this might lead to accidents.

Lack of Interest   If a person lacks interest in what she is doing, she becomes careless and doesn't follow the correct procedure for carrying out a task, leading to accidents.

Lack of Concentration   A person may not be able to concentrate on work due to personal problems, lack of interest, distractions, etc. The lack of concentration may lead to problems and accidents.

Failure to Apply Safety Rules   Safety rules, if followed, prevent accidents. Before operating any equipment, one should read and follow the operating instructions given in the product manual in order to eliminate the chances of accidents. The failure to apply safety rules may cause accidents.

Accidents in Hotels

In hotels, accidents usually happen in one of the following areas:
- Stairways
- Balconies or landings
- Ramps
- Parking lots
- Bathtubs or showers

To minimize the number of accidents and to avoid workplace injuries, the hotels should take care of the common problems, some of which are as follows:
- Presence of handrails/guardrails
- Presence of a non-slip surface
- Adequacy of landing areas

- The accident victim's field of vision
- The accident victim's health and behaviour
- Adequacy of lighting
- Weather conditions (wet, snowy) and maintenance (cleaned, recently polished)

Accident Report

In spite of all the precautions taken by hotels to prevent accidents, mishaps may still occur. If a staff member meets with an accident within the hotel premises, it must be reported to the management and a record of the accident must be entered in the accident book, as shown in Fig. 13.3.

A proper reporting of accidents is important for the following reasons:

- The accident-prone areas may be identified so that appropriate signs may be placed there to avoid any future accidents.

Hotel ABC

Accident Report

S. No.: 0123786

Name of the injured person:..

Occupation:.............................. Supervisor:......................................

Time of Accident	Date of Accident	Time of Report	Date of Report

Nature of injury or condition:...

....

....

Extent of injury (after medical attention):...

....

....

Place of accident or dangerous occurrence:..

Injured person's version of what happened (use separate sheet if required) :...........

....

....

Witness of evidence (I)	Witness of evidence (II)

Supervisor's recommendations: ....

....

Date:...........................   Authorized Signatory

Fig. 13.3   Accident report form

- First aid may be given to the injured person.
- If the injury is serious, an ambulance may be summoned.
- The damage/loss due to the accident can be assessed.

FIRST AID

According to the Oxford Advanced Learner's Dictionary, first aid is 'the simple medical treatment that is given to somebody before a doctor comes or before the person can be taken to a hospital'. It is mandatory for an establishment to have adequate first aid equipment, facilities, and trained personnel to provide first aid in the work area. If the injury is serious, the injured person should be treated by a doctor or a qualified nurse as soon as possible.

First Aid Box

There should be a first aid box in the work area and it should be easily identifiable and accessible. It should be in the charge of a responsible person, who should ensure that the consumed medicines are replenished and the expired medicines are replaced regularly. A first aid box must contain the following things:
- A card giving general first-aid guidance.
- Twenty individually wrapped, sterile, adhesive, waterproof dressings of various sizes.
- An antiseptic lotion and an antiseptic cream.
- Cotton wool packets (4 × 25 g).
- One dozen safety pins.
- Two triangular bandages.
- Two sterile eye pads, with attachment.
- Four medium-sized sterile unmedicated dressings.
- Two large-sized sterile unmedicated dressings.
- Two extra large-sized sterile unmedicated dressings.
- Scissors
- A report book to record all injuries.

First Aid for Some Common Problems

Shock　The signs of shock are faintness, sickness, clammy skin, and pale face. A person who has suffered a shock should be made to lie down. To make him comfortable and warm, he should be covered with a blanket or additional clothes.

Cuts　All cuts should be washed with an antiseptic lotion and covered with a waterproof dressing. In case of considerable bleeding, it should be stopped as soon as possible by bandaging firmly or by pressing the artery with thumb. If bleeding doesn't stop, immediate medical assistance should be sought.

Nose Bleeding In case of nose bleeding, the person should be asked to sit down with the head bent forward. His clothing should be loosened round the neck, chest, and waist. To stop bleeding, apply pressure and pinch the nostrils closed for about five minutes. Nose bleeding occurs due to the rupture of the fine capillary of artery; applying pressure and keeping the nostril closed provides sufficient time for blood coagulation. If bleeding persists, seek medical assistance.

Fainting A person may faint after standing for a long period in a hot, badly-ventilated area. The symptoms include whiteness, giddiness, and sweating. The person should be made to lie down and his legs should be raised slightly above the level of his head. When he regains consciousness, he should be kept in fresh air for a while and it should be ensured that he did not injure himself when he fainted.

Fractures In case of a suspected fracture, the first step should be to remove any pressure from the affected part and to make it immobile. One should not try to realign the bone and seek immediate medical assistance. If there is bleeding, apply pressure to the wound with a sterile bandage or a clean cloth. To prevent swelling and to relieve pain till the medical assistance arrives, apply ice packs wrapped in a towel or a piece of cloth. If the person feels faint or is breathing in short, rapid breaths, he should be made to lie down with the head slightly lower than the trunk, and, if possible, his legs should be elevated.

Burns and Scalds Burn is caused by a dry heat source like flame or hot articles, whereas scalds are caused by a wet heat source like steam or boiling liquids. The burnt part should be placed under running cold water or immersed in cold water till the pain ceases. If it's a major burn, seek the assistance of doctor.

Muscle Strain In case of a sprain, stop the activity that caused the injury and apply ice to the injured area to reduce swelling. Use a bandage to restrict the movement of the injured area, and, if possible, elevate the injured part to make the fluids drain away.

HANDLING UNUSUAL EVENTS AND EMERGENCY SITUATIONS

Besides accidents and injuries, the hotel staff should be equipped to handle unusual events and emergency situations like:
- Terrorist activities and bomb threat
- Robbery and theft
- Drunken guests

Terrorist Activities and Bomb Threat

In view of recent terrorist attacks in the top hotels of Mumbai, hotels have heightened their security levels for the safety of their guests and staff. It is a challenge for the hotel security staff face to strike the right balance between being hospitable and being alert to the activities of the resident and non-resident guests. They also have to go in for extra security measures (see Exhibit 13.1).

Hotels that cater to VIPs like cinestars, politicians, CEOs of key companies, etc. are potential targets of terrorist attacks and should be well equipped to handle terrorist threats. In case of a bomb threat, the hotel should liaise with the local police authorities and follow their instructions. If the bomb threat comes over the telephone, the person receiving such a call should follow the given procedure:

- Do not interrupt the caller.
- Write down the exact words of the caller.
- If possible find out:
  - The time by which the bomb is due to explode.
  - The place where the device is placed.
  - The description of the device.
  - The motive of the attackers.
  - The identity of the attackers.

Exhibit 13.1   Heightened Security Measures Post Mumbai Terror Attacks

The Mumbai terror attacks (26–29 November 2008) left more than 170 Indians and foreign nationals dead. Also, three of Mumbai's most famous hotels and notable landmarks—the Taj Mahal Palace and Tower, the Trident, and the Oberoi—were left looking like they had been through a war.

In the three hotels, the hotel staff took care of the guests of the hotel and laid down their lives while carrying out their duties. Many of the Taj and Oberoi staff were killed in indiscriminate firing. Instead of looking for ways to leave the hotel premises, the remaining hotel staff tried to ensure that the guests were safe and comfortable. When there were opportunities for escape, the staff made sure that the guests escaped, and after that only they tried to leave the hotel. The General Manager of Taj lost his wife and two children in the attacks, but still continued helping the guests escape from the hotel and took care of their needs.

As an aftermath of these attacks, security measures have been heightened to ensure that similar incidents do not occur again. Schools, railway stations, airports, hotels, government buildings, and market places have seen stepped up security with more closed circuit television cameras (CCTVs) being installed in vulnerable places.

All five-star hotels across the country have invested in beefed-up security, including metal detectors, baggage scanners, sniffer dogs, and other anti-terror and security arrangements. Even deluxe and medium grade hotels and important restaurants have upgraded safety measures. Many hotels have rows of cars lining up for security checks at the entrance, where security guards peer under the hood and in the back compartment. Dogs sniff bags at the entrance; baggage is passed through X-ray scanners; guests are patted down as they go through metal detectors at the entrance; soldiers are stationed behind embankments, on the alert with their high-powered rifles; and also teams from local police stations pay regular visits to hotels and other 'soft targets' within their jurisdiction.

- Write everything as soon as the call is disconnected. If available, a bomb threat form (shown in Fig. 13.4) may be used. Try to note down the following:
  - Caller's voice
  - Mannerism
  - Age and sex
  - Accent
  - Any background noise, etc.
- Do not alter the exact conversation between you and the caller while narrating the incident to the authorities.
- Inform the competent authority immediately.

Hotel ABC
Bomb Threat Form

S. No.:.....................

Date:.........................
Time call started:............................. Time call ended:............................
Caller's exact words:_____
_____
_____

Questions that may be asked:
When is the bomb due to explode?--
Where is the device placed?--
What does the device look like?--
What is the type of device? Time bomb/remote operated bomb
Why have you placed the device?--
Whom do you represent?--

Details of caller (Fill as soon as call ends)
Age:--------------------
Sex:--------------------
Voice :-----------------
Accent: local/foreigner/educated/other (specify)
Language used:---------------------
Manner:--------------------------------
Any background sounds:--------------------
Type of call: Local/long distance
Telephone/Mobile no. from which the call was received :----------------------------

Action Taken
Information to management:...Time....................
Information to local police station:...Time:................

Date & Time:..Signature............................

Fig. 13.4   Bomb threat form

- Do not spread any rumour.
- Do not attempt to defuse the bomb if you are able to locate the same. Contact the local police authority or bomb disposal squad for defusing the device.

Robbery and Theft

There is always a possibility of robbery in hotels as the front desk cash and bills section and the points of sale usually have large sums of money. Also, the valuables in the possession of guests may invite burglars. To discourage robbers, the guests should be asked to leave their valuables in the front office safety deposit locker or in the in-room locker. In the event of an armed robbery, the hotel employees should follow the below-mentioned procedure:

- Comply with the robbers' demand.
- Do not make any sudden movement as it may provoke the robbers to use weapons or firearms.
- Remain quiet, unless directed to talk by the robbers.
- Do not attempt to disarm the robbers, as this may jeopardize many lives.
- The cashier may switch on the secret alarm that might be installed in the cash drawer, while also following the direction of robbers so that they do not get suspicious of him.
- Observe the robbers carefully, noting the physical characteristics like height, build, eye colour, hair colour, mannerisms, complexion, clothing, scar marks, or anything that can be helpful in their identification.
- Note the direction of escape, and the type and registration number of the vehicle used by the robbers.
- Do not touch any object that might have been touched by the robbers and restrict the movement of people in the area in order to preserve fingerprints and other possible evidence left by the robbers.
- Gather the details of the robbers from the people who have witnessed the event and record them in the crime report form (shown in Fig. 13.5), if available.

Guests in Drunken State

A guest in a drunken state may disturb or trouble other guests and could be a cause of embarrassment for the hotel. To avoid problems, the hotel staff should politely remove the drunken guest from the hotel lobby at the earliest and escort him to an isolated place, like the back office. If the guest acts in an unruly manner, the hotel security must be called.

Every hotel has its own modus operandi to deal with emergency situations. It is very important to not to panic in emergency situations. The hotel staff should be trained to remain as calm as possible to avoid panic in guests. They should calmly handle the situation and try to defuse the threat to the security of guests till the expert help arrives.

Hotel ABC

Crime Report Form

S. No.:.....................

Area of the incident: ....

Number of people involved in robbery: ....

Weapons used: Knife/firearms (type)/gun/revolver/pistol/others

Description of the arms

Description of robbers:

Age:....................	Age:....................
Height:...............	Height:...............
Built:..................	Built:..................
Complexion:.........	Complexion:.........
Identification mark:..............	Identification mark:..............
Name (if used):................	Name (if used):................
Colour of eyes:...................	Colour of eyes:...................
Colour of clothes:...............	Colour of clothes:...............
Mannerism :....................	Mannerism :....................
Language used:...................	Language used:...................
Modus operandi:...............	Modus operandi:...............

Description of vehicle(s) used:

Type and make:.............Registration No.:..............Colour of Vehicle..............

Any other relevant thing:..

....

Authorized Signatory

Fig. 13.5   Format of crime report form

SUMMARY

It is the legal and moral responsibility of a hotel to ensure the safety and security of its guests and employees. Hotels control the access to guest rooms by maintaining a strict control over room keys. In case of fire or accidents, all the employees of the hotel should follow the standard procedure laid down by the authorities. Hotels should be equipped with smoke detectors, fire extinguishers, and fire exits to deal with an outbreak of fire. It is mandatory for all hotels to have adequate first aid equipment, facilities, and trained personnel to provide first aid to people injured in an accident. If the injury is serious, proper medical assistance should be sought. The security personnel in hotels should be trained to handle situations like vandalism, terrorist attacks, and bomb threats.

KEY TERMS

Double lock An internal safety locking device—if locked from inside the room, it cannot be opened from outside by its own key and master key.

Emergency key/Grand master key It opens all door locks, even if they are double locked.

First aid It is the simple medical treatment given to a person before a doctor arrives or before the person can be taken to a hospital.

Guest room key It opens the lock of an individual guest room.

Master key It opens all guest room locks, that are not double locked.

REVIEW QUESTIONS

Multiple Choice Questions

1. The hotel may have the following types of keys:

   a) Emergency key   b) Master key
   c) Guest room key   d) All of the above

2. The basic elements that are necessary for the outbreak of fire are:

   a) Fuel   b) Oxygen
   c) Ignition temperature
   d) All of the above

3. Fire can be extinguished by:

   a) Smothering   b) Starving
   c) Cooling   d) All of the above

4. Some of the causes of accidents are:

   a) Excessive haste   b) Anxiety
   c) Lack of interest   d) All

5. An outbreak of fire due to an electrical short circuit is classified as:

   a) Class A   b) Class B
   c) Class C   d) Class D

True/False

1. An emergency key is also known as grand master key.

2. A guest room key remains in possession of the floor supervisor.

3. Accidents may occur due to excessive haste.

4. A burn is caused by wet heat.

5. In an event of fire, one should try to extinguish fire even if one has not had any training.

Fill in the Blanks

1. A _____ key opens all guest room door locks which are not double locked.

2. A _____ key opens all guest room door locks, even those which are double locked.

3. Scalds are caused due to _____ heat.

4. _____ is the removal of the fuel from the vicinity of fire, so that there is nothing to burn.

5. The process in which the supply of oxygen is cut to extinguish fire is known as _____.

Discussion Questions

1. Describe the various types of room keys you may find in a hotel.

2. What is the reason for having different types of room keys?

3. What are the causes of fire? Explain the basic components of fire.

4. Classify fire. Explain the principles involved in extinguishing fire.

5. What do you understand by accident? What causes accidents? Explain.

6. What are the advantages of reporting accidents? Describe the accident report form with the format of the same.

7. What is first-aid? Name the articles that a first aid box should contain.

8. How will you deal with terrorist activity or bomb threat as a front desk employee?

Critical Thinking Questions

1. Suppose you are a cashier at the front desk of a hotel and a group of people comes with firearms to rob the cash. How you will handle the situation?

2. Rahul is a room attendant in a hotel. While routine cleaning a room, he sees smoke coming from the next room. He goes there and finds that flame and fumes are coming out of the air-conditioning duct. What should Rahul do? Give valid reasons for your answer.

CASE STUDIES

1. You are the security manager of Hotel Moonlight. A fire breaks out in a competing hotel, Hotel Sunrise, and causes great damage. Due to a lack of an evacuation plan and other security measures, the hotel suffers great loss. The front office manager of your hotel calls a meeting with you to discuss the need for security measures in your hotel. Prepare a discussion based on the following factors:
   a) Requirement for installing fire fighting equipment.
   b) Training of employees to prevent loss.
   c) Evacuation plan for occupants.

2. You are working in the night shift, when three drunken men stumble into the hotel and ask for two rooms to stay. The doorman does his best to not allow them to enter the lobby. But they create a lot of noise and disturbance and reach the lobby. You have only two rooms available and the duty manager is busy with a VIP guest.
   a) What would you do?
   b) Would you give them the rooms?
   c) Would the resident guests feel threatened by these drunken guests?
   d) Would you call the police?

3. You notice smoke coming from the window of a guest room. You alert the security personnel and rush to the room. On reaching the room, you find that the guest has placed a DND board outside the room. You knock on the room, but there is no response.
   a) What would you do?
   b) Would you use the emergency key and enter the room?
   c) Would you call the front office manager or duty manager?

Part III

Front Office Management

- Computer Applications in Front Office
- Evaluating Hotel Performance
- Yield Management and Forecasting
- Hospitality Marketing
- Human Resource Management
- Environmental Management
- Total Quality Management

CHAPTER 14

Computer Applications in Front Office

Learning Objectives:

After reading this chapter, you will be able to understand the following:
- Use of computers in hotels.
- Property management system.
- PMS application in front office—reservations module, front desk module, rooms module, cashier module, night audit module, set up module, reporting module, and back office module.
- PMS interface with stand-alone systems like points of sale, energy management system, call accounting system, and electronic locking system.
- Different property management systems by Micros, Amadeus, IDS Fortune, and ShawMan.

Information technology has revolutionized the way industries work the world over. The service industry also has been a beneficiary of this revolution. Computers have long been associated with this notion of work and organization, offering a way to organize data and perform business transactions. What is changing now is that computers are also being used for recreation and social contact.

Hotel industry is one place that has undergone a tremendous change in the past few years with the advent of computers. The Internet is growing so fast that people now find it easier to plan their holidays online than in person. Tourists staying in a hotel find it an inseparable part of their lives. This way the hotel guests are able to explore various options, compare prices, and make reservations from the comfort of hotel rooms rather than having to walk to the office of a tour operator.

To be a successful hotel today, it is not enough to provide great service with regard to room maintenance and meals; one needs to cater to the customers' expectations in terms of technology and communication as well. The days are over when a hotel just had to worry about its own computers that helped with the running of the business. Now a good hotel will offer Internet access to its guests either within a certain part of the hotel or as a hotspot zone that surrounds the entire building and can be accessed by individual rooms.

PROPERTY MANAGEMENT SYSTEM

Computers are used for many different purposes in hotels. The first use is at the front desk, where the computers are equipped with an intricate software called the property management system (PMS) to do all check-ins, guest accounting, check-outs, etc. In a restaurant, lounge, or bar of a hotel, the second type of computer system, called a point of sale (POS) system, is used. This system collaborates with a PMS to generate bills for meals and drinks consumed by guests, but it can also be used as a cash register. The third use of the computer is in the sales office, which has a booking terminal.

A PMS is a computer-based management system. In the hospitality industry, it is a computerized system used to manage guest bookings, online reservations, points of sale, telephone, and other amenities. A hotel PMS may interface with central reservation systems (CRS) and revenue or yield management systems, front office, back office, and POS systems. There are many types of PMSs—it is up to a hotel to choose the one that best fits its needs.

There are different modules of PMS to manage individual departments of a hotel, such as front office module, housekeeping module, restaurant management system, back office module, etc. These modules are supplied by a large number of vendors, who modify PMS solutions to meet the requirements of the hotel. The requirement for automation may vary for each hotel on the basis of its size, location, volume of business, operations, etc. The PMS should be able to interface with individual interfaces like call accounting system, energy management system, POS system, electronic door locking system, etc.

The networking of hotel computers—which may be linked by local area network, wide area network or metropolitan area network, depending upon the requirements of the hotel—is a pre-requisite for the installation of the PMS. The PMS terminals are located at the front desk, housekeeping, points of sale, stores, etc. Each individual user is given access to different modules, depending upon its area of work and its level in the hierarchy of the hotel. The general manager and the system administrator have full access to all PMS modules.

PMS APPLICATION IN FRONT OFFICE

The PMS application for the front office has different modules for the efficient functioning of the whole department. Some of the common modules used in front office are: reservations module, front desk module, rooms module, cashier module, night audit module, set up module, report generation module, and back office module.

Reservations Module

The reservations module is used to create and manage guest reservations, both for individuals as well as groups (Fig. 14.1). The reservations module includes the following features:

- It provides room status records when the date of arrival, date of departure, and type of guest room are entered in the system.
- It colour codes the room status by using different colours for, for example, sold out days and days on which particular room types are sold out.

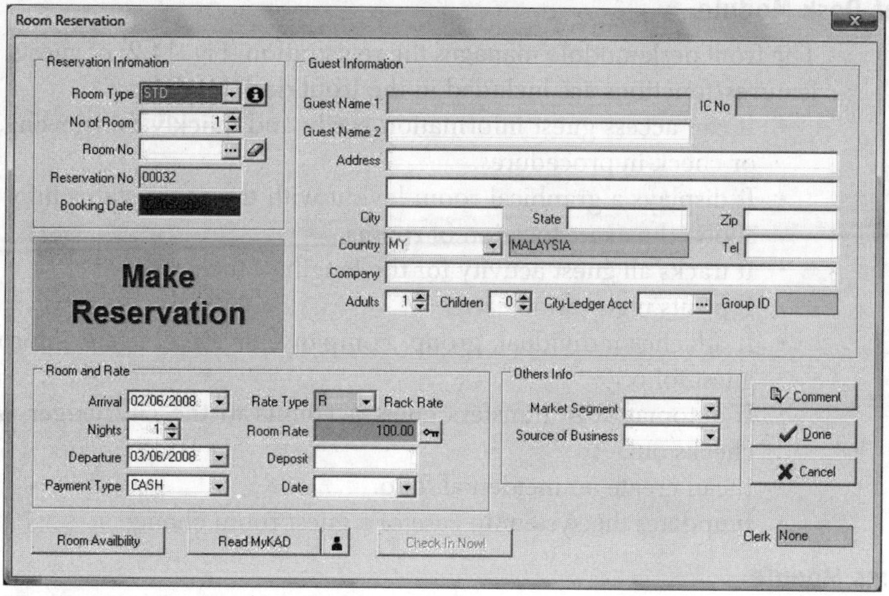

Fig. 14.1 Screenshot of reservation module

- It can check the reservation status of a guest quickly as it can search by guest name, company name, group ID, confirmation number, or arrival and departure dates.
- It displays room availability status (of up to 14 days at a time) by simply selecting a date.
- It can attach guest messages to relevant reservations, to be delivered to the guest upon arrival.
- It can automatically calculate rates based on the room type, the rate code, arrival and departure dates, and the number of adults and children.
- It can create group blocks and rooming lists for standard groups, tour series, and allotments.
- It can create special group rates.
- It can use the rooming list feature for rapid reservation pick-up.
- It can pre-assign rooms to guests when making a reservation or at any time using a graphical tape chart.
- It is able to define a 'share with' reservation in group bookings.
- It automatically transmits confirmation of a reservation via e-mail, fax, or Internet.
- It is able to post an advance deposit on a room.
- It can enter 'remarks', which are visible upon reservation retrieval.
- It can reserve and track the availability of service items such as rollaway beds, cribs, and refrigerators.

Front Desk Module

The front desk module manages the registration (Fig. 14.2) of guests. The following features/functions are included in the front desk module:

- It can access guest information easily and quickly for viewing, modification, or check-in procedures.
- It displays a graphical room layout with the room status information, which shows the exact location of rooms.
- It tracks all guest activity for the length of their stay.
- It prints registration cards.
- It attaches individual, group, company, or travel agent information to each guest folio.
- It automatically transfers guest accounts to the city ledger when the guest checks out.
- It can create an incidental folio.
- It updates the system in case of a guest room change.

Rooms Module

The rooms module allows the staff to manage the hotel's rooms and floor plans. The following are some of the functions performed by this module:

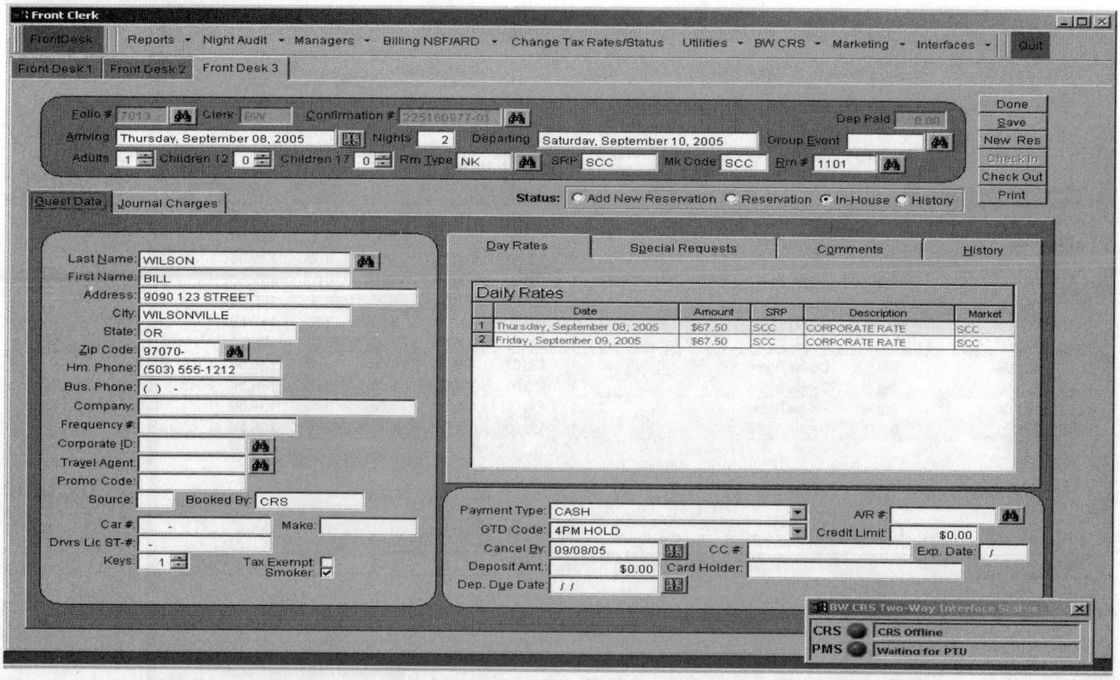

Fig. 14.2   Screenshot of front office module

- It displays the entire layout of a hotel, showing a single floor/wing at a time. One can easily go to another floor/wing by using the scroll buttons, and enlarge or reduce the size of floor plans by using the zoom buttons.
- The display of the floor plan can be changed to show housekeeping, front desk, or specific room status.
- It provides latest room status information to both housekeeping and front office departments.
- It schedules the maintenance work for rooms.
- It automatically adjusts room inventory.
- It schedules linen change in long-term stayovers.
- It can track discrepancies in the room status.

Cashier Module

The cashier module is used to manage guest folios, raise bills, and perform check-out procedures (Fig. 14.3). The following are some of the functions that can be performed with the cashier module:

- It can add incidental folios and move charges between folios with one click.
- It can locate any account by entering the room number or name.
- It manages all aspects of the guest folio, including debits, credits, adjustments, transfers, and voids.

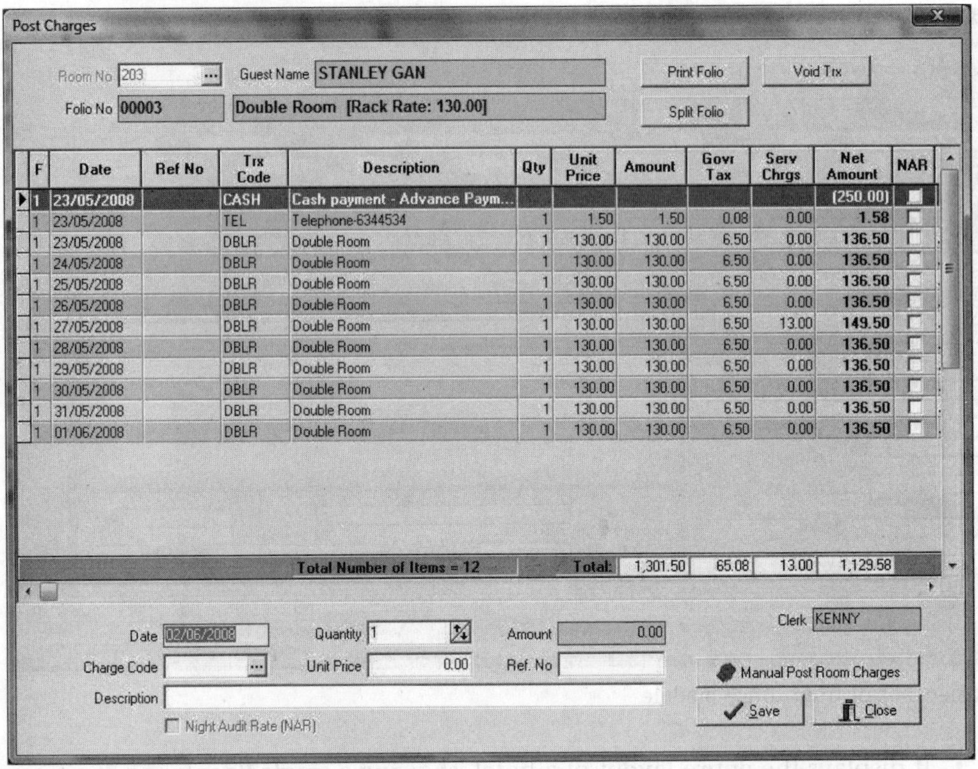

Fig. 14.3 Screenshot of posting charges

- It allows the viewing or printing of folio details and summary information.
- It consolidates all transactions and produces an accurate bill quickly, enabling a speedy check-out.
- It allows the attachment of unlimited folios to each guest account.
- It carriers out the transfer of charges from folio to folio, from one room to another, in amounts or by percentage.

Night Audit Module

The night audit module is used to balance the day's activity and complete the hotel's accounting functions for the day. The following are some of the features/functions of the night audit module:

- It can perform routine tasks of posting room charges, changing non-guaranteed rooms reservations to no-shows, and changing the status of guaranteed no-shows with one touch.
- It takes an automatic back-up of data to optical disk.

- It has the ability to rebuild room availability afresh in case there is a system failure.
- It has direct access to the reports module.
- It allows the auditor to view a scrolled display of various processing steps.
- It automatically posts service charges like garage fees, crib fees, etc.
- It automatically posts finance and recurring charges.
- If a room is scheduled for maintenance work, it automatically changes the room status to out of order.
- It automatically sets the housekeeping status of occupied rooms to dirty.
- It can do batch printing of registration cards.
- It has the ability to process no-shows with deposit payments.
- It can print customized reports automatically.
- It can archive all records.
- It has the ability to perform close-out without a system shut down; other users may perform any task while the audit is running.

Set-up Module

The set up module is used to define system settings. These settings allow for customization. Some of the key features/functions of this module are as follows:

- It can specify mandatory fields for required information and add custom information and forms.
- It can customize according to the market, source and rate codes, and can also define text for field selections.
- It can generate and customize colour codes.
- It allows the employees to access their function areas in the system using unique user IDs and passwords.
- It specifies rate codes, room rates, and rate availability along with the restriction of rate availability by date range, days of the week, or minimum stay.
- It creates and maintains profiles of individuals, groups, companies, and travel agents.
- It can define the phone extension for each room, including multiple phone extensions for a single room.
- It can display all message prompts and screen text in the local language.
- It creates a list of all room features available throughout the hotel and generates the display of attachments to specific room types and rooms.
- It can customize the reservations calendar with user-defined text for holidays, special events, and reminders.
- It sets a time limit for retaining the guest folios and profiles.
- It assigns request codes to anticipate the special needs of guests; these requests are either chargeable or complimentary.

- It creates an inventory of service items, such as roll-aways, cribs, and refrigerators. The availability of these items is also tracked.
- It uses a mix of standard and user-defined housekeeping codes.
- It configures printers and routes specific reports to specific printers.

Reporting Module

The reporting module has various reporting formats which allow the management to retrieve operating or financial information at any point of time. With this module, the management can quickly access information such as the availability of rooms on a particular day, the number of guests arriving on a specific day, listing of guests' folio balances, outstanding balance reports, etc. The access to reports can be customized through the use of filters.

Back Office Module

The back office module provides an integrated system for managing the hotel's financial and statistical information. It simplifies accounting processes such as posting of accounts payable, transfer of accounts receivables, compilation of the payroll, budget preparation, and the production of the hotel's profit-and-loss statement and balance sheet. The financial information entered on a terminal in back office updates all accounting records. The back office module is also linked with the night audit module, which helps in streamlining the accounting process.

PMS INTERFACE WITH STAND-ALONE SYSTEMS

When the PMS is integrated with other stand-alone automation systems like points of sale, energy management system, call accounting system, and electronic locking system, it becomes more effective and useful for hotel operations.

Point of Sales In a hotel, the points of sale (POS) are the products/services other than accommodation from where the hotel generates revenue. These include restaurants, bars, discotheque, night club, health centre, etc. Each point of sale is equipped with a stand-alone automated support for billings. If this is linked with the PMS, the data is immediately transferred to other modules for further processing. For example, a resident guest's credit sale in a restaurant will be immediately transferred to the cashier module, where it will be posted in the respective guest folio.

Call Accounting System Hotels provide telephone facility to their guests. The resident guests can make local as well as long distance calls from the comfort of their rooms. The call accounting system is a stand-alone automated system, which tracks all outgoing and incoming calls. It has the following features: identification of outward dialling, automatic route selection, and call rating programme. When the call accounting system is integrated with the PMS interface, the calls are automatically posted in the respective caller's account.

Energy Management System An energy management system is designed to manage the operations of equipments and instruments that consume energy. One typical function would be to shut down the operations of equipments that are not is use; for example, when a guest locks his room with the electronic key, the weather control system and lights are automatically turned off.

Electronic Locking System The electronic locking system is used widely nowadays. This system helps the hotels to control access to guest rooms. Only a person with the proper card key coded for the specific room can enter that room. When the electronic locking system is networked with the PMS, the front desk person is able to code the room keys for the guests. The coding is such that the key will become non-functional after the check-out time on the date of departure.

DIFFERENT PROPERTY MANAGEMENT SYSTEMS

There are several companies that provide the PMS software to hotels, with their own unique features to suit the different requirements of various hotels. Some of the companies providing PMS software also provide other tailor-made products to their clients. Micros, Amadeus, IDS Fortune, and ShawMan are some of the major companies that provide the PMS software. Let us discuss briefly about some of these softwares here:

Micros

Micros Systems provides PMS software solutions to the hospitality industry through:
  • Opera Enterprise Solutions
  • Micros Fidelio

Opera Enterprise Solutions The Opera Enterprise Solution (OES) is a fully integrated suite of products that can be easily combined for deployment at any size of organization—from a single-property hotel to a global, multi-branded hotel chain. Opera modules include:

Opera Reservation System The Opera Reservation System (ORS) is a centrally-managed computer reservation system that handles all types of reservations—individual, group and party, company, travel agent, multi-legged, multi-rate, and waitlisted (refer Exhibit 14.1).

Opera Customer Information System This gathers and manages profile data of guests, travel agents, sources, groups, and companies in a central database that can be shared by multiple properties.

Opera GDS Interface The Opera GDS Interface links the hotel's database and the global distribution systems (GDS) and web booking engines (WBEs) through a third-party switching company.

Opera Sales Force Automation Opera Sales Force Automation (SFA) is a central sales support tool for a hotel chain's regional or national sales team. SFA is fully integrated with Opera's central reservation system, ORS.

Micros Fidelio Micros Fidelio range of software products include property management systems (PMS), reservation systems, and points of sale (POS) systems.

Property Management System It takes care of tasks like guest information, night audits, inventory control, profit management, and report generation.

Reservation system Configured to a hotel's specification, it gives the hotel staff instant room status and availability report, leading to instant reservations.

POS systems Micros-Fidelio points of sale (POS) software systems facilitate faster information retrieval, which aids faster transactions.

Exhibit 14.1 Opera Reservation System (ORS): Login/Searching reservations

Step 1: Login
The screen asks for Username and Password

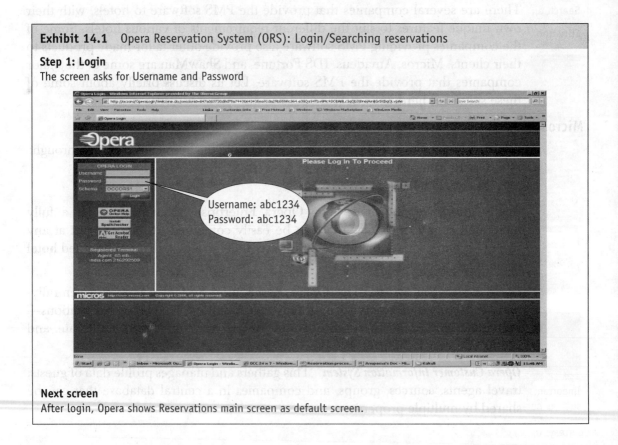

Next screen
After login, Opera shows Reservations main screen as default screen.

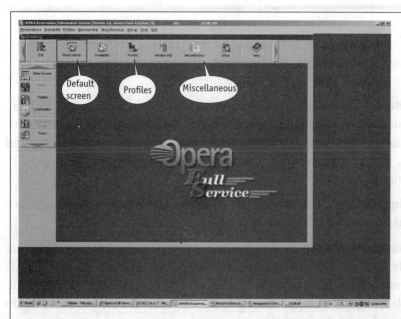

Search option

Click on Look up to search for existing reservations

Important: **Look up** – this option helps locate existing reservations on the basis of multiple search criterions, such as hotel name, guest name, arrival date, company/travel agent name, etc.

Courtesy: Oberoi contact centre

AMADEUS PMS

Amadeus property management system can be integrated with front office, sales/marketing, and financial management functions. It allows the user to move faster in all core aspects of guest experience management.

Front Office Module   This module offers full availability, reservation, yielding and billing functionalities, which in turn generate useful performance statistics. It provides data on performance indicators such as sales, accounts, source, and segment activity, which is monitored to analyse business efficiency and used to generate management reports.

Sales and Marketing Module   This module aids the sales and marketing professionals to target potential guests and effectively manage customer relationships.

Conference and Banqueting Module   Event planning is a feature that helps generate revenue for hotels. The key features of the conference management system include real-time conference/meeting room availability and equipment management. An interface with front office helps the sales agent to book rooms according to conference dates and guest preferences.

Financial Management   It is designed for liquidity planning and control along with comprehensive accounting, financial reporting, and analysis.

IDS Fortune

It offers the following three PMS for all categories of hotels:
- Fortune Enterprise
- Fortune Express
- Fortune Genie

Fortune Enterprise   It provides centralized data integration along with colourful displays to aid the absorption of the important facts at a glance.

Fortune Express   This has the flexibility needed to manage mid-segment and budget hotels. A single database keeps all aspects of management, speeding up information sharing for greater efficiency.

Fortune Genie   It has been designed to cater to the needs of limited service hotels, motels, and serviced apartments. A single database gives a clear overview of the entire enterprise, ensuring transparency.

SHAWMAN

The ShawMan PMS is an integrated front office management software that can host multiple properties and handle guest reservations simultaneously across many units, including an integrated web-based reservation agent and an auto confirmation manager.

Due to technological advances and globalization, hotel guests have high demands and their reliance on technology in office and at home has raised the bar for their travel expectations. Hotels are increasingly being asked by guests to provide them with the same quality of technology they have at home and the work place. In a dynamic industry such as hospitality, businesses require property management systems that deliver performance, scalability, and component integration. At the same time, these systems must be stable, intuitive, easy to manage, and ultimately help to drive revenue. Thus, hotels have to select property management systems that meet these tough requirements with care in order to improve guest experience while generating stronger revenues.

SUMMARY

Computers are used for many purposes in hotels like billing, reservations etc. A property management system (PMS) is a computer-based management system that is used to manage guest bookings, online reservations, points of sale, telephone, and other amenities. There are different modules of PMS to manage individual departments of a hotel, such as front office module, housekeeping module, restaurant management system, back office module, etc. The PMS should be able to interface with individual interfaces like call accounting system, energy management system, point of sales, electronic door locking system, etc. in order to be more useful to hotel operations. There are several companies that provide the PMS software to hotels, with their own unique features to suit the different requirements of various hotels. Micros, Amadeus, IDS Fortune, and ShawMan are some of the major companies that provide the PMS software.

KEY TERMS

Call accounting system It is a stand-alone automated system, which tracks all outgoing and incoming calls. Its features include identification of outward dialling, automatic route selection, and call rating programme.

Electronic locking system It is a stand-alone automated system in which the room key is electronically coded and access to a room is allowed only to a person with the proper card key.

Energy management system It is the practice of controlling the use of equipment that consumes energy.

Interface It is the meeting point between two computer systems or between a user and a computer system.

Points of sale All outlets—including restaurants, bars, discotheque, night club, health centre, etc.—from where hotels sell their products and services other than accommodation.

Property management system (PMS) A computerized system used to manage guest bookings, online reservations, point of sale, telephone, and other amenities.

REVIEW QUESTIONS

Multiple Choice Questions

1. What does PMS stands for?
   a) Proper management system
   b) Property management system
   c) Property managing society
   d) Positive motivation system

2. Which of the following compaines provides PMS software for hospitality industry?
   a) Micros   b) IDS Fortune
   c) ShawMan   d) All

3. PMS applications in the front office do not include:
   a) Reservation module
   b) Housekeeping module
   c) Cashier module
   d) Rooms module

4. PMS interfaces include:
   a) Point of sales
   b) Call accounting system
   c) Electronic locking system
   d) All

5. Which of the following is not provided by IDS Fortune?
   a) Fortune Enterprise   b) Fortune Genie
   c) Fortune Fidelio   d) Fortune Express

True/False

1. Amadeus provides PMS software for hospitality industry.

2. Assessing the needs of the hotel is very important for selecting the PMS for the hotel.

3. ShawMan is a computer software.

4. Information technology has revolutionized the hospitality industry.

5. Property management systems are not necessary for medium-sized hotels.

Discussion Questions

1. Write an essay on automation in hotels.

2. Write a note on :
   a) Property management system
   b) PMS applications in front office

3. Write an essay on PMS interfaces.

4. Explain the following modules of a PMS:
   a) Reservation module
   b) Cashier module
   c) Front desk module
   d) Night audit module
   e) Reporting module

CRITICAL THINKING QUESTIONS

1. Selecting a property management system requires skill and experience. Comment.

2. Hotel automation leads to the efficient management of hotel resources and to greater guest satisfaction. Discuss.

PROJECT WORK

Visit five hotels in your city and compare the property management systems of the different hotels on the basis of speed of the PMS, ease of operations, and retrieval of reservations.

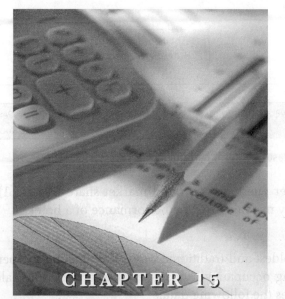

CHAPTER 15

Evaluating Hotel Performance

Learning Objectives:

After reading this chapter, you will be able to understand the following:
- Evaluation of hotel performance—its importance for investors, owners, and managers.
- Methods of measuring hotel performance—occupancy ratios, average daily rate, average room rate per guest, revenue per available room (rev-par), and market share index.
- Evaluation of hotels by guests.

easuring the performance of a hotel is important for its investors, owners, and managers. The investors want to assess the profitability of their investment in order to decide whether to continue to invest or to withdraw their investment from that venture. The owner(s) need to continuously evaluate the performance of the hotel with respect to revenue generation. The managers formulate strategies to improve the performance of the hotel and set targets to measure their success.

METHODS OF MEASURING HOTEL PERFORMANCE

There are different ways of measuring the performance of hotels. Hotels evaluate their performance by calculating occupancy ratios, average daily rate, average

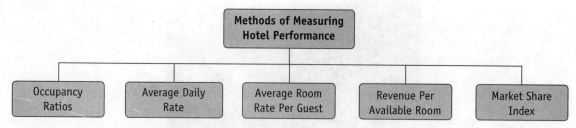

Fig. 15.1 Methods of measuring hotel performance

room rate per guest, rev-par, and market share (Fig. 15.1). Guests also have an important say in evaluating the performance of a hotel.

Occupancy Ratios

One of the oldest and traditional ways of evaluating the performance of a hotel is by calculating occupancy ratios (see Chapter 12). The calculation of occupancy ratios requires the following data:
- Total number of saleable rooms
- Number of rooms sold
- Number of guests (i.e. house count)
- Net room revenue generated

Occupancy percentage is the ratio of the total number of occupied rooms to the total number of rooms that are available for sale.

$$\text{Occupancy percentage} = \frac{\text{Number of rooms sold}}{\text{Total number of rooms available for sale}} \times 100$$

Let us suppose that a hotel with 350 rooms (all available for sale) manages to sell 245 rooms on a certain day. The occupancy percentage on that particular day will be:

Occupancy percentage = 245/350 × 100
= 70%

If in the above example, 25 rooms were blocked for spring cleaning and 25 rooms were under renovation, the total number of saleable rooms will reduce from 350 to 300. Then the occupancy percentage will be 245/300 ×100 = 82 per cent.

The occupancy percentage can be calculated for a particular day, or on a weekly, fortnightly, monthly, quarterly, half yearly, or annual basis. This yardstick helps the management to measure the performance of the hotel.

Average Daily Rate

Average daily rate—commonly referred to as ADR—is a statistical unit that is often used in the hospitality industry. It is the average rental income per occupied room for a given time period. It is calculated by dividing the total revenue generated in a specific duration of time by the total number of rooms sold in that duration.

Let us suppose that in the earlier example the total revenue generated was Rs 49,000. The average daily rate will be:

$$\text{ADR} = \frac{\text{Total revenue generated in a specific period}}{\text{Total number of rooms sold in that period}}$$

$$= \text{Rs } 49,000/245 \text{ rooms}$$
$$= \text{Rs } 200 \text{ per room}$$

Average Room Rate Per Guest

Average room rate per guest (ARG) is calculated by dividing the total room revenue by the total number of guests in the hotel, including children above five years. The formula to calculate the average room rate per guest is as under:

$$\text{Average room rate per guest (ARG)} = \frac{\text{Total revenue generated in a specific period}}{\text{Total number of guests in the hotel}}$$

In the above example, if the total number of guests is 280 on that particular day, the average room rate per guest will be:

$$\text{ARG} = \text{Rs } 49,000/280 \text{ guests}$$
$$= \text{Rs } 175 \text{ per guest}$$

Revenue Per Available Room (Rev-Par)

Rev-par is the revenue per available room. It is used to measure and compare the performance of two or more hotels. Rev-par is calculated by multiplying the average daily rate with the occupancy percentage.

$$\text{Rev-par} = \text{ADR} \times \text{Occupancy percentage}$$
$$= \text{Rs } 200 \times 70/100$$
$$= \text{Rs } 140$$

Rev-par can analyse the performance of a hotel over any timeframe—daily, weekly, monthly, quarterly, or yearly. The rev-par analysis can also be used to compare hotels of different sizes.

Let us take the following example:

The data collected on a particular day from three hotels is as under:

Hotel X (300 rooms): ADR is Rs 250 with an occupancy percentage of 75.

Hotel Y (200 rooms): ADR is Rs 275 with an occupancy percentage of 70.

Hotel Z (600 rooms): ADR is Rs 200 with an occupancy percentage of 65.

Let us evaluate the performance of the Hotels X, Y, and Z. The total revenue generated by a hotel is ADR × No. of rooms sold. The number of rooms sold can be calculated as:

$$\text{Number of rooms sold} = \frac{\text{Occupancy percentage} \times \text{Total number of rooms available for sale}}{100}$$

The number of rooms sold by Hotel X = 75 × 300/100 = 225 rooms
The number of rooms sold by Hotel Y = 70 × 200/100 = 140 rooms
The number of rooms sold by Hotel Z = 65 × 600/100 = 390 rooms

Thus, the total revenue generated by the hotels is as under:

Total revenue of a hotel: ADR × No. of rooms sold
Total revenue of Hotel X: Rs 250 × 225 = Rs 56,250
Total revenue of Hotel Y: Rs 275 × 140 = Rs 38,500
Total revenue of Hotel Z: Rs 200 × 390 = Rs 78,000

Thus, on the basis of revenue generated, one may reach a conclusion that Hotel Z has outperformed the other two hotels. However, let us now calculate the rev-par of each hotel, which is ADR × Occupancy percentage.

Rev-par of Hotel X: 250 × 75/100 = Rs 187.50
Rev-par of Hotel Y: 275 × 70/100 = Rs 192.50
Rev-par of Hotel Z: 200 × 65/100 = Rs 130.00

We see that on the basis of rev-par, Hotel Y has outperformed the other two hotels. Thus, rev-par is useful because of the above-mentioned flexibility of comparing hotels of different sizes and their respective rates.

Market Share Index

Rev-par is a useful tool to measure the performance of a hotel. It uses occupancy percentage and ADR for comparing the performance of hotels. However, in a competitive environment, hotels may not provide information about ADR. In such situations, the evaluation of the hotel's performance is done by using market share. Market share is defined as a hotel's occupancy performance in relation to other hotels within a predetermined competitive set.

A major task in calculating the market share is the determination of the competitive set. The answer to the question—if a guest is not staying at our hotel, where can he possibly stay?—constitutes the competitive set. The total market potential is the sum total of the number of rooms that are available in the total number of participating hotels.

Let's suppose there are five hotels in a competitive set, namely Hotel A, Hotel B, Hotel C, Hotel D, and Hotel E, with a total of 200, 300, 400, 500, 600 rooms respectively. The total market potential will be 2,000 rooms, and the individual market potential of each hotel in the set will be equal to the number of rooms available for sale in the hotel. The rightful market share of a hotel is the maximum share that can be occupied by the hotel, i.e. the number of rooms divided by the total market potential.

The rightful market share in this example can be summarized as under:

Hotel	Number of Rooms	Total Market Potential	Rightful Share (Number of rooms/Total market potential)
A	200	2,000	0.10 or 10%
B	300	2,000	0.15 or 15%
C	400	2,000	0.20 or 20%
D	500	2,000	0.25 or 25%
E	600	2,000	0.30 or 30%

If we feed the actual occupancy data of all the participating hotels of the competitive set, we will be able to know the actual market and share taken by each hotel, and can compare the performance of each participating hotel.

Let's suppose in the above example, Hotels A, B, C, D, and E have sold 1,300, 1,500, 2,100, 2,600, and 3,000 rooms respectively in one week. We can calculate the actual and potential market share as under:

Hotel	Number of rooms	Total number of rooms in a week (No. of rooms X No. of days)	Actual number of rooms sold in the week
A	200	1,400	1,300
B	300	2,100	1,500
C	400	2,800	2,100
D	500	3,500	2,600
E	600	4,200	3,000
		14,000 (potential)	10,500 (actual)

One can find out the performance of the entire set by dividing the actual number of rooms sold by the potential number of rooms available during that week.

$$10,500/14,000 = 0.75 \text{ or } 75\% \text{ occupancy}$$

From the available information, one can calculate the actual market share captured by each hotel in the set. The market captured by each hotel is as under:

Hotel	Market Share	Percentage
A	1,300/10,500	12.38%
B	1,500/10,500	14.28%
C	2,100/10,500	20.00%
D	2,600/10,500	24.77%
E	3,000/10,500	28.57%
	Total	100.00%

On comparing of the actual market share with the rightful market share, one can find the performance of each hotel in the competitive set. The comparative analysis of the present example is as under:

Hotel	Actual market share	Rightful share	Difference
A	12.38%	10%	+ 2.38
B	14.28%	15%	−0.72
C	20.00%	20%	Nil
D	24.77%	25%	−0.23
E	28.57%	30%	−1.43

From the above analysis, one can gauge that Hotel A's performance in better than Hotels B, D, and E, whereas Hotel C has been able to capture its rightful market share.

Market share index enables the managers to assess their hotel's performance with respect to the competitors. It assists the managers to develop plans to combat the loss of fair market share and also to gain market share from the competitors.

EVALUATION OF HOTELS BY GUESTS

We have looked at some methods by which hotels evaluate their performance. Let us also take a look at how guests evaluate a hotel (Exhibit 15.1). Guests base their evaluation of hotels on various criteria like location, hotel staff, service level, cleanliness, etc. A 2007 survey of the hotel and restaurant industry in Europe concluded that 80 per cent of UK consumers are now researching online before booking a hotel, and that half of them said they have refrained from booking a hotel as a direct result of a negative review on travel information websites such as TripAdvisor. Hence, it is very important that the hotel provides consistent excellent services to all the guests so that no guest leaves the hotel with a negative experience, which might lead to negative word-of-mouth publicity and to the lowering of hotel sales, and thus affecting the revenue and performance of the hotel.

Exhibit 15.1   Travel information website—TripAdvisor.com

About TripAdvisor

TripAdvisor.com is a travel information website, which covers more than 230,000 hotels and 76,000 attractions in over 33,000 destinations worldwide. With more than 15 million reviews and opinions and nearly 32 million visitors a month, TripAdvisor is also the largest travel community in the world. TripAdvisor has a wide range of content and provides recommendations for hotels, resorts, inns, vacation packages, and travel guides. Its mission is: Help people around the world plan and have the perfect trip.

Users can browse travel destinations across the world with the aid of a travel map and as the searches narrow down, the user is provided with a local map showing local attractions and the best deals for local hotels.

contd

Exhibit 15.1 *contd*

TripAdvisor is wiki-enabled, which facilitates millions of travellers to view, contribute, and edit the guides available on more than 33,000 destinations worldwide. The site also has photos and videos. The site has tie-ins with over 17 business partners in the travel industry, including Expedia, Sabre, Orbitz, and American Airlines.

TripAdvisor Hotel Survey

TripAdvisor announced the results of a hotel survey of more than 2200 travellers worldwide in September 2008.

The good

When asked what makes a hotel great, 30 percent of respondents said location is the most important factor, while 29 percent cited comfortable beds, and 24 percent said hotel staff/great service. When asked what makes a hotel bed comfortable, 64 percent said it's the mattress, 11 percent noted the linens, and another 11 percent said it's the pillows.

The bad

When asked what ruins a hotel stay, 54 percent said unclean rooms, 14 percent cited noisy hotel guests and 11 percent pointed to poor hotel staff/service.

The ugly

Sixty-eight percent of travellers have experienced a dirty carpet at a hotel, 64 percent have dealt with non-working appliances, and 59 percent have waited as their room was not ready at check-in. Thirty-eight percent of travellers think the dirtiest part of a hotel is the carpet, 37 percent speculate it's the bedspread, 11 percent believe it's the television remote and another 11 percent think it's the bathroom.

Honest and Truthful?

Seventy-eight percent of travellers said hotels are often "as advertised," 17 percent said they are rarely as advertised. Sixty-six percent of travellers said B&Bs are "as advertised," 20 percent said they are rarely so. A senior person at TripAdvisor summarized the results of the survey as, "Your hotel experience can make or break your vacation and we've found that travellers don't ask for much. Cleanliness is the top travel requirement among TripAdvisor members and that doesn't seem like too much to ask."

Adapted from:
http://www.hotelmarketing.com/index.php/content/article/tripadvisor_hotels_survey_reveals_the_good_the_bad_and_the_ugly/; http://www.tripadvisor.com/PressCenter-c4-Fact_Sheet.html; and http://www.readwriteweb.com/archives/tripadvisor_the.php, last accessed on 18 September 2008.

SUMMARY

It is important for the investors, owners, and managers of a hotel to continuously evaluate and assess the performance of the hotel with respect to revenue generation. Hotels measure their performance by calculating occupancy ratios, average daily rate, average room rate per guest, revpar, and market share. Guests also evaluate hotels on the basis of their experience, so hotels should provide excellent service to their guests.

KEY TERMS

Average daily rate (ADR) It is the average rental income per occupied room for a given time period.

Average room rate per guest (ARG) It is calculated by dividing the total room revenue by total number of guest in the hotel, including children.

Market share It is a hotel's occupancy performance in relation to other hotels within a predetermined competitive set.

Occupancy percentage It is the ratio of the total number of occupied rooms to the total number of rooms that are available for sale.

Revenue per available room (rev-par) It is obtained by multiplying the average daily rate with the occupancy percentage.

Rightful market share It is the maximum share of the market that can be occupied by a hotel, i.e., the number of rooms divided by the total market potential.

Total market potential It is the sum total of the number of rooms that are available in the total number of participating hotels.

REVIEW QUESTIONS

Multiple Choice Questions

1. Which of the following methods are used to measure hotel performance?
   a) Market share
   b) Rev-par
   c) Average daily rate
   d) All

2. Which of the following data is required for the calculation of occupancy percentage?
   a) Number of saleable rooms
   b) Number of rooms sold
   c) Both
   d) None

3. Average room rate per guest can be calculated by which of the following data?
   a) Total revenue generated in specific time
   b) Total number of guests who stayed in that duration
   c) Both
   d) None

4. On what bases do guests evaluate hotels?
   a) Cleanliness
   b) Location
   c) Hotel staff
   d) All

5. Rev-par stands for:
   a) Revenue percentage
   b) Renewal per guest
   c) Revenue per available room
   d) Actual revenue of room

True/False

1. ADR is the average rental income per occupied room for a given time period.

2. Average room rate per guest is calculated by dividing the total room revenue by the total number of guests in the hotel.

3. Market share index enables the managers to assess their hotel's performance with respect to the competitors.

4. ADR is not an important tool for assessing hotel performance.

5. Rev-par is used to compare the performance of two or more hotels.

Discussion Questions

1. What are the criteria for evaluating the performance of a hotel?

2. What is occupancy percentage? How can you calculate the occupancy percentage? Illustrate with an example.

3. Explain ADR in detail with examples.

4. What is rev-par? Explain rev-par with examples.

5. What do you understand by market share? How can it be used to analyse the performance of hotels?

CASE STUDIES

1. The data collected from three hotels is as under:

   Hotel A (300 rooms): ADR is Rs 255 with occupancy percentage 72.

   Hotel B (200 rooms): ADR is Rs 225 with occupancy percentage 75.

   Hotel C (600 rooms): ADR is Rs 290 with occupancy percentage 67.

   Evaluate the performance of Hotels A, B, and C using rev-par technique.

2. There are four hotels in a competitive set, namely Hotel Alpha, Hotel Beta, Hotel Gamma, and Hotel Delta, with 150, 250, 400, 500 rooms respectively. In a period of ten days, Hotel Alpha sold 1,250 rooms, Hotel Beta sold 1,850 rooms, Hotel Gamma sold 3,200 rooms, and Hotel Delta sold 3,500 rooms.

   Calculate the following:

   a) Total market potential
   b) Total individual potential
   c) Rightful market share of each hotel
   d) Actual market share of each hotel
   e) Compare the performance of the four hotels.

CHAPTER 16

Yield Management and Forecasting

Learning Objectives:

After reading this chapter, you will be able to understand the following:
- Concept of yield management.
- Application of yield management in the hotel industry.
- Elements and benefits of yield management.
- Yield management strategies in case of high demand and low demand periods.
- Measuring yield.
- Forecasting—benefits, data, and records required.
- Yield management prospects.

A s discussed in the previous chapter, hoteliers adopt various means to evaluate the performance of their hotels. Most of the hoteliers calculate the average daily rate to measure the performance of their hotels in terms of revenue generation. Hoteliers have realized that along with volume of business, they should also concentrate on revenue generation in each sale. The concept of yield is based on the basic economic principle of demand and supply. In this chapter, we will study the techniques used to maximize revenue generation. We will also study the various tools used to practice yield management and room availability forecasting.

YIELD MANAGEMENT

The concept of yield management was introduced by the airline industry. Yield is the revenue generated per statistical unit. For example, an airline's yield would be stated as the average revenue per mile per paying passenger. In 1985, American Airlines launched Ultimate Super Saver fares to compete with a low cost carrier. This was a very successful scheme. The airlines operators realized that their product (i.e. seat in the flight) was highly perishable—as a seat left unoccupied in a flight results in a loss of revenue of that seat forever. To maximize the revenue generated from selling the seats in a flight, the airlines adopted a technique based on demand and supply. When the demand for seats in a particular flight exceeded the supply (or availability) of seats, the airlines charged higher rates (close or equal to rack rate). But when the supply exceeded demand (available seats were much more than the demand), the airlines offered various types of discounts and package plans, resulting in the lowering of prices, which would lead to the selling of more seats on that particular flight. This way of maximizing revenue generation is termed as yield management. Soon, this concept gained popularity in various sectors selling highly perishable products and services like railways and hospitality.

Thus, yield management or revenue management is the process of understanding, anticipating, and influencing consumer behaviour in order to maximize revenue or profits from a fixed, perishable resource (such as airline seats or hotel rooms). The challenge is to sell the right resources to the right customer at the right time for the right price. This process can result in price discrimination, where a firm charges different prices from customers consuming otherwise identical goods or services. Airlines charge different airfares from travellers who are travelling in the same class of the same flight, depending upon the number of days in advance the tickets have been booked. In general, the tickets purchased much earlier than the date of travel are less expensive than bookings made a little in advance.

Measuring Yield in the Hotel Industry

Yield management is a tool to maximize the yield (revenue generated) of a hotel. Measuring yield is one of the various techniques employed by hotels to evaluate the performance of their business. The average daily rate (ADR) and occupancy percentages (discussed in Chapter 15) are commonly taken as indicators of a hotel's performance. While they do provide us with the basic tools, these figures can be taken a step further by utilizing them—together with a number of other formulae—to plan the hotel's pricing and booking strategies.

Let us understand the same by taking an example. Suppose we have a hotel with ten single rooms. Let the rack rate be Rs 100 (one hundred only). The potential revenue that can be earned by the hotel in one year (365 days) will be:

$$\text{Potential Revenue} = \text{Total no. of rooms} \times \text{No. of days in year} \times \text{Rack rate}$$
$$= 10 \times 365 \times \text{Rs } 100$$
$$= \text{Rs } 3,65,000$$

Let us suppose that the actual revenue generated by the same hotel during the previous year (365 days) was Rs 2,35,000. Then, the yield will be:

$$\text{Yield} = \text{Actual revenue produced/Potential revenue}$$
$$= \text{Rs } 2,35,000/\text{Rs } 3,65,000$$
$$= 0.64378 \text{ or } 64.38 \% \text{ of potential revenue}$$

This indicates that the actual revenue generated by the hotel is 0.64 times to its actual potential.

This can be further expanded as:

$$\text{Yield} = \frac{\text{Number of rooms sold}}{\text{Number of available rooms}} \times \frac{\text{Actual average room rate}}{\text{Room rate potential}}$$

Yield Management in the Hotel Industry

A guest room is one of the highly perishable products of the hospitality sector—if a room is not sold on a particular day, the entire potential revenue that could be generated from it is lost for ever. Hotels have come to realize that mere volume sales do not generate the desired revenue, and that they have to think of quality deals in terms of revenue generated per sale. Their focus is shifting from high volume reservations to high profit reservations. To maximize the revenue generated from rooms, hotels now sell their rooms at varying prices. Yield management is composed of a set of demand forecasting techniques, which are used to determine whether the room rates should be raised or lowered, and whether a reservation should be accepted or rejected in order to maximize revenue. Thus, we can define yield management in the hotel industry as 'a technique based on the principle of demand and supply, used to maximize the revenue generation of any hotel by lowering prices to increase sales during off season (low demand period) and raising the prices during peak season (high demand periods)'.

Hotels fulfil the three essential conditions for revenue management to be applicable:

- *There is a fixed amount of resources available for sale*: Hotels have a limited inventory of rooms available for sale to guests.
- *The resources sold are perishable*: In case the rooms are not sold on a particular day, the revenue is lost forever. This means that there is a time limit to selling the rooms, after which the revenue for the day is last.
- *Different customers are willing to pay a different price for using the same amount of resources*: Business customers would not mind paying higher room rates

and may book rooms closer to the stay dates, whereas families and guests on vacation are price sensitive and may book much ahead of the stay dates and would want to pay lower room rates.

Pricing and demand are inter-related and need to be coordinated. In the hospitality industry, demand for a room is cyclic in nature and follows a trend. Revenue management models help pinpoint demand by minimizing uncertainty and producing the best possible forecast. Revenue management helps in the allocation of the inventory of hotel rooms among the different segments of guests. For example, a hotel has two categories of rooms at Rs 2,000 and Rs 4,000. As the pricing is different for the two rooms, each of them is targeted at different customer sets. Based on the historical preference pattern of guests in each segment, it would be possible to estimate the number of guests who would be willing to buy these rooms at a given price with a reasonable variance. For example, an average of 100 guests may be willing to pay Rs 4,000 for some rooms, but it could also mean that the actual number of guests who arrive at the hotel for rooms at Rs 4,000 could be 110 or even 90 with some probability, or 120 or 70 with a lesser probability.

Revenue managers seek to maximize revenue by controlling forecast information with the help of the three tools illustrated in Fig. 16.1.

Selective Overbooking or Capacity Management Capacity management involves various methods of controlling and limiting room supply. The availability of rooms plays a vital role in taking advance booking of hotel rooms. Hotel managers, based on their experience and historical data available, often take chances to book more rooms than the total inventory of rooms in the hotel. Overbooking is the practice of intentionally selling more rooms than available, in order to offset the effect of cancellations, no-shows, and early departures. For example, though the total number of available rooms in a hotel are 200, 220 rooms may be booked on a certain day. Since the probability of exactly 200 guests turning up is low, the income from the additional guests generally compensates the loss of revenue. The availability of rooms increases in the following situations:

Early departure/understay When guests leave the hotel before their expected date of departure, the number of vacant rooms increases. If a provision is not made, the

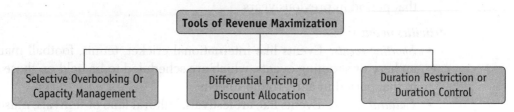

Fig. 16.1 Tools of revenue maximization

newly-vacated room will remain unsold, which would result in the loss of revenue. To avoid this situation, hotels generally discourage early departure.

Cancellations Cancellation is another major factor that increases the availability of rooms. The guests are free to cancel a booking made before a stipulated time. There are times when guests cancel their reservations after the stipulated time, which increases the number of available rooms. If a provision is not made, this would result in unsold rooms and loss of revenue.

No-shows It is a condition in which guests with confirmed bookings do not turn up at the hotel on the expected date of arrival, without any prior intimation. This also leads to the increase in the inventory of rooms. In case of non-guaranteed reservations, if the guest does not arrive on or before the cancellation hours (generally 6:00 p.m.), the room is released to waitlisted guests or walk-ins. In case of guaranteed reservations, if the guest does not arrive, the room is kept vacant and one day charge is levied on the guest and adjusted against the advance deposit. However, no-shows result in increasing the room availability of the hotel, which leads to the loss of revenue in case the room is not sold.

To avoid the loss of revenue from any of the above-mentioned situations, hotels generally prefer overbooking. Overbooking is not done by mere guesswork. Selective overbooking is done by considering the following factors:

Past history of data related to:
- *Cancellation statistics:* The number of cancellations received in those dates or that period (festival time or special events scheduled in the city, etc.) in previous years. For example, for a reservation for 31 December, the manager would check the previous year's statistics and also keep in mind that the day being the New Year's Eve, the hotel would be on high occupancy.
- *Understay statistics:* The number of guests who stayed for less than their reserved days in those dates or that period in previous years.
- *No-show statistics:* The number of no-shows during those dates or that period in previous years.
- *Turn away statistics:* The number of guests who were turned away or were denied reservations due to non-availability of rooms during those dates or that period in previous years.

Activities in town:
- *Sporting events:* Events like international cricket, tennis, football matches, or archery or shooting events, which are scheduled to be held on those dates or in that period in and around the city.
- *Cultural events:* Events like art festivals, cultural fairs or festivals, music shows, etc. which are scheduled to be held on those dates or in that period.

- *Business events:* Events like trade fairs, business conferences, which are scheduled to be held on those dates or in that period.
- *Protest/unrest/emergency etc.:* Events like curfews, bandhs, etc., scheduled to be held on those dates or in that period.

The experience of the reservation manager The reservation manager can tell from experience how many of the reserved guests will actually turn up.

Selective overbooking varies slightly with room types. The overbooking of lower priced rooms is advantageous because in case of oversell (i.e., there are no cancellations or no-shows, all the confirmed guests arrive at the hotel, and rooms are not available), the guests can be upgraded to a higher category room. The percentage of overbooking will depend upon the demand for higher-priced rooms in that duration. Overbooking should be avoided in cases where the hotel has only one or two rooms of the requested category, like presidential suites, luxury suites, etc. In case there is a reservation request for a suite, which has already been confirmed, the second reservation should be put on a waitlist. The guest should be informed that the confirmation of their waitlisted reservation is subject to cancellation. Selective overbooking or capacity management balances the risks of overbooking against potential loss of revenue from reservation cancellations, early departures, and no-shows.

Differential Pricing or Discount Allocation Price of goods or services may be defined as 'the value of the goods or services expressed in terms of money'. Price is a major criteria for a guest while choosing a hotel for stay. The pricing of a hotel's accommodation products is based on its demand in the market. Yield management attempts to get the right sales mix. It is next to impossible for a hotel to sell its rooms at rack rate at all times. A hotel must therefore have a sales strategy that will allow it to sell the maximum number of rooms at the best rates (to satisfy the projected demand for rooms at that rate), while at the same time filling the rooms that would have otherwise remained unsold at a discounted rate. Let us understand this by an example.

Let's suppose the Cricket World Cup final match is being organized at Mohali's (town adjacent to Chandigarh) PCA Stadium in the month of February. This is the peak season to visit north India. Moreover, during the month of February, Chandigarh celebrates 'Festival of Gardens'—a three day extravaganza that is flooded with various cultural programmes. During this period, hotels also sell packages for marriages.

From the above-mentioned situation, we can see that a large number of people will be coming to Chandigarh. These will include:

- People (Indians and foreigners) to watch the cricket match.
- Tourists, as it is the peak season for visiting the place.

- People to visit or participate in the Festival of Gardens.
- People to attend marriages.

This will lead to a high demand for rooms in Chandigarh during the above-mentioned period. In this situation, hotels may not offer any discount on room tariff and will prefer to charge the rack rate as they are confident that the demand for rooms would be more than the supply of available rooms.

During the lean time or off peak season, when the occupancy is low, the supply of rooms is more than its demand. In this situation, hotels offer discounted rates to attract more number of guests who otherwise might not have planned to stay at that hotel or visit that city. Hotels may offer off-season rates, package plans, special offers, etc. to attract more business.

A hotel normally offers discounts as under:

Rack rate (no discount) : Offered to walk-ins during peak season.

10% to 20% discount   : Offered to travel agents, groups, regular guests.

30% to 40% discount   : Offered to large travel agents and major companies.

50% to 60% discount   : Offered to very large multinational companies, holiday planners, conference and convention planners.

Duration Restriction or Duration Control Duration restriction is another tool of yield management. Duration control places time constraints on accepting reservations, in order to protect sufficient space for multi-day requests. For example, a hotel may refuse a reservation request for one-night stay, even though rooms are available for that night, as accepting such a reservation will block occupancy on adjacent days. Hotels located in a city generally witness lean occupancy during weekends and high occupancy during week days. Figure 16.2 shows the graphical representation of the occupancy trend in a downtown hotel during a week.

The situation is reverse for resort hotels at vacation destinations. Figure 16.3 shows the graphical representation of the occupancy trend in a holiday resort during a week. A hotel may exercise the length of stay restriction to control the imbalance of occupancy during the week. If the rooms of a hotel are sold out on one day of the week (e.g, on Wednesday in Fig. 16.2), the hotel will not be able to take bookings for two or more days including the sold-out day. As this will lead to a loss of potential revenue, hotels may turn down requests for single night booking on days of higher occupancy. Hotels may also offer special rates if the guests are willing to stay on lean days like weekends in downtown hotels. A similar practice may be used in hotels that are patronized by holidaymakers. The resorts located at holiday destinations like hill stations and sea beaches, where the hotels are almost sold out on weekends, may practice the length of stay restriction to neutralize the imbalance of occupancy during week days and weekends.

Normally, a hotel practices minimum length stay restrictions in case of a special event happening in the city. Let us suppose there is a mega show on Saturday.

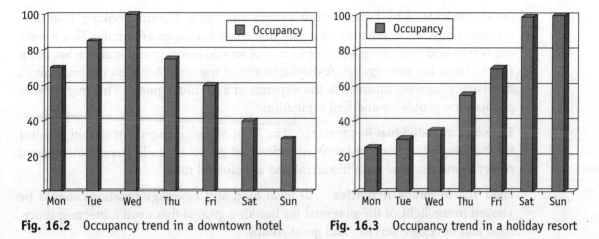

Fig. 16.2   Occupancy trend in a downtown hotel   **Fig. 16.3**   Occupancy trend in a holiday resort

The hotel's occupancy will adversely suffer on Sunday when guests, who've come specially for the event, leave. The hotel may exercise a minimum three-day stay restriction to take a booking for Saturday. This will bring down the imbalance of occupancy during the week. The hotel may also put restrictions of minimum and maximum lengths of stay to make a balance of occupancy throughout the duration. So, hotels may implement duration restriction on room bookings to protect rooms for multi-day reservations and thus higher levels of revenue.

Elements of Yield Management

While developing a successful yield strategy, the following elements (illustrated in Fig. 16.4) are very important:

Group Room Sales   By studying group booking data, hotels can anticipate group behaviour and accordingly make provisions (for cancellations, modifications, etc.) in group reservations. The group's booking pace indicates the rate at which group business is being booked as per the historical trends. Anticipated group business helps watch out for repetitive group patterns and accordingly forecast the pressure

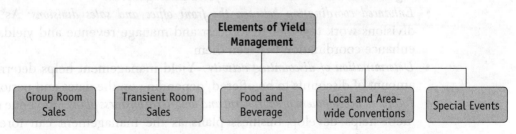

Fig. 16.4   Elements of yield management

on the market, and hence adjust selling strategies. Group booking lead-time measures how far in advance of a stay the group bookings are made. This is very important in determining whether to accept an additional group and at what room rate to book the new group. A displacement of transient business occurs when a hotel accepts group business at the expense of individual guests. This might cause profitability problems and bad reputation.

Transient or Individual Room sales   The front office management should monitor the booking pace and lead-time of individual guests to understand how current reservations compare with historical and anticipated rates.

Food and Beverage Activities   All local food and beverage functions should be viewed in the light of the potential for booking groups that need a meeting space, food and beverage service, and guest rooms.

Local and Area-wide Activities   Even when a hotel is not in the immediate vicinity of a convention, individual guests and small groups, who have been displaced by the convention, may be referred to your hotel (as an overflow facility) and this may have a tremendous impact on the hotel's revenue.

Special Events   During special events (like concerts, festivals, and sporting events), hotels might decide to benefit from high demand by restricting room rate discounts or requiring a minimum length of stay.

Benefits of Yield Management

There are a lot of benefits associated with the use of yield management in the hospitality sector, especially in hotels. These benefits include the following:
- *Improved forecasting*: Revenue management helps improve forecasting.
- *Improved seasonal pricing and inventory decisions:* It helps in deciding the season and off season pricing for accommodation products and also in making important inventory decisions like renovation.
- *Identification of new market segments:* New market segments can be identified on the basis of yield management.
- *Identification of market segment demands:* The demands of the targeted market segments can be identified with yield management.
- *Enhanced coordination between the front office and sales divisions:* As the two divisions work together to forecast and manage revenue and yield, it helps enhance coordination between them.
- *Determination of discounting activity:* Yield management helps determine the amount of discounts to be offered, depending on the dates and periods.
- *Improved development of short-term and long-term business plans:* Revenue management helps develop business plans as the management can forecast the revenue that can be generated and take measures to generate those figures.

- *Establishment of a value-based rate structure:* It helps define rates structures, based on perceived values.
- *Increased business and profits:* Good revenue management helps increase revenue and profits.
- *Savings in labour costs and other operating expenses:* As most of the revenue management tools are computerized, it helps in saving labour costs and other operating expenses.
- *Initiation of consistent guest-contact scripting:* Revenue management helps initiate consistent contact with guests.

Yield Management Strategies

Revenue management strategies differ during high demand and low demand periods.

High Demand During high demand periods, as indicated by the forecasts, the management would use the following tactics:

- Close or restrict discounts to generate more revenue.
- Apply minimum length of stay restrictions carefully.
- Reduce group room allocations as groups get very low room rates.
- Reduce or eliminate 6 p.m. holds to avoid last moment no-shows or cancellations.
- Tighten guarantee and cancellation policies to avoid last moment no-shows or cancellations.
- Raise rates as consistent with competitors to generate optimum revenue.
- Consider a rate increase for packages instead of giving more discounts.
- Apply rack rates to higher category of rooms like suites and executive rooms.
- Select dates that are to be closed-to-arrivals.
- Apply deposits and guarantees to the last night of stay.

Low Demand During low demand periods, as indicated by the forecasts, the management would use the following tactics:

- Sell value and benefits like spa treatments.
- Offer packages and special offers.
- Keep discount categories like advance purchase rates, corporate rates open.
- Encourage upgrades.
- Offer stay-sensitive price incentives.
- Remove stay restrictions.
- Establish relationships with competitors.
- Lower rates to attract more guests and to generate more revenue for the hotel.

In order to implement these tactics, the management establishes the hurdle rate (i.e., the lowest rate for a given day) below which it is impossible to sell any room.

Challenges or Problems in Yield Management

The yield management techniques and the models of overbooking, if applied aptly, would definitely maximize the revenue of the hospitality industry. But there are some challenges or problems in this, which include:

- *Measuring performance of a yield management system:* Occupancy rates and yield are measures that are affected by external competition. Therefore, an ideal measurement can be done using the opportunity model, i.e., if the hotel segments the market and fixes different rates for different guests, then it has to see that the revenue is generated from those rooms and it has to be utilized ideally.
- *Guest satisfaction:* Some guests do not like the practice of differential pricing. In evaluating the efficiency of yield management system, the trade off between generating short-term profits and creating long-term guest loyalty needs to be studied carefully.
- *Employee malpractice:* Revenue management may influence the employees to follow wrong practices. For example, hotels might offer incentives to the staff for selling higher category rooms and this might motivate the reservation agents to upsell while making reservations. So the agents might not sell the basic category rooms and offend certain guests.

MEASURING YIELD

The revenue generated by a hotel can be measured by yield management. As discussed earlier, yield is the ratio of actual revenue generated to the potential revenue that could have been generated by the hotel in a particular period. The hotel may determine its potential revenue as under:

1. All rooms sold at rack rate on double occupancy.
2. By taking an account of the percentage of rooms normally sold at single and double occupancy.

Let us understand this concept with the help of an example. Hotel Sun Star has 600 rooms (200 single rooms and 400 double rooms). The hotel is currently running on 75 per cent occupancy, with an average room rate of Rs 2,500. The hotel is offering:

- Single room at Rs 3,500 for single occupancy
- Single room at Rs 4,000 for double occupancy
- Double room at Rs 4,500 for single occupancy
- Double room at Rs 5,000 for double occupancy

Potential Average Single Rate   It is the ratio of the single occupancy revenue to the total number of rooms. Hotel Sun Star, as in the above case, is offering rooms for single occupancy at different rates, based on the category of the rooms. If the hotel sells all rooms in single occupancy, the potential room revenue will be:

Room Category	No. of Rooms	Room Rate (in Rs)	Revenue at 100% Single Occupancy (in Rs)
Single Room	200	Rs 3,500	7,00,000
Double Room	400	Rs 4,500	18,00,000
			25,00,000 (Total)

The potential average single rate can be calculated as under:

$$\text{Potential average single rate} = \frac{\text{Single occupancy room revenue}}{\text{Number of rooms (total)}}$$

$$= \text{Rs } 25,00,000/600$$
$$= \text{Rs } 4,166.67$$

Potential Average Double Rate   It is the ratio of the double occupancy revenue to the total number of rooms. Hotel Sun Star, as in the above case, is charging double occupancy at different rates, based on the category of the rooms. If the hotel sells all rooms in double occupancy, the potential room revenue will be:

Room Category	No. of Rooms	Room Rate (in Rs)	Revenue at 100% Double Occupancy (in Rs)
Single Room	200	Rs 4,000	8,00,000
Double Room	400	Rs 5,000	20,00,000
			28,00,000 (Total)

The potential average double rate can be calculated as under:

$$\text{Potential average double rate} = \frac{\text{Double occupancy room revenue}}{\text{Number of rooms (total)}}$$

$$= \text{Rs } 28,00,000/600$$
$$= \text{Rs } 4,666.66$$

Multiple Occupancy Percentage   Multiple occupancy percentage determines the average number of guests per room sold. It is calculated as the ratio of the number of rooms occupied by more than one guest to the number of occupied rooms. It represents the sales mix and helps in balancing rates with future demand for occupancy. Let's suppose in the case of Hotel Sun Star, 270 rooms are occupied by more than one guest. The multiple occupancy percentage can be calculated as under:

$$\text{Multiple occupancy percentage} = \frac{\text{No. of rooms occupied by more than one guest}}{\text{No. of occupied rooms}} \times 100$$

$$\text{Or,} \frac{\text{No. of rooms occupied by more than one guest}}{\text{Total number of rooms} \times \text{Occupancy ratio}}$$

$$
\begin{aligned}
\text{Total no. of occupied rooms} &= \text{No. of rooms} \times \text{occupancy percentage} \\
&= 600 \times 75\% \\
&= 450 \text{ rooms} \\
\text{Multiple occupancy percentage} &= 270/450 \\
&= 0.6 \text{ or } 60\%
\end{aligned}
$$

Rate Spread   The mathematical difference between potential average double rate and potential average single rate is called rate spread. The determination of a room rate spread among various room types plays a vital role in the use of yield decisions in targeting specific market segments for the hotel.

$$
\begin{aligned}
\text{Rate spread} &= \text{Potential average double rate} - \text{Potential average single rate} \\
&= \text{Rs } 4,666.66 - 4,166.67 \\
&= \text{Rs } 500
\end{aligned}
$$

Potential Average Rate   Potential average rate is a collective statistic that effectively combines the potential average single rate, multiple occupancy percentage, and rate spread. It is calculated as under:

$$
\begin{aligned}
\text{Potential average rate} &= (\text{Multiple occupancy percentage} \times \text{Rate spread}) + \\
&\quad \text{Potential average single rate} \\
&= \text{Rs } (0.6 \times 500) + 4166.67 \\
&= \text{Rs } 300 + 4166.67 \\
&= \text{Rs } 4466.67
\end{aligned}
$$

Room Rate Achiever Factor   The percentage of the rack rate a hotel actually receives is contained in the hotel's achievement factor, also referred to as the rate potential percentage. Yield management software computing this factor uses the weighted average of the rack rates of the rooms actually sold. It can also be calculated as under:

$$
\begin{aligned}
\text{Achievement factor} &= \text{Actual average rate/Potential average rate} \\
&= \text{Rs } 2500/\text{Rs } 4466.67 \\
&= 0.56
\end{aligned}
$$

Yield   Yield is the ratio of realized revenue to potential revenue. It can be expressed as under:

$$Yield = \frac{Actual\ revenue\ generated}{Potential\ revenue}$$

$$Or,\ Yield = \frac{Total\ rooms\ sold}{Total\ available\ rooms} \times \frac{Actual\ average\ room\ rate}{Potential\ average\ room\ rate}$$

Since, total rooms sold/total available rooms is the occupancy percentage and the actual average room rate/potential average room rate is the achievement factor, therefore, yield can also be calculated as:

$$Yield = Occupancy\ percentage \times Achievement\ factor$$

In the case of Hotel Sun Star, the yield will be:
$$Yield = 0.75 \times 0.56$$
$$= 0.42\ or\ 42\%$$

FORECASTING

According to New Oxford Intermediate Learner's Dictionary, forecast means 'to say (with the help of information) what will probably happen in future'. Thus, forecasting is the prediction of future happenings, based on the precise analysis of the data available rather than guesswork. Forecasting plays an important role in short-term planning.

Benefits of Forecasting

In the hotel industry, reservation forecasting is very useful in the following ways:
- It helps the reservation or revenue manager to project future volume of business and the revenue that would be generated by the hotel.
- The volume of reservations will help the front office manager and the management of the hotel to plan the following:
  - Staff requirement in each department for the smooth functioning of the hotel.
  - Minimum inventory of items required by each department to carry out their tasks efficiently.
  - Allocation of resources to serve the guests in the best possible way.
  - Maintenance and replacement requirements of the furniture, fixtures, and ultimately the property, as the wear and the tear of these depends on the number of people using it.
  - Special arrangements to be made for the arrival of groups, commercially important persons (CIPs) and VIPs.
- The reservation forecast will provide the necessary data to the reservation manager to practise yield management.

- The reservation manager will be able to take selective overbooking, based on the reservation forecast.
- The forecast data provides information about the lean days when the occupancy will be low; the sales department may take the necessary actions to attract the business for those durations.
- The forecast data will also reveal the sold out dates, which will ensure that the reservation agent does not accept reservations for those days.

Data Required for Forecasting

Forecasting gives an estimate of the revenue that should be generated by a hotel in near future. Forecasting, which is a difficult skill to develop, can be acquired through the effective and efficient tracking of records, by using accurate mathematical calculations, and through experience. The front office managers, by virtue of their experience, have found that the following information is necessary for making an accurate forecasting:

- Thorough product knowledge.
- A good judgement about what could happen in the future.
- Thorough knowledge about their area of operation in the hotel.
- The profile of the target market to which the hotel is catering.
- The events that are scheduled in the area during the forecasted period.
- Percentage of no-shows.
- Overstay percentage.
- Understay percentage.
- Turn-down statistics.
- Future plans for renovation or addition of more rooms in the property.
- Future plans regarding the opening of any new property in the vicinity of the hotel.
- A precise knowledge about the room status in competitor's property.
- Knowledge about competitor's plans with respect to activities (like renovations), which will reduce the supply of rooms in their property.
- Cancellation statistics.
- Wash out percentage (Travel agents normally book more number of rooms than the actual size of the group, to meet any last minute demand for the package tour. The same is cancelled, if they fail to sell those extra packages. The number of such cancellations is known as the wash out factor.)

Records Required for Forecasting Room Availability

The forecasting of room availability is not done on mere guesswork. Forecasting the availability of rooms requires the following information about the past trend in the same period:

- The number of arrivals on each day during the same periods.
- Number of walk-ins.
- Number of understays.
- Number of check-outs.
- Number of no-shows.
- Number of overstays.
- Cancellations.

Percentage of Walk-ins   The percentage of walk-ins is calculated by dividing the total number of walk-ins in that duration by the total number of arrivals in the same duration and then multiplying by 100. To understand the calculation, let us look at the occupancy history of Hotel ABC for the first week of June 2008 in Table 16.1

$$\text{Walk-in Percentage} = \frac{\text{Total no. of walk-ins in a specific duration}}{\text{Total no. of arrivals in that specific duration}} \times 100$$

$$= 100/325 \times 100$$

$$= 30.76\%$$

The higher percentage of walk-ins makes it difficult for the hotel to forecast accurate room availability as the number of walk-ins cannot be predetermined. The same would vary on a day to day basis, depending on various factors which are not in the control of the hotel.

Table. 16.1   Occupancy history of Hotel ABC

					Hotel ABC					
					Occupancy History					
First week of June 2008										
Day	Date	In House Guests	Arrivals	Walk-ins	Reservations	No-shows	Occupied Rooms	Overstay	Under-stays	Check-outs
Sun	1/6	120	75	15	70	5	95	7	1	35
Mon	2/6	150	50	20	45	10	120	9	5	45
Tue	3/6	175	65	18	50	12	115	12	4	34
Wed	4/6	115	55	16	45	9	90	5	3	75
Thu	5/6	85	40	9	35	7	50	3	0	85
Fri	6/6	80	25	7	25	5	55	2	8	21
Sat	7/6	50	15	15	15	2	40	4	5	40
Total		775	325	100	285	50	565	42	26	335

Percentage of Understay   When a guest checks out before his expected date of departure as mentioned at the time of the booking or at the time of registration, it is known as understay. The percentage of understay is calculated by dividing the total number of understays during the forecast period by the total number of check-outs in the same period, and then multiplying by 100.

$$\text{Understay percentage} = \frac{\text{Total no. of understays in a specific duration}}{\text{Total no. of check-outs in that duration}} \times 100$$

$$= 26/335 \times 100$$

$$= 7.76\%$$

Understays lead to the availability of more rooms at the last moment, which cannot be sold by the efforts of the front office and sales department. This results in the loss of revenue. The condition is reverse in the case of overstays when the occupancy is lean—then the hotel generates extra revenue. The front desk employees should always re-confirm the expected date of departure from the guest at the time of registration.

Percentage of No-shows   If a guest with a confirmed reservation does not arrive at the hotel on the date of arrival (and does not convey his change of plan to the hotel), it is known as no-show. The no-show percentage helps the front office manager to decide the early release of rooms to chance guests or walk-ins. The no-show percentage can be calculated by dividing the total number of no-shows in a specific duration by the total number of bookings made in the same period and then multiplying by 100.

$$\text{No-show percentage} = \frac{\text{Total no. of no-shows in a specific duration}}{\text{Total no. of reservations in that specific duration}} \times 100$$

$$= 50/285 \times 100$$

$$= 17.54\%$$

Percentage of Overstay   Guests staying beyond their expected date of departure are known as overstays. The percentage of overstays can be calculated by dividing the total number of overstays in a specific duration by the total number of check-outs in the same period and then multiplying by 100. Overstays result in lowering the room availability. This condition is favourable in lean season as hotels generally run on low occupancy levels and can accommodate the request for overstay. But it creates problems during peak season when the hotel might be booked to its capacity and cannot accommodate the request for overstay. The percentage of overstays, calculated from the data of Hotel ABC, is as under:

$$\text{Overstay percentage} = \frac{\text{Total no. of overstays in a specific duration}}{\text{Total no. of check-outs in that duration}} \times 100$$

$$= 42/335 \times 100$$

$$= 12.53\%$$

Once the above statistics are gathered, one can forecast the total availability of rooms for any particular day by processing the information as under:

Total availability of rooms = Total number of guest rooms – Out of order rooms – Total number of stayovers – Total number of reservations + Number of reservations × Percentage of no-shows + Number of understays – Number of overstays

Forecasting helps in developing revenue management strategies of the hotel. Accuracy in forecasting is achieved by the proper analysis of information available to the manager and also by the personal experience of the manager.

YIELD MANAGEMENT PROSPECTS

Yield management is a comparatively new concept. It has the following prospects in the future:

One-to-one revenue management

- Sophisticated hotels will move to one-to-one revenue management, where each individual will be a market segment in himself.
- In the future, technology will support calculating the total customer value and the potential total customer spend, based on history and future potential from demographics, to determine what rate and what availability should be offered to a potential guest.

Total customer value integration

- The future of revenue management will include a focus on the Revenue Per Available Guest (RevPAG) and total customer value.
- The next generation of revenue management systems will create offers based on the value or the potential value of each individual guest.

Function room yield

- Forecasting and yielding of function space will be a focus in the future for hotels.
- Many large hotel companies and revenue management systems are working to develop effective models in this area.

Cost of business analysis

- Different revenue streams and channels do not yield the same profit, even when the rate is exactly the same.

- In the future, channel cost will be incorporated into rate and inventory decisions for each channel individually.

Goal alignment

- The goals of the entire hotel team, from the property or hotel level to corporate, will need to be aligned in order for revenue management to reach its full potential.

Automation

- There is a gap between the sophistication of the revenue management practice and the technology available to support it.
- Adoption of the new available technologies and the use of minds to manipulate them expertly would help achieve ultimate success.

Yield management is thus a technique to optimize the revenue earned from a fixed, perishable resource. It tries to maximize revenues by managing the trade-off between a low occupancy and higher room rate scenario (for example business customers) versus a high occupancy and lower room rate (for example vacation customers). The challenge for revenue managers is to sell the right resources to the right customer at the right time. Revenue management adopts a systematic approach, ensures pricing and rate integrity, values sound inventory management, establishes a solid distribution network, recognizes total lifetime value of business, and recognizes superior service experiences affecting profitability.

SUMMARY

In this chapter, we have studied about yield and the various techniques are used to maximize revenue generation in the hospitality industry. Yield is the ratio of actual revenue generated to the potential revenue. The airlines industry pioneered the concept of yield management. These techniques are applicable to all highly perishable products and services. Yield management is a pricing strategy based on the principle of demand and supply. When demand exceeds supply, the prices are raised and when supply exceeds demand, the prices are lowered to attract more business. In hotel industry, the yield management tools are selective overbooking of rooms, differential pricing, and duration restriction. Forecasting provides information on projected revenue generation for a specific duration. In the later part of the chapter, we have discussed how forecasting for room availability is done and the future of yield management.

KEY TERMS

Differential pricing A pricing strategy in which a hotel charges different rates for the same product from different people.

Forecasting It is the prediction of future happenings based on a precise analysis of data available.

Hurdle rate Lowest rate for a given day.

Overbooking A situation when a hotel books more rooms than its total inventory of rooms.

Potential revenue The maximum revenue that can be generated from the operation of any business.

Understay When a guest departs from the hotel before his expected date of departure.

Upsell To try to persuade a customer to buy a more expensive item (room category) or to buy a related additional product at a discount.

Wash out factor Last-minute cancellation made by travel agents.

Yield The ratio of total output generated to actual potential.

Yield management A technique, based on the principle of demand and supply, used to maximize revenue generation of any hotel–by lowering prices to increase sales during low demand periods and raising prices during high demand periods.

REVIEW QUESTIONS

Multiple Choice Questions

1. Which of the following tools are utilized to practise yield management?
   a) Selective overbooking
   b) Differential pricing
   c) Duration restriction
   d) All

2. Yield management originated in
   a) Airlines   b) Cruise lines
   c) Railways   d) Hotels

3. Selective overbooking is also termed as:
   a) Booking management
   b) Capacity management
   c) Hotel management
   d) General management

4. For good forecasting one requires:
   a) Analysis of data   b) Future events in town
   c) Experience   d) All

5. ADR stands for
   a) Average Daily Rate
   b) Average Dormitory Rate
   c) All Day Rate
   d) Actual Daily Rate

True/False

1. Yield management is a technique based on the principle of demand and supply, used to maximize the revenue generation of any hotel.

2. Turn away means a situation when a hotel has to say no for reservation due to non-availability of rooms for sale.

3. No-show means the guest does not want to show their identity proof.

4. Forecasting can be done by any employee at the front desk.

5. Accurate forecasting requires careful analysis of data and experience of the front office manager.

Fill in the Blanks

1. The maximum revenue that can be generated from the operation of any business is known as _____ revenue.

2. When a guest departs from the hotel before his expected date of departure, it is called _____ stay.

3. When a guest departs from the hotel after his expected date of departure, it is called _____ stay.

4. The ratio of total output generated to actual potential is known as _____.

5. A situation when a hotel books more rooms than its total inventory of rooms is known as _____.

Discussion Questions

1. What do you understand by yield?

2. Explain how selective overbooking improves revenue generation.

3. Explain in which situations hotels should practice duration restriction for room reservation.

4. What pricing strategy should a hotel follow when the room demand is low and which strategy should be followed when the room demand is high?

5. What are the various factors which determine the availability of the rooms?

6. What is no-show percentage? How is it calculated?

7. What is meant by forecasting of room availability? What points should one keep in mind while forecasting?

8. What are the major benefits of forecasting?

9. What skills and information are required to make an accurate forecast?

CASE STUDIES

1. The reservation department of Hotel Taj View, located in Agra, has forecast lean occupancy during the months of June and July. This is the duration which has no festivals and is the peak of summer. The temperature of the city generally remains above 40°C. There are no group bookings in this duration. What measures will you take as the revenue manager to generate revenue in that lean season?

2. The peak season for Hotel Connaught Palace is during October to February. This duration has many festivals and marriages and is most suitable for visiting the place. Also, in the month of January, a national level athlete meet and an all India doctors conference are scheduled. Hotel Connaught Palace is booked to its capacity for most of the period. There are very few rooms available in the said month. Mr Sanjay Singh, a noted personality and a frequent visitor to the hotel, who has a discount card from the hotel, calls for reservation for a single room in that duration for a week. The reservation agent, as instructed by their supervisor, quotes the rack rate for the reservation. Mr Singh gets irritated and decides to stay somewhere else.

a) Discuss the impact of such an event on the future business of the hotel.

b) Was the reservation assistant right in quoting the rack rate?

3. Hotel Shanti Palace is located in the heart of a metropolitan city. The hotel has 100 rooms. The reservation manager, Subhash, found that the present policy of the hotel prevents the reservation department from taking more than 100% of the available rooms. On further analysis of past data, he found that 10% confirmed reservations turned into no-shows. On the analysis of the same, it was discovered that it resulted in the loss of 3,650 room nights during a year, resulting in a financial loss of Rs 91,25,000 (ADR being Rs 2,500). Subhash took the problem to the management and discussed with the General Manager of the hotel to formulate the policy for overbooking, so that the revenue loss can be minimized.

If you were the General Manager of the hotel, what policy would you make to cover the loss of revenue due to no-shows? Discuss in detail the following points:

a) Consequences if the no-show percentage is less than 10%

b) Accuracy of the formula for accepting overbooking

c) Strategy to combat overstays and no-shows.

4. The following occupancy history is available from Hotel Maurya Mahal for the first week of April.

Calculate the following:

a) No-show percentage

b) Walk-in percentage

c) Understay percentage

d) Overstay percentage

Hotel Maurya Mahal
Occupancy History

First week of April

Day	Date	In House Guests	Arrivals	Walk-ins	Reservations	No-shows	Occupied room	Overstay	Under-stay	Check-out
Mon	1/4	125	90	15	70	5	95	7	2	35
Tue	2/4	150	45	20	45	10	120	9	5	45
Wed	3/4	275	75	18	50	10	115	20	4	34
Thu	4/4	115	35	20	45	9	90	5	6	75
Fri	5/4	85	40	9	35	6	50	3	0	85
Sat	6/4	80	25	23	25	15	55	2	8	36
Sun	7/4	55	15	15	15	10	40	4	5	40
Total		885	325	120	285	65	565	50	30	350

REFERENCE

http://dspace.iimk.ac.in/bitstream/2259/566/1/ 270-278+Vani+Kamath+-+Revenue+Managemen t+techniques+in+hospitality+industr2.pdf, last accessed on 16 September 2008.

www.eiacademic.org/uploadedFiles/_Common/ppt/ Products/Books/TM13-333.ppt, last accessed on 17 September 2008.

CHAPTER 17

Hospitality Marketing

Learning Objectives:

After reading this chapter, you will be able to understand the following:
- Introduction to marketing.
- Basic concepts of marketing, elements of marketing mix, and market segmentation.
- Sales and marketing of hospitality products—sales and marketing team and sales techniques.
- Budget—types of budgets and budgetary control.

In the previous chapter, we learnt about yield management and forecasting techniques to help increase revenue generation. Nowadays, with cut-throat competition between hotels of the same competitive set, a hotel has to have a good sales and marketing team to gain maximum business from the market. In this chapter, we will look at the basic concepts of marketing and the elements of marketing mix.

It is important to exercise strict control over expenditure and to minimize costs in order to run any profitable business. Budgets play an important role in controlling costs. In this chapter, we will also understand budget, various types of budgets, and budgetary control.

INTRODUCTION TO MARKETING

Marketing is a comprehensive term that includes all resources and activities necessary to direct and facilitate the flow of goods and services from the producer to consumers in the process of distribution. Marketing is often regarded as a management function concerned with the promotion and sale of products to the end users. Other management functions like finance and human resources provide back-end support to marketing. The process of marketing is illustrated in Fig. 17.1.

The two most significant activities in marketing are:
1. Matching the product with the demand, i.e., matching the room, or conference hall, or restaurant with the consumer needs and desires or the target market.
2. Monitoring every stage of flow of goods from the primary producer to the end user.

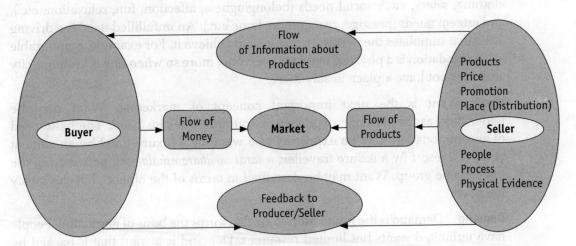

Fig. 17.1   The marketing process

Exhibit 17.1   Definitions of marketing

The American Marketing Association defines marketing as 'the process of planning and executing the conception, pricing, promotion and distribution of ideas, goods and services to create exchanges that satisfy individual and organizational objectives.'

The British Institute of Marketing defines marketing as 'the management process for identifying, anticipating and satisfying customers requirements profitably.'

According to Philip Kotler, 'marketing is the analysis, planning, implementation, and control of carefully formulated programs designed to bring about voluntary exchange of values with target markets for the purpose of achieving organizational objectives. It relies heavily on designing the organization's offerings in terms of the target markets' needs and desires, and on using effective pricing, communication, and distributions to inform, motivate, and service the markets.'

From the various definitions of marketing given in Exhibit 17.1, we can infer the following:

- Marketing is a managerial process that involves principles of management, like analysis, planning, implementation, and control.
- Marketing is identified as a process which identifies, expands, and serves the material need of the people.
- Marketing attempts to bring voluntary exchanges of goods and service with values.
- Marketing is the implementation of carefully formulated programmes.

Basic Concepts of Marketing

The key concepts of marketing are illustrated in Fig. 17.2.

Need Need is the basic concept of marketing. It is a positive, motivational factor that compels action for its satisfaction. It includes basic physical needs (food, warmth, clothing, safety, etc.), social needs (belongingness, affection, fun, relaxation, etc.), and esteem needs (prestige, recognition, fame etc.). An unfulfilled need is a driving force that stimulates the person to pursue and achieve it. For example, comfortable accommodation is a physical need for everyone, more so when one is visiting a city and does not have a place to stay there.

Want Want is the next important concept of marketing. Want may be understood as the way one expresses or communicates his need. The basic need of accommodation may be expressed as a want for a luxury hotel by an affluent person; a resort by a leisure traveller; a *sarai* or *dharamshala* by a person from the low-income group. Want may be described in terms of the objects that can satisfy the need.

Demand Demand is the foundation stone that forms the basis of marketing. People have unlimited wants but limited resources. Demand is a want that is backed by

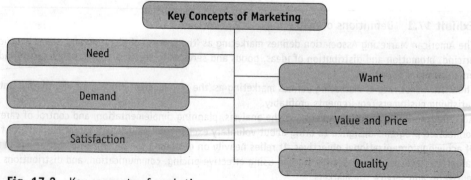

Fig. 17.2 Key concepts of marketing

the ability and willingness to pay for the product. Thus, only those wants become a demand that qualify the following:

- The ability to pay for the service or product that a person wants (if one wants something but is not in a position to pay for the same, the want will not turn into demand).
- The person should be willing to pay (if a person has enough amount to pay for a product but is not willing to pay the amount that is quoted by the seller/ producer, it will not qualify as effective demand. For example, if a person has Rs 10,00,000 but is not willing to pay the rent of Rs 25,000 for a suite in a hotel, it will not be an effective demand).

Product A product is a good or service that is the end-result of a process and serves as a need or want satisfier. It is usually a bundle of tangible and intangible attributes (benefits, features, functions, uses) that a seller offers to a buyer for purchase. People satisfy their needs and wants by using desired products. For example, when people stay in a five-star hotel, they satisfy their basic need of shelter, along with the needs of prestige, status, and ego. Thus, it is evident that a product should be able to satisfy the basic as well as hidden needs of the consumer.

Value Value is the extent to which a good or service is perceived by its customer to meet his needs or wants, measured by the customer's willingness to pay for it. It commonly depends more on the customer's perception of the worth of the product than on its intrinsic value. When the value of any item is expressed in terms of money, it is known as price. According to customers, value is the difference between the benefits that they will gain from owning and/or using a product and the cost of obtaining the product, which can be both monetary as well as non-monetary.

Satisfaction Satisfaction is an expression of a customer's approval that a product's performance meets his expectations. If the product/service meets the customer's expectation, it leads to customer satisfaction. If the product/service or its performance falls short of the customer's expectations, the buyer is dissatisfied. If the product/service exceeds the customer's expectations, it leads to customer delight. A delighted person is an unpaid advertiser for the product as he will give a positive feedback of the product to other potential users. A guest who is delighted with a hotel's service will come back to it and will also share his experience with his colleagues, friends, and family.

Quality Quality is the totality of features and characteristics of a product or service that bear on its ability to meet customers' needs. It has a direct impact on product or service performance and is closely linked to customer value and satisfaction. The fundamental aim of today's total quality movements has become total customer satisfaction.

Marketing Mix

Marketing mix is a planned mix of the controllable elements of a product's marketing plan, commonly known as 4 Ps: product, price, place, and promotion. The basic marketing mix is the blending of these four inputs which form the core of the marketing system. Apart from these, service marketing relies upon extra three Ps: people, process, and physical evidence (Fig. 17.3). These elements are adjusted until a right combination is found that serves the needs of the product's customers while generating optimum income. The task of a marketing manager is to integrate these variables into a marketing mix that meets the needs of each consumer group or market segment targeted by the organization.

In the marketing mix, the 7 Ps model can be represented by three concentric circles (Fig. 17.4). The innermost circle contains the focal point of marketing efforts—the consumer. The middle circle contains the marketing mix—product, price, promotion, place, people, process, and physical evidence (also called controllable variables). And the outer circle represents the uncontrollable variables like economic environment, political and legal situations, socio-cultural environment, etc.

Product/Service A product is a good or service that most closely meets the requirements of a particular market or segment and yields enough profit to justify its continued existence. It possesses utility for the end user. The product or service mix is always considered first, as without it the industry has nothing to distribute, promote, or price. The hospitality industry offers products like guest rooms, banquet halls, food and beverages; and services like valet parking, housekeeping, butler, express check-in and check-out services, etc.

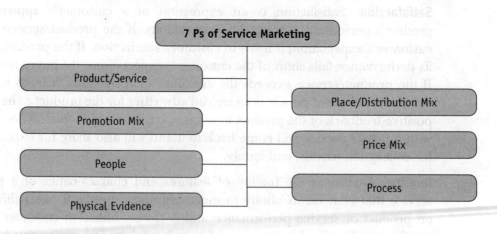

Fig. 17.3 The 7 Ps of service marketing

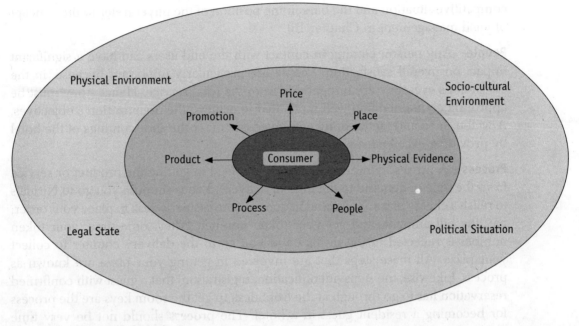

Fig. 17.4   The marketing mix

Place/Distribution Mix   In marketing mix, place is the location of the market and means of distribution used in reaching it. It refers to the accessibility of products to the end users. The distribution of consumer goods is achieved by shipping the products to the consumer, done through retail stores and local *kirana* shops. In the case of hospitality products, the consumer has to travel to a hotel to receive the benefits of the products and services that are offered by the hotel. The distribution channels of hospitality products may be direct (having their own sales team) or indirect (through travel agent, tour operators, intersell agencies, Internet, global distribution systems, etc.)

Promotion Mix   Promotion is the advancement of a product, idea, or point of view through publicity and/or advertising. A promotion mix includes all the means through which hotels communicate with their prospective guests. It consists of methods like advertisements in print and electronic media, sales promotions, personal selling, publicity, public relations, fam-tours, and exhibitions.

Price Mix   Price is the market value, or agreed exchange value, that will purchase a definite quantity, weight, or other measure of a good or service. Pricing is very important in the marketing mix. Hotels, especially large properties, often develop variable-rate policies to meet the needs of different market segments and charge different prices from different buyers of the same product, depending upon the competitive situation and the bargaining position of the buyer (refer to the concept of yield management in Chapter 16).

People   Any person coming in contact with the end-users can have a significant impact on overall satisfaction. People are particularly important because, in the consumer's eye, they are inseparable from the total service. Hence, they must be appropriately trained and well motivated to achieve the organization's objectives. A well-trained and tactful hotel employee can mask the shortcomings of the hotel by providing excellent services to guests.

Process   A process comprises the steps involved in getting the product or service from the time of demand to the time of delivery. Let us suppose you go to Nirula's to relish a cheese pizza. You stand in queue at the cashier's desk to place your order, pay the bill amount, and get your token number. After some time, your token number is reflected in the display and you go to the delivery counter to collect your pizza. All these steps that are involved in getting your pizza are known as process. Likewise, the steps (identification, registration) that a guest with confirmed reservation has to go through at the front desk to get the room keys are the process for becoming a resident guest in a hotel. The process should not be very time consuming, otherwise it will adversely affect guest satisfaction.

Physical Evidence   Unlike a product, a service cannot be experienced before it is delivered, which makes it intangible. So it is often vital to offer potential customers a physical equivalent of what a service would be like. The physical items that a customer will see must reflect the image that the service is trying to project. This will determine the customer's decision regarding the favouring and selection of a service. For a hotel, for example, towels, pens, notepads etc. all count as physical evidence and must portray the brand of the hotel. The brochures containing photographs, descriptions of the types of rooms with the facilities offered in each room type also act as physical evidence.

Market Segmentation

A market segment is an identifiable group of individuals, families, organizations or firms, sharing one or more characteristics or needs in an otherwise homogenous market. Market segments generally respond in a predictable manner to a marketing or promotion offer. Market segmentation is the process of defining and sub-dividing a large homogenous market into clearly identifiable segments having similar needs, wants, or demand characteristics. Its objective is to design a marketing mix that precisely matches the expectations of customers in the targeted segment. Segmentation is a consumer-oriented marketing strategy. Market segmentation gives formal recognition to the fact that wants and desires of consumers are diverse and we can formulate a specific market offering to a specific category or segment of the market, so that the supply will have the best correlation with demand. Varied and complex buyer behaviour is the root cause of market segmentation.

The hospitality market has two broad market segments: group market segment and transient market segment (Fig. 17.5).

Group Market Segment   The group market constitutes the segments that provide high volume and bulk business to hotels. The group market segments include: corporate market, tour operators, meetings/conferences/seminars, expositions, incentive travel, and extended stay market. As they provide high volume and continuous business to hotels, they generally get good tariff deals from hotels.

Corporate market   The corporate market provides bulk business to hotels as executives of business houses regularly visit different cities on official work. A contractual agreement is generally made between business houses and hotels to attract business from the corporate sector.

Tour operators   Tour operators generally purchase rooms in bulk at highly dis-counted prices because they provide a high volume of business to hotels. After making such bulk purchases, they prepare tour packages for their clients.

Meetings/Conferences/Seminars   Meetings, conferences, seminars are one of the major markets for the hotel industry. They provide bulk business to hotels and are generally organized by corporate sectors, institutions, and other organizations for the following reasons:
- To evaluate the performance of the company, departments, or employees.
- To discuss the introduction of new product/service by the company.
- To introduce new methods of operations.

These result in the requirement of a venue and other support services to hold these programmes. Hotels with well-appointed meeting halls and board rooms

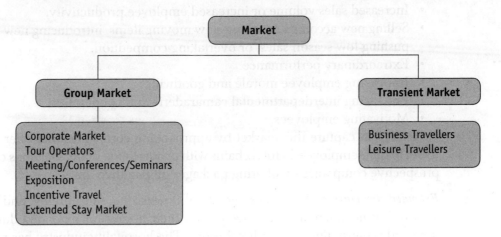

Fig. 17.5   Market segments

can capture this market. A conference centre is a specialized hospitality operation dedicated to facilitating and supporting conferences. It provides a venue for the conference, ministerial services required by the attendees as well as the organizer, telecommunication facilities, public address system, audio-visual aids, flip charts, white boards, projectors, screens, etc. In the case of residential conferences and meetings, the hotel or conference centre should have adequate number of guest rooms to accommodate the attendees of the conference.

Expositions   Trade shows and exhibitions bring together individuals and organizations associated with a common business or activity for the purpose of reviewing, demonstrating, marketing, and selling materials and products related to their common interest. The basic function of a trade fair is to facilitate the exchange of information between companies and prospective buyers. Trade fairs may be of the following types: industrial shows, trade shows, road shows, professional or scientific exhibitions.

Trade fairs and exhibitions cater to those who have a specific demonstrative relationship to the event and may or may not be open for the common public. They attract a large number of domestic as well as foreign attendees. The hotel may contact the officials arranging the trade show in order to become a co-sponsor or the official host of the show. This would help the hotel gain more room sale. Trade shows last for several days and thus have the scope for a large number of room sales.

Incentive travel   Incentive travel is travel that is given to employees as a reward for outstanding performance. This is a popular mode of motivating employees to outperform in their work and align their productivity to achieve the organization's objectives. Organizations may offer incentive tours to their employees for the following reasons:
- Increased sales volume or increased employee productivity.
- Selling new accounts or selling slow moving items, introducing new products, pushing low season sales, or overtaking competition.
- Extraordinary performance.
- Improving employee morale and goodwill.
- Enhancing interdepartmental camaraderie and cooperation.
- Motivating employees.

Hotels can capture this market by approaching companies that offer incentive travel to their employees. Hotel chains with properties at many locations can attract prospective companies by offering packages of incentive tours.

Extended stay market   In today's climate of downsizing, outsourcing, and mobility, a lot of businessmen are often away from their homes for extended durations of time and require more than a hotel room. The hospitality industry has responded to the growing demand for extended stay rooms. To capture this new segment, hotels feature rooms with full kitchen, safes, larger closets, and other amenities in rooms.

Transient Market Segments   The transient market segments provide comparatively low number of room sales as compared to the group market. This segment includes business and leisure travellers. They travel in smaller numbers and stay for shorter durations than group travellers. These segments provide less volume of business to the hotel and may be charged higher than the other segments that provide larger volume of business.

SALES AND MARKETING OF HOSPITALITY PRODUCTS

The sale of hotel rooms and other products is a joint effort of the hotel's sales and marketing division as well as the reservation department. The sales and marketing department is responsible for bulk sales of a hotel's major hospitality product— rooms. The reservation section deals with direct calls for the sale of rooms (room reservation). It can only get business that lands in the section through various modes of reservation requests—like in-person, telephone calls, e-mails, letters, faxes, etc.— and is not able to attract new business.

Sales and Marketing Team

In order to sell their products, hotels generally have their own sales and marketing teams or hire the service of any external agency specialized in this field. A team of sales and marketing personnel constitute the sales office of a hotel. The executives of the sales and marketing department make regular visits to existing corporate clients, travel agents, and tour operators, and generate new business.

The organization of the sales and marketing division depends upon the size, location, and volume of business of a hotel. Small hotels may have only sales persons; medium to large hotels may have a well-organized sales and marketing department with head of department, assistant sales manager, sales executives, and other administrative staff; and hotel chains may have a corporate office with vice president/director sales, regional managers, sales executives, and a well appointed office with administrative staff. The organization of sales and marketing department of small, medium, and large hotels is shown in Fig. 17.6.

Vice President of Sales and Marketing   The head of the sales and marketing division of a hotel chain with centralized marketing is designated as vice-president. He is involved in framing policy guidelines for the entire sales and marketing activity of the hotel.

Regional Sales and Marketing Manager   The regional manager of sales and marketing division of a hotel chain is responsible for the attainment of the sales

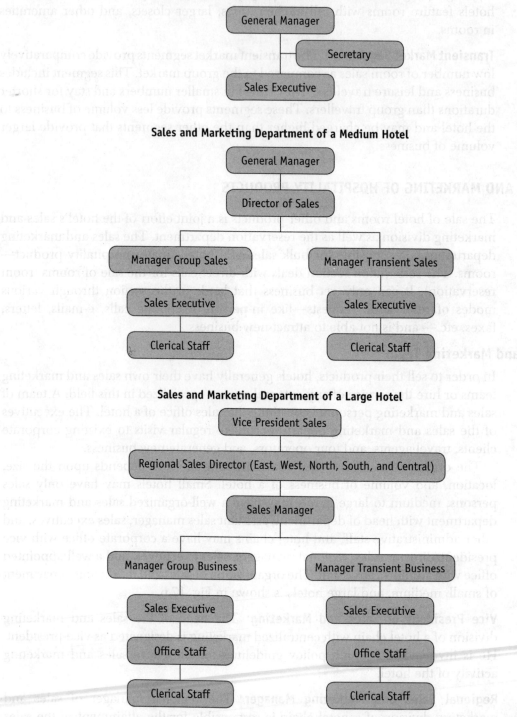

objectives of the hotel(s) within the purview of their region. A regional manager provides the directives to the sales managers of her region. She may call for regular meetings to discuss new guidelines, progress of the assigned assignments, and status of implementation of policy guidelines.

Sales and Marketing Managers   In small hotels, this position might be synonymous with the director of sales, whereas in a larger hotel, a sales manager will report to the director of sales. The sales and marketing manager usually assigns targets to sales executives, monitors their progress, and handles their own accounts. The specific duties of a sales manager will depend upon the size, location, and volume of business that the hotel receives from its market segments.

Sales Executives   Sales executives are the backbone of the sales department. They are the ones who give sales calls to the target market segments. They are responsible for contacting, soliciting, and providing follow-up services to the clients. In a small property, a sales executive handles all types of businesses. They give sales call to travel agents, tour operators, corporate clients, business houses, and other sources of potential business. In large hotels, they may be given specific tasks like individual or transient business, group business, crew business, domestic business, international business, etc.

Sales Techniques

A hotel may use various techniques to increase the sale of its room and other hospitality products. The most widely used techniques to boost sales of hotel rooms are personal sales and telephone sales.

Personal Sales   Personal sales technique is one of the most effective tools for selling hotel rooms. A personal sales call is used to build rapport with potential customers in order to sell the hospitality products offered by the hotel. The following steps are involved in personal sales techniques:

1. Prospecting.
2. Preparation for the presentation of a sales call.
3. Presentation of the sales call.
4. Overcoming objections.
5. Closing and follow up.

Prospecting   The first step of personal sales technique is estimating the possibility of opening a sales account. Prospecting is preparing a list of probable companies and individuals who might be contacted for getting business. A prospect may be from past referrals, community contacts, other property employees, etc.

Preparation for a sales call   A sales call may fail due to inadequate planning, anxiety, or nervousness of the sales person, and also the failure of the sales person to contact the decision-maker. The preparation for a sales call is very important in materializing the sales call. The proper planning for sales presentation includes:

- Thorough product knowledge.
- Competition research.
- Client research.

Presentation of a sales call The presentation of a sales call involves familiarizing clients with the prospects of your products and services, in order to convince them to use the same. It is the actual delivery of the facts and figures that you have prepared for presentation.

Overcoming objections Objections from prospective clients may arise at any point of time during the sales presentation. The client may have a doubt or might have misunderstood your point. It is important to overcome these objections and satisfy the client to win the business.

Closing sales and follow up One should evaluate a sales call by asking the prospects questions about their response towards the products or services offered to them. A favourable response shows the success of the sales call and you may close the deal. The next step is to constantly follow up with the client in future.

Telephone Sales Technology has enabled sales personnel to attract business without leaving their office—through telephone, Internet, etc, which can be an effective instrument for:

- Searching sales leads.
- Fixing sales appointment.
- Identifying target prospects.
- Selling additional services.
- Following up with the client.

A telephone sales call is made by an executive of the telemarketing team. Members of the telemarketing team are given proper training to carry out telephone sales calls. The mannerism and etiquette of a telesales person affect the response of the prospective clients. The call should be made after taking proper appointment from the client. A telephonic sales call is as good as a face-to-face interaction with a client and requires similar planning and preparation.

Hotels use a mix of the sales techniques to maximize hotel sales and generate optimum revenue for their organization. We have gained an understanding of various elements of hospitality marketing. Let us now understand the importance of budget and budgetary control, and various types of budgets.

BUDGET

According to Oxford Advanced Learner's Dictionary, budget is 'the money that is available to a person or an organization and a plan of how it will be spent over a period of time.' According to The Chartered Institute of Management Accountants, London, budget is defined as 'a financial and/or quantitative statement, prepared prior to a defined period of time, of the policy to be pursued during that period for the purpose of attaining a given objective'. Budget is a detailed estimated plan of operations for a specific future period. It acts as a yardstick for the evaluation of the performance of the organization as it is a complete programme of activities of the business for the period covered.

Thus, we find that the essentials of budget are:

- It is prepared in advance and is based on a future plan of action.
- It is based on objectives to be attained in future.
- It is a statement expressed in monetary and/or physical units.

Types of Budget

Budgets are generally prepared for the next financial year. There are several types of budgets that are prepared by an organization. Some of them are illustrated in Fig. 17.7.

Capital Expenditure Budget   The capital expenditure budget provides guidance as to the amount of capital (the overall assets of an individual/corporation less liabilities) needed for acquiring capital assets (assets with a lifespan of more than a year) during the budgeted period. Furniture, fixture, and equipments are among the constituents of capital expenditure budget. Some of the common items of the front office included in the capital expenditure budget are telecommunication equipments (such as EPABX, telephone instruments with special features), computers, new and improved software for front office department, billing machines, self service terminals, etc.

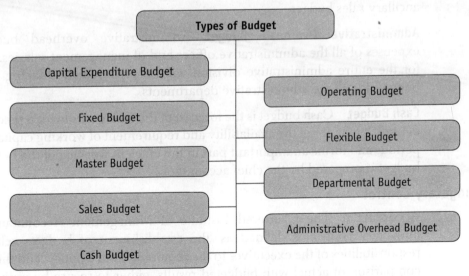

Fig. 17.7   Types of budget

Operating Budget   Operating budget is the financial statement that is associated with the routine operations of a hotel. Operating expenditure is the cost that a hotel incurs in the process of generating revenue during its normal operation. It includes salaries, wedges, and direct labour cost.

Fixed Budget   Fixed budget is a budget that is prepared on the basis of standard or fixed level of activity. It does not change with the level of activity.

Flexible Budget   Flexible budget is a budget prepared in a manner so as to give the budgeted cost for any level of activity. These are prepared after considering the fixed and semi-variable elements of cost and the changes that may be expected for each item at various levels of operation.

Master Budget   Master budget, known as final budget, is the summary of all the budgets that are prepared in the organization. According to The Chartered Institute of Management Accountants, London, master budget is defined as 'the summary budget, incorporating its component functional budgets, which is finally approved, adopted, and employed'.

Departmental Budget   Departmental budget is the budget that is prepared by individual departments of a hotel, containing the proposed estimates of revenue and expenditure for a specific duration of time. Examples of departmental budget include front office budget, housekeeping budget, food and beverage service budget, etc.

Sales Budget   Sales budget is essentially the forecast of the sales to be achieved in a budgeted period. The sales budget is generally prepared by the sales manager. The hotel may prepare the room sales budget, food and beverage sales budget, and ancillary sales budget.

Administrative Overhead Budget   Administrative overhead budget covers expenses of all the administrative offices and of management salaries. The budget for the entire administrative division will be prepared by totalling the separate budgets for all the administrative departments.

Cash Budget   Cash budget is the forecast of the cash position for a specific duration of time. It tells about the availability and requirement of working capital at different periods and forms an important part in the efficient working of the hotel. The cash budget is prepared by the chief accountant.

Budgetary Control

According to The Chartered Institute of Management Accountants, London, budgetary control is defined as 'the establishment of budgets relating to the responsibilities of the executives to the requirement of a policy, and the continuous comparison of actual with budgeted results, either to secure by individual action the objective of that policy or to provide a basis for its revision'. Budgetary control has now become an essential tool of the management for controlling costs and maximizing profits.

Thus, the budgetary control involves:

- Establishment of budgets.
- Continuous comparison of actual results with budgeted ones to attain the organization's objective.
- Ascertaining the responsibility for failure in the achievement of budgeted targets.
- Revision of budgets in the light of changed environment.

Advantages of Budgetary Control Budgetary control is a useful management tool for comparing actual results with the budgeted result. This practice has the following advantages:

- It brings efficiency and economy in the business enterprise.
- It establishes departmental responsibility.
- It acts as a safety signal for the management.

SUMMARY

The sales and marketing division of a hotel is responsible for procuring business for the hotel. This department works in close coordination with the front office because they both sell a common hospitality product—the room. In the present chapter, we have looked at basic marketing concepts, elements of marketing mix, market segmentation, sales and marketing team, and sales techniques.

Budgeting is essential for any organization. A budget is the blueprint of how the generated revenue will be utilized to achieve the objectives of the company. Budgets are of different types—such as capital expenditure budget, operating budget, fixed budget, flexible budget, master budget, departmental budget, sales budget, administrative overhead budget, and cash budget—and are an effective management tool for judging the performance of the organization. The management of a hotel may exercise budgetary control for controlling costs and maximizing profits.

KEY TERMS

Budget The money that is available to a person or an organization, and a plan of how it will be spent over a period of time.

Budgetary control The establishment of budgets relating to the responsibilities of the executives to the requirement of a policy, and the continuous comparison of actual with budgeted results, either to secure by individual action the

objective of that policy or to provide a basis for its revision.

Demand It is a want which is backed by the ability and willingness to pay for the product.

Marketing It is the management process for identifying, anticipating, and satisfying customers' requirements profitably.

Need It is a positive, motivational factor that compels action for its satisfaction.

Place/Distribution Mix It is the location of the market and means of distribution used in reaching it. It refers to the accessibility of products to the end users.

Price Mix It is the market value, or agreed exchange value, that will purchase a definite quantity, weight, or other measure of a good or service. Hotels, especially large properties, often develop variable-rate policies to meet the needs of the different market segments.

Product It is a good or service that is the end-result of a process and serves as a need or want satisfier. It is usually a bundle of tangible and intangible attributes that a seller offers to a buyer for purchase.

Promotion Mix Promotion is the advancement of a product, idea, or point of view through publicity and/or advertising. Promotion mix includes all the means through which hotels communicate with their prospective guests.

Prospecting Estimating and preparing a list of probable companies and individuals who might be contacted for getting business.

Quality It is the totality of features and characteristics of a product or service that bear on its ability to meet customers' needs.

Satisfaction An expression of a customers' approval that a product's performance meets his expectations.

Value It is the extent to which a good or service is perceived by its customers to meet their needs or wants, measured by the customers' willingness to pay for it.

Want: It may be understood as the way how one expresses or communicates his need.

REVIEW QUESTIONS

Multiple Choice Questions

1. The Ps of marketing are:
   - a) Product
   - b) Price
   - c) Promotion
   - d) All

2. The additional Ps related with service marketing are:
   - a) People
   - b) Process
   - c) Physical evidence
   - d) All

3. The group market segment includes:
   - a) Group
   - b) Tour operators
   - c) Travel agencies
   - d) All

4. Promotion-mix includes:
   - a) Advertisement
   - b) Personal sales
   - c) Publicity
   - d) All

5. The physical evidence for a hotel guest will be:
   - a) Hotel brochure
   - b) Air ticket
   - c) Rail pass
   - d) Theatre tickets

True/False

1. Budget is a plan of how to spend a mentioned amount of money over a particular period of time.

2. Budget can be used as a tool for control.

3. Master budget is also known as final budget.

4. Demand is a want which is backed by the ability and willingness to pay for the product.

5. Value of any item when expressed in terms of money is known as price.

Fill in the Blanks

1. The _____ possesses utility for the end user.

2. The steps involved in getting the product or service from the time of demand to the time of delivery are collectively known as _____ .

3. A travel trip to motivate employees at work is known as _____ .

4. _____ is guessing the possibility of opening a sales account.

5. The process of sorting target market to find the most suitable buyer is called _____ .

Discussion Questions

1. Define marketing. Explain the basic concepts of marketing.

2. What do you understand by the term 'marketing mix'? Explain with a suitable example.

3. Marketing segmentation is among the key factors of running a successful hospitality business. Comment.

4. Draw the organization chart of sales and marketing department of a hotel and explain the duties of a sales executive.

5. Explain the following sales techniques in detail:
   a) Personal sales
   b) Telephone sales

6. Define budget. What are the different types of budget? Explain each in detail.

7. What do you understand by the term 'budgetary control'? Explain its major advantages.

CRITICAL THINKING QUESTIONS

1. The sales and marketing department of a hotel is very essential for generating profitable business for the hotel. Comment.

2. Budget can be a tool for control. Explain.

CASE STUDY

1. Hotel Plaza has 150 rooms, three banquet halls, and one board room, and is located in the heart of the city. The hotel targets groups as well as business clients as its market segments. There are two more competitors for the same market: Hotel Starview and Hotel Grand. Both have larger banquet halls and more number of guest rooms. Hotel Grand opened the previous month and is located in the proximity of the business hub of the city. Assume you are the marketing manager of Hotel Plaza. Prepare the marketing plan for it to increase its market share. Focus on the following points:

   • Corporate market
   • Tour operators
   • Meeting/conferences/seminars
   • Exposition
   • Incentive travel
   • Extended stay market
   • Business traveller
   • Leisure traveller

CHAPTER 18

Human Resource Management

Learning Objectives:

After reading this chapter, you will be able to understand the following:
- Human resource management—human resource planning and human resource development.
- Job analysis—job description and job specification.
- Recruitment, selection, and orientation.
- Human resource challenges in the hospitality industry.
- Employee retention and employee motivation.

Efficient, hard working, and resourceful personnel are the backbone of any successful business. It is more so in the case of the service industry. Successful hotel operations are sustained by customer-oriented and hard working employees who have adequate competencies. The human resource department of a hotel is engaged in anticipation, acquisition, selection, and development of the present and future employee needs of the hotel. The present chapter discusses human resource planning and human resource development. It also includes the processes of job evaluation, recruitment, selection, and orientation. The challenges faced by the human resources department in the hospitality industry are also discussed, as also the ways to boost employee retention and employee motivation.

HUMAN RESOURCE MANAGEMENT

Human resource management (HRM) is the management of people to achieve behaviour and performance levels that will enhance an organization's effectiveness. It is a management function that helps managers plan, recruit, select, train, develop, remunerate, and maintain members for an organization. HRM encourages individuals to set personal goals and rewards, guiding them to shape their behaviour in accordance with the objectives of the organization that employs them.

HRM was traditionally called personnel management, a term which was used in the restricted sense of hiring and managing employees. The current trends place a greater emphasis on boosting the morale of employees and the ways of retaining employees—by using more sophisticated psychological tests in selecting employees, by training employees to do more than one job, and by encouraging all the members of a workforce to accept responsibility.

HRM can be studied under the following two subheads:
- Human resource planning
- Human resource development

Human Resource Planning

Human resource planning may be defined as 'a strategy for the acquisition, utilization, improvement, and preservation of the human resource of an organization'. The major activities of human resource planning include:

Forecasting   It is the process of estimating the future manpower requirements, which helps to allocate cost and plan recruitment activities accordingly.

Inventorying   Human resource planning also analyses the inventory of skills present and develops plans to utilize the same.

Planning   Human resource planning initiates the necessary programmes of recruitment, selection, training, development, motivation, and compensation so that the future needs of manpower will be met.

Human Resource Development

Human resource development (HRD) is the process of helping people acquire competencies and skills so as to ensure their usefulness to the organization in terms of both present and future organizational conditions. HRD also helps employees understand their own capabilities better, so that they can best utilize them and also fulfil their professional and personal expectations.

In an organizational context, HRM is a process that helps the employees of an organization in a continuous and planned way to:
- Acquire or sharpen capabilities required to perform various functions associated with their present or expected future roles.

- Develop their general capabilities as individuals and teams; discover and exploit their inner potential for their own and organizational growth and development purposes.
- Develop an organizational culture in which supervisor-subordinate relationships, teamwork, and collaboration among sub-units are strong and contribute to the professional well being, motivation, and pride of employees.

Job Analysis

Job analysis is the process of collecting information about a particular job position. It may be defined as 'a process of studying and collecting information relating to the operations and responsibilities of a specific job'. The process of job evaluation results in the generation of a large chunk of data related to a job position. The collected data can be grouped into the following sub categories:

- Job description
- Job specification

Job Description   Job description is a document that contains duties, responsibilities, and all the tasks that constitute a job position. It specifies the parameters within which a job is done. It not only includes duties and responsibilities but also contains report relationships, working conditions, authority and control, coordination with other departments, status within departmental hierarchy, equipments and materials to be used, and other information specific to the hotel. A sample job description of a front office manager is shown in Fig. 18.1.

Job Specification   Job specification is a document that contains information about the skills and qualities required for a position. It includes information such as personal qualities, skills, formal education, professional/technical qualification, work experience, general knowledge, previous training, physical skill, equipment skill, and communication skills of a person. A sample job specification of a bell boy is shown in Fig. 18.2.

Purpose of Job Analysis   Job analysis is useful for the overall activities of the HR department. The information generated during job analysis helps the department in the following activities:

Human resource planning   As discussed, human resource planning is the activity that assesses the present and future requirements of manpower for the organization. Job analysis helps the human resource manager to decide on the skills needed in the organization to carry out the present and future tasks in the organization.

Recruitment and selection   The recruitment process of the employees begins after the organization assesses its present and future manpower requirements. Once a

JOB DESCRIPTION

JOB TITLE   : Front Office Manager

DEPARTMENT   : Front Office

REPORTS TO   : General Manager

SUPERVISE   : Reservation Manager, Front Desk Supervisor, Lobby Manager, Telephone Supervisor, and all front office personnel

CO-ORDINATES WITH   : All the heads of departments of the hotel

SCOPE OF JOB (DUTIES AND RESPONSIBILITIES):
1. Directs and coordinates the activities of the front office department.
2. Performs the function of a link between management and front office employees.
3. Plans the present and future need of resources (men, money, material, and machine) to carry out the functions of the department.
4. Prepares the budget for the front office department.
5. Schedules tasks of the front office employees.
6. Conducts regular scheduled meetings of front office personnel.
7. Assesses the number and type of employees required in the department, and also participates in the selection process of front office employees.
8. Evaluates the job performance of front office employees and fills their appraisal forms.
9. Ascertains the training needs of the employees of the department and arranges training, refresher training, and cross training.
10. Resolves guest problems quickly, efficiently, and courteously.
11. Reviews all reports generated by all the sections of the department.
12. Ensures that all the standard procedures are followed.
13. Maintains good communication with other departments.
14. Holds regular meetings of the employees of the department.
15. Resolves employee grievances.
16. Motivates the front office employees to work in a team to attain organization objectives.
17. Coordinates with the sales and marketing department to work towards maximizing the sales of hotel rooms.

Fig. 18.1   Sample job description of front office manager

recruitment position has been identified, the job description and job specification of that position are drawn up, which define the scope of the job and the skills needed. This way managers are able to delegate job responsibilities more effectively and the HR managers have a better idea about the qualities that they should look for while selecting future employees.

Training and development   The training and development activities may be tailored as per the requirements of the job. Job analysis data helps to decide the training needs and the procedure of training for the present and future employees.

Job evaluation   Job evaluation involves the determination of relative worth of each job for the purpose of establishing wages and pay packages. Job description and job specification are the foundations for the determination of relative worth of a job.

JOB SPECIFICATION

JOB TITLE	:	Bell Boy
CATEGORY	:	Non-supervisory
EDUCATIONAL QUALIFICATION	:	High School
AGE LIMIT	:	18 Years–30 Years
EQUIPMENT SKILLS	:	Should know how to use luggage trolley, public address system, etc.
PHYSICAL ABILITY	:	Sound health and ability to carry luggage up to 50 kg.
PERSONALITY CONSIDERATION	:	Presentable, well groomed, good physique.
LANGUAGE SKILL	:	Ability to communicate in English and local language(s).
EXPERIENCE	:	None. One month job training is adequate.
SPECIAL REQUIREMENTS	:	• Proficiency in English language. • Should be able to lift luggage. • Willingness to assist guests. • Should be able to work in a team.

Fig. 18.2 Sample job specification of a bell boy

Performance appraisal The assessment of the performance of employees is judged on the basis of job description. Performance appraisal is the basis for awarding promotions, effecting transfers, or ascertaining the training needs of employees.

Recruitment

The need of personnel in any organization is fulfilled by attracting the right set of people for the existing as well as future job positions in the organization. The process of attracting people with desired qualifications and traits and motivating them to apply for suitable job positions is known as recruitment. Recruitment can be defined as 'a process of finding and attracting capable applicants for employment. The process begins when new recruits are sought and ends when their applications are submitted.'

Recruitment serves the following purposes:
- It attracts highly qualified and competent people.
- It provides a pool of potentially qualified candidates for various job positions at minimum cost.
- It meets the organization's legal and social obligations regarding the composition of its workforce.
- It identifies suitable candidates for various job positions.

Sources of Recruitment   The sources of recruitment may be broadly classified in the following two categories (Fig. 18.3):
- Internal sources
- External sources

Internal Sources   The internal sources of recruitment include present employees (who can be promoted or transferred), employee referrals, and former employees. Recruiting employees through internal sources has the following advantages:
- It builds good public relations.
- It increases the morale of the employees.
- It encourages the employees to develop the required competencies.
- The employees are already accustomed with the organization culture and find it easier to settle down.
- It is an economical way of hiring people.
- It reinforces loyalty in employees.

External Sources   The external sources of recruitment include professional or trade associations, advertisements, employment exchange, campus recruitments, walk-ins, consultants, contractors, acquisitions and mergers, competitors, and e-recruiting. They are more expensive as the cost of advertisement is higher. However, the external sources generate more applicants with the desired qualifications and make the selection process more effective.

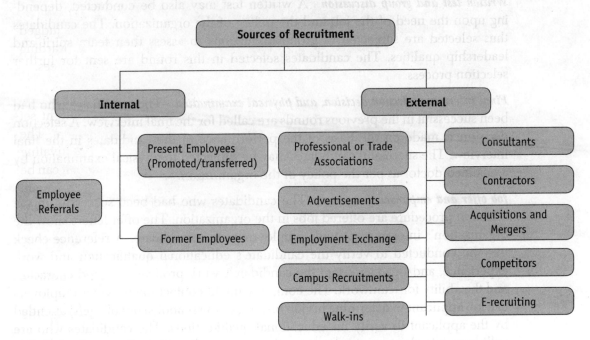

Fig. 18.3   Sources of recruitment

Selection

Selection is the process of choosing the right candidate from the pool of applications received in the recruitment process. The selection is done strictly on the basis of the skills and competencies required for the job position. A candidate with the right qualifications, skills, and traits is selected for the job. So selection may be defined as 'a process of differentiating between applicants in order to identify those with a greater likelihood of success in job'.

Selection Process Selection is a long process, depending on the policy of the organization. It starts with preliminary interviews and ends with the contract of employment and joining formalities. The sequence of the selection process is shown in Fig. 18.4.

Screening of applications The applications received during the recruitment process are screened for completeness, essential and desirable qualifications of the candidates, and the ratio of the number of vacancies to the number of candidates to be called for interviews.

Preliminary interviews A preliminary interview is conducted to pick the candidates with the desired traits. It is a screening round, which eliminates unsuitable candidates. After preliminary interviews, the desired set of candidates are subjected to further selection procedures till finally the selection of the right candidate is made.

Written test and group discussion A written test may also be conducted, depending upon the need of the job and the policy of the organization. The candidates thus selected are subjected to group discussions to assess their team spirit and leadership qualities. The candidates selected in this round are sent for further selection process.

Final interview, selection decision, and physical examination The candidates who had been successful in the previous rounds are called for the final interview. A selection decision is made on the basis of the performance of the candidates in the final interview. The successful candidates may be subjected to physical examination by a qualified doctor as per the policy of the organization.

Job offer and employment contract The candidates who had been successful in the selection procedure are offered jobs in the organization. The offer letters show the organization's interest to provide employment to a candidate. A reference check may be conducted to verify the candidate's educational qualification and work experience, and/or to ascertain the candidate's work proficiency, good character, and the ability for teamwork. The company might contact the previous employers of a job applicant to determine his job history, or the school(s) or college(s) attended by the applicant to verify his educational qualifications. The candidates who are willing to join the organization are asked to sign the employment contract. The

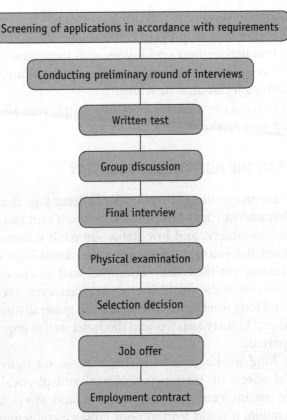

Fig. 18.4   Selection process

appointment letter mentions the following: job title, reporting relationship, joining date, salary and benefits, probationary period, notice periods, legal provisions, confidentiality clauses, job description, etc. The joining formalities include: submitting copies of original certificates and reference letters by the candidate, filling formal application forms, issuing of identity cards, and opening salary account for the new candidate by informing the accounts department.

Orientation

Orientation may be defined as 'a planned introduction of new employees to their jobs, their co-workers, the management, and the organization'. Orientation is also known as induction. It is designed to provide new employees with the information they need to work efficiently and effectively in the organization. Orientation may be informal where employees get introduced to co-workers while performing their job, or it may be a formal and structured which may extend from one week to several months.

Orientation serves the following purposes:
- It makes new employees comfortable in their new roles.
- It familiarizes new employees with their co-workers. It gives the employees on overview of the organization—work culture, functions of all departments, and organizational structure.
- It reduces the anxiety of the new employees and makes them feel at home in the new workplace.

HR CHALLENGES IN THE HOSPITALITY INDUSTRY

There are many human resource challenges in the hotel and tourism industry. The characteristic features of work in hotels and catering—long, anti-social hours, low pay, instability, and low status—make it unattractive as a career choice, and as a result the sector continues to suffer from high staff turnover and difficulties in recruiting qualified staff. The hotel staff works especially hard on those days when the rest of the world is enjoying vacations, such as Diwali, Christmas, New Year, and long weekends. The hotels are generally booked to capacity during such festival and holiday seasons and the hotel staff is required to work overtime during these periods.

The long working hours increase stress on individuals, and have potentially harmful effects on their psychological and physical health. Social effects might include an increase in family tension and stress in marital relations. For the organization, it could lead to poor labour productivity both in terms of increased absenteeism and declining marginal productivity of labour when present at the workplace but working long hours. This is sometimes referred to as presenteeism, which describes the phenomenon of being at work but achieving little or nothing.

Other key issues are: the lack of qualified staff at both operational and managerial levels, the unwillingness of university graduates to enter the industry, and the gap between what is taught in school and college and the realities of the industry itself. Together, these negative factors damage the reputation and perception of the sector. The primary challenge is to reverse this negative perception, first by improving working conditions to attract suitable staff and retain them, and second by investing in their development and taking interest in their well-being.

One of the challenges in improving working conditions is to ensure that both employees and employers engage in the process so that improvements are consistent with the aspirations and wishes of both groups—higher margins and productivity for businesses, and higher wages and a better work–life balance for employees.

Having set about improving working conditions, the next challenge is to attract and retain the correct staff. This is likely to prove difficult, as despite employees' vertical career aspirations, there is generally a lack of promotion prospects within the sector. To deal with this, some employers have focused on job satisfaction and designed systems to reward staff for their performance. In improving job satisfaction, one approach is to offer employees more variety by training them to do several tasks, i.e., so called 'multiskilling'. This way one person can do the jobs of several part-time people, which can be beneficial both for the employers and the employees.

Key employee retention is critical to the long-term success of any business. Retaining the best employees ensures customer satisfaction, product sales, satisfied co-workers and reporting staff, effective succession planning, and deeply imbedded organizational knowledge and learning. Exit interviews with departing employees provide valuable information that can be used to retain the remaining staff. The HR personnel should analyse the results of the exit interviews, come up with remedial solutions, and initiate action.

Employee Retention

The following factors are important in order to retain employees:

- *Employees should know what is expected from them every day at work*: Changing expectations keep people on the edge and create unhealthy stress. They rob the employees of the their confidence.
- *Effective supervisor*: People leave managers and supervisors more often than they leave companies or jobs. It is not enough that the supervisor is well-liked or is a nice person; he should be able to motivate and encourage his team members. Anything the supervisor does to make an employee feel unvalued will contribute to turnover.
- *Employee counselling*: The managers should have a goal to restore employees to full productivity. The HR department or the head of the department can provide confidential short-term counselling to identify an employee's problem and, when appropriate, make a referral to an outside organization, facility, or programme that can assist the employee in resolving his problem.
- *Employees should to speak their mind freely within the organization*: When organizations solicit ideas and provide an environment in which people are comfortable providing feedback, employees offer ideas, feel free to criticize, and are committed to continuous improvement. If not, they bite their tongues or find themselves constantly 'in trouble'—until they leave.
- *Talent and skill utilization*: A motivated employee wants to contribute to work areas outside of their specific job description. Many employees can contribute far more than they currently do. The HR manager and the supervisor should be able to identify their skills, talent and experience, and utilize them properly.
- *Fairness and equitable treatment*: In case one employee is given more raises or higher incentives, other staff members might find it unfair and start looking for other opportunities.

- *Tools, time, and training*: When an employee is failing at work, ask, 'What is it about the work system that is causing the person to fail?' Most frequently, employees need tools, time, and training to do their job well, which the organization must provide.
- *Frequent opportunities to learn and grow*: A career-oriented, valued employee must experience growth opportunities within the organization. Without the opportunity to grow in their careers, knowledge, and skill, they feel they will stagnate and look for better opportunities.
- *Employees should not be made to feel insecure about their jobs*: Even if a manager is aware that layoffs loom if the department's goals are not met, this information should not be shared with employees. They will get nervous and start looking for other job opportunities.
- *Employees should feel rewarded, recognized, and appreciated*: Frequently saying 'thank you' goes a long way. Monetary rewards, incentives, bonuses, and gifts make the 'thank you' even more appreciated. Salary raises, based on accomplishments and achievement, help motivate and retain staff.

Employee Motivation

Motivation may be defined as a driving and guiding force that makes people perform a particular activity to the best of their abilities. The word 'motivation' is based on the root word 'motive', which is derived from the Latin word *movere*, meaning to move. Motivation plays the following roles:

- It increases the performance level of the employees.
- It reduces employee turnover and absenteeism.
- It prepares the employees to accept organizational changes.

Motivating Employees Motivation is one of the most important factors that directly affect human behaviour and performance. Employees can be motivated by the following methods:

Training Training employees may convey to them that the organization takes necessary care of its employees. An employee who has received training has higher chances of promotions and other benefits. For example, some front office agents may be given training in the latest front office software available in the market, even if that software is not being used in the hotel at that point of time.

Cross-training Cross-training is training employees for roles other than their routine jobs. It helps the employees acquire new skills, which may lead to a career growth. For example, a housekeeping personnel may be given cross-training in front office if her interest lies in the same. Based on her success in the training, her future in the company can be charted out.

Recognition and incentives Every one wants to be recognized. Hotels generally have some employee recognition programmes like best performer of the month, best employee of the month, etc. The incentives may include:

- Certificate of appreciation
- Gift vouchers
- All expense paid holiday trips to domestic or foreign locations.

Also, as revenue management becomes increasingly integrated in hotel sales, it will need stronger human resources support. Thus, effective human resource management is the key to a hotel's success.

SUMMARY

Human resource management (HRM) is a management function that helps managers to plan, recruit, select, train, develop, remunerate, and maintain members for an organization. HRM comprises human resource planning and development. Human resource planning is a strategy for the acquisition, utilization, improvement, and preservation of the human resource of an organization. Human resource development is the process of helping people to acquire competencies and skills so as to ensure their usefulness to the organization in terms of both present and future organizational conditions. The human resource department of any organization carries out functions likes job analysis, recruitment, selection, orientation, and training. The department also faces many challenges, which include making employees cope with long working hours, finding qualified staff, etc. The means to retain and motivate employees are also discussed in the chapter.

KEY TERMS

Human Resource Management (HRM) It is a management function that helps managers to plan, recruit, select, train, develop, remunerate, and maintain members for an organization.

Human Resource Development It is the process of helping people acquire competencies and skills so as to ensure their usefulness to the organization in terms of both present and future organizational conditions.

Human Resource Planning It is a strategy for the acquisition, utilization, improvement, and preservation of the human resources of an organization.

Job analysis It is a process of studying and collecting information relating to the operations and responsibilities of a specific job.

Job description It is a document that contains a list of duties, responsibilities, and all tasks that constitute a job position.

Job evaluation It involves the determination of the relative worth of each job for the purpose of establishing wages and salary differentials.

Job specification It is a document that contains information about skills and attributes required for a particular job position, such as personal qualities, formal education, professional/technical qualification, work experience, general knowledge, previous training, physical skill, equipment skill, and communication skills.

Motivation It is a driving and guiding force that makes people perform a particular activity to the best of their ability.

Orientation It is a planned introduction of new employees to their jobs, their co-workers, the management, and the organization.

Recruitment It is a process of finding and attracting capable applicants for employment. The process begins when new recruits are sought and ends when their applications are submitted.

Selection A process of differentiating between applicants in order to identify those with a greater likelihood of success in the job.

Work-life balance A situation in which the demands of both a person's job and personal life are met.

REVIEW QUESTIONS

Multiple Choice Questions

1. The major activities of human resource planning are:

   a) Forecasting   b) Inventorying
   c) Planning   d) All

2. Sources of recruitment are:

   a) External   b) Internal
   c) Both   d) None

3. Internal sources of recruitment are:

   a) Promotions   b) Transfers
   c) Employee referrals   d) All

4. External sources of recruitment are:

   a) Employment Exchange
   b) Campus Recruitment
   c) Walk-in
   d) All

5. Motivation can be achieved by:

   a) Training   b) Cross-training
   c) Incentive   d) All

True/False

1. A strategy for the acquisition, utilization, improvement, and preservation of the human resource of an organization is known as human resource development.

2. Job specification is a process of collecting information about a particular job position.

3. Job description is a document that contains a list of duties, responsibilities, and all tasks that constitute a job position.

4. Selection has a negative approach.

5. Recruitment is also known as induction.

Fill in the Blanks

1. The process of studying and collecting information relating to the operations and responsibilities of a specific job is known as _____.

2. _____ is a document that contains information about the personal qualities, skills, and formal education required to perform a job efficiently.

3. A process of finding and attracting capable applicants for employment is known as _____.

4. _____ is the process of choosing the right candidate from the pool of applications received in the recruitment process.

5. _____ increases the performance level of employees.

Discussion Questions

1. Define human resources. Explain the importance of a human resource department of a hotel.

2. Define human resource planning. Explain the different functions performed in human resource planning.

3. What do you understand by human resource development? Explain the importance of the same.

4. Define job analysis. Explain the process of job analysis.

5. Define recruitment. Discuss the recruitment process in detail.

6. What do you understand by the term 'selection'? Explain the selection process in detail.

7. What are the challenges faced by the HR department in the hospitality sector? How can key staff be retained?

8. Explain the following in detail:
   - Orientation and induction
   - Employee motivation

CRITICAL THINKING QUESTIONS

1. Developing human resources of hotels leads to successful hotel operations. Comment.

2. Employee motivation is important for increasing the productivity of individual employees and ultimately results in better revenue generation for the hotel. Explain.

PROJECT WORK

Visit four hotels in your area and find the different employee motivation techniques being practised in the hotel. Compare the techniques of motivation being used at the hotels visited by you. Which technique of motivation is the best according to you? Explain with valid reasons.

CHAPTER 19

Environmental Management

Learning Objectives:

After reading this chapter, you will be able to understand the following:
- Environment and ecology.
- Environmental pollution—air and water pollution.
- Environmental education—formal and informal, and objectives.
- Environment legislations, environmental impact analysis, and environmental audit.
- Environment management systems, specially in the context of the hospitality industry—environment management programmes, international EMS standards.

The concern for the environment is increasing the world over day by day. Due to increased environmental pollution, most of the governments in the world have laid down certain regulations that are mandatory for industries to follow. Environmental studies is a branch of study that is concerned with environmental issues. It is essentially a multidisciplinary approach that brings about an appreciation of our natural world and the impacts of human beings on its integrity. It is an applied science that seeks practical answers to sustain the human civilization on the earth's finite resources. Its components include biology, geology, chemistry, physics, engineering, sociology, health, anthropology, economics, statistics, computers, and philosophy. In this chapter, we will discuss the concept of ecology, environmental pollution, and measures of mitigation to improve the environmental conditions. We will also discuss environment management systems, especially in the context of the hospitality industry.

ENVIRONMENT AND ECOLOGY

Environment is defined as 'the complex of physical, chemical, and biotic factors (as climate, soil, and living things) that act upon an organism or an ecological community, and ultimately determine its form and survival'. It includes land, water, and air. All the external conditions that affect the life of organisms in their natural habitats aggregate to form the environment. It may be divided into the following major heads:
- Physical or abiotic environment
- Living or biotic environment

Physical or abiotic environment   Physical or abiotic environment is composed of external physical factors such as water, minerals, temperature, gases, rainfall, earth surface, soil, humidity, etc.

Living or biotic environment   The biotic environment is composed of all the living components including plants, animals, and micro-organisms.

Beside the biotic and abiotic components, the environment is made up of the following main constituents: atmosphere, hydrosphere, lithosphere, and biosphere (Fig. 19.1).

Lithosphere   The lithosphere includes rocks, earth surface, sand, and the exposed part of earth that is not covered by water. The lithosphere began as a hot ball of matter that formed the earth about 4.6 billion years ago. About 3.2 billion years ago, the earth cooled down considerably and life began on our planet. The crust of the earth is 6 or 7 km thick and lies under the continents. Of the 92 elements in the lithosphere, only eight are common constituents of crystal rocks. Of these constituents, 47 per cent is oxygen, 28 per cent is silicon, 8 per cent is aluminium, 5 per cent is iron, while sodium, magnesium, potassium, and calcium constitute 4 per cent each. Together, these elements form about 200 common mineral compounds. Rocks, when broken down, form soil on which man is dependent for his agriculture. Their minerals are also the raw material used in various industries.

Hydrosphere   Hydrosphere is the part of lithosphere that is covered by water. It includes rivers, streams, glaciers, lakes, and sea. The hydrosphere covers three quarters of the earth's surface. A major part of the hydrosphere is the marine ecosystem in the ocean, while only a small part occurs in fresh water. Fresh water in rivers, lakes and glaciers, is perpetually being renewed by a process of evaporation

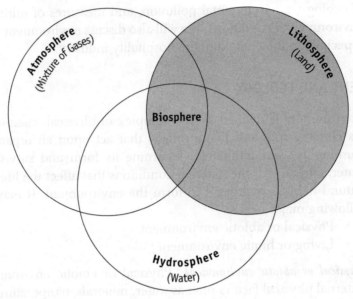

Fig. 19.1 The environment

and rainfall. Some of this fresh water lies in underground aquifers. Human activities such as deforestation damage the hydrosphere severely.

Atmosphere The lithosphere and hydrosphere are surrounded by about a 200-km thick envelope of a mixture of various gases known as atmosphere, which forms a protective shell over the earth. The lowest layer, the troposphere, the only part warm enough for us to survive in, is only 12-km thick. The stratosphere is 50-km thick and contains a layer of sulphates that is important for the formation of rain. It also contains a layer of ozone, which absorbs ultra-violet light known to cause cancer and without which no life could exist on earth. The atmosphere is not uniformly warmed by the sun. This leads to air flows and variations in climate, temperature, and rainfall in different parts of the earth. It is a complex dynamic system. If its nature is disrupted, it affects all mankind.

Biosphere This is the relatively thin layer on the earth in which life can exist. Within it, air, water, rocks, soil, and living creatures form structural and functional ecological units, which together can be considered as one giant global living system, that of our earth itself. Within this framework, those characterized by broadly similar geography and climate, as well as communities such as plant and animal life, can be divided for convenience into different bio-geographical realms. These occur on different continents. Within these, smaller bio-geographical units can be identified on the basis of structural differences and functional aspects into distinctive recognizable ecosystems, which give a distinctive character to a landscape or waterscape. Their easily visible and identifiable characteristics can be described at different scales such as those of a country, a state, a district, or even an individual valley, hill range, river or lake.

The term ecology is derived from the root words *oikos* (meaning 'house or dwelling place') and *logos* (meaning 'study'). Thus, ecology is the study of interrelationships between living organisms and their environment. The main theme of ecological studies is the relationship between organisms and their environments; hence ecology may also be called environmental science.

The two major aspects of ecology, recognized by ecologists, are:

Autecology: It is concerned with the study of individual living component or the population of the same living component in relation to environment.

Synecology: It is the study of communities, their composition, behaviour, and relationship to the environment.

ENVIRONMENTAL POLLUTION

All the living organisms depend upon a balanced environment for growth, development, and to complete their life cycle in an orderly manner. The components of environment are present in a balanced ratio; a variation in the composition of environment may hamper the normal living of people. The change that causes hindrance in the normal living of organisms is known as pollution. The agent that causes that change is known as pollutant. Environmental pollution may be defined as 'an undesirable change of physical, chemical, or biological characteristics in the atmosphere, lithosphere, and hydrosphere which is harmful to man directly or indirectly'. Pollutants include solid, liquid, or gaseous substances present in greater than natural abundance in the environment. These are produced due to human activity and have a detrimental effect on the environment. The nature and concentration of a pollutant determines the severity of detrimental effects on human health. Pollutants that enter water have the ability to spread to distant places, especially in the marine ecosystem.

From an ecological perspective, pollutants can be classified as follows:

Degradable or non-persistent pollutants   These can be rapidly broken down by natural processes, e.g., domestic sewage, discarded vegetables, etc.

Slowly degradable or persistent pollutants   Pollutants that remain in the environment for many years in an unchanged condition and take decades or longer to degrade, e.g., DDT and most plastics.

Non-degradable pollutants   These cannot be degraded by natural processes. Once they are released into the environment they are difficult to eradicate and continue to accumulate, e.g., toxic elements like lead or mercury.

Air Pollution

Any harmful change in the composition of atmospheric gases results in air pollution. The origin of air pollution on the earth can be traced from the times when man started using firewood as a means of cooking and heating. Hippocrates has mentioned air pollution in 400 BC. With the discovery and increasing use of coal, air pollution became more pronounced, especially in urban areas. It was recognized as a problem 700 years ago in London in the form of smoke pollution, which prompted King Edward I to make the first anti-pollution law to restrict people from using coal for domestic heating in the year 1273.

Air pollution occurs due to the presence of undesirable solid or gaseous particles in the air in quantities that are harmful to human health and the environment. Air may get polluted by natural causes such as volcanoes, which release ash, dust, sulphur, and other gases, or by forest fires may be caused by lightning. However, unlike pollutants from human activity, naturally occurring pollutants tend to remain in the atmosphere for a short time and do not lead to permanent atmospheric change. Pollutants that are emitted directly from identifiable sources are produced both by natural events (for example, dust storms and volcanic eruptions) and human activities (emission from vehicles, industries, etc.). These are called primary pollutants. There are five primary pollutants that together contribute about 90 per cent of the global air pollution. These are: carbon monoxide and carbon dioxide (CO and CO_2), nitrogen oxides, sulphur dioxides, volatile organic compounds (mostly hydrocarbons), and suspended particulate matter.

Pollutants that are produced in the atmosphere when certain chemical reactions take place among the primary pollutants are called secondary pollutants; e.g., sulphuric acid, nitric acid, carbonic acid, etc. Figure 19.2 shows the causes of air pollution.

Air pollution began to increase in the beginning of the twentieth century with the development of the transportation systems and intense use of petrol and diesel. The severe air quality problems due to the formation of photochemical smog from the combustion residues of diesel and petrol engines were felt for the first time in Los Angeles. Pollution due to auto-exhaust remains a serious environmental issue in many developed and developing countries, including India. The Air Pollution Control Act in India was passed in 1981 and the Motor Vehicle Act for controlling the air pollution, very recently. These laws are intended to prevent air from being polluted. The greatest industrial disaster leading to serious air pollution took place in Bhopal, where extremely poisonous methyl isocyanate (MIC) gas was accidentally released from the Union Carbide's pesticide manufacturing plant on the night of 3 December 1984. The effects of this disaster on human health and the soil are felt even today.

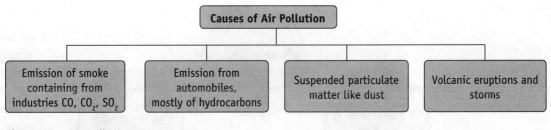

Fig. 19.2   Air pollution

Water Pollution

Water is the essential element that makes life on earth possible. Without water, there would be no life. Although 71 per cent of the earth's surface is covered by water, only a tiny fraction of this water is available to us as fresh water. About 97 per cent of the total water available on earth is found in oceans and is too salty for drinking or irrigation. The remaining 3 per cent is fresh water. Of this, 2.997 per cent is locked in ice caps or glaciers. Thus, only 0.003 per cent of the earth's total volume of water is available to us in the form of soil moisture, groundwater, water vapour, and water in lakes, streams, rivers, and wetlands.

When the quality or composition of water changes directly or indirectly as a result of man's activities, such that it becomes unfit for any purpose, it is said to be polluted. Water pollution is mainly caused by the pollutants given in Fig. 19.3.

Disease-causing Agents   The disease-causing agents include bacteria, viruses, protozoa and parasitic worms that enter water from domestic sewage and untreated human and animal wastes. Human wastes contain concentrated populations of coliform bacteria such as *Escherichia coli* and *Streptococcus faecalis*. These bacteria normally grow in the large intestine of humans. A large amount of human waste in water increases the number of these bacteria, which cause gastro-intestinal diseases.

Oxygen-depleting Agents   These are another category of water pollutants. Oxygen depleting agents are organic wastes that can be decomposed by aerobic (oxygen requiring) bacteria. The amount of oxygen required to break down a certain amount of organic matter is called the biological oxygen demand (BOD). The amount of BOD in the water is an indicator of the level of pollution. If too much organic matter is added to the water, all the available oxygen is used up. This causes fish and other forms of aquatic life dependent on oxygen to die.

Plant Nutrients   These are water soluble nitrates and phosphates that cause excessive growth of algae and other aquatic plants, a phenomena known as eutrophication. This may interfere with the use of water by clogging water intake

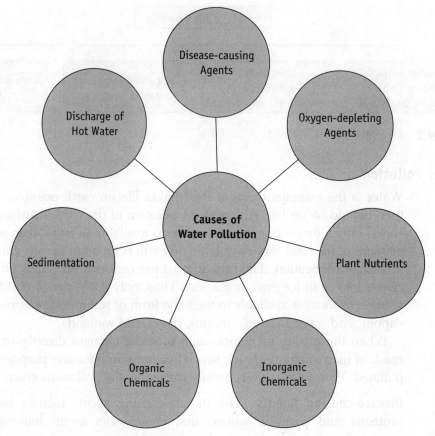

Fig. 19.3 Causes of water pollution

pipes, changing the taste and odour of water, and causing a build-up of organic matter. As the organic matter decays, oxygen levels decrease, and fish and other aquatic species die. The quantity of fertilizers applied in a field is often many times more than is actually required by the plants. The chemicals in fertilizers and pesticides pollute soil and water. While excess fertilizers cause eutrophication, pesticides cause bioaccumulation and biomagnification.

Inorganic Chemicals The water polluting chemicals are acids, salts, and compounds of toxic metals such as mercury and lead. High levels of these chemicals can make the water unfit to drink, harm fish and other aquatic life, reduce crop yields, and accelerate corrosion of equipment that use this water.

Organic Chemicals The organic chemicals include oil, gasoline, plastics, pesticides, cleaning solvents, detergents, and many other chemicals. These are harmful to aquatic life and human health. They get into the water directly from industrial activity—either from the improper handling of chemicals in industries or, more often, from the illegal disposal of chemical wastes.

Sedimentation of Suspended Matter   It is another class of water pollutants. These are insoluble articles of soil and other solids that become suspended in water. This occurs when soil is eroded from the land. High levels of soil particles suspended in water interfere with the penetration of sunlight. This reduces the photosynthetic activity of aquatic plants and algae, disrupting the ecological balance of the aquatic bodies. When the velocity of water in streams and rivers decreases, the suspended particles settle down at the bottom as sediments.

Discharge of Hot Water   Thermal pollution occurs when industry returns heated water to a water source. Power plants heat water to convert it into steam, to drive the turbines that generate electricity. For the efficient functioning of steam turbines, the steam is condensed into water after it leaves the turbines. This condensation is done by taking water from a water body to absorb the heat. This heated water is discharged back into the water body. The warm water not only decreases the solubility of oxygen but also adversely affects the breeding cycles of various aquatic organisms.

ENVIRONMENTAL EDUCATION

Rapid industrialization, development, consumerism, and population explosion have upset the ecological balance. Affluent sections of the population increase pollution level in the process of raising their living standard (by acquring refrigerators and air-conditioners that release hydrocarbons), whereas the poor sections of the society destroy their immediate environment in order to survive (by cutting down forests and letting their livestock to overgraze the grassland). People hare now realizing the threat that is posed by environmental pollution. Out of this realization has emerged the concept of environmental education.

Objectives of Environmental Education

According to UNESCO, the objectives of environmental education are:
- Creating awareness about environmental problems among people.
- Imparting basic knowledge about the environment and its allied problems.
- Developing an attitude of concern for the environment.
- Motivating people to participate in environment protection and environment improvement.
- Acquiring skills to help the concerned individuals in identifying and solving the environmental problems.
- Striving to attain harmony with nature.

The environmental education can be imparted in the following ways:

Formal Education   Environmental education is given formally in schools, colleges, and universities, etc. It is limited to a specific period and a well defined and structured curriculum.

Informal Education   Providing informal education is an answer for the majority of population that still does not have adequate access to formal education. Environmental education may be imparted by programmes that fall outside the formal education system, like *nukkad naataks, chaupal* discussions, puppet shows, eco-development camps, posters, essay writing competitions, seminars, nature camps, audio-visual slides, mobile exhibition, etc.

ENVIRONMENTAL LEGISLATIONS

The rapid growth of human populations and unbalanced distribution leads to depletion in resources and creates environmental pollution. The serious environmental degradation during the last century has urged the need for taking effective steps towards the protection of environment. In order to achieve a clean environment, there should be effective laws to protect the environment, coupled with willing cooperation and active participation of the citizens. Thus, all the governments should have a sound environmental policy. India's concern for the environment is evident from the fact that the Indian constitution has provision for environmental protection; the same can be seen in:

- Fundamental rights
- Directive principles of states policy
- Fundamental duties
- Article 47, 48-A and article 51-A of the Indian constitution

The Indian government has established an individual department—namely, Department of Environment—to take care of the issues that pose threats to the environment. The Indian Parliament has passed many acts to protect the environment; some of them are as under:

- Wildlife Protection Act, 1972
- The Water (Prevention and Control of Pollution) Act, 1974
- The Forest (Conservation) Act, 1980
- The Air (Prevention and Control of Pollution) Act, 1981
- The Environmental (Protection) Act, 1986
- The Motor Vehicles Acts, 1988 (to limit the hazardous emission of gases from automobiles)
- Environmental (Protection) Rules—Environmental statement, 1992–93
- Environmental (Protection) Rules—Environmental standard, 1993
- The National Environmental Tribunal Act, 1995

Environmental Impact Analysis

Environmental impact assessment is a study of the probable changes in socio-economic and bio-physical characteristics of the environment that may result from a proposed action. It has become indispensable to introduce environmental aspects in planning, especially in hotel planning, during the construction phase. For efficient environmental management, environmental impact assessment must be conducted for a wide range of projects and activities which may be inadvertent environmental intrusions, such as highways, airport, and canals etc., or intentional environmental manipulations, like the construction of dams, streams, pesticide application programme, clearing forest, etc. The purpose of environmental impact analysis is to help design the projects that enhance the quality of the environment as well as examine alternatives and mitigation measures for the development of mega projects such as hotels.

Environmental Audit

The environmental audit checks the organization's environment management systems and status on compliance requirement and standards. It also incorporates an assessment of risks and study for waste utilization/minimization. Environmental audit is a proactive activity wherein, apart from finding faults, weak areas in the system are identified and measures are undertaken for improving overall productivity of the industry. There are two components of environmental audit: assessment and verification.

Assessment: The assessment activity identifies potential hazards, estimates the significance of risks, assesses current practices and capabilities, and provides the basis for recommendations to improve the organization's perception and approach to environmental management.

Verification: The verification activity can confirm whether the management control systems are in place to manage environmental hazards, verifies that regulations and policies are being adhered to, and assists in identifying gaps in organizational policies and standards.

ENVIRONMENTAL MANAGEMENT

Environmental management is a systematic approach to finding practical ways for saving water, energy, and materials, and reducing negative environmental impacts. An environment management system (EMS) is a framework that helps management assign responsibilities, motivate staff, implement best practices, and monitor performance. It typically involves a set of activities, led by a core group of staff, that includes meetings, planning, training, incentive programmes, utility monitoring, and reporting progress.

Environmental Management in the Hospitality Industry

In the hotel industry, activities such as the construction of buildings and landscaping, cooking and disposal of waste, use of water and energy, tend to affect the environment adversely, if not properly managed. Hotels and resorts around the world use large amounts of water, energy, chemicals, supplies, and disposable items. They also generate a lot of waste, such as waste water and solid waste. The major pollutants (refer Fig. 19.4) that are added to the environment from hotels include the following:

- Hazardous chemicals like pesticides, disinfectants, acids, soaps, and detergents.
- Gases like green house gases (CO_2), ozone depleting gases (CCl_2F_2), and acid rain causing gases (SO_2).
- Waste materials from bathrooms, flushing cisterns, laundry, kitchen, and rooms.
- Noise from equipment like generator, AC plant, laundry, etc.

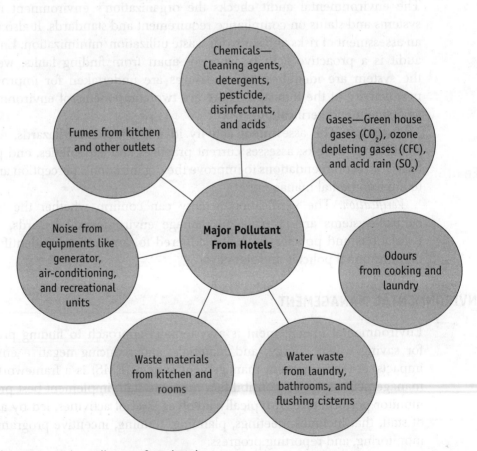

Fig. 19.4 Major pollutants from hotels

Service sector businesses like hotels, resorts, and restaurants have some inherent characteristics that aggravate their impact on the environment, namely time perishable capacity, heterogeneity, labour intensity, and customer involvement in the production process. The size of the hotel facility also influences the environmental impact. For instance, the impact of a hundred room limited service hotel will be different from a six-hundred room full service hotel.

Because of this, small efficiency gains can lead to large cost savings and environmental performance improvements. The use of natural resources (e.g. water, energy, materials, chemicals, etc.) produce the main environmental impacts of the hotel industry. Therefore, indicators of sustainability for the hotel industry should include indexes of the consumption of these resources. In addition, the use of resources constitutes a significant portion of a hotel's operating cost, thus, this type of indicators allow hotels to closely monitor expenses associated with the inefficient use of resources, and take corrective measures when necessary.

Globally, the tourism industry is under pressure to adopt more environmentally sound practices. This arose out of concerns that tourism could and often did have negative impacts on the host communities and their environments. Increasing environmental awareness on the part of consumers has added to the pressure on hotels to adopt sound environmental practices. Tourists are becoming more discerning, seeking activities, arrangements, and experiences which depend crucially on a high quality physical and cultural environment. One of the most critical elements of becoming an environmentally friendly hotel is the adoption of a new culture that extends throughout the hotel organization, and between the hotel and its guest, local community, and even its vendors.

Environmental Management Programmes

Environmental management has become an important issue in the hospitality industry, with a number of hotels adopting sound environmental management practices in response to the growing concerns for sustainable tourism products. The increasing adoption of environmental management in hotel firms seems to have been sparked off by growing concerns over the impacts of tourism on the environment. Let us look at the forces exerting pressure on hotels to adopt environmental management practices and some environmental initiatives that have changed the nature of environmental management practices in hotels.

An environmental management programme is based on practical steps to conserve water and energy, and minimize waste. Typical strategies include:

- Water conservation devices and equipment such as efficient shower-heads and faucet aerators.
- Energy-efficient lighting and lighting controls.
- Weather-stripping and insulation of hot water pipes, refrigerant lines, and air-conditioned areas.

- Timers and occupancy sensors for lighting and air-conditioning equipment.

In addition to engineering 'fixes' and efficient equipment, a property can get a quick start by implementing key operational measures such as:

- Adopting an environmental policy.
- Appointing an environmental officer.
- Establishing a 'Green Team'.
- Establishing a preventative maintenance programme.
- Adopting best practices (staff procedures) for conservation and waste minimization in hotel operations.
- Developing a utility monitoring programme.

After implementing the initial steps outlined above, a hotel may decide to take additional steps to achieve greater cost savings and environmental improvements. This typically involves:

- An environmental assessment of the hotel;
- The adoption of an integrated tool—an environment management system;
- Seeking third party certification by a recognized programme such as Green Globe 21.

Although improving the efficiency of hotel facilities and equipment is essential to becoming an environmentally-friendly hotel, 'engineering fixes' alone are only a part of the puzzle. Hotel staff is the other part (Exhibit 19.1). Some of the most significant water, energy, and materials savings are achieved not by installing new equipment, but by improving standard operating procedures and training and motivating staff to use resources efficiently. Most of these measures have a very low implementation cost and a payback period of close to zero!

A proactive environmental management programme is a three-win proposition because it can help a property save money, get recognized for environmental leadership, and preserve and protect unique destinations.

1. *Save money:* Environmental management reduces operating costs and improves profitability. Most hotels can quickly achieve substantial cost savings with a modest investment in simple, low-cost technologies and practices.

2. *Get recognized for environmental leadership:* Adopting environmental best practices can help hotels stand out from the competition and be recognized through certification programmes, awards, tour operator programmes, and other special promotions. Getting recognized for your commitment to environmental management can enhance the property's image with environmentally conscious guests and tour operators.

3. *Protect and preserve destinations:* Each year millions of tourists go to experience the natural and cultural treasures that a region has to offer. The hospitality industry, while a critical engine for economic growth, also puts a tremendous strain on the natural 'assets' such as beaches, reefs, rivers, and forests.

> **Exhibit 19.1**   Environment-friendly staff
>
> The hotel staff can contribute in a big way to making a hotel eco sensitive. Each member of the staff should be made aware of the organization's concern regarding the consumption of energy. All the representatives of the various departments should work together to formulate guidelines for conserving energy in the hotel. The staff can contribute in the following ways:
>
> - Most five-star hotels wash bed linen on a daily basis. Since the linen is generally very lightly soiled, the management may draw up a policy for laundering bed linen only once in two to three days, unless perceptibly soiled. This practice can save a large amount of water. The ideal way to introduce this policy would be to leave the option to guests. A tent card that states the purpose behind the same encourages guests to oblige. Towels can also be reused.
> - Switch off lights and fans that are not in use.
> - Immediately report any leaky faucets or pipes.
> - Ensure that only the correct wattage of bulbs is used and that light shades are clean.
> - Ensure that drapes are closed to maximize the effect of air-conditioning or heating.
> - Use products with a significant proportion of recycled content.
> - Ensure preventive maintenance of equipment. All equipment should be maintained and kept clean for the highest efficiency levels.
> - Use biodegradable and eco-friendly chemicals in all cleaning and laundry operations. Use non-toxic cleaners, sanitizers, paints, pesticides, and so on throughout the hotel.
> - No aerosol dispensers should be used in dispensing or applying cleaning materials and air fresheners.
> - Guest supplies and amenities should be biodegradable and eco-friendly.
> - Minimize the amount of paper used for each guest—that is, reduce the size of paper invoices and similar documents.
> - Water from the laundry can be treated and used for watering plants.
> - Whenever possible, buy guest amenities in bulk. Use refillable dispensers for hair and skincare products.
> - Buy guest products that contain recycled materials.
> - For guest stationery, use recycled-paper products.
> - Reusable, non-disposable cups and mugs should be provided to guests for in-room beverages. Provide cloth napkins and ceramic dishes too, as these are reusable.
> - Provide morning newspapers in public areas for community access instead of individual room distribution. This reduces paper waste by 60 per cent.
> - Replace paper hand towels with air dryers in restrooms.
> - Donate leftover guest amenities, mattresses, old furniture, and so on to charities.
> - The management should create an incentive programme to encourage staff to participate in and improve upon environment-friendly practices.

Identifying opportunities for cost savings and improved environmental management is best achieved through an all-encompassing and step-by-step process that addresses all aspects of hotel operations and facilities. There are examples of transportation companies, hotels, and restaurants that have taken steps to recycle and reduce the consumption of energy, thereby reducing costs, increasing profits, and taking some steps towards sustainability. A survey carried out by the American Hotel and Motel Association (AH&MA) revealed that hotel managers rated reduction of energy consumption as well as waste management through recycling to be their most important concerns.

As exemplified by Table 19.1, the thrust of the green campaign in the hospitality sector focuses mainly on energy savings as demonstrated by the number of hotels engaging in energy-saving measures, which range from the use of compact fluorescent bulbs to shutting down unused appliances.

In effect, hotels are gradually responding to concerns for environmental sustainability on the part of customers, international organizations, NGOs, and governments. However, environmental management practices have often been geared towards saving costs on energy and water. There have been diverse initiatives by hotels, international organizations, NGOs, and trade associations in the form of ecolabelling, certification, publications, and awards. These initiatives have created greater awareness of environmental management in hotels. Environmental responsibility not only safeguards the environment on which hotels depend but also insulates them from legal tussles, saves costs, promotes customer loyalty, and enhances the reputation of hotels.

International EMS Standards

Hotels are becoming increasingly keen to achieve and demonstrate sound environmental performance by controlling the impact of their activities, products, and services on environment. The International Standards Organization (ISO) 14000 series is an international standard for EMS. The World Travel and Tourism Council's Green Globe international certification has developed an EMS standard specifically for the travel and tourism industry.

The principal components of an EMS, as defined by Green Globe, include the following: an environmental policy that clearly communicates the organization's commitment to maintaining the social, cultural and physical environment; an action plan to guide the property's actions and expenditure of resources; the implementation of operations of the EMS that encompass all of the property's actions relative to the environment, including awareness and training, staff procedures, incentive programmes, and community outreach, among other things; corrective action or monitoring to ensure that the EMS performs as expected, allowing for responsive actions to capture things such as leaking toilets and chemical spills, and review, typically by senior management, to determine how to improve the EMS and the level of compliance with the hotel's environmental policy.

The International Organization Standards on EMS are of direct interest to firms in developing countries, for compliance with the standard is increasingly becoming a competitive factor for the companies selling in the international market. International environmental management standards are intended to provide organizations with the elements of an effective EMS, which can be integrated with other management requirements to assist organizations to achieve environmental and economic goals. These standards, like other international standards, are not

Table 19.1 Cost-cutting environmental management measures by US hotels

Hotel	Practice Initiated	Impact
Westin, Seattle	Changed incandescent bulbs to energy saving compact fluorescent light bulbs and improving control mechanisms.	Achieved 66 per cent reduction in guest room wattage and an annual savings of $400,000.
Apple Farm Inn and Restaurant, California	Uses discharged water from washing machines to flush toilets.	Saving 15,900 litres (4,200 gallons) of water per day and approximately $5,000 per year.
Disney World, Florida	Recycles 15.2 million litres (4 million gallons) of wastewater a day for irrigation of landscaping and golf courses.	More cost-effective as using municipal treated water would have been much more expensive.
Hotel Bel Air	Undertook a comprehensive environmental programme.	Saved $10,000 in 10 months, plus increased revenue from the sale of cardboards.
Hyatt Regency, Chicago	A comprehensive waste reduction and recycling programme.	Recovered approximately 70 per cent of recyclable materials and cut waste hauling costs in half. Recycling programme has resulted in the recovery of $120,000 in hotel items.
Inter-Continental, LA	Installed a power monitoring system.	Saved some $12,000 in electricity costs.
Intercontinental, Miami	Recycling programme involving 30 materials.	Diverts 65 per cent of the waste stream with annual savings of $31,000.
	Recycling waste water for watering gardens as well as use of aerators on water outlets.	Saved over 400 gallons of water per year, amounting to $4,000.
	Reduced energy consumption by using energy efficient appliances.	Saved 400,000 kwh of energy annually, which amounted to $2,400.
Habitat Suites Hotel, Austin, Texas	Water conservation programmes such as use of low-flow sink and shower aerators, water-saving toilets, and water saving sprinklers.	Combined water-saving measures led to savings of $9,000.
	Use of fluorescent and air-conditioning units.	Saved over 122,000 kw of energy per year, which equals $10,954.
Boston Park Plaza	Installed 1,686 thermopane windows at a cost of $1.2 million.	Each window saves the hotel $75 per year in energy costs and the guests benefit from quieter rooms.

Source: http://www.hotel-online.com/News/PR2004_2nd/May04_EnvironmentalPractices.html, last accessed on 20 October 2008.

intended to be used to create non-tariff trade barriers or to increase or change an organization's legal obligations. The standards in ISO 14000 series are:

ISO 14001 Environment Management Systems—specifications with guidance for use. This standard is applicable to any organization that wishes to:

1. Implement, maintain, and improve an environment management system.
2. Assure itself of its conformance with its own stated environmental policy.
3. Demonstrate conformance.

4. Ensure compliance with environmental laws and regulations.
5. Seek certification of its environment management system by an external third party organization.
6. Make a self-determination of conformance.

ISO 14004   General guidelines on environmental management principles, systems, and supporting techniques. It is for information only and is not to be used for registration. It is for the use of the organizations for internal guidance; some of them are as under:

  • Establishes key principles for managers to use in implementing an EMS.
  • Sets forth the benefits of an EMS.
  • Suggest implementation plan.

ISO 14010   Guidelines for environmental auditing—general principles.

ISO 14011   Guidelines for environmental auditing—audit procedures for auditing of EMS.

ISO 14012   Guidelines for environmental auditing—qualification criteria for environmental auditors.

The above mentioned are the standards in the ISO 14000 series that are directed at organizations. They constitute the core documents that will provide guidance to managers and their staff on the establishment, maintenance, auditing, and continual improvement of the hotel's EMS. ITC Maurya, New Delhi is India's first hotel to be accorded the ISO 14001 certification for its environment management systems.

Governments should begin laying out the necessary incentives and standards to move the industry in this direction. Banks should open special lines of credit to finance the improvements. And hotel associations, tourism organizations, and the tourist boards of countries should find ways to link the marketing of their hotels directly to the computers of the millions of so-called 'eco-tourists' in the US and Europe who are beginning to plan their next family vacations.

SUMMARY

Environment is 'the complex of physical, chemical, and biotic factors (as climate, soil, and living things) that act upon an organism or an ecological community, and ultimately determine its form and survival.' Ecology is the study of interrelationships between living organisms and their environment.

Environmental pollution is a major threat to humanity and should be combated with imparting environmental education and implementing sound environmental policy.

It is important to take environmental protection measures at the stage of planning a project.

Environmental impact assessment is a study of the probable changes in socio-economic and bio-physical characteristics of the environment that may result from a proposed action. It should be an integral part of hotel planning during the construction phase. In addition, environment audit analyses a hotel's environment management systems and suggests ways to overcome shortcomings.

Hotels and resorts use large amounts of water, energy, chemicals, and disposable items. They also generate a lot of waste, such as waste water and solid waste. All of these affect the environment adversely, if not properly managed. Environmental management is a systematic approach to finding practical ways for saving water, energy, and materials, and reducing negative environmental impacts. An environment management system (EMS) is a framework that helps management assign responsibilities, motivate staff, implement best practices, and monitor performance. It typically involves a set of activities, led by a core group of staff that includes meetings, planning, training, incentive programmes, utility monitoring, and reporting progress. Hotels are becoming increasingly concerned to achieve and demonstrate sound environmental performance by controlling the impact of their activities, products, and services on environment. The International Standards Organization (ISO) 14000 series is an international standard for EMS. The World Travel and Tourism Council's Green Globe international certification has developed an EMS standard specifically for the travel and tourism industry. The International Organization Standards on EMS are of direct interest to firms in developing countries, for compliance with the standard is increasingly becoming a competitive factor for the companies selling in the international market. International environment management standards are intended to provide organizations with the elements of an effective EMS which can be integrated with other management requirements, to assist organizations to achieve environmental and economic goals.

KEY TERMS

Atmosphere The lithosphere and hydrosphere are surrounded by an about 200-km thick envelope of mixture of various gases known as atmosphere.

Ecology It is the study of interrelationship between living organisms and their environment.

Environment Management System (EMS) It is a framework that helps management assign responsibilities, motivate staff, implement best practices, and monitor performance.

Environmental audit It checks an organization's EMS and status on compliance requirement and standards.

Environmental impact assessment It is a study of the probable changes in socio-economic and bio-physical characteristics of the environment that may result from the proposed action.

Hydrosphere The part of lithosphere that is covered by water; it includes rivers, streams, glaciers, lakes, and sea.

Lithosphere It includes rocks, earth surface, sand, and exposed part of earth that is not covered by water.

REVIEW QUESTIONS

Multiple Choice Questions

1. Hippocrates has mentioned air pollution in the year:
   a) 400 BC
   b) 200 BC
   c) AD 200
   d) AD 400

2. King Edward I made the first anti-pollution law in the year:
   a) 1273 BC
   b) AD 1273
   c) AD 1274
   d) AD 1275

3. The major causes of air pollution are:
   a) Emission from industry
   b) Automobile emission
   c) Volcanic eruptions
   d) All

4. The major causes of water pollution are:
   a) Organic chemicals
   b) Oil discharge
   c) Sewage discharge without treatment
   d) All

5. The informal mode of environmental education includes
   a) *Nukkad naataks*
   b) Puppet shows
   c) Nature camps
   d) All

True/False

1. The study of individual living component or the population of same living component in relation to environment is known as autecology.

2. Any harmful change in the composition of atmospheric gases results in air pollution.

3. Air pollution may lead to acid rains.

4. Seventy-one per cent of the earth's surface is covered by water.

5. Environmental audit involves checking the information about the organization's environment management systems.

Fill in the Blanks

1. _____ is the study of communities, their composition, behaviour, and relationship to the environment.

2. The Air Pollution Control Act in India was passed in _____.

3. _____ gas was accidentally released from the Union Carbide's pesticide manufacturing plant at Bhopal.

4. _____ is a study of the probable changes in socio-economic and bio-physical characteristics of the environment that may result from the proposed action.

Discussion Questions

1. Define ecology. Explain different types of ecology with examples.

2. What do you understand by environmental pollution? Write a short note on environmental pollution.

3. What do you understand by environment education?

4. What are the environmental legislations prevailing in India?

5. What do you understand by environmental impact analysis?

6. What is the environmental audit? What are the benefits of environmental audit?

7. What is an environment management system?

8. What are the benefits of hotels adopting EMS?

9. Does the hotel staff play a role in conserving energy in the hotel? Explain.

CRITICAL THINKING QUESTIONS

1. Environmental studies is important for hospitality management students. Comment.

2. How can a hotel adversely affect our environment? What are the remedial measures that a hotel adopts to minimize the negative impact on environment?

PROJECT WORK

Visit a hotel that is certified by ISO 14000 series and study the environment management system implemented in the hotel. Write a report on the same.

BIBLIOGRAPHY

http://www.hotel-online.com/News/PR2004_2nd/May04_EnvironmentalPractices.html, last accessed on 16 October 2008.

http://www.hotel-online.com/Trends/PanAmer ProceedingsMay99/EnviroManagmt.html, last accessed on 16 October 2008.

www.ecobalt.lv/request.php?536, last accessed on 16 October 2008.

Raghubalan G. and Smritee Raghubalan, *Hotel Housekeeping: Operations and Management*, Oxford University Press, New Delhi, 2007.

CHAPTER 20

Total Quality Management

Learning Objectives:

After reading this chapter, you will be able to understand the following:

- Quality.
- Total quality management (TQM).
- Practices in TQM—Japanese 5-S practice, business process re-engineering, quality control circles, kaizen, and benchmarking.
- Benefits of TQM.

With the boom in the tourism industry, many hotels offer similar products. The most important asset for these hospitality organizations is their guests, and their success depends upon the number of loyal guests and their frequency of patronizing the hotel. Meeting guest satisfaction and exceeding their expectations are an important part of the hospitality business. Guests distinguish between hotels on the basis of the range and quality of services and facilities offered by them. Therefore, quality plays an important role in satisfying guests and achieving customer delight.

The word 'quality' means different things to different people. Quality can be defined as 'the strict and consistent adherence to measurable and verifiable standards to achieve uniformity of output that satisfies specific customer or user requirements'. Quality is aimed at the needs of the present and future guests. According to ISO 8402, quality is 'the totality of features and characteristics of a product or service that bear on its ability to satisfy stated or implied needs'.

There are two types of customers: external and internal.

External customer   An external customer is the one who purchases or uses a particular product or service and who influences the sales of that product or service. An external customer exists outside the organization and generally falls in three categories, viz. current customers (existing guests), prospective customers (potential guests who fall in the target segment of a hotel), and lost customers (guests who did not have a satisfactory experience at the hotel and have moved their business to another hotel).

Internal customer   Internal customers (employees) are also very important for an organization as they exist within the organization. Every function has an internal customer as each employee receives a product or service and, in exchange, provides a product or service. Every person working in the organization may be considered a customer of the preceding operation and every employee's goal is to make sure that the product/service quality meets the expectations of the next person. When this is achieved throughout production, sales, and distribution chains, the satisfaction of external customers can also be achieved easily.

Guests' Perception of Quality

A quality product or service should fulfil or exceed the users' expectations. The expectations are based on the intended use and the selling price of the product or service. If a product exceeds guest expectations, it is considered to be a quality product. Quality may be measured in dimensions like performance, features, conformance, reliability, durability, service, response, aesthetics, and reputation. These dimensions are somewhat independent in nature, hence a product can be excellent in one dimension and may be average or poor in another. For example, a restaurant may serve excellent quality food but its ambience may lack aesthetic appeal. A hotel offering limited services and catering to the needs of a budget segment will be considered a good quality hotel, though it may lack facilities like swimming pool, speciality restaurants, bar, limousine service, valet attendant, etc. that are available in a five-star hotel.

Although it is very tough to define quality, but broadly quality is quantified as follows (refer Fig. 20.1).

Fitness of Use   Products and services are considered to be of good quality when every component of the product is working properly. For example, when all furniture and fixtures, equipments, and other amenities of a hotel room are in perfectly working order, the room is considered to be of good quality. The efficiency and tactfulness of service personnel also determine the quality of a product.

Performance   Performance is related with the fitness of the product/service for consumption by the end user. Other considerations for performance are:
- *Availability*: the probability that a product/service will be available when needed.
- *Reliability*: freedom from failure over time.
- *Maintainability*: the ease of keeping the product in operation.

The hospitality industry offers products like accommodation, food and beverage, and services like travel assistance, facilities like fitness centre, yoga, entertainment, sports, etc. Among these, accommodation is the major hospitality product that constitutes the major part of hotel revenue. In case of accommodation, the quality concern with respect to performance is reliability, i.e., the room that is assigned to the guest should be in a good condition and all the fittings and fixtures that are installed in the room should work properly. The performance in relation with the front desk is that an employee should be available at the desk all the time to assist the guest and should be able to respond to guest queries and resolve problems.

Service   An emphasis on customer service is emerging as a means of organizations giving customers added value. However, customer service is intangible—it is made up of many small things, all geared to changing the customer's perception. Intangible characteristics are those traits that are not quantifiable, yet contribute greatly to

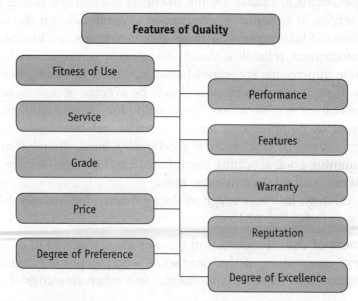

Fig. 20.1   Features of quality

customer satisfaction. Providing excellent customer service is different from and more difficult to achieve than providing excellent product quality. Organizations that emphasize service never stop looking for ways to serve their customers better, even if their customers are not complaining. Some of the services provided by the hotel front desk to guests include: room reservation, reception of guests, registration and assigning rooms to guests, luggage handling, and other services during the stay of the guest, such as maintenance of guest accounts, and preparation, presentation, and settlement of guest bills. Guests look for polite and courteous behaviour of the front desk employees while receiving the above-mentioned services.

Features   Identifiable features or attributes of a product/service are psychological, time oriented, contractual, ethical, and technological. Features are secondary characteristics of a product/service. For example, the primary product of the hotel is a guest room, whereas the furniture and fixtures placed in a room are the features of the room. The design and décor of the front desk, hotel, and lobby are the key features of a hotel.

Grade   The grade of the product or service is also considered a measure of the quality of the product/service. Hotels and restaurants are graded according to the services and facilities provided by them. A hotel graded as five-star deluxe is considered as a hotel that offers the most luxurious and best quality products and services.

Warranty   The product warranty represents an organization's public promise of a quality product backed up by a guarantee of customer satisfaction. Ideally, it also represents a commitment to provide a level of service that meets the satisfaction of the customer. The warranty that a guest expects from a hotel is that the quality of the services will be of the highest standards. Some hotels offer guarantee of satisfaction to their guests.

Price   Today's discerning customers are willing to pay a higher price to obtain value for their money. Customers are constantly evaluating one organization's products and services against those of its competitors to determine who provides the greatest value. Thus, it is very important to provide high quality products and service to competetive rates in order to retain guests and get repeat business.

Reputation   Most of us rate organizations by our overall experience with them. Total customer satisfaction is based on the entire experience with the organization, not just the product. It is human nature that one shares good experiences with few people and bad experiences with many, therefore it is more difficult to create a favourable reputation.

Degree of Preference   Quality is the degree to which a particular product is preferred over competing products of equivalent grade. In the hotel industry, this is based on comparative tests by guests and is normally called guest preference. There may be several hotels in the same category in a town but the hotel that is most preferred by guests will be considered as a good quality hotel in the town.

Degree of Excellence Quality is a measure of the degree of general excellence of the products or services that are offered by a hotel.

TOTAL QUALITY MANAGEMENT

Total quality management (TQM) is a set of systematic activities carried out by the entire organization to effectively and efficiently achieve company objectives so as to provide products and services at a level of quality that satisfies customers, at the appropriate time and price. It is a holistic approach to long-term success that views continuous improvement in all aspects of an organization as a journey and not as a short-term destination. It aims to radically transform the organization through progressive changes in the attitudes, practices, structures, and systems. TQM transcends the 'product quality' approach, involves everyone in the organization, and encompasses every function—administration, communications, distribution, manufacturing, marketing, planning, training, etc.

TQM, as we can see from the various meanings given in Exhibit 20.1, is the art of managing the whole (sum total attributes of the product or service) to achieve excellence. It is a management approach that tries to achieve and sustain long-term organizational success by encouraging employee feedback and participation, satisfying guest needs and expectations, respecting societal values and beliefs, and obeying governmental statutes and regulations. Product/service, process, organization, leadership, and commitment form the five pillars of TQM (Fig. 20.2).

TQM may be defined as a philosophy and also as a set of guiding principles that represent the foundation of a continuously improving organization. It is the application of quantitative methods and human resources to improve all the

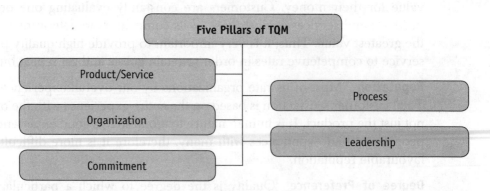

Fig. 20.2 Five pillars of total quality management

Exhibit 20.1 Various meanings of total quality management (TQM)

Coined by the US Naval Air Systems Command in early 1980s, the term 'total quality management' has now taken on several meanings and includes:

1. Commitment and direct involvement of highest-level executives in setting quality goals and policies, allocation of resources, and monitoring of results.
2. Realization that transforming an organization means fundamental changes in basic beliefs and practices, and that this transformation is everyone's job.
3. Building quality into products and practices right from the beginning—doing things right the first time.
4. Understanding the changing needs of the internal and external customers, and stakeholders, and satisfying them in a cost-effective manner.
5. Instituting leadership in place of mere supervision so that every individual performs in the best possible manner to improve quality and productivity, thereby continually reducing total cost.
6. Eliminating barriers between people and departments so that they work as teams to achieve common objectives.
7. Instituting flexible programmes for training and education, and providing meaningful measures of performance that guide the self-improvement efforts of everyone involved.

---

processes within an organization and exceed guest needs in the present as well as in the future. TQM integrates fundamental management techniques, existing improvement efforts, and technical tools under a disciplined approach.

The implementation of TQM involves:

- A systematic and long-term commitment, in particular by senior management.
- A commitment to getting things right the first time.
- An understanding of both internal and external customer-supplier relationships.
- An understanding of the total costs involved in the purchase of products and services, e.g., cheap inputs of low quality can cause serious faults in processes and products.
- A commitment to aligning systems to the organizational needs.
- Appropriate management and training techniques to improve communication between sections and between staff and management.
- Meaningful measures of performance to enable workers to understand what they are contributing and how they can improve.

TQM is a necessity in the hospitality industry. Its purpose is to provide quality product/service to a guest, which will, in turn, increase productivity and lower the cost. This will help to place a higher quality product at a lower price in the market, which will give the hotel a cutting edge over competitors' products and services. Discerning guests are willing to pay higher prices if the hotel can assure them that it offers high quality products and service.

The best practices in TQM implementation, particularly in the travel services are: providing information to reduce transaction and waiting time, using feedback to identify new segments and customer expectations, designing various customer opinion capturing devices for different operational needs and logging, monitoring, analysing, and stipulating deadlines for solving problems and implementing schemes.

Modern methods of quality control were developed and matured in manufacturing industries. These involve the processing and fabrication of materials into finished durable and non-durable goods. Service, however, is a relatively distinct non-manufacturing activity. It is performed for someone else. The major distinctions between service and manufacturing organizations are that the product in the service industry is intangible, perishable, and temporary; it involves the customer in the delivery of the product; and is not perceived as a product by employees. The intangible nature of the service as a product means that it could be very difficult to place quantifiable terms on the features that contribute to the quality of the product. This could make the measurement of the quality of the product a problem for TQM.

As service products are perishable, they cannot be stockpiled and must be produced 'on demand'. The result is that the process for delivering a service may be highly complex, involving the coordination of primary and support systems in what is usually a very time-sensitive relationship with the customer. This is in contrast to manufacturing organizations, where although time may be an important aspect in the delivery of the goods, it is rarely regarded as a feature of the goods will affect its quality.

In the case of a service organization, time is regarded as an assessable quality or feature of the product. For example, people usually book flights based on the departure and arrival times that are most convenient to them. If a traveller is expecting to arrive at a destination at a specified time, and the plane is two hours late, the guest will not be satisfied. This is irrespective of how comfortable the plane was, how good the in-flight service was, or the fact that the flight had reached the destination safely.

The customer is frequently and directly involved in the delivery of the service and as such introduces an unknown and unpredictable influence on the process. It is also often difficult to determine the exact requirements of customers and what they regard as an acceptable standard of service. This problem is magnified by the fact that standards are often judgemental; they may be based on personal preferences or even mood of the guest, rather than on technical performance that can be measured. While a service completely satisfied a customer yesterday, the same service may not do so today because of the mood of the customer. Therefore, there is a problem of the unpredictable customer.

PRACTICES IN TOTAL QUALITY MANAGEMENT

Total quality management is the process of identifying and administrating the activities that are needed to achieve the quality objective of a hotel, which is contained in the statement of the quality as well as in the mission statement. To have a systematic approach to TQM, it is necessary to develop a conceptual model. Generally, a model is a sequence of steps arranged logically to guide the implementation of a process in order to achieve the ultimate goal of quality assurance. The following are the recognized practices in TQM, as illustrated in Fig. 20.3:

Japanese 5-S Practice

The 5-S stand for five Japanese words—*seiri* (sort), *seiton* (systematize), *seiso* (sanitize), *seiketsu* (standardize), and *shitsuke* (self-discipline). The 5-S practice (Fig. 20.4) is a

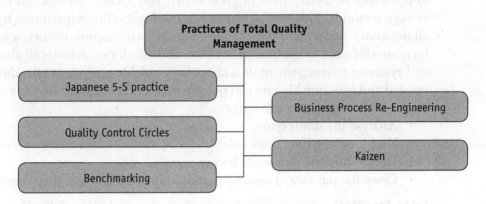

Fig. 20.3 Practices of total quality management

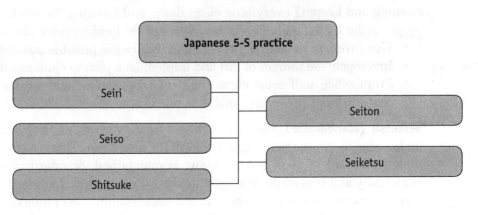

Fig. 20.4 Japanese 5-S practice

Japanese technique for establishing and maintaining quality environment in an organization. Japanese factories, well known for their cleanliness and orderliness, follow the 5-S practice.

Seiri (sort)   *Seiri* is sorting through the contents of the workplace and removing unnecessary items. It is about separating the things that are necessary for the job from those that are not and discarding the latter. Some of the necessary items may be:
- Unnecessary tools and equipments in the work area.
- Unused machinery in the area.
- Defective products, such as stationery like staplers.
- Papers and documents such as forms and formats that are not in use.

Seiton (systematize)   *Seiton* is putting the necessary items in their place and providing easy access so that they are ready for use when needed. This is an action to put every necessary item in good order, and focuses on efficient and effective storage methods. This can be applied in the front office department by arranging all necessary papers and documents in an orderly manner in such a way so as to increase efficiency at the time of check-in and check-out. *Seiton* is all about neatness and systematic arrangement. It is about how quickly one can get the things that are needed and how quickly one can put them away. There are four ways of achieving neatness and increasing efficiency:
- Analyse the status quo.
- Decide where the things belong.
- Decide how things should be put away.
- Obey the put-away rules (by putting things back where they belong).

Seiso (sanitize)   *Seiso* is an action to clean the workplace daily. Everyone in the organization from the managing director to the cleaner should undertake this job. It is believed that while cleaning, one is cleaning one's mind as well. This involves cleaning and keeping everything clean daily, and bringing the work desk back to proper order by the end of each day. Some of the guiding principles are:
- Use covers or devices to prevent and reduce the possible amount of dirt.
- Investigate the sources of dirt and implement a plan to eliminate these causes.
- Front office staff must clean their own equipment and working area, and perform basic preventive maintenance.

Seiketsu (standardize)   *Seiketsu* involves creating visual controls and guidelines for keeping the workplace organized, orderly, and clean. This is a condition where a high standard of good housekeeping is maintained. Standardization means to continually and repeatedly maintain the first three Ss. In other words, one should maintain neatness and cleanliness in the organization. The emphasis is on visual management and standardization. Put systems in place to ensure that what has been accomplished remains intact. Establish standardized procedures and practices, and make them into habits. You can use labels, signs, posters, and banners to make people aware and to remind them about the standards.

Shitsuke (self-discipline) *Shitsuke* involves training and discipline to ensure that everyone follows the 5-S standards. This is a condition where all members practise the first four Ss spontaneously and willingly as a way of life. Accordingly, it becomes a culture in the organization. Self-discipline is important because it reaches beyond discipline. The emphasis here is on creating a workforce with good habits. Everyone should follow the procedure in the work area of their respective job locations.

Once the 5-S system is set up, one needs to establish a formal system for monitoring and evaluating the results of the system. Maintaining correct procedures should become a habit. Following the 5-S system ensures effective and quality production. It improves efficiency and productivity, quality, safety, reduces breakdowns, and reduces inventory and supply costs. Finally, it spreads a positive and healthy attitude by creating a clean and organized work environment.

Business Process Re-engineering

Business process re-engineering (BPR) is a thorough rethinking of all business processes, job definitions, management systems, organizational structure, work flow, and underlying assumptions and beliefs. BPR's main objective is to break away from old ways of working, and effect radical (not incremental) redesign of processes to achieve dramatic improvements in critical areas (such as cost, quality, service, and response time) through the indepth use of information technology. It is also called business process redesign. It is a management process used to redefine mission statement, analyse critical success factors, redesign organizational structure, and re-engineer critical processes to improve customer satisfaction. BPR is the radical redesign of business as a whole or individual work processes to maximize business effectiveness. It challenges managers to rethink traditional work methods and commit themselves to customer focused processes. It uses recognized techniques for improving business results and questions the effectiveness of the traditional organizational structure.

BPR is the analysis and redesign of workflow within and between enterprises. The process reached its heyday in the early 1990s when Hammer and Champy (1993) promoted the idea that sometimes radical redesign and reorganization of an enterprise (wiping the slate clean) was necessary to lower costs and increase the quality of service, and that information technology was the key enabler for that radical change. They felt that the design of workflow in most large corporations was based on assumptions about technology, people, and organizational goals that were no longer valid. They suggested seven principles of re-engineering to streamline the work process and thereby achieve significant levels of improvement in quality, time management, and cost:

1. Organize around outcomes, not tasks.
2. Identify all the processes in an organization and prioritize them in order of redesign urgency.
3. Integrate information processing work into the real work that produces the final information.
4. Treat geographically dispersed resources as though they were centralized.
5. Link parallel activities in the workflow process instead of just integrating their results.
6. Put the decision point where the work is performed, and build control into the process.
7. Capture information once and at the source.

Although it is difficult to figure out whether an organization needs a BRP, some factors that can be considered are:

- Does the competition clearly outperform the hotel?
- Are there many conflicts in the organization?
- Is there excessive use of non-structured communication (e.g., memos, e-mails, etc.)?
- Is it possible to consider a more continuous approach of gradual, incremental improvements?

Rapid technological changes and competitive pressures of modern markets increases demands for quality, service cycle times, and innovation. Business process re-engineering is designed to help with these situations.

Quality Control Circles

Quality control is maintenance of standards of quality of manufactured goods or services provided. It is the set of activities and techniques used to achieve and maintain a high standard of quality in a transformation process. In traditional organizations, management has to balance the costs incurred against the customer's goodwill. Quality control is also concerned with finding and eliminating the causes of quality problems.

Quality control circles (QCC) originated in Japan in the 1950s. A QCC is a small group of people working together to contribute to the improvement of the enterprise, to respect humanity, and to build a cheerful workgroup through the development of the infinite potential of its workers. A QCC team usually comes from the same work area and voluntarily meets on a regular basis to identify, investigate, analyse, and solve work-related problems. The basic concepts behind QCC activities as part of company-wide quality control efforts are:

- To contribute to the improvement and development of the enterprise.

- To respect humanity and to build worthwhile lives and cheerful work areas.
- To give fullest recognition to human capabilities and to draw out each individual's infinite potential.

Kaizen

Kaizen is the Japanese concept of continuous overall improvement. It is a Japanese term for a gradual approach to ever-higher standards in quality enhancement and waste reduction through small but continual improvements, involving everyone from the chief executive to the lowest level workers. Its prime consideration is to ensure that problems are continuously sought out and rectified, and that opportunities for improvement, in any aspect of the system, are exploited. It is a process that, when done correctly, humanizes the workplace, eliminates overly hard work *(muri)*, and teaches people how to perform experiments on their work using the scientific method and how to learn to spot and eliminate waste in business processes.

It defines the management's role in continuously encouraging and implementing small improvements, involving everyone that make the process efficient, effective, under control, and adaptable. It focuses on simplification by breaking down complex processes into their sub-processes and then improving them. Improvements are usually accomplished at little or no expense, without sophisticated techniques or expensive equipment.

The Kaizen improvement focuses on the use of:
1. Value-added and non-value-added work activities.
2. *Muda*, which refers to the seven classes of waste—over-production, delay, transportation, over processing, inventory, wasted motion, and defective parts.
3. Principles of motion study and the use of cell technology.
4. Principle of materials handling and use of one-piece flow.
5. Documentation of standard operating procedure.
6. The Japanese 5-S practice for workplace organizations.
7. Visual management by means of visual display that everyone in the hotel can use for better communication.

Kaizen relies heavily on a culture that encourages suggestions by operators who continually try to incrementally improve their jobs or processes. Rather than concealing problems, staff is encouraged to bring them to the surface.

Benchmarking

Benchmarking is the process of identifying the best practice in relation to products and processes, both within an industry and outside it, with the objective of using this as a guide and reference point for improving the practice of one's own organization. Through this systematic method, organizations can measure themselves against the best industry practices. It promotes superior performance by providing an organized framework through which organizations learn how the 'best-in-class' do things, understand how these best practices differ from their own, and implement change to close the gap. The essence of benchmarking, which is a tool for continuous improvement, is the process of borrowing ideas and adapting them to gain competitive advantage.

Benchmarking, an increasingly popular tool, is used extensively by manufacturing as well as service organizations, including AT&T, Motorola, and Toyota. Benchmarking is a common element of quality standards such as the Chrysler, Ford, and General Motors Quality System Requirements. These standards stipulate that quality goals and objectives be based on competitive products and benchmarking, both inside and outside the automotive industry. The Malcolm Baldrige National Quality Award similarly requires that the applicants benchmark external organizations.

Benchmarking is the systematic search for best practices, innovative ideas, and highly effective operating procedures. It considers the experience of others, learns what they did right, and then imitates them to avoid reinventing the wheel. Benchmarking is not new and has been around for a long time. In fact, in the 1800s, Francis Lowell, a New England colonist, studied British textile mills and imported many ideas, along with his own improvements, for the burgeoning American Textile Mills.

Benchmarking measures performance against that of the best-in-class organizations, determines how the best-in-class achieve those performance levels, and uses the information as the basis for adaptive creativity and breakthrough performance.

Implicit in the definition of benchmarking are two key elements. First, measuring performance requires some unit of measures. These are called metrics and are usually expressed numerically. The numbers achieved by the best-in-class set the target. An organization seeking improvement then plots its own performance against the targets. Second, benchmarking requires that managers understand why their performance differs. Benchmarkers must develop a thorough and indepth knowledge of their own processes as well as the processes of the best-in-class organizations. An understanding of the differences allows the managers to organize their improvement efforts to meet the goal. Benchmarking is about setting goals and objectives, and about meeting them by improving processes.

BENEFITS OF TQM

TQM is a business management strategy aimed at embedding awareness of quality in all organizational processes. The practice is used in manufacturing, education, call centres, government, and service industries, as well as NASA space and science programmes. Some of the major benefits of TQM (Fig. 20.5) are as follows:

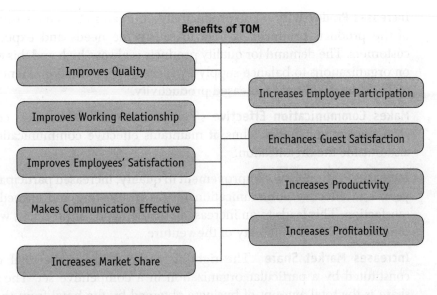

Fig. 20.5 Benefits of TQM

Improves Quality TQM revolves around the quality of products and services. Improvement of quality of the products and services is a direct outcome of TQM. Emphasis is laid on improving the dimensions of quality like performance, conformance, aesthetics, reliability, reputation, etc.

Increases Employee Participation Success in TQM can only be achieved if all the people in the organization participate in the process. Thus, TQM helps increase employee participation in achieving quality dimensions.

Improves Working Relationship The participation of each employee in enhancing the quality of products and services poses the responsibility of quality concerns on each of them. Each employee has to contribute in maintaining the quality of products and services. This leads to the development of good working relationships between employees.

Enhances Guest Satisfaction When the quality of products and services meet or exceed guest expectations, it results in guest satisfaction. The purpose of TQM is to enhance of the quality dimensions of products and services, thus increasing guest satisfaction.

Improves Employees' Satisfaction People who produce quality products or deliver quality services are recognized and awarded by organizations. The creation of quality products itself increases the morale and satisfaction level of the employees. Every creator feels a sense of satisfaction when the quality of their products/ services is appreciated by others. Thus, TQM helps to improve satisfaction levels of employees.

Increases Productivity   The productivity of organizations increases as the quality of the products produced is able to satisfy the needs and expectations of the customers. The demand for quality products is always high and this exerts pressure on organizations to balance supply by increasing production. Hence, the practice of TQM leads towards increased productivity.

Makes Communication Effective   The practice of TQM makes communication clear and unambiguous. Thus, it maintains effective communication within and also outside the organization.

Increases Profitability   Improvement in quality, increased participation of employees, and effective communication results in meeting and exceeding consumer satisfaction. This leads to an increase in the demand for products, which increases productivity and profitability of the venture.

Increases Market Share   The rightful market share is the total market that is constituted by a particular organization in a competitive set. The actual market share is the total amount of business obtained by the hotel from the total pool of business. If a hotel is able to suppress the business of other hotels in the competitive set by virtue of its quality, its market share will increase. Thus, TQM practices lead to an increase in the market share of organizations.

SUMMARY

Quality is the strict and consistent adherence to measurable and verifiable standards to achieve uniformity of output that satisfies specific customer or user requirements. It is an important aspect of the products and services offered by a hotel. Total quality management (TQM) is a management philosophy where every individual in an organization is motivated to work towards a common vision, in an ideal environment, continuously improving one's performance, resulting in better business opportunities. Product/service, process, organization, leadership, and commitment form the five pillars of TQM. The practices in TQM include—Japanese 5-S practice, business process re-engineering, quality control circles, kaizen, and benchmarking. There are several benefits of TQM, such as it improves quality, enhances guest satisfaction, and increases productivity and profitability.

KEY TERMS

Business process re-engineering (BPR) It is a thorough rethinking of all business processes, job definitions, management systems, organizational structure, work flow, and underlying assumptions and beliefs.

Kaizen It is a Japanese term for a gradual approach to ever-higher standards in quality enhancement and waste reduction, through small but continual improvements, involving everyone from the chief executive to the lowest level workers.

Quality It is the strict and consistent adherence to measurable and verifiable standards to achieve uniformity of output that satisfies specific customer or user requirements.

Quality control circles It is a small group of people working together to contribute to the improvement of the enterprise, to respect humanity, and to build a cheerful workgroup through the development of the infinite potential of its workers.

Seiri (sort) It is sorting through the contents of the workplace and removing unnecessary items.

Seiton (systematize) It is putting the necessary items in their place and providing easy access so that they are ready for use when needed.

Seiso (sanitize) It involves cleaning everything, keeping it clean daily, and using cleaning to inspect the workplace and equipment for defects.

Seiketsu (standardize) It involves creating visual controls and guidelines for keeping the workplace organized, orderly, and clean.

Shitsuke (self-discipline) It involves training and discipline to ensure that everyone follows the 5-S standards.

Total quality management (TQM) It is a set of systematic activities, carried out by the entire organization, to effectively and efficiently achieve company objectives by providing products and services at a level of quality that satisfies customers, at the appropriate time and price.

REVIEW QUESTIONS

Multiple Choice Questions

1. The five S of Japanese 5-S practice include:
   - a) Seiri
   - b) Seiton
   - c) Seiso
   - d) All

2. Quality Control Circles originated in:
   - a) America
   - b) Britain
   - c) Japan
   - d) India

3. Benefits of TQM are:
   - a) Improvement in quality
   - b) Improvement in participation
   - c) Enhancement of guest satisfactions
   - d) All

4. The various aspects of quality are:
   - a) Performance
   - b) Reliability
   - c) Availability
   - d) All

True/False

1. The totality of features and characteristic of product or service that bear on its ability to satisfy stated or implied needs is known as quality.

2. Business process re-engineering is a management process used to redefine mission statement, analyse critical success factors, redesign organizational structure, and reengineer critical processes to improve customer satisfaction.

3. Kaizen is the process of continuous improvement in small increments that make the process efficient, effective, under control, and adaptable.

4. Benchmarking is an increasingly popular tool.

5. Seiso is the systematic search for best practices, innovative ideas, and highly effective operating procedures.

Discussion Questions

1. Define quality, especially in the context of the hotel industry.

2. Explain total quality management.

3. Explain the following:
   a) Japanese 5-S practice

b) Business process re-engineering
c) Quality control circles
d) Kaizen
e) Benchmarking

CRITICAL THINKING QUESTIONS

1. What are the benefits of total quality management in hotels?

2. How does the quality of products and services affect guest's satisfaction? Explain in the context of the hospitality industry.

CASE STUDY

You are the General Manager of a hotel that is renowned for its quality service. You are standing in the lobby foyer and are discretely observing the activities at the nearby front desk where guests are being checked in. From your vantage point, you can hear the front desk agent confirming the arrangements of a booking with a guest:

'Sir, I would like to reconfirm that your accommodation charges would be billed to your company and the rest would be on direct payment as per actuals.'

The guest responds by saying, 'No, all the expenses will be paid by the company.'

The agent checks the guest details on his computer and says, 'I am sorry sir, but according to this we only have authorized charge of the accommodation.'

The guest reiterates, 'Last time I stayed here I had the same problem. In order to avoid such a problem this time, I had personally called up last week to sort this out. All expenses are to be charged to my company.'

The clerk goes to get authorization on the account and the disgruntled guest turns to his companion and says in exasperation:

'See, it's exactly like I had said. I stay here every month, but still every time I have the same problem.'

You consider the exchange with concern. The guest has apparently not received the quality service the hotel was aiming to provide, and if the guest continually faces this problem, it would simply be a matter of time before he decides to try one of the competitors. Not only could that one guest be lost, but he could also be the manager of a company whose employees frequently stay at the hotel and hold functions there.

1. How will you react to this situation? Find out if this is a problem that only this particular guest faces or is it a common problem experienced by many guests.

2. Whose fault is it that the problem arose initially?

3. What appropriate action should be taken?

4. How can you ensure that such situations do not occur again?

Index

THE LEARNING CENTRE
HAMMERSMITH AND WEST
LONDON COLLEGE
GLIDDON ROAD
LONDON W14 9BL